Research and Survey on Mental Health of Children and Adolescents

Research and Survey on Mental Health of Children and Adolescents

Editor

Roberta Frontini

MDPI • Basel • Beijing • Wuhan • Barcelona • Belgrade • Novi Sad • Cluj • Manchester

Editor
Roberta Frontini
Faculdade de Ciências Humanas
Universidade Católica Portuguesa
Lisboa
Portugal

Editorial Office
MDPI
St. Alban-Anlage 66
4052 Basel, Switzerland

This is a reprint of articles from the Special Issue published online in the open access journal *Healthcare* (ISSN 2227-9032) (available at: www.mdpi.com/journal/healthcare/special_issues/9CN29919WA).

For citation purposes, cite each article independently as indicated on the article page online and as indicated below:

Lastname, A.A.; Lastname, B.B. Article Title. *Journal Name* **Year**, *Volume Number*, Page Range.

ISBN 978-3-7258-0992-9 (Hbk)
ISBN 978-3-7258-0991-2 (PDF)
doi.org/10.3390/books978-3-7258-0991-2

Contents

About the Editor

Roberta Frontini

Roberta Frontini has a PhD from the Inter-University PhD Program in Clinical and Health Psychology from the University of Coimbra and the University of Lisbon (approved unanimously with distinction and honour). Roberta has conducted research at Loughborough University, London as part of her PhD. She has published articles in specialized journals with an impact factor. Although her main work is in the area of psychology, she extensively collaborates in multidisciplinary projects in the scientific area of health and wellbeing.

healthcare

MDPI

Case Report

The Practice of Physical Exercise and Sports in Portuguese Trans Youth: A Case Study

Joana Oliveira [1], Roberta Frontini [2,3,*], Miguel Jacinto [1,2,4] and Raul Antunes [1,2,3]

1 ESECS, Polytechnic of Leiria, 2411 Leiria, Portugal
2 CIEQV-Life Quality Research Centre, Polytechnic of Leiria, 2411 Leiria, Portugal
3 Center for Innovative Care and Health Technology (ciTechCare), Polytechnic of Leiria, 2411 Leiria, Portugal
4 Faculty of Sport Sciences and Physical Education, University of Coimbra, 3040 Coimbra, Portugal
* Correspondence: roberta.frontini@ipleiria.pt

Abstract: The following case study aims to analyze the experience of a Portuguese trans individual regarding their practice of physical exercise (PE) and sports in Portuguese gyms and sports clubs. A 30-min interview was conducted through the Zoom platform. Before the interview, four questionnaires—Satisfaction with Life Scale (SWLS), Positive and Negative Affect Schedule (PANAS), Hospital Anxiety and Depression Scale (HADS), and EUROHIS-QOL 8-item index—were also applied, all in their Portuguese version. The interview was digitally video recorded after consent was obtained, transcribed verbatim, and subject to thematic analysis. Findings suggest positive values for satisfaction with life and quality of life. The values of positive affect were higher than those of negative affect, and there was an absence of depressive and anxious symptomatology. In the qualitative analysis, mental health was the main motive for the practice, while locker rooms separated by gender and university life were the main barriers mentioned. Mixed changing rooms were identified as facilitators of PE practice. This study highlights the importance of developing strategies for the creation of mixed changing rooms and sports teams in order to promote a comfortable and safe practice for all individuals.

Keywords: transgender; gender identity; barriers; motives; facilitators; exercise; sport

check for updates

Citation: Oliveira, J.; Frontini, R.; Jacinto, M.; Antunes, R. The Practice of Physical Exercise and Sports in Portuguese Trans Youth: A Case Study. *Healthcare* **2023**, *11*, 668. https://doi.org/10.3390/healthcare11050668

Academic Editor: José Carmelo Adsuar Sala

Received: 18 January 2023
Revised: 19 February 2023
Accepted: 22 February 2023
Published: 24 February 2023

1. Introduction

The trans community represents between 0.1% and 0.2% of the general population [1]. In Portugal, trans individuals have been identified as one of the most discriminated against and excluded populations [2]. In fact, studies report situations of discrimination, violence and transphobia toward trans individuals [3–5], which leads this population to avoid particular spaces and public facilities, such as gyms [6,7].

The term transgender or trans refers to a person whose gender identity differs from the sex assigned to them at birth [8–10]. A trans man is an individual with female birth-assigned sex but identifies as male, and a trans woman is a person with male birth-assigned sex but identifies as female [9].

In the 2015 U.S. Transgender Survey, 14% of respondents reported that they did not go to a gym or health club in the past year because they were afraid of meeting a trans person [11]. Nearly one in five (18%) trans individuals who went to a gym or health club where staff knew or thought they were trans reported being denied equal treatment or service, being verbally harassed or physically attacked because of being trans [11]. In the study by Symons and colleagues [12], almost half of the participants from mainstream clubs (48.2%) reported that their club was unwelcoming to trans individuals, and 58.3% of trans respondents reported that there were sports that they did not play because of their gender identity. In the same study, the two-sexed/gendered sports model was presented several times as difficult for trans people [12]. Participants of the study also highlighted general ignorance and prejudice concerning trans issues within many of the sporting communities, experiences of discrimination, a lack of policies to enable their participation in sports, concerns with using changing rooms and concerns regarding being accepted and fitting in [12].

Trans people have more barriers than reasons to engage in PE and sports, the most frequent being body image dissatisfaction [13]. This is not surprising, as trans people tend to be more dissatisfied with body image and have a higher prevalence of eating disorders [14]. In addition, changing rooms are frequently reported as unsafe and uncomfortable spaces that limit the regular practice of PE and sports among trans individuals [13,15–17]. In 2017, in the British school context, it was reported that 29% of trans students are bullied during sports lessons, especially in changing rooms (25%) [18]. Negative past experiences are also an aspect reported in the literature as one of the main barriers to the practice of physical exercise [12,19], which cause acute feelings of gender dysmorphia, especially in a school context [19]. In elite competitive sports, the debate and discussion about the participation or not of trans athletes have increased, as well as scientific evidence on the possible advantages of trans women in sports competitions [20,21]. Although the policies and regulations for participation in the Olympic Games have changed over the years [22], participation rules still discriminate against and exclude transgender people from sports [12]. On the other hand, despite the immense barriers identified in the literature, it seems that the practice of PE and sports activities is empowering and may play a fundamental role in the gender identification process [23].

Therefore, and considering the aforementioned data, research must address these issues in order to achieve a more inclusive and comfortable practice for all individuals. However, there is still a long way to go, since this is a field that has been that has been neglected for many years. A recent systematic review [13] included articles mainly from the UK and USA, with results related to their population. To the best of our knowledge, there is no evidence of studies on this topic in Portugal. With the purpose of knowing the reality of the Portuguese context and helping make it more inclusive and safer for the trans population, the present study aims to shed light and analyze the experience of a Portuguese trans individual regarding his practice of PE and sports in Portuguese gyms and sports clubs, identifying possible barriers, motives and facilitators for the practice.

2. Materials and Methods

The present study was conducted in accordance with the Declaration of Helsinki and its subsequent amendments [24]. In order to report qualitative data, the COREQ (Consolidated Criteria for Reporting Qualitative research) checklist was followed [25].

2.1. Study Design and Participant

This was a qualitative exploratory case study conducted with a trans male participant (n = 1) who was involved in the practice of PE and had a history of sports practice. The participant was 17 years old, identified as transgender, and was a practitioner of physical activity (PA) and/or PE and/or sport. The participant was recruited via advertisements on social media. After expressing interest, the participant contacted the authors for a more detailed explanation of the study.

The participant met all criteria and agreed to participate. A meeting was scheduled through the Zoom platform and was video recorded. Written informed consent forms were obtained before any data collection took place.

2.2. Data Collection

Data were collected in June 2022. Before the interview, four questionnaires were also completed—the Portuguese version of the Satisfaction with Life Scale [26]; the short Portuguese version of the Positive and Negative Affect Schedule (PANAS) [27]; the Portuguese version [28] of the Hospital Anxiety and Depression Scale; and the Portuguese version of the EUROHIS-QOL 8-item index [29]—to measure global life satisfaction, both positive and negative affect, anxiety and depressive symptoms and quality of life, respectively.

Information on gender, age, marital status, physical activity (PA), physical exercise (PE) and sports practiced was collected. For the purpose of this study, the participant was asked about five domains: the frequency and type of PA, PE and sports practiced before and after gender affirmation; barriers to its practice; facilitators of its practice; motives for its practice; and safety of the practice spaces. The participant was free to respond in ways he felt comfortable with and was encouraged to present his own understandings and meanings. The researcher could explore a particular meaning or sentence and could clarify any question raised. The interview was conducted by one health and clinical psychologist and psychological field (RF) with qualifications in qualitative research, experience in sport and exercise psychology research and interviewing. To reduce any influence on the participant's responses, the researcher had no previous contact with the participant, and only the participant and the researcher were present during the interview. A semi-structured guide was used to explore the participant's perspectives. Specialists reviewed this interview in both areas of psychology and sports. The session lasted 30 min. A digital video and audio recording of the interview was made with the participant's permission, for later transcription and analysis.

2.3. Data Analysis

The interview was transcribed verbatim and analyzed using thematic analysis [30]. Two authors independently performed data analysis. However, the entire research team organized and conducted regular online meetings to examine and discuss topics regarding data analysis to ensure reflexivity. Data analysis occurred in three phases: data reduction, data display, and conclusion drawing/verification [30]. In the first phase (i.e., data reduction), significant sections of the answers were coded into themes using a deductive–inductive approach. All responses were meticulously read in order to obtain a complete picture of the participant. Furthermore, interpretative notes were made. Subsequently, emerging subthemes were grouped into major themes. The data display permitted drawing conclusions. The map's themes and quotations were created to organize and facilitate data analysis. In "conclusion drawing/verification" researchers reviewed the meaning and significance of the data analyzed. Emergent conclusions were confirmed as a means of testing the validity of the findings [30]. Both themes and subthemes were examined, reviewed and iterated to guarantee that they reflected the data collected. After independent analysis, researchers compared and discussed the findings to reach a consensus.

3. Results

At the time of the study, the participant was a young trans male who was regularly engaged in PA and PE practice. On average, the participant practiced PE for five years, three times/week and four hours/week. Regarding the practice of PA, the participant practiced physical activities, such as running and cycling, three hours/per week.

Table 1 summarizes the descriptive statistics related to subjective well-being values (life satisfaction, positive and negative affect), anxiety and depression symptoms and quality of life.

Table 1. Summary of the descriptive statistics.

Hours of weekly PA practice	3.00
Years of PE practice	5.00
Number of weekly PE practice	3.00
Hours of weekly PE practice	4.00
Satisfaction with life	4.60
Positive affect	2.80
Negative affect	1.40
Anxiety symptoms	6.00
Depression symptoms	3.00
Quality of life	81.25

Regarding satisfaction with life, the average was 4.60, while regarding the emotional dimension of subjective well-being, the values of positive affect were higher than those of negative affect. Regarding anxiety and depressive symptomatology, anxiety symptoms (6.00) had a higher score than depressive symptoms (3.00). Finally, the quality of life mean value was 81.25 (on a scale ranging from 0 to 100).

Thematic analysis revealed five main themes: practice of PE and sports, barriers to engaging in PA and sports, facilitators of PE, motives for PE practice and safety of the places. Nineteen subthemes were also identified. The results, organized by themes, subthemes, illustrative expressions of the interview, and the number of times the theme appeared, can be found in Table 2.

Table 2. Qualitative analysis of the interview.

Main Theme	Subthemes	Illustrative Expression	N
Practice of physical exercise and sports	Previous	*"I started to practice sports and physical exercise when I was 14/15 years old. (...) Sports were karate and futsal. And physical exercise, gym. (...) And dance, yes."*	1
	After gender affirmation	*"I don't do any sports anymore; I just go to the gym. (...) I usually go 2/3/4 times. I want to go; I will go. Other times, "I have to go on this day to have regularity. (...) I stay as long as I can. I always try to stay 2 h, but sometimes it's only for 45 min, 1 h and a half ... I do more weight training and cardio and occasionally do cycling or something else."*	1
Barriers	Locker rooms divided by gender	*I haven't had the courage to take a shower yet because I still don't have a mastectomy. After the mastectomy, I don't mind showering there, but other than that, there's nothing stopping me from being there and doing my thing."*	7
	University life	*"It's about the college. I had a very irregular schedule. Now, as I will be in exams, it will be easier to be regular, at more certain times, but I had a very irregular schedule in college, so that was a barrier."*	4
	COVID-19 pandemic	*"Yes, I live in a village, and here we have a gym, and we signed up for that gym, but because of the pandemic, it was impossible to continue."*	1
	PT behaviour	*"The worst was perhaps when I went to do my first physical evaluation in the gym. I was a little overweight, and an instructor treated me a bit ... I don't know if it was because I was trans, or I don't know if he noticed, but I felt a little lack of sensitivity from him ... (...) he called me obese, and I felt a little bit sick. When I started the treatment, I started to eat a lot more and with the pandemic, it made it a little difficult to lose weight or maintain weight. I missed his sensitivity a bit, but other than that I haven't had any negative experiences (...). He was very insensitive. I didn't like him at all."*	1
	Sports characteristics	*"I didn't want to go to the gym, I wanted to do swimming, but obviously, it was a bit more impossible to do this sport for obvious reasons, but of course, yes, of course, there are barriers."*	1

Table 2. *Cont.*

Main Theme	Subthemes	Illustrative Expression	N
	Gender division in the sport	*"For example, when there are places that have a football team that until a certain age is all together, boys and girls, and then from that age onwards you start to divide, boys on one side, girls on the other. There is no sport that is totally mixed, or if there is, I don't know which one, but it is always divided. For example, we are talking more about trans people who identify with their own gender, because that's my perspective, but if I were a non-binary person, I would come here and say, "I don't feel comfortable playing football because there is no team that we are all ... that is everything". It's either a girl or a boy. So yes, it's still a barrier, even for people like me, who identify as male and I have that in my head, and that's what I am, but even so, I could want to do football but not want to play in a male team, I might want to play in a mixed team. These issues still exist. We have already seen several examples of trans people who practiced a modality in the Olympic games and who now practice the same modality, but in a male or female team, contrary to what they practiced before, we saw that it does not matter if that person is trans or not because there are cis women who will be "stronger" than cis men, so I feel that the gender issue doesn't make much sense, because it has already been proven that there will be people of other genders who will be stronger, more agile than you, even if you are of the opposite gender, then I feel like the gender question doesn't make much sense."*	1
Facilitators of physical exercise	Mixed changing rooms	*"Portugal is still conservative, I feel that we have made some progress, but even so, people are still very closed to these issues. If there were neutral changing rooms, it would be ok to have a man, a woman, and a non-binary all together in there. It's a basic need, it's the bathroom, and it's for showering. That's what the locker room is for, it's not to divide up genders, but obviously, it's all for the safety of all parties. I don't mind sharing a locker room with another woman, obviously, but there are people who do, so it might not be safe for us or them."*	3
	Gym environment	*"And although in this city there are a lot of sports, there are infinite sports there. But I didn't feel the need to continue in any. As I wanted to maintain my physical shape or wanted to improve, I decided to go to the gym, because I also think it's more neutral. ... in terms of gender."*	2
	City environment	*"I think it would also depend a lot on where you live, because, for example, I exercise in this city, which is a city where young people from all over the country come to study, and so there ends up being a great flow of diversity of people. I don't know if there are more trans people in that gym, there probably are, but I've never seen them, or I've never noticed them, but from my perspective, from what I can say, I feel like it's safer. Now, for example, a person who is from a more closed city, who has a higher rate of transphobia, I think there may be security issues that can compromise the person."*	1
	Social Experiences	*"I enjoyed going with my male colleagues. It was very natural. They knew me before I came out of the closet as a trans person, and it was all very natural, and I enjoyed going with them and having that locker room conversation. It was all very natural. I think that was the best experience I had."*	1
	Mastectomy	*"The mastectomy will open many doors."*	1

Table 2. *Cont.*

Main Theme	Subthemes	Illustrative Expression	N
Motives for physical exercise practice	Mental health	*"I exercise to take a moment for myself, to think about my stuff, and I think we're all like that, no matter the gender, no matter cis or trans. I think everyone will do physical exercise also for a mental issue."*	3
	Energy release	*"I've never liked being quiet, so it's a good way to spend energy."*	2
	Health	*"For health too."*	1
	Desire to achieve a specific physical form	*"As I am already on my hormonal treatment, physical exercise will help me a lot to get what I want, the body I want."*	1
	Pleasure	*"It's because I like it."*	1
Safety of the places	Gyms as safe places	*"I cannot generalize. I've only had experiences in two; one was, literally, a garage. I don't have much to go on. I feel that, in my experience, they are safe, despite the issue of the changing room. In the exercise itself, people don't want to know who you are."*	1

Note: N = frequency response in each subtheme.

3.1. The Practice of Physical Exercise and Sports

In this topic, subthemes emerged before gender affirmation (N = 1) and after gender affirmation (N = 1). Before gender affirmation, the participant practiced sports (specifically karate and futsal) and PE at a gym. After gender affirmation, the participant abandoned sports and remained only in the gym.

3.2. Barriers to Engaging in Physical Activity and Sports

Regarding barriers, six subthemes were identified: locker rooms divided by gender (N = 7), university life (N = 4), COVID-19 pandemic (N = 1), PT behavior (N = 1), sports characteristics (N = 1) and gender division in sport (N = 1). The most discussed subtopic throughout the interview was locker rooms, followed by university life. The participant feels uncomfortable taking a bath in the changing rooms. In addition, the participant presents the irregular college schedulers as a factor that hinders a more assiduous practice of PE.

3.3. Facilitators of Physical Exercise

Regarding facilitators of PE, five subthemes were identified: mixed changing rooms (N = 3), gym environment (N = 2), city environment (N = 1), social experiences (N = 1) and mastectomy (N = 1).

3.4. Motives for Physical Exercise

Five subthemes related to motives for PE practice were identified: mental health (N = 3), energy release (N = 2), health (N = 1), desire to achieve a specific physical form (N = 1) and pleasure (N = 1). The participant reported mental health maintenance as the main motive for exercise practice.

3.5. Safety of the Places

Regarding the safety of the places, one subtheme was identified: gyms as a safe place (N = 1).

4. Discussion

The present study case aimed to fill a gap in the literature regarding knowledge of the experience of the practice of PA, PE and sports in trans individuals. This study aimed to help create more inclusive and safer spaces for the practice of PE and sports, explicitly considering the higher levels of sedentary behaviors and the lower practice of PE and sports of the entire population. Thus, some barriers were identified in the present study, which can also be found in a recent systematic review of the topic by Oliveira et al. [13].

4.1. Satisfaction with Life

Regarding satisfaction with life, the average was 4.60, which means that the individual was slightly satisfied with life. However, the literature indicates that trans individuals tend to report reduced levels of satisfaction with life [31], which is easily explained since trans individuals tend to experience situations of discrimination [5], abuse and violence [4], and difficulties in accessing health and employment opportunities [3]. However, the slight satisfaction reported by the participant in the present study can be explained by the results of the study by Drydakis [32], which suggest that changing one's appearance to match gender identity and transitioning can be positively associated with life satisfaction. In addition, parental support regarding gender identity and expression seems to be related to greater life satisfaction in trans individuals [33].

4.2. Well-Being and Quality of Life

In the emotional dimension of subjective well-being, the values of positive affect were higher than those of negative affect, and there was an absence of depressive and anxious symptomatology. The participant seemed to be slightly satisfied with life, and this topic was positively related to positive affect [34] and negatively correlated with depression and anxiety [35]; in the same sense, these results were also not in accordance with the literature, since this population presents high levels of mental health problems [3,36,37], namely, with the presence of anxious and depressive symptomatology [38]. With regard to the quality of life, despite the participant in the present study having a good quality of life, evidence suggests that transgender people have a lower quality of life than the general population [39]. Hormone therapy has been associated with increased quality of life and decreased depression and anxiety [40,41], which may explain all the positive values that the participant presented related to these topics, since hormone treatment had already started.

4.3. Type of PA Practiced

The differences regarding this aspect before and after gender affirmation seemed to play an essential role in characterizing transgender individuals' participation in PE and sports [42]. Individual activities, such as the gym, and collective and individual sports, such as futsal, karate, and dance, were the activities that the participant of this study performed until his gender affirmation. After that, sports were no longer part of his PE routine. In a study by López-Cañada and colleagues [42], their results revealed that the participation of trans people in unorganized PA and sports activities is higher than in organized activities after gender disclosure. In the same study, it was also reported that the activities most practiced after gender disclosure were jogging, walking and bodybuilding [42]. These results can be justified by the fact that trans individuals tend to avoid social interaction [17] due to fear and anxiety about the reaction of other people [43–45].

4.4. Barriers to Practice

The results of this study were in accordance with the recent systematic review by Oliveira and colleagues [13], especially regarding external barriers. Inadequate changing facilities and regulations surrounding gender were some of the obstacles mentioned in the present study, corroborating the findings of the previous systematic review. The bathhouse continued to be the most mentioned subject, with the structure and gender division of the changing rooms mentioned seven times by the participant and presented as the barrier that generates the most concern. This is supported by previous literature [12,13,16,43,46,47] and, consequently, the aspect that should have most attention in the context of practice. Changing rooms and bathrooms, characterized as awkward or unsafe places that produce a fear of social rejection [17,42], and where many trans people experience embarrassment and stress [15], are sites of hateful violence against trans and non-conforming people [48].

Furthermore, the binary system and the lack of private curtains are factors that create inequality and exclusion of trans children in the school context [49]. In order to solve this problem, *"there could even be mixed changing rooms"* as suggested by our participant. Neutral or mixed changing rooms with structures that provide greater privacy are the PE facilitator most mentioned in this study, and also a strategy presented several times in other articles (e.g., [16,17,47]. To make changing rooms more comfortable and safer for everyone, strategies, such as those mentioned above, should be considered and implemented in different contexts of PE and sports by fitness organizations and sports clubs, or even in educational contexts.

The binary structure is not only a characteristic of changing rooms but also of the sports context and culture [19]. The gender division in sports is based on the assumption that sex and gender are binary and immutable characteristics and that physical differences between men and women substantially affect athletic performance [50]. In this study, it was reported as a barrier to trans individuals' participation in sports, as it limits participation to people whose sex does not match their gender identity. This is an important aspect for sports organizations to consider. Mixed sports should be a strategy for fair and inclusive participation.

Some sports, notably swimming (as confirmed by the participant in the present study), are less popular among transgender individuals due to excessive body exposure [51], and swimming pools are often considered unsafe spaces in both pre- and post-transition phases [15]. Therefore, it is important that sports organizations create inclusive strategies and spaces where everyone feels comfortable during practice. *"The mastectomy will open me many doors"*. In this study, performing upper surgery is presented as one of the facilitators of PE practice. This is a factor also presented in the study by Jones and colleagues [44], where two participants who had chest reconstructive surgery reported feeling more comfortable and engaged in more PA. This is important data for healthcare systems in order to provide conditions and quick access to gender affirmation programs. A qualitative study by Elling-Machartzki [15] also demonstrated the importance that the transition phase has in PA and sports engagement. In fact, participants felt more comfortable with their bodies during PE and sports after the transition [15]. These data are extremely important, especially for healthcare systems. New inclusive policies and conditions should be considered to facilitate the process of gender-affirming surgery and care, as it seems to influence the quality of life of trans individuals.

University life was another barrier mentioned several times (n = 4) in this study. The transition from high school to university, lack of time, and irregular schedules characteristic of college life seem to be the main reasons that prevented more active participation [52–54]. In addition, the COVID-19 pandemic was also presented as one of the factors limiting practice, which is not surprising, since it negatively impacted PA [55]. This is supported by a recent systematic review [56], where the results report a decrease in PA and an increase in sedentary behaviors of several populations during confinement.

In the present study, the worst experience mentioned by the participant in the context of PE was related to the behavior of a personal trainer, which presented itself as another barrier to practice, and this professional may determine their continuity or drop out [57]. This is important, especially when dealing with a sexual minority, such as trans people, who mostly have negative experiences in the context of sports and PE [13,19,58]. On the other hand, social experiences, in addition to being a facilitator of PE identified in this study, were also the participant's best experiences. In a study by Unger and Johnson [59], the results suggested that friendships that involve exercising together and the social contacts that result from the practice of PE can motivate exercise behavior.

4.5. Reasons to Practice

The practice of PE has numerous benefits regarding the maintenance or improvement of mental health [60], and this was the most discussed theme throughout this study. In the literature, regular practice of PE and PA is associated with improved mental health and the prevention of anxiety and depression disorders [61–63]. In addition to this topic, physical health was also mentioned as one of the reasons to practice. The importance of practicing PA and PE in order to prevent several diseases, such as cardiovascular diseases, diabetes and obesity, was evident [64–66]. The fact that physical and mental health were the main reasons for practicing PE in this study suggests that people, especially trans people, are increasingly recognizing the key role that PA and PE can play in maintaining and improving mental and physical health. This awareness is extremely important to promote more active and healthier lifestyles in the future.

In the present study, pleasure was identified as one of the reasons for the practice: *"Because I like it"*. Although the trans population does not refer to it as one of the main factors that promote the practice [47], the link between enjoyment and adherence and continuity of practice in different contexts of PA has been studied over time. Studies suggest that enjoyment seems to be a relevant predictor for the continuity and adherence to PA in gyms [57,67] and in the sports context [68]. Moreover, the desire to achieve a specific physical form, which was another reason for the practice identified in this study, is one of the most mentioned topics in the literature [15,45,47,69]. In this case, similar to those studies, the aesthetic issue is not only related to a construction of their body image with a social stereotype, but with the need to accelerate the changes produced by hormonal treatment.

4.6. Facilitators to Practice

The gym and city environment were also identified as facilitators of practice. The fact that there is no sex segregation in the gym makes it a more neutral space compared to sports that are divided between men and women. This finding in the present study may explain the results of the study by López-Cañada and colleagues [42,46], who reported a decrease in the participation of transgender individuals in sports such as football and basketball, and an increase in bodybuilding after gender disclosure. In addition, geographic factors seem to influence the practice of PE and sports. The results of this study suggest that cities with a greater diversity of people end up becoming safer and more comfortable spaces for trans people compared to cities with higher rates of transphobia and lower diversity. In fact, the environment in which the exercise takes place seems to influence the practice experience and the practitioner's behavior [57], especially in trans individuals who frequently experience situations of discrimination, abuse and violence [3,4].

In the present study, there were no reports of harassment, discrimination or transphobia. According to the participant of this study, Portuguese gyms and sports clubs are usually safe places where *"people don't want to know who you are"*. Although the experience reported in the present study was mostly good, there are still aspects, which are also reported in the existing literature, that require the attention of the sports and fitness community, especially regarding sports and PE facilities. The binary system of changing rooms and the lack of privacy in them is something that seems to concern trans individuals, as well as the sex segregation existing in sports. It is necessary to find strategies that correspond to the needs of practitioners and that guarantee safety, comfort and inclusion for all, considering the creation of mixed changing rooms with private cubicles for bathing and changing, and the creation of mixed teams.

5. Practical Implications

Case studies are important for research, since they capture a wider range of perspectives, contrary to the use of surveys. Therefore, this study may have important implications for the practice. Firstly, it may be important for gyms and sports clubs to have a greater sensitivity to these issues. They may minimize some behaviors so that trans individuals can feel safer during the practice of sports. For example, it may be important to consider creating specific spaces for non-binary people (e.g., gender-neutral changing rooms). It is also crucial that both gyms and sports clubs assess these perceptions of their members very carefully in order to enhance the benefits of sports and physical exercise. Namely, the importance of focusing on the benefits for mental health is highlighted, since this was an emerging point from this study. On the other hand, this study draws attention to possible threats and barriers to the practice of sports that must be addressed. The presence of friendlier spaces for showering and changing clothes and the decrease of gender division in team sports (or the creation of mixed teams) should be strategies to be considered. In addition, improving inappropriate behaviour by PTs is important and should be a priority. In an increasingly inclusive world, where barriers are being broken down, and it is becoming easier to assume one's gender identity, it is possible that the number of difficulties for trans individuals to participate in PE and sporting activities will increase. Thus, it is of the utmost importance to better understand the specific challenges that a transgender individual may experience when engaging in sports activities and PE. This study draws attention to research questions that should be further explored. It is important that future studies look into these issues, so that exercise and sports are safe practices for all individuals and enjoyable moments. This way, their benefits (not only physical but also psychological) will be enhanced.

6. Limitations and Future Research

Despite its contributions to research and practical implications, this study has some limitations that should be acknowledged, and that can guide future research. Firstly, as a case study, the present study only analyzed the experiences of one trans individual and cannot be generalized, which means that the results should not be generalized to the entire trans community. Thus, it is important that future research includes larger samples in various contexts. Reaching out to LGBTQ+ associations or other kind of organizations where these issues are important could be a way to achieve a more representative sample. Secondly, this study only provided the perspective of trans men in its specific context. In future research, it is important to identify the barriers, motives and facilitators that trans women may also be facing, as well as the differences between the experiences of trans women and trans men in sports and exercise contexts. Finally, the inclusion of people surrounding the trans individuals (e.g., coaches, fitness and sports managers, physical education teachers, etc.) should be considered in order to have the perspectives of sports and PE professionals and a better understanding of the existing sports policies in these contexts.

7. Conclusions

After gender affirmation, there are changes in the amount and type of physical activities practiced by trans individuals. Changing rooms divided by gender and university life may be factors that hinder a comfortable and regular practice of PE and sports. The characteristics of the sports, the behavior of personal trainers, and the COVID-19 pandemic were also identified as possible barriers to practice. Furthermore, mental health was the most frequently mentioned reason to practice PE throughout this study. Besides this, it seems that the creation of mixed changing rooms and mixed sports teams would be an inclusive strategy that would facilitate the practice of PE for transgender people.

Author Contributions: Conceptualization, J.O., R.F., M.J. and R.A.; methodology, J.O. and R.F.; validation, M.J., and R.A.; investigation, J.O., R.F., M.J. and R.A.; resources, J.O., R.F., M.J. and R.A.; data curation, J.O., R.F., M.J. and R.A.; writing—original draft preparation, J.O. and R.F.; writing—review and editing, M.J. and R.A.; visualization, J.O., R.F., M.J. and R.A.; supervision, R.F., and R.A. All authors have read and agreed to the published version of the manuscript.

Funding: This work was funded by Portuguese national funds provided by Fundação para a Ciência e Tecnologia (FCT) (UIDB/04748/2020 and UIDP/05704/2020).

Institutional Review Board Statement: The study was conducted in accordance with the Declaration of Helsinki and approved by the Ethics Committee of the Polytechnic of Leiria (reference number: CE/IPLEIRIA/20/2022).

Informed Consent Statement: Informed consent was obtained from all subjects involved in the study.

Data Availability Statement: Additional data are available to the corresponding author upon request.

Conflicts of Interest: The authors declare no conflict of interest.

References

1. Goodman, M.; Adams, N.; Cornell, T.; Kreukels, B.; Motmans, J.; Coleman, E. Size and Distribution of Transgender and Gender Nonconforming Populations: A Narrative Review. *Endocrinol. Metab. Clin. N. Am.* **2019**, *48*, 303–321. [CrossRef] [PubMed]
2. Costa, C.; Pereira, M.; de Oliveira, J.; Nogueira, C. Imagens Sociais Das Pessoas LGBT. In *Estudo Sobre a Discriminação em Função da Orientação Sexual e da Identidade de Género*; Comissão para a Cidadania e a Igualdade de Género, Ed.; Clássica Artes Gráficas: Porto, Portugal, 2010; pp. 93–147.
3. Klemmer, C.L.; Arayasirikul, S.; Raymond, H.F. Transphobia-Based Violence, Depression, and Anxiety in Transgender Women: The Role of Body Satisfaction. *J. Interpers. Violence* **2021**, *36*, 2633–2655. [CrossRef]
4. Lombardi, E.L.; Malouf, D. Gender Violence: Transgender Experiences with Violence and Discrimination. *J. Homosex.* **2001**, *42*, 89–101. [CrossRef]
5. Owen-Smith, A.A.; Sineath, C.; Sanchez, T.; Dea, R.; Giammattei, S.; Gillespie, T.; Helms, M.F.; Hunkeler, E.M.; Quinn, V.P.; Roblin, D.; et al. Perception of Community Tolerance and Prevalence of Depression among Transgender Persons. *J. Gay Lesbian Ment. Health* **2017**, *21*, 64–76. [CrossRef]
6. Ellis, S.J.; McNeil, J.; Bailey, L. Gender, Stage of Transition and Situational Avoidance: A UK Study of Trans People's Experiences. *Sex. Relatsh. Ther.* **2014**, *29*, 351–364. [CrossRef]
7. Herrick, S.S.C.; Duncan, L.R. A Systematic Scoping Review of Engagement in Physical Activity among LGBTQ+ Adults. *J. Phys. Act. Health* **2018**, *15*, 226–232. [CrossRef]
8. American Psychologist Association; Guidelines for Psychological Practice With Transgender and Gender Nonconforming People. *Am. Psychol.* **2015**, *70*, 832–864. [CrossRef]
9. Guidelines for the Primary and Gender-Affirming Care of Transgender and Gender Nonbinary People. Available online: https://transcare.ucsf.edu/guidelines (accessed on 3 November 2022).
10. Coleman, E.; Bockting, W.; Botzer, M.; Cohen-Kettenis, P.; DeCuypere, G.; Feldman, J.; Fraser, L.; Green, J.; Knudson, G.; Meyer, W.J. Standards of Care for the Health of Transsexual, Transgender, and Gender Nonconforming People. *Int. J. Transgend.* **2012**, *7*, 165–232. [CrossRef]
11. James, S.E.; Herman, J.L.; Rankin, S.; Keisling, M.; Mottet, L.; Anafi, M. *About the National Center for Transgender Equality*; National Center for Transgender Equality: Washington, DC, USA, 2016.
12. Symons, C.; Sbaraglia, M.; Hillier, L.; Mitchell, A. *Come out to Play: The Sports Experiences of Lesbian, Gay, Bisexual and Transgender LGBT) People in Victoria*; Institute of Sport, Exercise and Active Living: Melbourne, Australia, 2010; ISBN 9781921377860.
13. Oliveira, J.; Frontini, R.; Jacinto, M.; Antunes, R. Barriers and Motives for Physical Activity and Sports Practice among Trans People: A Systematic Review. *Sustainability* **2022**, *14*, 5295. [CrossRef]
14. Witcomb, G.L.; Bouman, W.P.; Brewin, N.; Richards, C.; Fernandez-Aranda, F.; Arcelus, J. Body Image Dissatisfaction and Eating-Related Psychopathology in Trans Individuals: A Matched Control Study. *Eur. Eat. Disord. Rev.* **2015**, *23*, 287–293. [CrossRef]
15. Elling-Machartzki, A. Extraordinary Body-Self Narratives: Sport and Physical Activity in the Lives of Transgender People. *Leis. Stud.* **2017**, *36*, 256–268. [CrossRef]
16. Pérez-Samaniego, V.; Fuentes-Miguel, J.; Pereira-García, S.; López-Cañada, E.; Devís-Devís, J. Experiences of Trans Persons in Physical Activity and Sport: A Qualitative Meta-Synthesis. *Sport Manag. Rev.* **2019**, *22*, 439–451. [CrossRef]
17. López-Cañada, E.; Devís-Devís, J.; Pereira-García, S.; Pérez-Samaniego, V. Socio-Ecological Analysis of Trans People's Participation in Physical Activity and Sport. *Int. Rev. Sociol. Sport* **2021**, *56*, 62–80. [CrossRef]
18. Bradlow, J.; Bartram, F.; Stonewall, A.; Jadva, V. School Report: The Experiences of Lesbian, Gay, Bi and Trans People in Britain's in 2017. Available online: https://healtheducationresources.unesco.org/library/documents/school-report-experiences-lesbian-gay-bi-and-trans-young-people-britains-schools (accessed on 3 November 2022).
19. Hargie, O.D.W.; Mitchell, D.H.; Somerville, I.J.A. 'People Have a Knack of Making You Feel Excluded If They Catch on to Your Difference': Transgender Experiences of Exclusion in Sport. *Int. Rev. Sociol. Sport* **2017**, *52*, 223–239. [CrossRef]
20. Harper, J.; O'Donnell, E.; Sorouri Khorashad, B.; McDermott, H.; Witcomb, G.L. How Does Hormone Transition in Transgender Women Change Body Composition, Muscle Strength and Haemoglobin? Systematic Review with a Focus on the Implications for Sport Participation. *Br. J. Sports Med.* **2021**, *55*, 865–872. [CrossRef]
21. Roberts, J.L.; Williams, J.; Griffith, G.M.; Jones, R.S.P.; Hastings, R.P.; Crane, R.; Bryning, L.; Hoare, Z.; Edwards, R.T. Soles of the Feet Meditation Intervention for People with Intellectual and Problems with Anger and Aggression-a Feasibility Study. *Mindfulness* **2020**, *11*, 2371–2385. [CrossRef]
22. Harper, J.; Hirschberg, A.L.; Jose, M.; Patino, M.; Ritzén, M.; Vilain, E.; Partner, J.T.; Bird, B.; Riley, L.; Thill, C. IOC Consensus Meeting on Sex Reassignment and Hyperandrogenism. Available online: https://stillmed.olympic.org/Documents/Commissions_PDFfiles/Medical_commission/2015-11_ioc_consensus_meeting_on_sex_reassignment_and_hyperandrogenism-en.pdf (accessed on 3 November 2022).

23. Elling, A.; Collot d'Escury, K. Between Stigmatization and Empowerment. Meanings of Physical Activity and Sport in the Lives of Transgender People. In *Transgender Athletes in Competitive Sport*; Anderson, E.A.T.A., Ed.; Routledge: New York, NY, USA, 2017; pp. 54–67.
24. World Medical Association World Medical Association Declaration of Helsinki: Ethical Principles for Medical Research Involving Human Subjects. *JAMA* **2013**, *310*, 2191–2194. [CrossRef]
25. Tong, A.; Sainsbury, P.; Craig, J. Consolidated Criteria for Reporting Qualitative Research (COREQ): A 32-Item Checklist for Interviews and Focus Groups. *Int. J. Qual. Health Care* **2007**, *19*, 349–357. [CrossRef]
26. Neto, F. The Satisfaction with Life Scale: Psychometrics Properties in an Adolescent Sample. *J. Youth Adolesc.* **1993**, *22*, 125–134. [CrossRef]
27. Galinha, I.C.; Pereira, C.R.; Esteves, F. Versão Reduzida Da Escala Portuguesa de Afeto Positivo e Negativo-PANAS-¬-VRP: Análise Fatorial Confirmatória e Invariância Temporal. Available online: https://repositorio.ul.pt/handle/10451/11477 (accessed on 3 November 2022).
28. Pais-Ribeiro, J.; Silva, I.; Ferreira, T.; Martins, A.; Meneses, R.; Baltar, M. Validation Study of a Portuguese Version of the Hospital Anxiety and Depression Scale. *Psychol. Health Med.* **2007**, *12*, 225–237. [CrossRef]
29. Pereira, M.; Melo, C.; Gameiro, S.; Canavarro, M.C. Estudos Psicométricos Da Versão Em Português Europeu Do Índice de Qualidade de Vida EUROHIS-QOL-8. Available online: https://www.scielo.br/j/rbp/a/4rMkYnHFQ5BtHfs5TjPcmkM/?lang=en (accessed on 5 November 2022).
30. Miles, M.B.; Huberman, M.; Miles, M.B.; Huberman, A.M. *Qualitative Data Analysis: An Expanded Sourcebook*, 2nd ed.; Sage: Newbury Park, CA, USA, 1994.
31. Anderssen, N.; Sivertsen, B.; Lønning, K.J.; Malterud, K. Life Satisfaction and Mental Health among Transgender Students in Norway. *BMC Public Health* **2020**, *20*, 138. [CrossRef] [PubMed]
32. Drydakis, N. Trans People, Transitioning, Mental Health, Life, and Job Satisfaction. In *Handbook of Labor, Human Resources and Population Economics*; Springer: Berlin/Heidelberg, Germany, 2020; pp. 1–22.
33. Robb, T. *Impacts of Strong Parental Support for Trans Youth. A Report Prepared for Children's Aid Society of Toronto and Delisle Youth Services Purpose of Report*; Trans PULSE: Toronto, ON, Canada, 2012.
34. Jovanović, V.; Joshanloo, M. The Contribution of Positive and Negative Affect to Life Satisfaction across Age. *Appl. Res. Qual. Life* **2022**, *17*, 511–524. [CrossRef]
35. Hoseini-Esfidarjani, S.S.; Tanha, K.; Negarandeh, R. Satisfaction with Life, Depression, Anxiety, and Stress among Adolescent Girls in Tehran: A Cross Sectional Study. *BMC Psychiatry* **2022**, *22*, 109. [CrossRef]
36. Connolly, M.D.; Zervos, M.J.; Barone, C.J.; Johnson, C.C.; Joseph, C.L.M. The Mental Health of Transgender Youth: Advances in Understanding. *J. Adolesc. Health* **2016**, *59*, 489–495. [CrossRef]
37. Budge, S.L.; Adelson, J.L.; Howard, K.A.S. Anxiety and Depression in Transgender Individuals: The Roles of Transition Status, Loss, Social Support, and Coping. *J. Consult. Clin. Psychol.* **2013**, *81*, 545–557. [CrossRef]
38. Watson, D.; Clark, L.A.; Carey, G. Positive and Negative Affectivity and Their Relation to Anxiety and Depressive Disorders. *J. Abnorm. Psychol.* **1988**, *97*, 346–353. [CrossRef]
39. Nobili, A.; Glazebrook, C.; Arcelus, J. Quality of Life of Treatment-Seeking Transgender Adults: A Systematic Review and Meta-Analysis. *Rev. Endocr. Metab. Disord.* **2018**, *19*, 199–220. [CrossRef]
40. White Hughto, J.M.; Reisner, S.L. A Systematic Review of the Effects of Hormone Therapy on Psychological Functioning and Quality of Life in Transgender Individuals. *Transgend. Health* **2016**, *1*, 21–31. [CrossRef] [PubMed]
41. Wilson, L.M.; Sharma, R.; Dukhanin, V.; McArthur, K.; Robinson, K.A.; Baker, K.E. Hormone Therapy, Mental Health, and Quality of Life among Transgender People: A Systematic Review. *J. Endocr. Soc.* **2021**, *5*, bvab011. [CrossRef]
42. López-Cañada, E.; Devís-Devís, J.; Valencia-Peris, A.; Pereira-García, S.; Fuentes-Miguel, J.; Pérez-Samaniego, V. Physical Activity and Sport in Trans Persons before and after Gender Disclosure: Prevalence, Frequency, and Type of Activities. *J. Phys. Act. Health* **2020**, *17*, 650–656. [CrossRef]
43. Gilani, M.; Wallach, P.; Kyriakou, A. Levels of Physical Activity and Barriers to Sport Participation in Young People with Gender Dysphoria. *J. Pediatr. Endocrinol. Metab.* **2021**, *34*, 747–753. [CrossRef] [PubMed]
44. Jones, B.A.; Arcelus, J.; Bouman, W.P.; Haycraft, E. Barriers and Facilitators of Physical Activity and Sport Participation among Young Transgender Adults Who Are Medically Transitioning. *Int. J. Transgend.* **2017**, *18*, 227–238. [CrossRef]
45. Teti, M.; Bauerband, L.A.; Rolbiecki, A.; Young, C. Physical Activity and Body Image: Intertwined Health Priorities Identified by Transmasculine Young People in a Non-Metropolitan Area. *Int. J. Transgend. Health* **2020**, *21*, 209–219. [CrossRef] [PubMed]
46. Herrick, S.S.C.; Rocchi, M.A.; Couture, A.L. A Case Study Exploring the Experiences of a Transgender Athlete in Synchronized Skating, a Subdiscipline of Figure Skating. *J. Sport Soc. Issues* **2020**, *44*, 421–449. [CrossRef]
47. Jones, B.A.; Arcelus, J.; Bouman, W.P.; Haycraft, E. Sport and Transgender People: A Systematic Review of the Literature Relating to Sport Participation and Competitive Sport Policies. *Sport Med.* **2017**, *47*, 701–716. [CrossRef]
48. Bender-Baird, K. Punto de Vista Orinando Bajo Vigilancia: Baños, Vigilancia de Género y Violencia de Odio. *Gend. Place Cult.* **2016**, *23*, 983–988. [CrossRef]
49. Sørlie, A. Transgender Children's Right to Non-Discrimination in Schools: The Case of Changing-Room Facilities. *Int. J. Child. Rights* **2020**, *28*, 221–242. [CrossRef]

50. Griffi, P. "Ain't I a Woman?" Transgender and Intersex Student athletes in Women's Collegiate Sports. In *Transfeminis Perspectives in and Beyond Transgender and Gender Studies*; Enke, A., Ed.; Temple University Press: Philadelphia, PA, USA, 2012; pp. 98–111.
51. National Union of Students (NUS). *Out in Sport: LGBT Students' Experiences of Sport*; National Union of Students: London, UK, 2012.
52. Bray, S.R.; Born, H.A. Transition to University and Vigorous Physical Activity: Implications for Health and Psychological Well-Being. *J. Am. Coll. Health* **2004**, *52*, 181–188. [CrossRef]
53. Kljajević, V.; Stanković, M.; Đorđević, D.; Trkulja-Petković, D.; Jovanović, R.; Plazibat, K.; Oršolić, M.; Čurić, M.; Sporiš, G. Physical Activity and Physical Fitness among University Students—A Systematic Review. *Int. J. Environ. Res. Public Health* **2022**, *19*, 158. [CrossRef]
54. Wilson, O.W.A.; Walters, S.R.; Naylor, M.E.; Clarke, J.C. Changes in Physical Activity and Motives Following the Transition from High School to University. *Int. J. Kinesiol. High. Educ.* **2022**, *6*, 56–67. [CrossRef]
55. Puccinelli, P.J.; da Costa, T.S.; Seffrin, A.; de Lira, C.A.B.; Vancini, R.L.; Nikolaidis, P.T.; Knechtle, B.; Rosemann, T.; Hill, L.; Andrade, M.S. Reduced Level of Physical Activity during COVID-19 Pandemic Is Associated with Depression and Anxiety Levels: An Internet-Based Survey. *BMC Public Health* **2021**, *21*, 425. [CrossRef]
56. Stockwell, S.; Trott, M.; Tully, M.; Shin, J.; Barnett, Y.; Butler, L.; McDermott, D.; Schuch, F.; Smith, L. Changes in Physical Activity and Sedentary Behaviours from before to during the COVID-19 Pandemic Lockdown: A Systematic Review. *BMJ Open Sport Exerc. Med.* **2021**, *7*, e000960. [CrossRef] [PubMed]
57. Rodrigues, F.; Teixeira, D.S.; Neiva, H.P.; Cid, L.; Monteiro, D. The Bright and Dark Sides of Motivation as Predictors of Enjoyment, Intention, and Exercise Persistence. *Scand. J. Med. Sci. Sports* **2020**, *30*, 787–800. [CrossRef] [PubMed]
58. Hartmann-Tews, I.; Menzel, T.; Braumüller, B. Experiences of LGBTQ+ Individuals in Sports in Germany. *Ger. J. Exerc. Sport Res.* **2022**, *52*, 39–49. [CrossRef]
59. Unger, J.B.; Johnson, C.A. Social Relationships and Physical Activity in Health Club Members. *Am. J. Health Promot.* **1995**, *9*, 340–343. [CrossRef]
60. Mikkelsen, K.; Stojanovska, L.; Polenakovic, M.; Bosevski, M.; Apostolopoulos, V. Exercise and Mental Health. *Maturitas* **2017**, *106*, 48–56. [CrossRef]
61. Carek, P.J.; Laibstain, S.E.; Carek, S.M. Exercise for the Treatment of Depression and Anxiety. *Int. J. Psychiatry Med.* **2011**, *41*, 15–28. [CrossRef]
62. de Mello, M.T.; Lemos, V.D.A.; Antunes, H.K.M.; Bittencourt, L.; Santos-Silva, R.; Tufik, S. Relationship between Physical Activity and Depression and Anxiety Symptoms: A Population Study. *J. Affect. Disord.* **2013**, *149*, 241–246. [CrossRef]
63. Ströhle, A. Physical Activity, Exercise, Depression and Anxiety Disorders. *J. Neural Transm.* **2009**, *116*, 777–784. [CrossRef]
64. Myers, J. Exercise and Cardiovascular Health. *Circulation* **2003**, *107*, 2–5. [CrossRef]
65. Pinckard, K.; Baskin, K.K.; Stanford, K.I. Effects of Exercise to Improve Cardiovascular Health. *Front. Cardiovasc. Med.* **2019**, *6*, 69. [CrossRef] [PubMed]
66. Warburton, D.E.R.; Nicol, C.W.; Bredin, S.S.D. Health Benefits of Physical Activity: The Evidence. *CMAJ* **2006**, *174*, 801–809. [CrossRef] [PubMed]
67. Calder, A.J.; Hargreaves, E.A.; Hodge, K. Great Expectations: A Qualitative Analysis of the Factors That Influence Affective Forecasts for Exercise. *Int. J. Environ. Res. Public Health* **2020**, *17*, 551. [CrossRef] [PubMed]
68. Nielsen, G.; Wikman, J.M.; Jensen, C.J.; Schmidt, J.F.; Gliemann, L.; Andersen, T.R. Health Promotion: The Impact of Beliefs of Health Benefits, Social Relations and Enjoyment on Exercise Continuation. *Scand. J. Med. Sci. Sports* **2014**, *24*, 66–75. [CrossRef] [PubMed]
69. Robinson, K.H.; Bansel, P.; Denson, N.; Ovenden, G.; Davies, C. Growing up Queer: Issues Facing Young Australians Who Are Gender Variant and Sexuality Diverse. Available online: http://www.youngandwellcrc.org.au/wp-content/uploads/2014/02/Robinson_2014_GrowingUpQueer.pdf. (accessed on 3 November 2022).

healthcare

MDPI

Article

Attachment Style and Emotional Regulation as Protective and Risk Factors in Mutual Dating Violence among Youngsters: A Moderated Mediation Model

Jessica Morales-Sanhueza *, Guadalupe Martín-Mora-Parra * and Isabel Cuadrado-Gordillo

Department of Psychology and Anthropology, Faculty of Education and Psychology, University of Extremadura, 06071 Badajoz, Spain; cuadrado@unex.es

* Correspondence: prof.moralessanhueza@gmail.com (J.M.-S.); gumartinxmop@unex.es (G.M.-M.-P.)

Abstract: Violence in intimate partner relationships among young adults has become a global health problem given its prevalence and its negative effects on physical and psychological well-being. The severity of the problem has given rise to a large body of research that has attempted to find the variables associated with victimization in young couples (for example, attachment style, emotional regulation skills or empathy, among others). Moreover, traditionally, many of these investigations have only considered the point of view of female victims within a gender violence approach. However, in recent times, more and more evidence of the existence of mutual violence in young relationships has been found. These findings, combined with simplistic explanations of the phenomenon, have proven to be insufficient to prevent it. In this context, the main objective of this study was to investigate how some variables linked to dating violence interact with each other, modifying the mutual violence young people suffer and exercise. Considering this, different instruments were administered (the Experience in Close Relationships Scale (ECR-R); Difficulties in Emotional Regulation Scale (DERS-E); Basic Empathy Scale (BES); and Multidimensional Couple Violence Scale (EMVN)) to a sample of 557 young Chileans. The analysis of the results, based on the construction of a moderated mediation model, reveals that difficulties in emotional regulation are a predictor of violence in intimate partner relationships, whose direct and indirect effects on the violence exercised can be moderated by that partner's attachment style. The findings also reveal that there is no association between empathy and violence, and they highlight that both men and women are victims and aggressors at the same time. This demonstrate the need to consider prevention and intervention strategies aimed at both sexes, since intimate partner violence is mutual and reciprocal.

Keywords: young adults; difficulties in emotional regulation; attachment styles; well-being; mutual violence

check for updates

Citation: Morales-Sanhueza, J.; Martín-Mora-Parra, G.; Cuadrado-Gordillo, I. Attachment Style and Emotional Regulation as Protective and Risk Factors in Mutual Dating Violence among Youngsters: A Moderated Mediation Model. *Healthcare* **2024**, *12*, 605. https://doi.org/10.3390/healthcare12060605

Academic Editors: Victor R. Prybutok and Roberta Frontini

Received: 29 September 2023
Revised: 1 March 2024
Accepted: 4 March 2024
Published: 7 March 2024

1. Introduction

Intimate partner violence in young adults has become a highly relevant social health problem, with growing research interest due to its high prevalence in different countries around the world [1,2]. The interest in addressing this phenomenon in young people is crucial since, at this stage of life, the relationship patterns that determine the way young people will interrelate with others in the future are established [3]. In this context, it is important to highlight that intimate partner violence is any behavior causing physical, psychological, or sexual harm to one of the partners in an intimate relationship, regardless of sex, gender, or who plays the role of the victim or perpetrator [4,5].

The severity of violence in intimate partner relationships between young people is related to the continuity over time of these violent behaviors due to, generally, the fact that the first aggressions do not usually lead to a breakup and cause, in the long term, adverse effects on young peoples' physical health as well as on their social and psychological well-being [6–8]. In fact, it is common for the partners to maintain the relationship, disregarding the abuse based on strongly held beliefs, ideas, or myths about romantic love. In this situation, many victims even justify violent behaviors by mistakenly confusing them with displays of an idealized romantic love [9,10]. These circumstances frequently lead to the normalization of aggressions, which are considered an inherent part of the relationship, or to strategies to cope with their couple conflicts, even minimizing or denying them, especially when these violent episodes are sporadic or conducted through social networks [11–16].

In relation to the prevalence of these violent behaviors in couples, women have traditionally been considered as the victims, a fact that may stem from sexist behaviors maintained by men, and by women themselves, who frequently demonstrate benevolent sexist attitudes [17]. Hence, many women involved in violent relationships consider that the role of men is to protect and care for them, placing themselves in a position of inferiority with respect to men, and behaving in accordance with sexist expectations [18–20]. However, currently, other research has pointed out that women also play the role of the aggressor, finding that the phenomenon of violence in young couple relationships affects both men and women in a reciprocal and bidirectional way [1,21–25].

Considering the above, several studies have analyzed the possible causes underlying the development of these abusive partner relationships and found that the causes are diverse. A theoretical review of 113 investigations identified 30 different variables related to violence in intimate partner relationships. This study allowed for the identification of relevant variables that seem to have an important effect on the establishment and maintenance of abusive relationships, such as the attachment style of the partners and their emotional regulation skills, as well as empathy [26].

Focusing attention on empathy, which is defined as the ability to understand and experience the emotions, thoughts and experiences of another person, which entails experiencing an emotional response and establishing an empathic connection to both emotional and cognitive experiences [27], it is cataloged as one of the most important precipitating factors in intimate partner violence, with the importance of its inhibitory role against violent impulses emphasized, considering that this variable is a protective factor that reduces the probability of aggression [28,29]. In contrast, a low level of empathy, or its absence, would increase the probability of a person assaulting their partner, becoming a facilitator of violence [28–30].

Another factor linked to dating violence among adolescents and young people is attachment style. Adult attachment styles are emotional and behavioral patterns that significantly influence how people engage in affective relationships and manage conflict within their intimate and romantic relationships. These styles are based on early attachment experiences in infancy and associated with abandonment anxiety and intimacy avoidance. Secure-attachment people trust their partner; they are comfortable with intimacy and have low levels of attachment anxiety and avoidance. On the other hand, people with a dismissing attachment style fear intimacy and dependence, are distant with their partners and present high levels of avoidance. Preoccupied-attachment people search for security and constant displays of affection from their partners, fear abandonment and present high levels of anxiety. Finally, fearful-attachment people present high levels of anxiety and avoidance, tending to engage in contradictory behaviors that alternate between anxious and avoidant attachment behaviors [31].

In this regard, several studies have highlighted a connection between secure attachments and the absence of violence in couple relationships. Likewise, secure attachment has been related to better mental and physical health, and, therefore, to well-being [32–34]. Instead, it has been documented that those with an insecure attachment style are more likely to suffer from physical diseases, as well as poor psychological and neurobiological functioning, which continues from childhood into adulthood [35]. Furthermore, many investigations have indicated that attachment styles characterized by high levels of anxiety and avoidance are significantly related to both aggression and victimization during physical violence in an intimate relationship. Thus, attachment style has a crucial role in the way emotions are managed in couples, while also being a moderating factor that could influence, in turn, their emotional regulation, as well as the processes of the functional and dysfunctional expression of anger [36–41].

Regarding the difficulty with emotional regulation, understood as the difficulty for a person to effectively manage their emotions or their inability to maintain emotional balance in times of stress, by not being able to control their impulsive reactions [42], this variable has also been associated with aggressive behaviors. In this way, several authors have indicated that aggressive attitudes are correlated with low levels of emotional regulation, while the absence of violent behavior is associated with greater emotional regulation. Likewise, they point out that difficulties in emotional regulation cause not only various health problems, but they also negatively affect cognitive processes and behavior, facts that can finally lead to the development of different psychopathologies [43–46].

Finally, sexual orientation refers to a person's sexual attraction to men, women, or both. In general, people who are attracted to the opposite sex are considered heterosexual, while those who are attracted to the same sex, or both sexes, are considered non-heterosexual [47]. In this regard, although violence in intimate partner relationships can affect people of any sexual orientation, research focused on young people indicates that heterosexual couples have a higher prevalence of violence in both men and women [48–51], with this prevalence being similar in different countries. In this context, Chile is no exception, since there is evidence that indicates that violence among young Chileans is a problem equivalent (in magnitude) to what has been reported in Latin America and the rest of the world [2]. Specifically, the seriousness of this phenomenon in the country has been proven due to the high prevalence of violence in romantic relationships among young people (psychological violence 51% and physical violence 25%) [2], as well as the consequences derived from this phenomenon that threaten the well-being of young Chileans.

Despite the evidence found, few studies have focused on analyzing the variables that influence the initiation and maintenance of abusive dating relationships in Latin America, and the way those factors interact with each other, as they mainly focus on describing the prevalence and the factors associated with the phenomenon. Additionally, even fewer studies have focused on mutual violence in the dating relationships of young couples. Consequently, more specific studies are needed to analyze the influence and interactions of less-explored variables, such as difficulties in emotional regulation, attachment style, empathy, and sexual orientation, to determine their importance in the prediction of violence and in the promotion of well-being in young couples. In this context, the main objectives of this study are (i) to analyze the prevalence of mutual violence in young university students, and (ii) to study the influence that variables such as difficulties in emotional regulation, attachment style, or empathy have on the violence exercised or suffered in intimate partner relationships between young adult couples, analyzing, additionally, which variables are mediators and moderators. Considering this, the following hypothesis were posited:

H1: *Men and women are both victims and perpetrators of violence in their intimate partner relationships.*

H2: *Attachment styles are related to the violence exercised and suffered in intimate partner relationships.*

H3: *Difficulty with emotional regulation is a predictor of violence in intimate partner relationships in young people, and its influence is also mediated by the attachment styles and empathy that the partners have.*

2. Materials and Methods

2.1. Sample

The sample size required was calculated using G*power 3.1 software's [52,53] recommendations (statistical power = 80%; Effect size = 0.02; $\alpha = 0.05$). The minimum sample size recommended by this software was 395. The final sample consisted of 557 participants,

171 of whom were men (30.7%) and 386 of whom were women (69.2%), aged between 18 and 29 years old (M = 21.62; SD = 2.44).

The sample was selected in three phases. In the first phase, the Universidad Católica de Temuco was chosen, considering the age of the students and the objectives of the study. The first phase ended after contacting the university to explain the characteristics of the research and to ask for permission to administer the questionnaires. The second phase consisted of selecting, randomly, some classes from different grades and majors. The researchers themselves went to every class to obtain informed consent and assure the anonymity and voluntary participation of the students. In each class, the questionnaires were administered collectively. Finally, the third phase consisted of determining the final sample based on the inclusion and exclusion criteria; the inclusion criteria were that participants were university students who had had a previous relationship and were no older than 29 years of age. Therefore, since all participants were university students, only students who had never been in a relationship and who were older than 29 years of age were excluded from the sample.

2.2. *Instruments*

The participants answered a brief survey with questions about their sociodemographic characteristics: age, biological sex, sexual orientation and gender identity, as well as the Spanish version of the Experiences in Close Relationships, the Spanish version of the Difficulties in Emotion Regulation Scale, the Spanish version of the Basic Empathy Scale and the Multidimensional Scale of Dating Violence.

2.2.1. Experience of Close Relationships Scale (ECR-R)

This questionnaire is the Spanish version of the Experiences in Close Relationships (ECR). The Spanish version that was used in the research was a self-reporting instrument comprising a total of 36 items grouped in two Likert-type scales with 7 anchor points, where 1 means "totally disagree" and 7 means "totally agree".

Thus, based on its avoidance and anxiety scales, the ECR-R makes it possible to establish 4 adult attachment styles depending on the level of avoidance and anxiety obtained: secure attachment; preoccupied; dismissing; and fearful [54].

The validation of the ECR-R questionnaire carried out by Alonso-Arbiol et al. in 2007; they performed an exploratory factor analysis with oblique rotation, obtaining two factors that explained 34.65% of the accumulated variance (avoidance 18.9% and anxiety 15.7%). Cronbach's alpha was 0.87 for avoidance and 0.85 for anxiety [55].

2.2.2. Difficulties in Emotion Regulation Scale (DERS-E)

This instrument corresponds to the adapted Spanish version of the Difficulties in Emotion Regulation Scale (DERS), developed by Gratz and Roemer in 2004. This instrument is a self-report questionnaire that allows for the evaluation of emotional regulation difficulties. The scale used is a Likert-type scale with five anchor points, in which 1 corresponds to "almost never" and 5 to "almost always". Higher scores are indicative of a greater degree of difficulty with emotional regulation [56].

The review and adaptation of the DERS-E to the Chilean population, composed of 25 items, confirmed, in general terms, that it is an instrument with reliable and valid psychometric properties, presenting internal consistency indexes that fluctuated between 0.66 and 0.89 [57].

2.2.3. Basic Empathy Scale (BES)

The original self-report scale (Basic Empathy Scale) consists of 20 items that allow for the individual or collective assessment of affective, cognitive and global empathy. This questionnaire includes a Likert-type scale with five anchor points (1 = totally disagree and 5 = totally agree) [58]. A review carried out in the Spanish adolescent population performed an exploratory factor analysis to validate this scale, checking the adequacy of the sample for performing an analysis by means of the Kaiser–Meyer–Olkin test (KMO = 0.83). Subsequently, items with communalities below 0.40 were followed, as well as those whose highest factor weight was below 0.32, those with weights above 0.32 in more than one factor, and those in which the difference between the highest factor weight and the next was below 0.15. In this way, only 9 of the original items were retained. The final factorial solution performed on the nine items revealed the existence of two factors that explain 34.7% of the variance.

2.2.4. Multidimensional Scale of Dating Violence (EMVN)

The EMVN is a valid and reliable scale that measures violent behaviors in the dating relationships that are established among young people. It is a 32-item self-report scale made up of two subscales that measure the violence exerted and suffered by university student couples (with three dimensions: physical and sexual assault, behavioral control and psycho-emotional abuse, as a victim or as an aggressor). The questionnaire includes a Likert-type scale with five anchor points (1 = totally disagree and 5 = totally agree) and the higher the score, the more violence exerted or suffered. This is an instrument with reliable and valid psychometric properties; presenting internal consistency indices that fluctuate between 0.88 and 0.80, it stands out for its easy application, correction and interpretation [13].

2.3. Procedure

Prior to the distribution of the questionnaires, both the research objectives and the procedures, instruments and techniques used were checked and approved by the Bioethics and Biosafety Committee of the University of Extremadura (Spain) (Ref. 95/2023). Subsequently, authorization from the University was obtained and, after that, the potential participants were informed of the objectives, methods and mechanisms used to guarantee anonymity, as well as the confidentiality of their responses and the voluntary nature of the study.

Once informed consent was obtained from the university students, the researchers went themselves to every class at a fixed date and time to administer the questionnaires. A QR code and a link to access the questionnaires (that were administered through the Google Forms platform) were shared. This platform allowed the information to be collected and sorted quickly and easily, also allowing participants to complete the questionnaires using their mobile phones or laptops. The instructions given by the researchers were the same in every class. Additionally, we stayed in the class while the students filled out the different questionnaires to clarify any possible doubts they could have.

2.4. Analysis of Data

To obtain the final sample, a preliminary analysis was conducted to identify participants whose responses to the questionnaire met the inclusion criteria (having previously been in a relationship). In addition, the descriptive and correlational analyses of the different variables included in the sample (attachment, difficulties in emotional regulation, empathy and violence exercised and suffered) were carried out by means of calculating the mean and standard deviation, as well as Spearman's correlation coefficient.

Thereafter, to verify the existence of an association between attachment styles, difficulties in emotional regulation and empathy, the chi-square test was used, as well as Cramer's V statistic, to measure the strength of the association.

Finally, a moderated mediation analysis was performed using "Process" V3.3 to determine the mediating effect of attachment style, as well as the moderating effect of sexual orientation, on the relationship between emotional regulation difficulties and violence in dating relationships [59] (Model 14) (Figure 1).

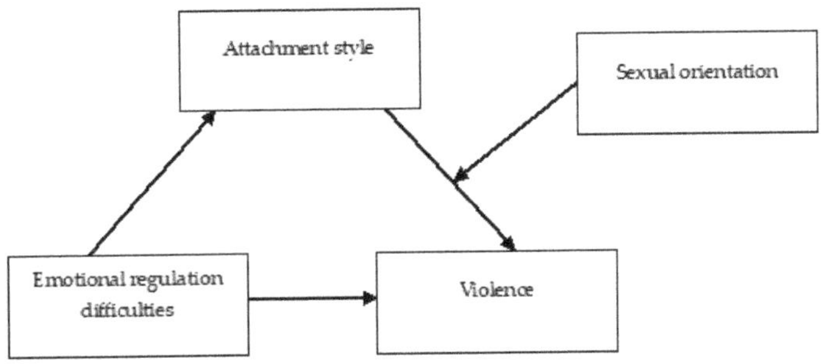

Figure 1. Serial mediation model 14.

Process is an interface used in SPSS that employs least squares regression to estimate the significance and size of the direct and indirect effects in mediation models. With this tool, indirect effects are inferred using bootstrapping after generating an empirical representation of the sampling distribution of the indirect effects. Bootstrapping is suitable for linear hypotheses when the variables are not normally distributed [60]. All analyses were performed using the IBM SPSS v. 24 statistical package.

3. Results

3.1. Descriptive Statistics

The analysis of the results reveals that the sexual orientation of the participants was heterosexual (86%), homosexual (2.2%), bisexual (11.2%), pansexual (0.4%) and demi-sexual (0.2%). In relation to their gender orientation, 68.76% were female, 30.52% were male, 0.17% were fluid and 0.53% were non-binary.

The analysis also shows that all the men in the sample have exercised violence in their intimate partner relationships. On the other hand, the analysis reveals that 99.2% of the women have also committed violence towards their partners. Considering the frequency of violence, this analysis shows that 99.4% of men report being occasional aggressors, while only 6% acknowledge that they have committed violence on a frequent basis. On the other hand, 97.4% of women reported being occasional aggressors. Finally, 1.8% of women reported the frequent violence of their partners (Table 1).

Table 1. Descriptive statistics: exercised and suffered violence.

	Exercised Violence		Suffered Violence	
Frequency	**Men**	**Women**	**Men**	**Women**
Never	0 (0%)	3 (0.8%)	0 (0%)	3 (0.8%)
Occasionally	170 (99.4%)	376 (97.4%)	164 (95.9%)	361 (93.5%)
Frequently	1 (0.6%)	7 (1.8%)	7 (4.1%)	22 (5.7%)

In addition to the above, the data analysis revealed that 302 people in the sample (80 men and 222 women) said they were in a relationship at the time they participated in the study (54.3%).

In the case of the violence suffered, 100% of the men indicated that they had been victims of violence by their partners, 95.9% of them suffered occasional aggression and 4.1% frequent abuse. The responses of the women revealed that 99.2% of them had suffered violence in a dating relationship, with a frequency of occasional violence in 93.5% of the cases and frequent violence in 5.7% (Table 1). These results allow us to conclude that the subjects, regardless of sex, become aggressors and victims at the same time, thus revealing that dating relationships are characterized by mutual aggression and abuse.

Furthermore, considering the dimensions of violence, our analysis of the data reveals that, although violence is bidirectional, abusive behavior is different in men and women.

Women experience a higher prevalence of psycho-emotional, physical and sexual violence. Men, on the other hand, exercise more physical and sexual violence, but experience more behavioral control than women (see Table 2).

Table 2. Descriptive statistics: dimensions of violence exercised and suffered by men and woman.

Dimensions of Violence	Men	Woman
Exercised Violence		
Physical and sexual	14.6%	10.3%
Behavioral control	100%	99%
Psycho-emotional	73.6%	73.1%
Suffered Violence		
Physical and sexual	21.6%	32.1%
Behavioral control	100%	98.7%
Psycho-emotional	44.4%	46.8%

Regarding their attachment style, the results revealed that 27.8% of the participants had a secure attachment, 21.5% had a dismissing attachment, 25% had a preoccupied attachment and, finally, 25.7% had a fearful attachment style. Focusing attention on sex, a higher prevalence of secure attachment was found in men (33.9%) compared to women (25.1%). In addition, the results show that women more often have a fearful attachment (27.2%) or preoccupied attachment style (25.6%) (Table 3).

Table 3. Frequency of attachment styles in men and women.

Attachment Styles	Men	Women
Fearful	38 (22.2%)	105 (27.2%)
Preoccupied	40 (23.4%)	99 (25.6%)
Dismissing	35 (20.5%)	85 (22.0%)
Secure	58 (33.9%)	97 (25.1%)

Complementary to the above, our analysis of the results shows that 66.9% of those who state that they are not in a romantic relationship have a fearful attachment style. Likewise, 74% of those who say they currently have a partner have a secure attachment style (Table 4).

Table 4. Frequency of attachment styles and a current partner.

Current Partner	Fearful	Preoccupied	Dismissing	Secure
No	95 (66.9%)	41 (29.5%)	78 (65.0%)	40 (25.8%)
Yes	47 (33.1%)	98 (70.5%)	42 (35.0%)	115 (4.2%)

Furthermore, our analysis of the results reveals that 49.1% of the sample presented difficulties in emotional regulation. In relation to its prevalence by sex, 55% of women and 36% of men, respectively, present difficulties in emotional regulation. Likewise, 66.7% of those who have never used violence against their partners do not present difficulties in emotional regulation; on the other hand, 50.3% of those who have used violence in their intimate partner relationships have difficulty regulating their emotions. Added to the above, 87.2% of those who present insecure attachment styles present difficulties in emotional regulation (Table 5).

Finally, regarding empathy, the findings indicate that 46.65% of the sample have low levels of empathy and that women have higher levels compared to men (Table 6).

Table 5. Descriptive statistics: attachment styles and difficulties in emotional regulation.

Attachment Style	Difficulties in Emotional Regulation
Fearful	38.3%
Preoccupied	31.8.%
Dismissing	17.1.%
Secure	12.8.%

Table 6. Descriptive statistics: empathy levels in men and woman.

Empathy Level	Men	Women
Low empathy	48.5%	44.8%
High empathy	51.5%	55.2%

3.2. Association Analysis

As for the association analysis, a statistically significant association was found between the variable "difficulties in emotional regulation" (D.E.R.) and "attachment style" ($\chi^2 = 345.378$; $p < 0.01$), with the finding that the strength of the association, measured using Cramer's V coefficient, is moderate (V = 0.455; $p < 0.01$). Likewise, a statistically significant relationship was found between "attachment style" and "exercised violence" ($\chi^2 = 181.395$; $p < 0.01$), with the strength of the association established as moderate (V = 0.329; $p < 0.01$).

On the other hand, a statistically significant relationship was found between "sexual orientation" and "exercised violence" ($\chi^2 = 329.928$; $p < 0.01$), with moderate associative strength (V = 0.386; $p < 0.01$), as well as between "attachment style" and "currently having a partner" ($\chi^2 = 83.166$; $p < 0.01$; V = 0.387; $p < 0.01$).

The analysis also reveals that there is no association between "sex" and "exercised violence or suffered" in intimate partner relationships ($p > 0.05$), between "sex" and "attachment style" ($p > 0.05$), between "empathy" and "exercised violence or suffered" ($p > 0.05$), or between "sex" and "emotional regulation difficulties" ($p > 0.05$).

Finally, our analysis of the correlation matrix (Table 7) indicated that "exercised violence" shows a positive correlation with "difficulties in emotional regulation" (D.E.R.).

Table 7. Spearman correlations.

	1	2	3	4	5
D.E.R.	-				
Attachment	−0.475 **	-			
Sexual Orientation	0.113 **	−0.058	-		
Exercised Violence	0.269 **	−0.343 **	0.056	-	
Suffered Violence	0.164 **	−0.190 **	−0.005	0.681 **	-

Note: 1 = difficulty with emotional regulation; 2 = attachment; 3 = sexual orientation; 4 = exercised violence; 5 = suffered violence; ** $p < 0.01$.

Similarly, "exercised violence" correlates with "suffered violence". Thus, young people who report having performed a high degree of violence against their partners show a high level of difficulty in regulating their emotions. These young adults also suffer a high degree of violence, being victimized themselves, both in the case of males and females. Additionally, a statistically significant and negative correlation was found between "attachment" and "D.E.R.". This finding indicates that a secure attachment style is linked to fewer difficulties in emotional regulation. Finally, the variable "attachment" shows a negative correlation with "exercised violence", revealing that secure attachment styles are related to less violence exercised in intimate partner relationships. In contrast, attachment styles characterized by high anxiety or avoidance are linked to the violence exercised and suffered in intimate partner relationships (Table 7).

3.3. Moderated Mediation Analysis

Two moderated mediation analyses were performed with 10,000 bootstraps, taking both exercised and suffered violence as the dependent variables. The coefficients of the moderated mediation model on exercised violence can be seen in Table 8.

Table 8. Model of moderated mediation on violence exercised.

	Model 1. Attachment		**Model 2. Exercised Violence**	
	B	**T**	***B***	**T**
D.E.R.	−0.03 ***	−12.29	0.003 ***	2.69
Attachment			−0.012	−0.40
Sexual Orientation			0.19 **	3.74
Attachment × Sexual Orientation			−0.07 **	−3.28
R^2	0.21		0.15	
F	151.16		24.43	

Note: ** $p < 0.01$; *** $p < 0.001$.

The direct effect of "emotional regulation difficulties" on "attachment style" (Model 1) is statistically significant (β = −0.003; t = −12.29; $p < 0.001$).

Model 2 shows the effect of "emotional regulation difficulties", "attachment style" and "sexual orientation" on "violence exercised ". In this regard, a direct effect of "emotional regulation difficulties" on "exercised violence" (β = 0.003; t = 2.69; $p < 0.001$) is found, as well as of "sexual orientation" on the degree of "exercised violence" in a dating relationship (β = 0.19; t = 3.74; $p > 0.01$). As for the interaction between "attachment" and "sexual orientation", it is also statistically significant (β = −0.07; t = −3.28; $p > 0.01$).

Then, "sexual orientation" moderates the relationship between the style of "attachment" and the exercising of "violence" in dating relationships. The results have also shown that a difficulty with emotional regulation is a predictor of violence ($R^2 = 0.21$) and mediated by the type of attachment.

A bootstrap procedure was used to evaluate the indirect effects and the confidence intervals (CIs). An indirect effect is significant if the CI does not include the value 0. For the pathway "difficulties in emotional regulation" → "attachment style" → "exercised violence," a significant indirect effect, β = 0.0028; 95% CI [0.0012, 0.0045], was obtained.

Meanwhile, the coefficients of the moderated mediation model on violence suffered can be seen in Table 9.

Table 9. Moderated mediation model on violence suffered.

	Model 1. Attachment		**Model 2. Suffered Violence**	
	B	**T**	***B***	**T**
D.E.R.	−0.03 ***	−12.29	0.002	1.26
Attachment			−0.05	−0.99
Sexual Orientation			0.09	1.13
Attachment × Sexual Orientation			−0.04	−1.23
R^2	0.21		0.05	
F	151.16		7.57	

Note: *** $p < 0.001$.

The direct effect of "emotional regulation difficulties" on "attachment style" (Model 1) is statistically significant (β = −0.03; t = −12.29; $p > 0.001$). Therefore, "attachment style" has a partial mediating effect on "exercised violence".

On the other hand, the effect of "emotional regulation difficulties", "attachment style" and "sexual orientation" was analyzed in Model 2. The results reveal that these variables do not exert any statistically significant effect on "suffered violence". Likewise, the interaction between "attachment styles" and "sexual orientation" is also not statistically significant (Table 9).

Finally, regarding indirect effects, for the pathway "emotional regulation difficulties" → "attachment style" → "suffered violence", a significant indirect effect, β = 0.0028; 95% CI [0.0012, 0.0045], was obtained. Therefore, "attachment style" also exerts a partial mediating effect on "suffered violence".

4. Discussion

The results found in this study indicate a high prevalence of violence exercised and suffered by young people in their intimate partner relationships, with a higher prevalence in the dimensions of behavioral control and psycho-emotional violence. Likewise, the findings reveal that both young men and women exercise and suffer violence, becoming victims and victimizers at the same time. Consequently, our first hypothesis is confirmed. In this way, the results are consistent with previous research, which has also highlighted that the aggressions that occur in relationships between young people can be mutual and reciprocal [2,21–25,48–51]. Moreover, it is important to highlight that, far from being a phenomenon confined to Latin America, more and more studies reveal similar results in different countries and places around the world [13,21–25].

However, these findings are not without controversy, due to the great tradition of research that has considered women as the only victims of violence in intimate partner relationships [50]. In this sense, the invisibility of the mistreatment that a man may receive from a woman is due to the smaller social repercussion that this entails. This fact can be seen, for example, in the social acceptance of certain physical aggressions committed by a woman against her male partner (for example, a slap in the face) when the latter has been offended. On the contrary, similar behaviors could hardly be considered non-harmful or unimportant if this type of aggression were committed the other way around. Thus, from this perspective, and in line with a patriarchal model, a woman could react violently towards a man without major social consequences [31,50].

On the other hand, in accordance with our second hypothesis, our results reveal interrelationships between violence and attachment styles. Thus, attachment styles characterized by high levels of anxiety and avoidance increase the risk of violence in intimate partner relationships. These results are consistent with those previously suggested by different researchers, indicating that people with insecure attachment styles may react aggressively towards their partners when they see their relationship threatened. Likewise, several studies have revealed that this reaction would occur mainly in those who present high anxiety about abandonment, since violent behavior would be used to demonstrate unsatisfied needs for closeness, while also becoming a maladaptive response to a possible abandonment by their partner [36–40,61–65].

The next relevant finding of this study confirms the interrelation between difficulties in emotional regulation and violence. In this sense, several authors have shown that difficulties in emotional regulation are a factor that hinders the prevention of violence [45–47,66,67]. In addition, it has been pointed out that people who present difficulties in emotional regulation do have greater difficulty in managing their negative emotions in stressful situations, especially among those with insecure attachment styles [46,61–68]. These studies are consistent with our findings, which show a high prevalence of insecure attachment styles in subjects with emotional regulation difficulties. These facts seem to explain the connection found between difficulties in emotional regulation, violence and the presence of insecure attachment styles [32–47]. Therefore, this combination of factors could translate into violent responses towards their partners when the aggressors feel that their attachment needs are not satisfied [68].

On the other hand, our analysis also reveals that there are no interrelationships between empathy and exercised or suffered dating violence. Consequently, our third hypothesis is partially confirmed, since the interaction between difficulties in emotional regulation, attachment style and empathy is not a key predictor of violence. These results are inconsistent with prior research that has highlighted the role of empathy, considering it a protective factor that reduces the probability of aggression [27–30]. A possible explanation of this fact could be related to the high prevalence of controlling behavior and psycho-emotional violence exercised and suffered by both young men and women. These kinds of conduct, which would mainly occur at present in a virtual context (for example, through social networks), where the levels of empathy generated are lower (especially considering that these interactions are mediated by a screen), may be the key to preventing empathy from exercising its protective role [16,27,28].

Finally, another relevant finding of our research is related to the construction of a moderated mediation model. Specifically, our analysis reveals that difficulties in emotional regulation, attachment styles and sexual orientation interact with each other, becoming moderating and modulating factors that modify the effect that these intersecting variables have on the precipitation of violent events. In this sense, the results show that difficulties in emotional regulation have a direct effect on the precipitation of violence. In addition, this effect seems to be mediated by a person's style of attachment. Likewise, the results indicate that sexual orientation moderates the relationship between attachment styles and the perpetration of violence in dating relationships, with a partial mediating effect on the perpetration of violence. This analysis also determines that difficulties in emotional regulation are a predictor of violence in dating relationships.

Although the above results regarding the influence of difficulties in emotional regulation and attachment styles on violence were expected, given the evidence that had previously linked these variables to violence [41–47,61–68], the role of sexual orientation is noteworthy. In this regard, we can mention that, although violence in couple relationships can come from any person regardless their sexual orientation, recent studies focused on intimate partner relationships agree that heterosexual couples are characterized by a high prevalence of violence in both men and women [49–51]. This relational phenomenon could be linked to the normalization of the aggressive patterns of these partners due to an inadequate way of resolving conflicts, a situation that leads to the normalization of violence [48].

According to this, the influence of sexual orientation could be attributed to the fact that neither member of these couples identifies with gender-based violence. For example, many women justify their partners' violent or abusive behaviors, misinterpreting them as signs of an idealized love influenced by benevolent sexism [17,69]. Likewise, some young women play the role of aggressors in their relationships by imitating the controlling and aggressive behaviors of young men. Furthermore, some studies have suggested that these girls may become victimizers by justifying their behavior based on female empowerment, which represents a rupture of the traditional gender paradigm in the context of more egalitarian relationships, such as the relationships between young university students [51].

Concurrently, many men may use violence to reaffirm their dominant position within their relationship, in accordance with the stereotypes of hostile sexism. At the same time, these young men may have a lower perception of victimization, not interpreting the violence they receive as severe due to a lower perception of the seriousness of these events or because the stereotypes of gender violence traditionally describe partner violence as exercised unilaterally by men [49–51,70–74]. Consequently, mutual violence in heterosexual young people could be traced back to a functionally violent and sexist family environment or to the context of increased social violence, such that their experiences during childhood and youth could have contributed to normalizing not only victimization, but also aggression, so that both men and women could consider abusive behavior as a normal way of interacting with their partner [75,76].

These findings have important practical applications, since the high prevalence of violence exercised and suffered by young people in their intimate relationships should be considered as a risk factor for their health, given its negative effects on physical and psychological well-being. Likewise, the existence of mutual violence in young people should lead to a new model of the interactions between aggression and victimization in violent couple relationships, introducing changes to the preventive measures adopted both at the political level and in health and educational contexts. Thus, the key to prevention would not lie in the design of programs aimed only at victimized women, but in the inclusion of men, understanding that both sexes can play the roles of aggressor and victim.

These prevention programs should be focused on the promotion of coeducation models from early childhood for both sexes, considering the variables traditionally linked to the phenomenon of dating violence (sexism, the normalization of violence, moral disengagement, etc.), but they should also incorporate work focused on fostering emotional regulation skills as an essential part of the development of coping strategies. Giving visibility to the importance of creating secure emotional bonds with parents and/or caregivers during early childhood will be a protective factor that will allow young men and women to maintain healthy interactions based on trust, security, and independence in their future relationships.

5. Conclusions

To date, the association between difficulties in emotional regulation and attachment styles in relation to the violence in young couple relationships has been poorly studied. However, it cannot be denied that these variables have a great relevance in the general well-being of young people. Furthermore, the dating violence phenomenon has become a source of mental and physical health problems for teenagers and young adults. In this context, one of the main contributions of this research is its integration of some of the less studied variables to understand the factors that contribute to violence in couple relationships. Likewise, this study succeeds in exploring the links between these variables by establishing how some of them may influence others, seeking complex explanations rather than focusing on simpler, unidirectional relationships.

Another major finding proves that difficulty with emotional regulation is a key factor in understanding the phenomenon of violence in dating relationships, since it was possible to determine both its association with and its direct and indirect effects on the violence exercised. Moreover, it was established that difficulty with emotional regulation is a predictor of violence, and that its role is mediated by the type of attachment style a person has. Likewise, sexual orientation moderates the relationship between attachment style and the perpetration of violence in dating relationships.

Our findings also allow us to conclude that young people, regardless of their sex, become aggressors and victims at the same time, thus revealing that dating relationships are characterized by a bidirectionality in partner violence, implying that both sexes mutually become the aggressors and victims of violence in intimate relationships, fostering and validating the normalization of aggressive behaviors, while being equally influenced by the network of relationships that we have established between the variables analyzed in this study. However, these findings must not be interpreted as an attempt to deny or minimize the existence of violence against women, but rather as a complementary finding which reveals the dynamics of the phenomenon of dating violence in a changing society.

Therefore, it is necessary to indicate that any attempt to prevent violence in intimate partner relationships, as well as to promote well-being and health in young people, should consider the incorporation of strategies that promote the development of emotional regulation from an early age and should be extended to both young men and women.

Finally, future lines of research should focus on LGTBI+ couples to explore in depth the phenomenon of violence, due to the high prevalence observed in these relationships [77–80], which highlights the need for us to better understand the factors that mediate and moderate the perpetration of intimate partner violence and understand the possible differences between heterosexual couples and LGTBI+ couples.

6. Limitations

The present study has some limitations that should be considered. First, it is a cross-sectional study, which makes it impossible to infer causality in this study. Longitudinal research could offer a complementary view of the findings provided by this study, and also allow us to observe the way in which emotional regulation difficulties and attachment styles evolve in terms of their influence on abuse in violent intimate partner relationships. Also, analyzing whether the bidirectionality of violence in couples is a phenomenon that is occurring across all types of abuse (physical, psychological and sexual) would help us to understand more deeply the mediating and modulating influence that attachment and emotional regulation exert on violence. In addition, when interpreting the results and implications of this study, it should be considered that the sample included only university students, so the results may not be representative of all young people. Therefore, studies that include samples of non-university students are recommended to extend the generalizability of these results.

Author Contributions: J.M.-S., G.M.-M.-P. and I.C.-G. contributed to the design, writing and supervision of the article. All authors have read and agreed to the published version of the manuscript.

Funding: This research received no external funding.

Institutional Review Board Statement: This research was conducted according to the guidelines of the Declaration of Helsinki and approved on 15 June 2023 by the Bioethics and Biosafety Committee of the University of Extremadura (Spain) (Ref. 95/2023).

Informed Consent Statement: Informed consent was obtained from all the subjects involved in the study.

Data Availability Statement: The data presented in this study are not available due to privacy reasons.

Conflicts of Interest: The authors declare no conflicts of interest.

References

1. Rivara, F.; Adhia, A.; Lyons, V.; Massey, A.; Mills, B.; Morgan, E.; Simckes, M.; Rowhani-Rahbar, A. The effects of Violence on health. *Health Aff.* **2019**, *38*, 1622–1629. [CrossRef] [PubMed]
2. Valdivia-Peralta, M.; Fonseca-Pedrero, E.; González, L.; Paíno, M. Invisibilización de la violencia en el noviazgo en Chile: Evidencia desde la investigación empírica. *Perfiles Latinoam.* **2019**, *27*, 00012. [CrossRef]
3. Zimmermann, P.; Iwanski, A. Emotion regulation from early adolescence to emerging adulthood and middle adulthood: Age differences, gender differences, and emotion specific developmental variations. *Int. J. Behav. Dev.* **2014**, *38*, 182–194. [CrossRef]
4. World Health Organization Violence against Women. Available online: http://www.who.int/news-room/fact-sheets/detail/violence-against-women (accessed on 30 August 2023).
5. Centers for Disease Control and Prevention. Intimate Partner Violence: Risk and Protective Factors. 2017. Available online: https://www.cdc.gov/violenceprevention/intimatepartnerviolence/riskprotectivefactors.html (accessed on 30 August 2023).
6. Hernando-Gómez, A.; Maraver-López, P.; Pazos-Gómez, M. Experiencias positivas y negativas en relaciones de pareja de jóvenes y adolescentes. *Rev. Psicol.* **2016**, *25*, 1–19. [CrossRef]
7. McLaughlin, J.; O'Carrol, R.E.; O'Connor, R.C. Intimate partner abuse and suicidality: A systematic review. *Clin. Psychol. Rev.* **2012**, *32*, 677–689. [CrossRef] [PubMed]
8. Vizoso-Gómez, C.; Fernández-Gutiérrez, A. Programa socioeducativo de prevención de la violencia en el noviazgo en adolescentes. *Int. J. New Educ.* **2022**, *10*, 87–102. [CrossRef]
9. Pérez-Marco, A.; Soares, P.; Davó-Blanes, M.; Vives-Cases, C. Identifying types of dating violence and protective factors among adolescents in Spain: A qualitative analysis of Lights-4Violence materials. *Int. J. Environ. Res. Public Health* **2020**, *17*, 2443. [CrossRef]
10. Rebollo-Catalán, A.; De los Santos-Martínez, P.; Jiménez-Cortés, R. Recursos que ayudan a las adolescentes a recuperarse de una experiencia de violencia de género en el noviazgo. *Rev. Investig. Educ.* **2022**, *40*, 203–218. [CrossRef]
11. Avery-Leaf, S.; Cascardi, M.; O'Leary, K.; Cano, A. Efficay of a dating violence prevention program on attitudes justifying aggression. *J. Adolesc. Health* **1997**, *21*, 11–17. [CrossRef] [PubMed]
12. Bonache, H.; Ramírez-Santana, G.; Gonzalez-Mendez, R. Estilos de resolución de conflictos y violencia en parejas de adolescentes. *Int. J. Clin. Health Psychol.* **2016**, *16*, 276–286. [CrossRef] [PubMed]
13. García-Carpintero, M.; Rodríguez-Santero, Y.; Pórcel-Gálvez, A. Diseño y validación de la escala para la detección de violencia en el noviazgo en jóvenes en la Universidad de Sevilla. *Gac. Sanit.* **2018**, *32*, 121–128. [CrossRef] [PubMed]
14. Bonache, H.; Gonzalez-Mendez, R.; Krahé, B. Romantic Attachment, Conflict Resolution Styles, and Teen Dating Violence Victimization. *J. Youth Adolesc.* **2017**, *46*, 1905–1917. [CrossRef] [PubMed]
15. Rodríguez-Franco, L.; Gracia, C.; Juarros-Baterretxea, J.; Fernández-Suárez, A.; Rodríguez-Díaz, F.J. Generalist and Specialist Batterers in Teen and Young Dating Violence: Implications for Development of Prevention Programs. *Acción Psicol.* **2017**, *14*, 1–16. [CrossRef]

16. Martín Montilla, A.; Pazos Gómez, M.; Montilla Coronado, M.V.C.; Romero Oliva, C. Una modalidad actual de violencia de género en parejas de jóvenes: Las redes sociales. *Educ. XX1* **2016**, *19*, 405–429. [CrossRef]
17. Orozco, A.; Venebra, A.; Aguilera, U.; García, G. Análisis de trayectoria de las creencias patriarcales y sexistas, actitudes favorables a la violencia y violencia en el noviazgo. *Psicol. Conduct.* **2022**, *30*, 309–331. [CrossRef]
18. Rodríguez-Castro, Y.; Lameiras, M.; Carrera, M.V. Amor y Sexismo: Una peligrosa relación en los y las adolescentes gallegos/as. Rev. Estud. *Investig. Psicol. Educ.* **2015**, *02*, 11–14. [CrossRef]
19. Dosil, M.; Jaureguizar, J.; Bernaras, E.; Sbicigo, J.B. Teen dating violence, sexism, and resilience: A multivariate analysis. *Int. J. Environ. Res. Public Health* **2020**, *17*, 2652. [CrossRef]
20. Cuadrado-Gordillo, I.; Fernández-Antelo, I.; Martín-Mora Parra, G. Search for the Profile of the Victim of Adolescent Dating Violence: An Intersection of Cognitive, Emotional, and Behavioral Variables. *Int. J. Environ. Res. Public Health* **2020**, *17*, 8004. [CrossRef] [PubMed]
21. López-Barranco, P.J.; Jiménez-Ruiz, I.; Pérez-Martínez, M.J.; Ruiz-Penin, A.; Jiménez-Barbero, J.A. Systematic review and meta-analysis of the violence in dating relationships in adolescents and young adults. *Rev. Iberoam. Psicol. Salud.* **2022**, *13*, 73–84. [CrossRef]
22. Rubio-Garay, F.; López-González, M.; Carrasco, M.; Amor, P. The prevalence of dating violence: A systematic review. *Papeles Psicol.* **2017**, *38*, 135–148. [CrossRef]
23. Herrero, J.; Rodríguez-Franco, L.; Rejano-Hernández, L.; Juarros-Basterretxea, J.; Rodríguez-Díaz, F.J. The actor-partner interdependence model in the study of aggression and victimization within couples; an empirical examination in 361 dyads. *Psychosoc. Interv.* **2020**, *29*, 165–174. [CrossRef]
24. Rubio-Garay, F.; Carrasco, M.A.; García-Rodríguez, B. Moral disengagement and violence in adolescent and young dating relationship: An exploratory study. *Rev. Argent. Clín. Psychol.* **2019**, *28*, 22–31. [CrossRef]
25. Langhinrichsen-Rohling, J.; Selwyn, C.; Rohling, M.L. Rates of bidirectional versus unidirectional intimate partner violence across samples, sexual orientations, and race/ethnicities: A comprehensive review. *Partn. Abus.* **2012**, *3*, 199–230. [CrossRef]
26. Rubio-Garay, F.; Carrasco, M.; Amor, P.; López-González, M. Factores asociados a la violencia en el noviazgo entre adolescentes: Una revisión crítica. *Anu. Psicol. Jurid.* **2015**, *25*, 47–56. [CrossRef]
27. Decety, J.; Jackson, P. A social-neuroscience perspective on empathy. *Curr. Dir. Psychol. Sci.* **2006**, *15*, 54–58. [CrossRef]
28. Espelage, D.; Leemis, R.; Niolon, P.; Kearns, M.; Basile, K.; Davis, J.P. Teen dating violence perpetration: Protective factor trajectories from middle to high school among adolescents. *J. Res. Adolesc.* **2020**, *30*, 170–188. [CrossRef] [PubMed]
29. Glowacz, F.; Curtain, A. Perpetration of dating violence among Belgian youth: Impulsivity, verbal skills, and empathy as risk and protective factors? *Violence Vict.* **2021**, *36*, 110–131. [CrossRef]
30. Valdivia-Salas, S.; Lombas, A.S.; Jiménez, T.I.; Lucas-Alba, A.; Villanueva-Blasco, V.J. Profiles and Risk Factors for Teen Dating Violence in Spain. *J. Interpers. Violence* **2023**, *38*, 4267–4292. [CrossRef]
31. Mikulincer, M.; Shaver, P.R. *Attachment in Adulthood: Structure, Dynamics, and Change*; Guilford Press: New York, NY, USA, 2016.
32. Spencer, C.M.; Keilholtz, B.M.; Stith, S.M. The Association between Attachment Styles and Physical Intimate Partner Violence Perpetration and Victimization: A Meta-Analysis. *Fam. Process.* **2021**, *60*, 270–284. [CrossRef]
33. Farrell, A.K.; Waters, T.E.A.; Young, E.S.; Englund, M.M.; Carlson, E.E.; Roisman, G.I.; Simpson, J.A. Early maternal sensitivity, attachment security in young adulthood, and cardiometabolic risk at midlife. *Attach. Hum. Dev.* **2019**, *21*, 70–86. [CrossRef]
34. Gause, N.K.; Sales, J.M.; Brown, J.L.; Pelham, W.E.; Liu, Y.; West, S.G. The protective role of secure attachment in the relationship between experiences of childhood abuse, emotion dysregulation and coping, and behavioral and mental health problems among emerging adult Black women: A moderated mediation analysis. *J. Psychopathol. Clin. Sci.* **2022**, *131*, 716–726. [CrossRef] [PubMed]
35. Hornor, G. Attachment Disorders. *J. Pediatr. Health Care* **2019**, *33*, 612–622. [CrossRef] [PubMed]
36. González-Ortega, E.; Orgaz, B.; Vicario-Molina, I.; Fuertes, A. Adult Attachment, Conflict Resolution Style and Relationship Quality among Spanish Young-adult Couples. *Span. J. Psychol.* **2021**, *24*, e5. [CrossRef] [PubMed]
37. Sandberg, D.A.; Valdez, C.E.; Engle, J.L.; Menghrajani, E. Attachment Anxiety as a Risk Factor for Subsequent Intimate Partner Violence Victimization: A 6-Month Prospective Study Among College Women. *J. Interpers. Violence* **2019**, *34*, 1410–1427. [CrossRef] [PubMed]
38. Bonache, H.; Gonzalez-Mendez, R.; Krahé, B. Adult Attachment Styles, Destructive Conflict Resolution, and the Experience of Intimate Partner Violence. *J. Interpers. Violence* **2019**, *34*, 287–309. [CrossRef]
39. Rholes, S.W.; Paetzold, R.L.; Kohn, J.L. Disorganized attachment mediates the link from early trauma to externalizing behavior in adult relationships. *Personal. Individ. Differ.* **2016**, *90*, 61–65. [CrossRef]
40. Mikulincer, M.; Shaver, P.R. Attachment orientations and emotion regulation. *Curr. Opin. Psychol.* **2019**, *25*, 6–10. [CrossRef]
41. Gardner, A.A.; Zimmer-Gembeck, M.J.; Campbell, S.M. Attachment and emotion regulation: A person-centred examination and relations with coping with rejection, friendship closeness, and emotional adjustment. *Br. J. Dev. Psychol.* **2020**, *38*, 125–143. [CrossRef]
42. Hervás, G.; Vázquez, C. La regulación afectiva: Modelos, investigación e implicaciones para la salud mental y física. *Rev. Psicol. Gen. Apl.* **2006**, *59*, 9–36.
43. Vatan, S.; Pellitteri, J. The relationship between attachment styles, emotion regulation and psychopathology symptoms in Turkish and American Students. *J. Psychol. Res.* **2016**, *6*, 14–23. [CrossRef]

44. Caiozzo, C.N.; Houston, J.; Grych, J. Predicting aggression in late adolescent romantic relationships: A short-term longitudinal study. *J. Adolesc.* **2016**, *53*, 237–248. [CrossRef] [PubMed]
45. Gutiérrez-Cobo, M.J.; Megías-Robles, A.; Gómez-Leal, R.; Cabello, R.; Fernández-Berrocal, P. Emotion regulation strategies and aggression in youngsters: The mediating role of negative affect. *Heliyon* **2023**, *9*, e14048. [CrossRef] [PubMed]
46. Gómez-Leal, R.; Megías-Robles, A.; Gutiérrez-Cobo, M.J.; Cabello, R.; Fernández-Berrocal, P. Personal risk and protective factors involved in aggressive behavior. *J. Interpers. Violence* **2020**, *37*, 3–4. [CrossRef] [PubMed]
47. Bailey, J.M.; Vasey, P.L.; Diamond, L.M.; Breedlove, S.M.; Vilain, E.; Epprecht, M. Sexual Orientation, Controversy, and Science. *Psychol. Sci. Public Interest* **2016**, *17*, 45–101. [CrossRef]
48. Aguilera-Jiménez, N.; Rodríguez-Franco, L.; Rohlfs-Domínguez, P.; Alameda-Bailén, J.R.; Paíno-Quesada, S.G. Relationships of Adolescent and Young Couples with Violent Behaviors: Conflict Resolution Strategies. *Int. J. Environ. Res. Public Health* **2021**, *18*, 3201. [CrossRef]
49. Hine, B.; Noku, L.; Bates, E.A.; Jayes, K. But, who is the victim here? Exploring judgments toward hypothetical bidirectional domestic violence scenarios. *J. Interpers. Violence* **2022**, *37*, NP5495–NP5516. [CrossRef]
50. Alegria, M.; Rodriguez, A. Violencia en el noviazgo: Perpetración, victimización y violencia mutua. Una revisión. *Actual. Psicol.* **2015**, *29*, 57–72. [CrossRef]
51. Kidman, R.; Kohler, H.P. Emerging partner violence among young adolescents in a low-income country: Perpetration, victimization and adversity. *PLoS ONE* **2020**, *15*, e0230085. [CrossRef]
52. Faul, F.; Erdfelder, E.; Lang, A.-G.; Buchner, A. G*Power 3: A flexible statistical power analysis program for the social, Behavioral, and Biomedical Sciences. *Behav. Res. Methods* **2007**, *39*, 175–191. [CrossRef] [PubMed]
53. Hair, J.F.; Hult, G.T.M.; Ringle, C.M.; Sarstedt, M. *A Primer on Partial Least Squares Structural Equation Modeling (PLS-SEM)*; Sage: Thousand Oaks, CA, USA, 2016.
54. Brassard, A.; Darveau, V.; Péloquin, K.; Lussier, Y.; Shaver, P.R. Childhood sexual abuse and intimate partner violence in a clinical sample of men: The mediating roles of adult attachment and anger management. *J. Aggress. Maltreatment Trauma* **2014**, *23*, 683–704. [CrossRef]
55. Alonso-Arbiol, I.; Balluerka, N.; Shaver, P. A Spanish version of the Experiences in Close Relationships (ECR) adult attachment questionnaire. *Pers. Relatsh.* **2007**, *14*, 45–63. [CrossRef]
56. Gratz, K.; Roemer, L. Multidimensional assessment of emotion regulation and dysregulation: Development, factor structure, and initial validation of the difficulties in emotion regulation scale. *J. Psychopathol. Behav. Assess.* **2004**, *26*, 41–54. [CrossRef]
57. Guzmán-González, M.; Trabucco, C.; Urzúa, A.; Garrido, L.; Leiva, J. Validez y Confiabilidad de la Versión Adaptada al Español de la Escala de Dificultades de Regulación Emocional (DERS-E) en Población Chilena. *Ter. Psicol.* **2014**, *32*, 19–29. [CrossRef]
58. Jolliffe, D.; Farrington, D. Development and validation of the Basic Empathy Scale. *J. Adolesc.* **2006**, *29*, 589–611. [CrossRef] [PubMed]
59. Hayes, A. *Introduction to Mediation, Moderation, and Conditional Process Analysis*; Guilford: New York, NY, USA, 2013.
60. Chernick, M. *Bootstrap Methods: A Guide for Practitioners and Researchers*, 2nd ed.; Wiley-Interscience: Hoboken, NJ, USA, 2008.
61. Lee, M.; Reese-Weber, M.; Kahn, J. Exposure to family violence and attachment styles as predictors of dating violence perpetration among men and women: A mediational model. *J. Interpers. Violence* **2014**, *29*, 20–43. [CrossRef] [PubMed]
62. Péloquin, K.; Lafontaine, M.; Brassard, A. A dyadic approach to the study of romantic attachment, dyadic empathy and psychological partner aggression. *J. Soc. Pers. Relatsh.* **2011**, *28*, 915–942. [CrossRef]
63. Pollard, D.L.; Cantos, A.L. Attachment, Emotion Dysregulation, and Physical IPV in Predominantly Hispanic, Young Adult Couples. *Int. J. Environ. Res. Public Health* **2021**, *18*, 7241. [CrossRef]
64. Velotti, P.; Beomonte Zobel, S.; Rogier, G.; Tambelli, R. Exploring relationships: A systematic review on intimate partner violence and attachment. *Front. Psychol.* **2018**, *9*, 1166. [CrossRef]
65. Velotti, P.; Rogier, G.; Beomonte Zobel, S.; Chirumbolo, A.; Zavattini, G.C. The Relation of Anxiety and Avoidance Dimensions of Attachment to Intimate Partner Violence: A Meta-Analysis about Perpetrators. *Trauma Violence Abus.* **2022**, *23*, 196–212. [CrossRef]
66. Neilson, E.C.; Gulati, N.K.; Stappenbeck, C.A.; George, W.H.; Davis, K.C. Emotion Regulation and Intimate Partner Violence Perpetration in Undergraduate Samples: A Review of the Literature. *Trauma Violence Abus.* **2023**, *24*, 576–596. [CrossRef]
67. Birkley, E.L.; Eckhardt, C.I. Effects of instigation, anger, and emotion regulation on intimate partner aggression: Examination of "perfect storm" theory. *Psychol. Violence* **2019**, *9*, 186–195. [CrossRef]
68. Kayha, Y.; Taskale, N. Difficulties in emotion regulation, separation anxiety, and impulsivity as predictors of women's intimate partner violence experiences. Dusunen Adam. *J. Psychiatry Neurol. Sci.* **2019**, *32*, 101–112.
69. Cuadrado-Gordillo, I.; Martín-Mora-Parra, G. Influence of Cross-Cultural Factors about Sexism, Perception of Severity, Victimization, and Gender Violence in Adolescent Dating Relationships. *Int. J. Environ. Res. Public Health* **2022**, *19*, 10356. [CrossRef]
70. Cuadrado-Gordillo, I.; Martín-Mora-Parra, G.; Puig-Amores, I. Victimization Perceived and Experienced by Teens in an Abusive Dating Relationship: The Need to Tear down Social Myths. *Healthcare* **2023**, *11*, 1639. [CrossRef]
71. Paíno-Quesada, S.G.; Aguilera-Jiménez, N.; Rodríguez-Franco, L.; Rodríguez-Díaz, F.J.; Alameda-Bailén, J.R. Adolescent conflict and young adult couple relationships: Directionality of Violence. *Int. J. Psychol. Res.* **2020**, *12*, 36–48. [CrossRef]
72. Rojas-Solís, J.L.; Guzmán-Pimentel, M.; Jiménez-Castro, M.P.; Martínez-Ruiz, L.; Flores-Hernández, B.G. La violencia hacia los hombres en la pareja heterosexual: Una revisión de revisiones. *Cienc. Soc.* **2019**, *44*, 57–70. [CrossRef]

73. Fernández de Juan, T.; Florez Madan, L. Bidirectional Violence among Male and Female University Students: Comparison of Observations and Results between Two Countries. *Masculinities Soc. Chang.* **2018**, *7*, 279–312. [CrossRef]
74. Pereira, R.; López, D.; Campuzano, J. Violencia de género bidireccional: Resultados preliminares de investigación. *Temas Soc.* **2017**, *40*, 115–138.
75. Godbout, N.; Daspe, M.È.; Lussier, Y.; Sabourin, S.; Dutton, D.; Hébert, M. Early exposure to violence, relationship violence, and relationship satisfaction in adolescents and emerging adults: The role of romantic attachment. *Psychol. Trauma* **2017**, *9*, 127–137. [CrossRef]
76. Moral-de la Rubia, J.; López, F. Relación de violencia en la familia de origen y machismo con violencia en la pareja. *Med. Univ.* **2013**, *15*, 3–9.
77. Stephenson, R.; Finneran, C. Minority Stress and Intimate Partner Violence Among Gay and Bisexual Men in Atlanta. *Am. J. Mens Health* **2017**, *11*, 952–961. [CrossRef] [PubMed]
78. Whitton, S.W.; Dyar, C.; Mustanski, B.; Newcomb, M.E. Intimate Partner Violence Experiences of Sexual and Gender Minority Adolescents and Young Adults Assigned Female at Birth. *Psychol. Women Q.* **2019**, *43*, 232–249. [CrossRef] [PubMed]
79. Olsen, E.O.; Vivolo-Kantor, A.; Kann, L. Physical and Sexual Teen Dating Violence Victimization and Sexual Identity among U.S. High School Students, 2015. *J. Interpers. Violence* **2020**, *35*, 3581–3600. [CrossRef] [PubMed]
80. Dyar, C.; Feinstein, B.A.; Zimmerman, A.R.; Newcomb, M.E.; Mustanski, B.; Whitton, S.W. Dimensions of sexual orientation and rates of intimate partner violence among young sexual minority individuals assigned female at birth: The role of perceived partner jealousy. *Psychol. Violence* **2020**, *10*, 411–421. [CrossRef]

healthcare

MDPI

Article

Preschool Emotional Problems in the Post-Pandemic Era between Parental Risk and Protective Factors

Laura Elvira Prino *, Angelica Arace, Paola Zonca, Protima Agostini and Donatella Scarzello

Department of Philosophy and Education Sciences, University of Turin, 10124 Turin, Italy; angelica.arace@unito.it (A.A.); paola.zonca@unito.it (P.Z.); protima.agostini@unito.it (P.A.); donatella.scarzello@unito.it (D.S.)
* Correspondence: lauraelvira.prino@unito.it

Abstract: The psychosocial adaptation of children born or experiencing their early years during the COVID-19 pandemic remains uncertain. In order to implement prevention strategies, it is, therefore, a priority to deeply analyze children's mental health in this post-pandemic phase and to identify family risk and protective factors. Indeed, recent studies reveal that children's emotional distress increased with the COVID-19 pandemic, especially in situations of high parental stress. The study investigates associations between some parental characteristics (coping strategies, parental burnout, resilience, perception of social support, and promotion of children's social-emotional competence) and children's emotional symptoms, considering gender differences. A total of 358 parents of children aged 2 to 6 years participated in this study. Regression analyses show that parental burnout is a predictor of emotional symptoms; moreover, for females, higher levels of emotional symptoms are associated with parental maladaptive coping strategies, whereas for males, the parent's ability to promote children's emotional competence is a protective factor. Results emphasize the importance of supporting parental well-being as a critical factor in shielding children from the repercussions of adverse situations.

Keywords: emotional problems; parental burnout; coping strategies; resilience; emotional competence; COVID-19

check for updates

Citation: Prino, L.E.; Arace, A.; Zonca, P.; Agostini, P.; Scarzello, D. Preschool Emotional Problems in the Post-Pandemic Era between Parental Risk and Protective Factors. *Healthcare* **2023**, *11*, 2862. https://doi.org/10.3390/healthcare11212862

Academic Editors: Ines Aguinaga-Ontoso, John H. Foster and Roberta Frontini

Received: 13 September 2023
Revised: 25 October 2023
Accepted: 27 October 2023
Published: 30 October 2023

1. Introduction

1.1. The Impact of the Pandemic on Children's Emotional Well-Being

The COVID-19 pandemic constituted a critical paranormative, that is, an unforeseen event that suddenly disrupted personal and family balances and routines. It was a potentially traumatic event, a universal introduction of risk [1] that negatively affected the mental health of both adults [2–5] and children [6–9].

With respect to children, available data from the pandemic indicate a significant increase in emotional symptoms, such as irritability, anger, anxiety, mood alterations, sleep disturbances, feeding-related issues, and hyperactivity [6,10–15].

A recent systematic review of Italian studies on children in the 0–12 age group [15] found that the children most adversely affected by the lockdown's impact on emotional processes are those between the ages of 3 and 5 years. Preschool-aged children observed a 73.3% increase in emotional disturbances, with lower percentages observed in other age groups (35% for children under one year and 40.5% for primary school children). Preschool age also appears to be a particularly critical period for subsequent developmental trajectories and is a key target for prevention programs [15]. Indeed, mental health problems have an early onset in childhood [16,17], and longitudinal studies showed a continuous pattern of mental health sphere issues from preschool onward [18–21].

The pandemic generation (the cohort of children born during the pandemic or who experienced their first years of life under this phenomenon) has been deprived of essential relational and learning experiences due to the social isolation resulting from contagion prevention measures.

It is, therefore, essential to intervene early to identify the risk and protective factors that may affect these children's emotional symptoms, considering the complex interaction between personal factors and experiences in the relational sphere. In terms of these relational experiences, the literature found that parents play a fundamental role in mediating the impact of a stressful event on their children's developmental outcomes. Children's ability to cope with a stressful and potentially traumatic event, such as a pandemic, is indeed closely interrelated with family functioning, parenting practices, and the quality of the caregiver–child relationship [10,22–25]. Children's emotional responses to stressful events are influenced by parental reactions, and according to the spillover hypothesis, such reactions may increase children's emotional vulnerability or, conversely, decrease it by functioning as a protective buffer [26].

Especially in the case of young children, the findings indicate that the well-being of key adults is critical to ensuring the well-being of children, so much so that supporting parents through targeted prevention programs is equivalent to investing in a "parenting vaccine" [27] meaning that it constitutes an intervention that protects children's mental health in addition to safeguarding parental well-being. Parenting education programs can support families in daily and exceptional challenges, such as the pandemic, to interrupt the intergenerational transmission of toxic stress.

Indeed, it has long been recognized that problems in parental mental health are associated with negative outcomes in children's mental health [28–31]. The pandemic has highlighted and intensified the already-known process of transgenerational transmission of mental disorders. The occurrence of psychopathological disorders in parents (e.g., depression and anxiety) has been found to be associated with internalizing and externalizing symptoms in their children [32,33], consistent with studies addressing the pre-pandemic period. This association is so significant, in fact, that we might borrow the title of a paper by Stracke and colleagues [33] to assert that "Mental health is a family affair" since the well-being of children is closely linked to that of parents.

Several authors have pinpointed parental stress as the key factor explaining the association between parental and children's symptoms [24,34]. In keeping with these observations, research data show that children's symptoms during the pandemic increased, particularly during moments of elevated parental stress levels [33,35,36]. As emphasized by attachment theory [37], children need their safe base in moments of stress, but stressed parents find it more difficult to understand their children's needs and respond sensitively and appropriately by providing protection and reassurance. Many studies have, therefore, focused on analyzing parental stress associated with COVID-19 and its possible effects.

1.2. Parental Stress and Burnout

Studies on the psychological outcomes of the pandemic have shown that parents experienced high levels of stress [38,39], greater than the general population of adults [40,41].

Parents were indeed faced with multiple sources of stress during the pandemic: the tasks of providing physical care, emotional support, and financial support for children became much more difficult to cope with [42]. The lockdown and contagion-prevention measures also deprived families of support from informal networks and hampered their access to various types of services (health care, mental health, education and schooling, social services) that enable households to seek support under normal conditions; the resulting social disconnect exacerbated the burden on parents. Research has found that parents harbored numerous concerns: fears of falling ill, be it themselves, their children, or other family members; a lack of social relationships; mental health consequences; and economic and work-related problems [43,44].

Stress levels were highest among the parents of very young, preschool-aged children, probably due to their greater needs, especially during the lockdown period, considering that educational services were closed and it was not possible to take advantage of the support provided by informal networks, it fell wholly on parents to meet these needs [45,46].

Excessive parenting stress levels increased the risk of adults manifesting post-traumatic stress, anxiety, and depression [9,47,48] and practicing harsh parenting in interactions with their children; in the worst cases, they resulted in intra-familial physical and psychological violence [24,49] and the phenomenon of parental burnout [42,50,51].

Parental burnout is a chronic stress condition characterized by intense exhaustion tied to one's parental role, leading to emotional detachment from one's children and self-doubt about one's parenting abilities [52]. There is a high risk of burnout when a parent perceives a significant discrepancy between what would be required to practice optimal parenting and the resources actually available to them [53].

The lockdown exacerbated the gap between the tasks required for child care and education and the resources available to meet these demands; this caused an increased risk of burnout [42,54], especially among parents with at least one young child under the age of 4 [55]. Burnout can have serious consequences on parents and the family as a whole, including in the long term [55,56]; it is therefore imperative that parental burnout risk be evaluated, and such evaluation requires a careful and systematic assessment.

1.3. Parental Well-Being: Coping and Protective Factors

The psychological impact of the pandemic varies considerably due to differences in the availability of resources—personal and social—both before and during the pandemic. While some families turned out to be more vulnerable, in part due to pre-existing factors (economic-social marginality, mental health problems, or family members with special needs) and limited opportunities to avail themselves of support, for many parents, the stress they experienced during the early phase of the pandemic diminished in the later phases [57,58] and did not result in lasting or clinically significant mental health problems [44]. Some families can even be said to have exhibited "post-traumatic growth" [59], that is, the ability to thrive in the face of adversity [60,61].

It is, therefore, necessary to analyze what protective factors can act as a buffer against the impact of stress on families, preventing such stress from resulting in mental health problems. Of these factors, parental emotional competence is associated with a lower risk of burnout [62]; in fact, parents with higher emotional regulation skills were better able to cope with stress during the pandemic period [63,64]. In addition, it is important to note that parental emotional competence influences how children respond to stress [65].

In addition, several studies showed that social support helps parents cope with stress [66]; its role as a protective factor for parents' perceived stress has also been emphasized for the pandemic period [67]. These findings are consistent with studies conducted on the general population from which the protective effect of social support on mental health in stressful situations and its buffer function on the negative effects of a low level of resilience are shown [68,69].

The literature, in fact, points to the central role played by parental resilience, understood as the ability to bounce back during the pandemic [25], thereby enabling parents to provide competent and quality parenting for their children despite adverse circumstances [70,71]. Highly resilient families were able to maintain their daily routines, adapt to change, and solve problems creatively [72]. Some research data show that a high level of parental resilience protects against the risk of parental burnout [25,73] and is associated with fewer emotional symptoms in both caregivers and children [74]. Parental resilience is related to child resilience, as resilient parents are better able to foster children's adaptation and coping skills in dealing with stressful situations [71,75,76], but there are still few studies on this issue, and the results they present are inconsistent [25].

Although many families proved resilient, as Whaley and Pfefferbaum [44] argued, the long-term effects of the pandemic are still beginning to emerge. A better understanding of risk and protective factors is therefore needed in the long term as well.

1.4. Current Study

The pandemic was an unprecedented event; hence, it is difficult to make predictions about the long-term effects it might have on the psychosocial adaptation of children who were born or experienced their early years during the pandemic. It is, therefore, necessary to continue to monitor such children's well-being over time in order to identify risk and protective factors on the basis of which to design programs and services to increase their resilience to adverse events.

The first objective of this pilot study is thus to analyze the emotional symptoms of a sample of children between the ages of two and six years: the "lingering impact" of the pandemic may reveal different specificities than seen in previous phases. We also aim to analyze gender differences in emotional symptoms because the previous data are not conclusive, perhaps due in part to heterogeneity in the methodologies used and the age groups considered: some studies found that it is boys who exhibit more emotional symptoms [77,78], while others instead pointed to girls [79]. It is, therefore, useful to proceed by adopting a more gender-specific analysis of the pandemic's impact on children.

Given that young children's emotional well-being is closely intertwined with parental well-being and the way parents cope with stressful events while also taking into consideration the resources available to parents, the second objective of this study is to investigate the level of parental burnout, coping strategies used, and protective factors (specifically parental resilience, social support and the promotion of children's emotional competence) while also analyzing possible associations between these aspects and parents' socio-demographic characteristics. Available studies show that mothers suffered more negative consequences than fathers during the pandemic, exhibiting higher levels of stress and mental health problems [58,80,81], whereas the association between parental age and exhibited symptoms is unclear. According to some research, it is younger parents who present more problems [44,82], while other studies found it is older ones [9]. With respect to socioeconomic status, strain arising from financial problems increased parental stress; precarious and unfavorable economic conditions, such as low SES, may, therefore, be associated with a higher risk of both parental and child maladjustment [15,44,59].

Studies mainly focused on the association between socio-demographic characteristics and levels of stress and mental health problems, while little research investigated the specific association between parental socio-demographic characteristics, coping strategies used to deal with the pandemic, and protective factors.

As a third objective, we aim to analyze whether parental adjustment predicts children's emotional symptoms and, if so, what dimensions of it. Many studies focused on stress, mental health problems, and parental burnout in influencing children's emotional well-being and attempted to identify which family factors are protective for children, but to our knowledge, no research simultaneously considered the role of parental burnout, pandemic-related coping strategies, resilience, emotional competence, and social support (emotional and practical) in influencing children's well-being, including analyzing possible differences between boys and girls.

2. Materials and Methods

2.1. Participants

Participants included 358 parents (84.9% mothers) aged 24 to 48 years old (M = 38.04; SD = 5.69), almost all of whom were Italian (92.2%). Most of the participants (64.8%) had high educational attainment (bachelor's or postgraduate degree), 31.3% completed upper secondary school, and 3.9% completed only junior high school. Of these parents, 40.2% were employed in a white-collar profession, 11.2% were teachers, 11.7% were entrepreneurs, 5% were managers, and 5.6% were homemakers. Parents who worked exclusively from home were in the minority (7.3%). Their socioeconomic status (SES) was upper-middle level (M = 51.68; SD = 10.06), as measured by Hollingshead's index (1975), which is a cultural and economic index based on an algorithm that combines individuals' educational level and their profession.

Regarding marital status, most participants were married (62.1%) or cohabiting (32.9%); a limited number were single parents (2%), separated/divorced (2.5%), or widowed (0.5%).

The children for whom responses were provided (females: 50.3%) were aged between 2 and 6 years (M = 3.82; SD = 1.22); 57.8% were aged between 2 and 4 years, while 42.2% were between 4 and 6 years old.

2.2. *Instruments*

To detect children's emotional difficulties, we used the ***Emotional symptoms*** scale from the **Strengths and Difficulties Questionnaire** (SDQ) [83], an instrument that is employed widely to investigate strengths and weaknesses in children's behavior. Specifically, the scale is composed of 5 items (i.e., "Nervous or clingy in new situations, easily loses confidence") rated on a 3-point Likert scale (0: Not true, 1: Somewhat true, 2: Certainly true). Higher scores on the scale indicate that the parent filling out the questionnaire perceives that their child exhibits more behaviors relating to emotional distress. In this research, Cronbach's α for this scale is $\alpha = 0.72$.

To investigate levels of parental burnout, the **Parental Burnout Assessment** (PBA) [84] was used. This instrument consists of 23 items assessed on a 7-point Likert scale (0 = never to 6 = every day) investigating 4 dimensions of parental burnout: *Exhaustion in one's parental role* (i.e., "I feel completely run down by my role as a parent"); *Contrast with previous parental self* (i.e., "I'm ashamed of the parent that I've become"); *Feelings of being fed up with one's parental role* (i.e., "I don't enjoy being with my child/children"); and *Emotional distancing from one's children* (i.e., "outside the usual routines—lifts in the car, bedtime, meals—I'm no longer able to make an effort for my child/children"). In addition to the scores for the individual scales, the total score can also be used. This tool showed excellent psychometric properties in studies using it in many different countries, including Italy [85]. For our study, the reliability coefficients of the scales were: *Exhaustion in one's parental role*: $\alpha = 0.89$; *Contrast with previous parental self*: $\alpha = 0.86$; *Feelings of being fed up with one's parental role*: $\alpha = 0.81$; *Emotional distancing from one's children*: $\alpha = 0.77$; and Overall score for the scale: $\alpha = 0.93$.

To capture the coping strategies parents used in dealing with the pandemic, the **Robust—Pandemic Coping Scale** (R-PCS) [86] was administered. This consists of 20 items scored on a 5-point Likert scale (from 1 = never to 5 = always) and has 4 subscales, each consisting of 5 items: *Adjustment*, *Proactivity*, *Despair*, and *Aversion*. The first two measure adaptive coping strategies related to pandemics and epidemics, while the second two examine maladaptive coping strategies. In this research, the totals of adaptive and maladaptive strategies calculated as the sum of the two related subscales were also considered. The reliability coefficients of the subscales for this study are: $\alpha = 0.74$ for the *Adjustment* subscale, $\alpha = 0.75$ for the *Proactivity* subscale, $\alpha = 0.72$ for the *Despair* subscale, and $\alpha = 0.74$ for the *Aversion* subscale.

Finally, the **Parents Assessment of Protective Factors scale** (PAPF) [87] was used to analyze the existence of family protective factors. The scale consists of 36 items on a 5-point Likert scale (ranging from 0, "This is not at all like me or what I believe", to 4, "This is very much like me or what I believe") that assess four types of protective factors: (1) *Parental resilience*, (2) *Social connections*, (3) *Concrete support in times of need*, and (4) *Social and emotional competence of children*. The latter scale measures the parent's ability to recognize and respond consistently to children's emotions and promote their emotional competence. Average scores for the subscales and full measure can be interpreted as Low (0–1.99), Moderate (2.00–2.99), High (3.00–3.99), and Maximum (4.00), with higher scores representing a higher level of that protective factor. This instrument has sound psychometric properties, and the subscale reliability index (Cronbach's α) ranges between 0.87 and 0.93 (Kiplinger & Browne, 2014). In our study, the reliability coefficients were: $\alpha = 0.88$ for the *Parental resilience* subscale, $\alpha = 0.95$ for the *Social connections* subscale, $\alpha = 0.89$ for the *Concrete support in times of need* subscale, $\alpha = 0.93$ for the *Social and emotional competence of children* subscale, and $\alpha = 0.95$ for the total scale.

2.3. Procedure

After obtaining approval from the Ethics Committee of the home university, nurseries and preschools in the Piedmont region were contacted, and the link to the online Google Form was disseminated to families through them. The link was active from May to November 2022. All research participants gave their informed consent after receiving information about the objectives and methods of the study. Data were processed in accordance with privacy regulations.

2.4. Data Analysis

Data analysis was performed using the statistical package SPSS version 28.

First, descriptive analyses were carried out for all variables considered, and gender differences and associations with socio-demographic characteristics were investigated. Next, correlations between girls' and boys' emotional symptoms and different dimensions of parental adjustment were analyzed. Finally, several stepwise regression analyses, separate for boys and girls, were performed to investigate whether any dimensions of parental adjustment were predictors of emotional symptoms and, if so, which ones.

3. Results

3.1. Emotional Symptoms

The mean score for the sample (M = 1.68; sd = 1.84) was in line with the averages reported in the literature and indicated in studies on the Italian population as well [88]. Parents, therefore, do not detect significant problems in their children's emotional domain. There was a slight significant difference in the mean scores obtained by girls and boys (F = 5.875; $p < 0.05$); it was the girls who scored slightly higher on this scale. Taking into consideration the age of the children, younger children scored lower on average on this scale (F = 9.279; $p < 0.01$).

3.2. Parental Burnout

The scores measured by the various scales of the PBA indicate low levels of parental burnout in our sample. The two subscales showing the highest scores (see Table 1) were that of *Parental role exhaustion* and *Contrast with previous parental self*, which reflect, on the one hand, the feeling that parenting requires too much commitment and that the parental role is emotionally draining and, on the other hand, the feeling of not being as good a parent as one used to be and shame around one's parenting.

Table 1. Parental Burnout Assessment (PBA) descriptive statistics.

	Min	Max	Mean	S.D.
Exhaustion in one's parental role	0.00	5.00	0.872	0.949
Contrast with previous parental self	0.00	4.67	0.449	0.726
Feelings of being fed up with one's parental role	0.00	4.60	0.248	0.518
Emotional distancing from one's children	0.00	5.67	0.323	0.663
Total scale	0.00	4.11	0.473	0.624

In line with previous research [89], using an analysis of variance, this study found that mothers exhibited a higher level of parental burnout than fathers, both in their total score (F = 6.59; $p < 0.05$) and in the two subscales with a higher average score in the sample, namely *Exhaustion in one's parental role* (F = 8.05; $p < 0.01$) and *Contrast with previous parental self* (F = 6.49; $p < 0.05$). The parent's age had a slight significant negative correlation with the total scale score (r = −0.113; $p < 0.05$) and, specifically, with the subscale *Contrast with previous parental self* (r = −0.114; $p < 0.05$). There were no associations with other socio-demographic variables, such as socioeconomic status (SES), working outside the home vs. smart working, and having one or more children. There were no differences between those who contracted COVID-19 and those who did not, even when the individual was hospitalized.

3.3. Coping Strategies

Consistent with previous research [86], the mean scores (Table 2) for the two challenge-focused adaptive coping dimensions, namely *Adjustment* and *Proactivity*, were higher than those for the threat-focused maladaptive coping strategies, namely *Despair* and *Aversion*. Parents who participated in the questionnaire thus perceived in the post-pandemic period that they possessed adaptive coping resources.

Table 2. Robust—Pandemic Coping Scale (R-PCS) descriptive statistics.

	Min	Max	Mean	S.D.
Adjustment	1.00	5.00	3.64	0.75
Proactivity	1.00	5.00	4.05	0.69
Despair	1.00	4.60	1.94	0.72
Aversion	1.00	5.00	2.11	0.73
Adaptive coping strategies	2.00	10.00	7.68	1.26
Maladaptive coping strategies	2.00	8.80	4.06	1.12

Differences between mothers and fathers were not significant under the analysis of variance, unlike the findings reported for previous research. Working at home or outside also did not appear to be associated with the coping strategies parents use. Age appeared to be weakly negatively correlated with the *Aversion* subscale ($r = -0.114$; $p < 0.05$). The *Proactivity* subscale was weakly associated with two socio-demographic characteristics of the parent: it showed positive correlations with SES ($r = 0.267$; $p < 0.05$) and a negative correlation with the number of children ($r = -0.126$; $p < 0.019$). For the *Aversion* scale, significant correlations were found in the opposite direction: with SES ($r = -0.128$; $p < 0.05$) and number of children ($r = 0.173$; $p < 0.01$). Finally, there were no differences related to having contracted COVID-19 or not and having been hospitalized due to the virus.

3.4. Familial Protective Factors

Administration of the instrument shows that, on average, the sample of parents participating in the research scored high on all the subscales (Table 3); only the score for the *Concrete support in times of need* scale presented an average at the upper end of "moderate" [87].

Table 3. Parents Assessment of Protective Factors scale (PAPF) descriptive statistics.

	Min	Max	Mean	S.D.
Parental resilience	0.00	4.00	3.31	0.56
Social connections	0.00	4.00	3.05	0.92
Concrete support in times of need	0.11	4.00	2.99	0.73
Social and emotional competence of children	0.00	4.00	3.06	0.67
Total scale	0.11	16.00	12.41	2.32

In terms of socio-demographic differences, only a few slight significant associations were found. SES correlated weakly with the *Social connections* ($r = 0.117$; $p < 0.05$) and *Concrete support in times of need* ($r = 0.150$; $p < 0.05$) subscales. Finally, having only one child was associated with higher scores on the *Children's social and emotional competence* subscale ($F = 6.63$; $p < 0.05$). There were no differences associated with having contracted COVID-19 and having been hospitalized.

3.5. Children's Emotional Problems and Familial Adjustment

Based on correlation analyses, the emotional symptoms of girls and boys were correlated with all scales of parental adjustment (Table 4). Emotional symptoms were positively associated with all dimensions of parental burnout and the use of maladaptive coping strategies and negatively correlated with adaptive coping strategies and all familial protective factors. As can be seen from the table, there were differences in the correlations calculated here depending on the sex of the child. The results for coping strategies and familial protective factors are worth noting. In relation to coping strategies, maladaptive strategies significantly correlated with emotional symptoms scores, especially for girls; in relation to familial protective factors, the results showed that family protective factors were more correlated with emotional symptoms for boys.

Table 4. Correlations between sons' and daughters' emotional symptoms and parental adjustment.

		Emotional Symptoms Scale (SDQ)		
		Total Sample	**M**	**F**
PBA	Exhaustion in one's parental role	0.301 **	0.298 **	0.333 **
	Contrast with previous parental self	0.292 **	0.354 **	0.251 **
	Feelings of being fed up with one's parental role	0.210 **	0.284 **	0.166 *
	Emotional distancing from one's children	0.221 **	0.278 **	0.180 *
	Total scale	0.301 **	0.348 **	0.281 **
R-PCS	Adjustment	−0.183 **	−0.215 **	−0.174 *
	Proactivity	−0.123 *	n.s.	−0.151 *
	Despair	0.195 **	0.204 **	0.207 **
	Aversion	0.183 **	n.s.	0.275 **
	Adaptive coping strategies	−0.176 **	−0.186 *	−0.187 *
	Maladaptive coping strategies	0.246 **	0.182 *	0.307 **
PAPF	Parental resilience	−0.280 **	−0.348 **	−0.241 **
	Social connections	−0.124 *	−0.168 *	n.s.
	Concrete support in times of need	−0.168 **	−0.187 *	−0.157 *
	Social and emotional competence of children	−0.236 **	−0.352 **	−0.155 *
	Total scale	−0.237 **	−0.303 **	−0.199 **

** $p < 0.01$, * $p < 0.05$.

To ascertain whether parental adjustment is a predictor of the occurrence of emotional problems in children, several stepwise regression analyses were conducted. In the first analysis, the total scales for the different instruments (parental burnout, adaptive coping strategies, maladaptive coping strategies, and familial protective factors) were included as independent variables. Three different regression analyses were then carried out considering the subscales of each of the three instruments as predictors to investigate the specific dimensions of parental adjustment in more depth. To highlight possible gender differences, given the discrepancies already observed in the correlations, the analyses were carried out separately for male and female children.

Based on the first regression, for boys, emotional symptoms were predicted by parental burnout ($\beta = 0.269$; $p < 0.001$) and familial protective factors ($\beta = -0.194$; $p < 0.05$), while coping strategies were not significant predictors. For girls, parental burnout also turned out to be a predictor of emotional symptoms ($\beta = 0.235$; $p < 0.01$), but familial protective factors were not significant predictors; for female children, maladaptive coping strategies play an important role in predicting the level of emotional symptoms ($\beta = 0.266$; $p < 0.001$).

The second regression analysis focused on the dimensions of parental burnout. For boys, the *Contrast with former parental self* scale was a predictor of emotional symptoms ($\beta = 0.354$; $p < 0.001$), while for girls, it was a different aspect of burnout that predicted emotional symptoms, namely *Exhaustion in one's parental role* ($\beta = 0.333$; $p < 0.001$).

With regard to coping strategies, in boys, *Despair* ($\beta = 0.174$; $p < 0.05$) was positively associated with emotional symptoms, while *Adjustment* was negatively associated with symptoms ($\beta = -0.187$; $p < 0.05$); for girls, both of the scales referring to maladaptive coping strategies were predictors of emotional symptoms (*Despair*: $\beta = 0.150$; $p < 0.05$; *Aversion*: $\beta = 0.240$; $p < 0.01$).

Among the family protective factors negatively associated with emotional symptoms, the role of *Social and emotional competence* is significant for boys ($\beta = -0.352$; $p < 0.001$), and that of *Parental resilience* is significant for girls ($\beta = -0.241$; $p < 0.01$).

4. Discussion

Although the pandemic represented a universal introduction of risk [1], the consequences were not the same for all individuals. As argued by Rosenfeld and colleagues, "the pandemic has affected everyone, but not everyone has been affected equally" [90] (p. 316); therefore, it is vital to identify which risk and protective factors explain the pandemic's differential impact on families and children in order to implement ever more effective prevention and support measures.

This study's first objective was to analyze, in the post-pandemic period, the prevalence of emotional symptoms in a sample of preschool children so as to also highlight possible gender differences since there are discrepancies among the data presented in the literature. Our results are consistent with studies that show a greater frequency of emotional symptoms among girls in this age group [79]. Higher scores in parent-reported emotional symptoms for daughters could also be a reflection of a differential emotional socialization process and a different focus on and interpretation of certain emotions exhibited by sons and daughters on the part of parents, which in turn reflect stereotypical gender differences and tend to reproduce culturally accepted gender roles, widespread even today, framing girls as more emotional, more prone to mood swings, more fearful, and less confident (e.g., [91–94]).

The second research objective was to analyze the level of burnout, coping strategies used, promotion of children's emotional competence, resilience, and social support reported by parents, relating each of these aspects to the socio-demographic characteristics of the parents.

In comparison with fathers, mothers have a higher level of burnout. This result is consistent with studies showing that the negative consequences of the pandemic were more severe for mothers [58,80,81]. In contrast, no differences were found between mothers and fathers in terms of the coping strategies they used and the protective factors investigated. The higher level of maternal burnout does not depend on these aspects, therefore, but might be attributed to the unequal burden of parenting borne by mothers and fathers on a daily basis; generally, mothers are entrusted with most of the caregiving tasks. The temporary closure of schools and educational services made it particularly strenuous for them to manage their children and, in the case of working mothers, to also maintain an effective work–life balance.

Younger parents seem to be in greater distress: they have higher burnout scores and use the maladaptive coping strategy of aversion more frequently. This finding is in line with some previous studies indicating that younger parents have higher levels of stress and emotional exhaustion and increased mental health problems [44,82,95].

According to previous studies, having more than one child is a risk factor for the onset of parental burnout [95]. In our sample, in contrast, the number of children was not found to affect the level of burnout and is instead associated with coping; parents with more children are more likely to use the maladaptive coping strategy of aversion and less likely to use the adaptive coping strategy of proactivity. Furthermore, we found an association between promoting children's emotional competence and having only one child. Having more than one child multiplies the demands children make on their parents, and thereby makes it more difficult for parents to manage stressors and use effective coping strategies. Having only one child allows more opportunities for observation and dialogue, which facilitate emotional socialization processes.

With respect to socioeconomic status, there is evidence in the literature that strain related to financial problems increases parental stress and that, in the face of the critical event of the pandemic, precarious and unfavorable economic conditions such as low SES can lead to an increased risk of maladjustment on the part of both parents and children [15,44,59]. Our results also suggest that socioeconomic status influences parental adaptation; a higher level of SES is associated with coping characterized by greater proactivity and less aversion, as well as more social, concrete, and emotional support. Contrary to findings in other studies [82] conducted in earlier periods of the pandemic, the fact of having contracted COVID-19 or not does not influence any of the variables considered. Presumably, COVID-19 has come to constitute a commonplace experience, and contracting the virus no longer qualifies as an exceptional or traumatic event capable of affecting parental adjustment.

The third and final research objective was to investigate some predictors of girls' and boys' emotional symptoms by considering parental burnout, pandemic-related coping strategies, resilience, promotion of children's emotional competence, and the social support perceived.

Different predictors emerged for male and female children, with the exception of parental burnout, which was significant for both girls and boys, consistent with the many findings in the literature that show a close link between the emotional symptoms manifested by children and the level of burnout and parental stress experienced by parents [96,97]. There are no data on parental burnout in the literature that take into account gender differences in children. However, in our study analyzing the specific dimensions of burnout that predict girls' and boys' emotional symptoms, we did find a difference linked to the children's gender; in the case of sons, it is the feeling of not being as good a parent as one used to be and shame around one's parenting that is a predictor of emotional symptoms, while for daughters, it is the feeling that the parental role is emotionally draining and that parenting requires too much commitment.

The results indicate that pandemic coping strategies are a predictor of emotional symptoms only for daughters; specifically, it is the enactment of maladaptive coping strategies that predicts emotional symptoms for female children. Looking specifically at the various coping strategies, differences emerge between sons and daughters here as well; for females, both parental maladaptive strategies are significantly associated with emotional symptoms. Therefore, both Despair (i.e., feeling overwhelmed by fear, tending to fixate on the emergency, and not being able to recognize solutions and avenues for coping with problems) and Aversion (i.e., the degree of rejecting the public health protection measures established by applicable authorities, perceiving such rules as a threat to the need for autonomy) are significant. For boys, in contrast, the significant aspects are one parental maladaptive strategy (Despair) and one parental adaptive strategy (Adaptation), each of which has the opposite effect on emotional issues. Analyzing which coping strategies parents use in relation to the pandemic is highly important. According to the family stress model, environmental stressors, such as those related to the pandemic situation (e.g., social isolation, difficult balancing work time and family time due to smart working, financial difficulties, risk of job loss, trouble managing homeschooling, and increased parenting duties) interfere with family dynamics, can negatively affect parenting [98–100]. Due to a spillover effect, parental stress leads to intensified negative interactions between parents and children and, as a cascade, an increased risk of negative outcomes in children [100]. Individuals respond to stress differently depending on their subjective perception of the situation and the coping strategies they employ [101,102]. Parents who are able to enact functional coping strategies in dealing with stressors may become positive role models from whom children learn by observation, thus acquiring their own functional coping strategies for dealing with stress. The differing effects observed on male and female children are worth investigating further, with a view to calibrating parenting support efforts to children's characteristics so as to make them more effective.

Finally, family protective factors are negatively associated with emotional symptoms in boys and not in girls in the analysis that considered the broader dimensions of the constructs investigated. Looking in detail at the various family protective factors, parental resilience, namely the process of coping with stress and functioning well in the face of stressors, challenges, or adversity, was significant for females. The result of parental resilience is personal growth and positive change. This finding is in line with the literature on resilience, in which it is shown to play a key role as a protective factor for child development [70,103].

For boys, on the other hand, the family protective factor associated with decreased emotional symptoms is the parental ability to promote children's social and emotional competence. Children's emotional competence, in fact, is developed through an environment and experiences that allow them to establish close and secure relationships with adults and peers and to experience, regulate, and express their emotions. The fostering of this dimension requires the parent to have a strong degree of social and emotional competence. Indeed, the literature points out that parents must have emotional competence in order to foster this quality in their children [104,105]. Children learn to understand, express, and regulate emotions thanks to parental support [106,107], and such support is especially important in the early years of life [108,109], during which the caregiver acts as an external regulator of the child's emotions [110]. Our results are thus consistent with a number of studies indicating that parents who have enacted "emotion coaching" processes in relation to their children's negative emotions were better able to buffer the effects of stress on children and that, as a result, such children exhibited fewer symptoms [111]. In addition, the findings agree with studies showing that, at preschool age, boys, more so than girls, are in need of nurturing environments in which sensitive caregivers act as external regulators of their emotions [112,113].

Limitations of the Study

The study has some limitations. First of all, as a cross-sectional study, it does not allow for the identification of cause-and-effect relationships; a possible bidirectionality of influence between the variables must also be considered possible. For example, children's emotional symptoms could increase parental burnout: in fact, some studies show that children's emotional dysregulation predicts parental stress [114], and so, as suggested by Johnson and colleagues [57], one must be cautious in positing a one-sided relationship. Second, the questionnaire link was disseminated through nurseries and preschools in the area; the participants are thus residents of a region in northern Italy, which means that the results cannot be generalized to the Italian population as a whole, also because most respondents have medium or high SES and there are few fathers in the sample. The fact that participation was voluntary probably favored the participation of parents who were attentive and sensitive to the issues at hand and familiar with computers and other electronic devices. The difficulty in involving representative samples of the general population is common to many studies on this topic, as reported in several systematic reviews [9,15,75]. It would be interesting to replicate the study on a more heterogeneous sample in terms of socio-demographic characteristics that also include high-risk families so as to test the link between the constructs investigated and the occurrence of clinically significant symptomatology, aspects that could not be explored in our study given the small number of children with high emotional symptom scores and parents with high levels of parental burnout, prone to dysfunctional coping strategies and possessing few protective factors. Finally, it would also be interesting to take into account the assessment of children's emotional symptoms by an independent observer to be compared with the parent's evaluation.

5. Conclusions

Our study shows that in order to counteract the risk of negative effects on the emotional development of this "pandemic generation" of children, it is essential to invest in parental well-being that can serve as a kind of parenting vaccine against the repercussions of adverse events. In particular, according to our data, parenting support programs should aim to strengthen the ability to manage stress and the use of adaptive coping strategies. Another important dimension of family intervention is to promote parents' emotional competence and their ability to recognize children's needs and respond to them sensitively by promoting their emotional competence through a cascading effect.

Consistent with currently available studies on the psychological effects of the pandemic, the analysis of our data led to the conclusion that a range of risk and protective factors need to be considered—there is no single dominant factor that predicts outcomes [44]—and further research in this area is needed in order to field interventions aimed at protecting the mental health of boys, girls, and families so as to foster their resilience in the face of highly stressful situations, such as the one we have just experienced, that might arise in the future.

Author Contributions: Conceptualization, L.E.P., A.A. and D.S.; methodology, L.E.P., A.A., P.Z., P.A. and D.S.; recruitment of the sample, L.E.P., A.A., P.Z., P.A. and D.S.; data analyses, L.E.P., A.A. and D.S.; writing L.E.P., A.A. and D.S. All authors have read and agreed to the published version of the manuscript.

Funding: This research was funded by Fondazione CRT, Protocol: 2021.AI701.U793, 8 July 2021, RF = 2021.0526.

Institutional Review Board Statement: The study was conducted in accordance with the Declaration of Helsinki and approved by the Ethics Committee of the University of Turin (protocol n. 0197535, 11 April 2022).

Informed Consent Statement: Informed consent was obtained from all subjects involved in the study.

Data Availability Statement: The data presented in this study are available on request from the corresponding author.

Conflicts of Interest: The authors declare no conflict of interest. The funders had no role in the design of the study; in the collection, analyses, or interpretation of data; in the writing of the manuscript; or in the decision to publish the results.

References

1. Zalewski, M.; Liu, S.; Gunnar, M.; Lengua, L.J.; Fisher, P.A. Mental-Health Trajectories of US Parents with Young Children During the COVID-19 Pandemic: A Universal Introduction of Risk. *Clin. Psychol. Sci.* **2023**, *11*, 183–196. [CrossRef] [PubMed]
2. Cénat, J.M.; Blais-Rochette, C.; Kokou-Kpolou, C.K.; Noorishad, P.-G.; Mukunzi, J.N.; McIntee, S.-E.; Dalexis, R.D.; Goulet, M.-A.; Labelle, P.R. Prevalence of Symptoms of Depression, Anxiety, Insomnia, Posttraumatic Stress Disorder, and Psychological Distress among Populations Affected by the COVID-19 Pandemic: A Systematic Review and Meta-Analysis. *Psychiatry Res.* **2021**, *295*, 113599. [CrossRef] [PubMed]
3. Santomauro, D.F.; Herrera, A.M.M.; Shadid, J.; Zheng, P.; Ashbaugh, C.; Pigott, D.M.; Abbafati, C.; Adolph, C.; Amlag, J.O.; Aravkin, A.Y. Global Prevalence and Burden of Depressive and Anxiety Disorders in 204 Countries and Territories in 2020 Due to the COVID-19 Pandemic. *Lancet* **2021**, *398*, 1700–1712. [CrossRef]
4. Wu, T.; Jia, X.; Shi, H.; Niu, J.; Yin, X.; Xie, J.; Wang, X. Prevalence of Mental Health Problems during the COVID-19 Pandemic: A Systematic Review and Meta-Analysis. *J. Affect. Disord.* **2021**, *281*, 91–98. [CrossRef] [PubMed]
5. Xiong, J.; Lipsitz, O.; Nasri, F.; Lui, L.M.; Gill, H.; Phan, L.; Chen-Li, D.; Iacobucci, M.; Ho, R.; Majeed, A. Impact of COVID-19 Pandemic on Mental Health in the General Population: A Systematic Review. *J. Affect. Disord.* **2020**, *277*, 55–64. [CrossRef] [PubMed]
6. Meherali, S.; Punjani, N.; Louie-Poon, S.; Abdul Rahim, K.; Das, J.K.; Salam, R.A.; Lassi, Z.S. Mental Health of Children and Adolescents amidst COVID-19 and Past Pandemics: A Rapid Systematic Review. *Int. J. Environ. Res. Public Health* **2021**, *18*, 3432. [CrossRef]

7. Panchal, U.; Salazar de Pablo, G.; Franco, M.; Moreno, C.; Parellada, M.; Arango, C.; Fusar-Poli, P. The Impact of COVID-19 Lockdown on Child and Adolescent Mental Health: Systematic Review. *Eur. Child Adolesc. Psychiatry* **2023**, *32*, 1151–1177. [CrossRef]
8. Panda, P.K.; Gupta, J.; Chowdhury, S.R.; Kumar, R.; Meena, A.K.; Madaan, P.; Sharawat, I.K.; Gulati, S. Psychological and Behavioral Impact of Lockdown and Quarantine Measures for COVID-19 Pandemic on Children, Adolescents and Caregivers: A Systematic Review and Meta-Analysis. *J. Trop. Pediatr.* **2021**, *67*, fmaa122. [CrossRef]
9. Racine, N.; Eirich, R.; Cooke, J.; Zhu, J.; Pador, P.; Dunnewold, N.; Madigan, S. When the Bough Breaks: A Systematic Review and Meta-Analysis of Mental Health Symptoms in Mothers of Young Children during the COVID-19 Pandemic. *Infant Ment. Health J.* **2022**, *43*, 36–54. [CrossRef]
10. Arace, A.; Agostini, P.; Zonca, P.; Scarzello, D. Disagio Psichico e Sociale in Genitori e Bambini 0–6 Anni Durante La Pandemia Da COVID-19: Conseguenze Emotive e Comportamentali Tra Lockdown e Post-Lockdown. *Maltrattamento Abus. All'Infanzia Riv. Interdiscip.* **2021**, *23*, 11–31. [CrossRef]
11. Deolmi, M.; Pisani, F. Psychological and Psychiatric Impact of COVID-19 Pandemic among Children and Adolescents. *Acta Bio Medica Atenei Parm.* **2020**, *91*, e2020149.
12. Ma, L.; Mazidi, M.; Li, K.; Li, Y.; Chen, S.; Kirwan, R.; Zhou, H.; Yan, N.; Rahman, A.; Wang, W. Prevalence of Mental Health Problems among Children and Adolescents during the COVID-19 Pandemic: A Systematic Review and Meta-Analysis. *J. Affect. Disord.* **2021**, *293*, 78–89. [CrossRef] [PubMed]
13. Viner, R.; Russell, S.; Saulle, R.; Croker, H.; Stansfield, C.; Packer, J.; Nicholls, D.; Goddings, A.-L.; Bonell, C.; Hudson, L. School Closures during Social Lockdown and Mental Health, Health Behaviors, and Well-Being among Children and Adolescents during the First COVID-19 Wave: A Systematic Review. *JAMA Pediatr.* **2022**, *176*, 400–409. [CrossRef] [PubMed]
14. World Health Organization (WHO). *World Health Statistics 2022: Monitoring Health for the SDGs, Sustainable Development Goals*; WHO: Geneva, Switzerland, 2022; ISBN 978-92-4-005114-0.
15. Bonvino, A.; Calvio, A.; Stallone, R.; Marinelli, C.V.; Quarto, T.; Petito, A.; Palladino, P.; Monacis, L. Emotions in Times of Pandemic Crisis among Italian Children: A Systematic Review. *Int. J. Environ. Res. Public Health* **2023**, *20*, 6168. [CrossRef] [PubMed]
16. Bosquet, M.; Egeland, B. The Development and Maintenance of Anxiety Symptoms from Infancy through Adolescence in a Longitudinal Sample. *Dev. Psychopathol.* **2006**, *18*, 517–550. [CrossRef]
17. Räikkönen, K.; Pesonen, A.-K.; Roseboom, T.J.; Eriksson, J.G. Early Determinants of Mental Health. *Best Pract. Res. Clin. Endocrinol. Metab.* **2012**, *26*, 599–611. [CrossRef]
18. Beyer, T.; Postert, C.; Müller, J.M.; Furniss, T. Prognosis and Continuity of Child Mental Health Problems from Preschool to Primary School: Results of a Four-Year Longitudinal Study. *Child Psychiatry Hum. Dev.* **2012**, *43*, 533–543. [CrossRef]
19. Bufferd, S.J.; Dougherty, L.R.; Carlson, G.A.; Rose, S.; Klein, D.N. Psychiatric Disorders in Preschoolers: Continuity from Ages 3 to 6. *Am. J. Psychiatry* **2012**, *169*, 1157–1164. [CrossRef]
20. Goodwin, R.D.; Fergusson, D.M.; Horwood, L.J. Early Anxious/Withdrawn Behaviours Predict Later Internalising Disorders. *J. Child Psychol. Psychiatry* **2004**, *45*, 874–883. [CrossRef]
21. Supke, M.; Ferling, C.; Hahlweg, K.; Schulz, W. Persistence and Course of Mental Health Problems from Childhood into Adolescence: Results of a 10-Year Longitudinal Study. *BMC Psychol.* **2021**, *9*, 38. [CrossRef]
22. Canzi, E.; Ferrari, L.; Ranieri, S.; Vittoria Danioni, F.; Lopez, G. Essere Genitori Durante l'emergenza COVID-19: Stress Percepito e Difficoltà Emotive Dei Figli. *Maltrattamento Abus. All'Infanzia Riv. Interdiscip.* **2021**, *23*, 29–46. [CrossRef]
23. Morelli, M.; Cattelino, E.; Trumello, C.; Longobardi, E.; Baiocco, R. Parents' Psychological Factors Promoting Children's Mental Health and Emotional Regulation during the COVID-19 Lockdown. *Maltrattamento Abus. All'Infanzia Riv. Interdiscip.* **2021**, *23*, 47–63. [CrossRef]
24. Spinelli, M.; Lionetti, F.; Pastore, M.; Fasolo, M. Parents' Stress and Children's Psychological Problems in Families Facing the COVID-19 Outbreak in Italy. *Front. Psychol.* **2020**, *11*, 1713. [CrossRef] [PubMed]
25. Yates, J.; Mantler, T. The Resilience of Caregivers and Children in the Context of COVID-19: A Systematic Review. *J. Child Adolesc. Trauma* **2023**, 1–20. [CrossRef] [PubMed]
26. Brooks, S.K.; Webster, R.K.; Smith, L.E.; Woodland, L.; Wessely, S.; Greenberg, N.; Rubin, G.J. The Psychological Impact of Quarantine and How to Reduce It: Rapid Review of the Evidence. *Lancet* **2020**, *395*, 912–920. [CrossRef]
27. Perks, B.; Cluver, L.D. The Parenting 'Vaccine'. *Nat. Hum. Behav.* **2020**, *4*, 985. [CrossRef] [PubMed]
28. Connell, A.M.; Goodman, S.H. The Association between Psychopathology in Fathers versus Mothers and Children's Internalizing and Externalizing Behavior Problems: A Meta-Analysis. *Psychol. Bull.* **2002**, *128*, 746. [CrossRef]
29. Goodman, S.H. Intergenerational Transmission of Depression. *Annu. Rev. Clin. Psychol.* **2020**, *16*, 213–238. [CrossRef]
30. Van Santvoort, F.; Hosman, C.M.; Janssens, J.M.; Van Doesum, K.T.; Reupert, A.; Van Loon, L.M. The Impact of Various Parental Mental Disorders on Children's Diagnoses: A Systematic Review. *Clin. Child Fam. Psychol. Rev.* **2015**, *18*, 281–299. [CrossRef]
31. Wille, N.; Bettge, S.; Ravens-Sieberer, U.; Group, B.S. Risk and Protective Factors for Children's and Adolescents' Mental Health: Results of the BELLA Study. *Eur. Child Adolesc. Psychiatry* **2008**, *17*, 133–147. [CrossRef]
32. Bate, J.; Pham, P.T.; Borelli, J.L. Be My Safe Haven: Parent–Child Relationships and Emotional Health during COVID-19. *J. Pediatr. Psychol.* **2021**, *46*, 624–634. [CrossRef] [PubMed]

33. Stracke, M.; Heinzl, M.; Müller, A.D.; Gilbert, K.; Thorup, A.A.E.; Paul, J.L.; Christiansen, H. Mental Health Is a Family Affair—Systematic Review and Meta-Analysis on the Associations between Mental Health Problems in Parents and Children during the COVID-19 Pandemic. *Int. J. Environ. Res. Public. Health* **2023**, *20*, 4485. [CrossRef] [PubMed]
34. Babore, A.; Trumello, C.; Lombardi, L.; Candelori, C.; Chirumbolo, A.; Cattelino, E.; Baiocco, R.; Bramanti, S.M.; Viceconti, M.L.; Pignataro, S. Mothers' and Children's Mental Health during the COVID-19 Pandemic Lockdown: The Mediating Role of Parenting Stress. *Child Psychiatry Hum. Dev.* **2023**, *54*, 134–146. [CrossRef]
35. Dillmann, J.; Sensoy, Ö.; Schwarzer, G. Parental Perceived Stress and Its Consequences on Early Social-Emotional Child Development during COVID-19 Pandemic. *J. Early Child. Res.* **2022**, *20*, 524–538. [CrossRef]
36. Hendry, A.; Gibson, S.P.; Davies, C.; McGillion, M.; Gonzalez-Gomez, N. Toward a Dimensional Model of Risk and Protective Factors Influencing Children's Early Cognitive, Social, and Emotional Development during the COVID-19 Pandemic. *Infancy* **2023**, *28*, 158–186. [CrossRef] [PubMed]
37. Bowlby, J. *A Secure Base: Parent-Child Attachment and Healthy Human Development*; Basic Books: New York, NY, USA, 2008; ISBN 0-7867-2257-6.
38. Adams, E.L.; Smith, D.; Caccavale, L.J.; Bean, M.K. Parents Are Stressed! Patterns of Parent Stress across COVID-19. *Front. Psychiatry* **2021**, *12*, 626456. [CrossRef] [PubMed]
39. Brown, S.M.; Doom, J.R.; Lechuga-Peña, S.; Watamura, S.E.; Koppels, T. Stress and Parenting during the Global COVID-19 Pandemic. *Child Abuse Negl.* **2020**, *110*, 104699. [CrossRef]
40. Gadermann, A.C.; Thomson, K.C.; Richardson, C.G.; Gagné, M.; McAuliffe, C.; Hirani, S.; Jenkins, E. Examining the Impacts of the COVID-19 Pandemic on Family Mental Health in Canada: Findings from a National Cross-Sectional Study. *BMJ Open* **2021**, *11*, e042871. [CrossRef]
41. Lateef, R.; Alaggia, R.; Collin-Vézina, D. A Scoping Review on Psychosocial Consequences of Pandemics on Parents and Children: Planning for Today and the Future. *Child. Youth Serv. Rev.* **2021**, *125*, 106002. [CrossRef]
42. Griffith, A.K. Parental Burnout and Child Maltreatment during the COVID-19 Pandemic. *J. Fam. Violence* **2022**, *37*, 725–731. [CrossRef]
43. Scarzello, D.; Prino, L.E.; Arace, A. Pandemic and Educational Relationships in the 0–6 Age Group: An Italian Study on Children, Families and Childhood Educational Services. *J. Psychol. Educ. Res.* **2022**, *30*, 71–92.
44. Whaley, G.L.; Pfefferbaum, B. Parental Challenges during the COVID-19 Pandemic: Psychological Outcomes and Risk and Protective Factors. *Curr. Psychiatry Rep.* **2023**, *25*, 165–174. [CrossRef] [PubMed]
45. Cusinato, M.; Iannattone, S.; Spoto, A.; Poli, M.; Moretti, C.; Gatta, M.; Miscioscia, M. Stress, Resilience, and Well-Being in Italian Children and Their Parents during the COVID-19 Pandemic. *Int. J. Environ. Res. Public Health* **2020**, *17*, 8297. [CrossRef] [PubMed]
46. Freisthler, B.; Gruenewald, P.J.; Tebben, E.; McCarthy, K.S.; Wolf, J.P. Understanding At-the-Moment Stress for Parents during COVID-19 Stay-at-Home Restrictions. *Soc. Sci. Med.* **2021**, *279*, 114025. [CrossRef]
47. Crescentini, C.; Feruglio, S.; Matiz, A.; Paschetto, A.; Vidal, E.; Cogo, P.; Fabbro, F. Stuck Outside and inside: An Exploratory Study on the Effects of the COVID-19 Outbreak on Italian Parents and Children's Internalizing Symptoms. *Front. Psychol.* **2020**, *11*, 586074. [CrossRef]
48. Mohler-Kuo, M.; Dzemaili, S.; Foster, S.; Werlen, L.; Walitza, S. Stress and Mental Health among Children/Adolescents, Their Parents, and Young Adults during the First COVID-19 Lockdown in Switzerland. *Int. J. Environ. Res. Public Health* **2021**, *18*, 4668. [CrossRef]
49. Clemens, V.; Köhler-Dauner, F.; Ziegenhain, U.; Fegert, J.M. Predictors of Parental Coping during the Covid-19 Pandemic: A Survey in Germany. *Front. Psychol.* **2021**, *12*, 715327. [CrossRef]
50. Joyce, A. Controlling the Uncontrollable: Stress, Burnout, and Parenting during a Pandemic. *Fam. J.* **2022**, *30*, 605–610. [CrossRef]
51. Skjerdingstad, N.; Johnson, M.S.; Johnson, S.U.; Hoffart, A.; Ebrahimi, O.V. Parental Burnout during the COVID-19 Pandemic. *Fam. Process* **2022**, *61*, 1715–1729. [CrossRef]
52. Mikolajczak, M.; Gross, J.J.; Roskam, I. Parental Burnout: What Is It, and Why Does It Matter? *Clin. Psychol. Sci.* **2019**, *7*, 1319–1329. [CrossRef]
53. Mikolajczak, M.; Brianda, M.E.; Avalosse, H.; Roskam, I. Consequences of Parental Burnout: Its Specific Effect on Child Neglect and Violence. *Child Abuse Negl.* **2018**, *80*, 134–145. [CrossRef] [PubMed]
54. Fontanesi, L.; Marchetti, D.; Mazza, C.; Di Giandomenico, S.; Roma, P.; Verrocchio, M.C. The Effect of the COVID-19 Lockdown on Parents: A Call to Adopt Urgent Measures. *Psychol. Trauma Theory Res. Pract. Policy* **2020**, *12*, S79. [CrossRef] [PubMed]
55. Holmes, C.; Iwanaga, K. Parental Burnout, Quality of Life, and Pregnancy during COVID-19. *Fam. J.* **2023**, 10664807231173693. [CrossRef]
56. Giraldo, C.P.; Santelices, M.P.; Oyarce, D., Chalco, E.F.; Escobar, M.J. Children's Age Matters: Parental Burnout in Chilean Families during the COVID-19 Pandemic. *Front. Psychol.* **2022**, *13*, 946705. [CrossRef]
57. Johnson, M.S.; Skjerdingstad, N.; Ebrahimi, O.V.; Hoffart, A.; Urnes Johnson, S. Mechanisms of Parental Distress during and after the First COVID-19 Lockdown Phase: A Two-Wave Longitudinal Study. *PLoS ONE* **2021**, *16*, e0253087. [CrossRef] [PubMed]
58. Zhou, X.; Shein, B.W.; Khalil, A.; Duncan, R.J. Parent and Child Adjustment Dual Trajectories at the Beginning of the COVID-19 Syndemic. *Fam. Process* **2023**, *62*, 352–367. [CrossRef]
59. Prime, H.; Wade, M.; Browne, D.T. Risk and Resilience in Family Well-Being during the COVID-19 Pandemic. *Am. Psychol.* **2020**, *75*, 631–643. [CrossRef]

60. Calhoun, L.G.; Tedeschi, R.G. *Handbook of Posttraumatic Growth: Research and Practice*; Routledge: London, UK, 2014; ISBN 1-317-77801-4.
61. Masten, A.S.; Narayan, A.J. Child Development in the Context of Disaster, War, and Terrorism: Pathways of Risk and Resilience. *Annu. Rev. Psychol.* **2012**, *63*, 227–257. [CrossRef]
62. Mikolajczak, M.; Raes, M.-E.; Avalosse, H.; Roskam, I. Exhausted Parents: Sociodemographic, Child-Related, Parent-Related, Parenting and Family-Functioning Correlates of Parental Burnout. *J. Child Fam. Stud.* **2018**, *27*, 602–614. [CrossRef]
63. Dhieni, N.; Mayuni, I.; Juriana, J. Emotional Intelligence of Early Childhood Parents during the COVID-19 Pandemic in Indonesia. *Psychosophia J. Psychol. Relig. Humanit.* **2022**, *4*, 1–9. [CrossRef]
64. Restubog, S.L.D.; Ocampo, A.C.G.; Wang, L. Taking Control amidst the Chaos: Emotion Regulation during the COVID-19 Pandemic. *J. Vocat. Behav.* **2020**, *119*, 103440. [CrossRef] [PubMed]
65. Shorer, M.; Leibovich, L. Young Children's Emotional Stress Reactions during the COVID-19 Outbreak and Their Associations with Parental Emotion Regulation and Parental Playfulness. *Early Child Dev. Care* **2022**, *192*, 861–871. [CrossRef]
66. Masarik, A.S.; Conger, R.D. Stress and Child Development: A Review of the Family Stress Model. *Curr. Opin. Psychol.* **2017**, *13*, 85–90. [CrossRef] [PubMed]
67. Oppermann, E.; Cohen, F.; Wolf, K.; Burghardt, L.; Anders, Y. Changes in Parents' Home Learning Activities with Their Children during the COVID-19 Lockdown—The Role of Parental Stress, Parents' Self-Efficacy and Social Support. *Front. Psychol.* **2021**, *12*, 682540. [CrossRef]
68. Li, F.; Luo, S.; Mu, W.; Li, Y.; Ye, L.; Zheng, X.; Xu, B.; Ding, Y.; Ling, P.; Zhou, M.; et al. Effects of Sources of Social Support and Resilience on the Mental Health of Different Age Groups during the COVID-19 Pandemic. *BMC Psychiatry* **2021**, *21*, 16. [CrossRef]
69. Khan, A.; Husain, A. Social Support as a Moderator of Positive Psychological Strengths and Subjective Well-Being. *Psychol. Rep.* **2010**, *106*, 534–538. [CrossRef]
70. Gavidia-Payne, S.; Denny, B.; Davis, K.; Francis, A.; Jackson, M. Parental Resilience: A Neglected Construct in Resilience Research. *Clin. Psychol.* **2015**, *19*, 111–121. [CrossRef]
71. Mariani Wigley, I.L.C.; Mascheroni, E.; Bulletti, F.; Bonichini, S. COPEWithME: The Role of Parental Ability to Support and Promote Child Resilient Behaviors during the COVID-19 Emergency. *Front. Psychol.* **2021**, *12*, 732745. [CrossRef]
72. Koskela, T.; Pihlainen, K.; Piispa-Hakala, S.; Vornanen, R.; Hämäläinen, J. Parents' Views on Family Resiliency in Sustainable Remote Schooling during the COVID-19 Outbreak in Finland. *Sustainability* **2020**, *12*, 8844. [CrossRef]
73. Sorkkila, M.; Aunola, K. Resilience and Parental Burnout among Finnish Parents during the COVID-19 Pandemic: Variable and Person-Oriented Approaches. *Fam. J.* **2022**, *30*, 139–147. [CrossRef]
74. Gayatri, M.; Irawaty, D.K. Family Resilience during COVID-19 Pandemic: A Literature Review. *Fam. J.* **2022**, *30*, 132–138. [CrossRef] [PubMed]
75. Ng, C.S.M.; Ng, S.S.L. Impact of the COVID-19 Pandemic on Children's Mental Health: A Systematic Review. *Front. Psychiatry* **2022**, *13*, 975936. [CrossRef] [PubMed]
76. Russell, B.S.; Tomkunas, A.J.; Hutchison, M.; Tambling, R.R.; Horton, A.L. The Protective Role of Parent Resilience on Mental Health and the Parent–Child Relationship during COVID-19. *Child Psychiatry Hum. Dev.* **2022**, *53*, 183–196. [CrossRef] [PubMed]
77. Ishimoto, Y.; Yamane, T.; Matsumoto, Y.; Takizawa, Y.; Kobayashi, K. The Impact of Gender Differences, School Adjustment, Social Interactions, and Social Activities on Emotional and Behavioral Reactions to the COVID-19 Pandemic among Japanese School Children. *SSM-Ment. Health* **2022**, *2*, 100077. [CrossRef]
78. Wang, J.; Chen, Y.; Guo, X.; Lin, H.; Richards, M.; Wang, H.; Chen, X.; Fu, C. Impact of COVID-19 Related Knowledge and Precautions on Emotional and Behavioral Problems among Children during the Post-Pandemic in China: The Explanatory Value of Emotional Problems among Caregivers. *Front. Psychol.* **2021**, *12*, 712529. [CrossRef]
79. Mendolia, S.; Suziedelyte, A.; Zhu, A. Have Girls Been Left behind during the COVID-19 Pandemic? Gender Differences in Pandemic Effects on Children's Mental Wellbeing. *Econ. Lett.* **2022**, *214*, 110458. [CrossRef]
80. Giannotti, M.; Mazzoni, N.; Bentenuto, A.; Venuti, P.; de Falco, S. Family Adjustment to COVID-19 Lockdown in Italy: Parental Stress, Coparenting, and Child Externalizing Behavior. *Fam. Process* **2022**, *61*, 745–763. [CrossRef]
81. Wade, M.; Prime, H.; Johnson, D.; May, S.S.; Jenkins, J.M.; Browne, D.T. The Disparate Impact of COVID-19 on the Mental Health of Female and Male Caregivers. *Soc. Sci. Med.* **2021**, *275*, 113801. [CrossRef]
82. Calvano, C.; Engelke, L.; Holl-Etten, A.K.; Renneberg, B.; Winter, S.M. Almost 2 Years into the COVID-19 Pandemic: An Update on Parental Stress, Parent Mental Health, and the Occurrence of Child Maltreatment. *Eur. Child Adolesc. Psychiatry* **2023**, 1–17. [CrossRef]
83. Goodman, R. The Strengths and Difficulties Questionnaire: A Research Note. *J. Child Psychol. Psychiatry* **1997**, *38*, 581–586. [CrossRef]
84. Roskam, I.; Brianda, M.-E.; Mikolajczak, M. A Step Forward in the Conceptualization and Measurement of Parental Burnout: The Parental Burnout Assessment (PBA). *Front. Psychol.* **2018**, *9*, 758. [CrossRef]
85. Roskam, I.; Aguiar, J.; Akgun, E.; Arikan, G.; Artavia, M.; Avalosse, H.; Aunola, K.; Bader, M.; Bahati, C.; Barham, E.J. Parental Burnout around the Globe: A 42-Country Study. *Affect. Sci.* **2021**, *2*, 58–79. [CrossRef] [PubMed]
86. Burro, R.; Vicentini, G.; Rocca, E.; Barnaba, V.; Hall, R.; Raccanello, D. Development and Validation of the Robust-Pandemic Coping Scale (R-PCS). *Front. Psychol.* **2021**, *12*, 725344. [CrossRef] [PubMed]

87. Kiplinger, V.L.; Browne, C.H. Parents' Assessment of Protective Factors. In *User's Guide and Technical Report*; Center for the Study of Social Policy: Washington, DC, USA, 2014.
88. Tobia, V.; Marzocchi, G.M. The Strengths and Difficulties Questionnaire-Parents for Italian School-Aged Children: Psychometric Properties and Norms. *Child Psychiatry Hum. Dev.* **2018**, *49*, 1–8. [CrossRef] [PubMed]
89. Bastiaansen, C.; Verspeek, E.; van Bakel, H. Gender Differences in the Mitigating Effect of Co-Parenting on Parental Burnout: The Gender Dimension Applied to COVID-19 Restrictions and Parental Burnout Levels. *Soc. Sci.* **2021**, *10*, 127. [CrossRef]
90. Rosenfeld, D.L.; Balcetis, E.; Bastian, B.; Berkman, E.T.; Bosson, J.K.; Brannon, T.N.; Burrow, A.L.; Cameron, C.D.; Chen, S.; Cook, J.E. Psychological Science in the Wake of COVID-19: Social, Methodological, and Metascientific Considerations. *Perspect. Psychol. Sci.* **2022**, *17*, 311–333. [CrossRef]
91. Brody, L.R. The Socialization of Gender Differences in Emotional Expression: Display Rules, Infant Temperament, and Differentiation. In *Gender and Emotion: Social Psychological Perspectives*; Cambridge University Press: Cambridge, UK, 2000; pp. 24–47.
92. Chaplin, T.M.; Aldao, A. Gender Differences in Emotion Expression in Children: A Meta-Analytic Review. *Psychol. Bull.* **2013**, *139*, 735–765. [CrossRef]
93. Morawska, A. The Effects of Gendered Parenting on Child Development Outcomes: A Systematic Review. *Clin. Child Fam. Psychol. Rev.* **2020**, *23*, 553–576. [CrossRef]
94. Thomassin, K.; Seddon, J.A.; Vaughn-Coaxum, R. Development and Validation of the Parents' Gendered Emotion Beliefs Scale. *J. Child Fam. Stud.* **2020**, *29*, 855–866. [CrossRef]
95. Vigouroux, S.L.; Scola, C. Differences in Parental Burnout: Influence of Demographic Factors and Personality of Parents and Children. *Front. Psychol.* **2018**, *9*, 887. [CrossRef]
96. Deater-Deckard, K. Parenting Stress and Child Adjustment: Some Old Hypotheses and New Questions. *Clin. Psychol. Sci. Pract.* **1998**, *5*, 314–332. [CrossRef]
97. Kerr, M.L.; Fanning, K.A.; Huynh, T.; Botto, I.; Kim, C.N. Parents' Self-Reported Psychological Impacts of COVID-19: Associations with Parental Burnout, Child Behavior, and Income. *J. Pediatr. Psychol.* **2021**, *46*, 1162–1171. [CrossRef] [PubMed]
98. Browne, D.T.; Wade, M.; May, S.S.; Jenkins, J.M.; Prime, H. COVID-19 Disruption Gets inside the Family: A Two-Month Multilevel Study of Family Stress during the Pandemic. *Dev. Psychol.* **2021**, *57*, 1681. [CrossRef] [PubMed]
99. Shelleby, E.C.; Pittman, L.D.; Bridgett, D.J.; Keane, J.; Zolinski, S.; Caradec, J. Associations between Local COVID-19 Case Rates, Pandemic-Related Financial Stress and Parent and Child Functioning. *J. Fam. Psychol.* **2022**, *36*, 932–942. [CrossRef] [PubMed]
100. Ünsal, F.O.; Acar, I.H. Pathways to Children's Behavioral Problems during the COVID-19 Pandemic: Fathers' Parenting Stress and Parenting Approaches. *Children* **2023**, *10*, 639. [CrossRef] [PubMed]
101. Folkman, S. Stress, Coping, and Hope. In *Psychological Aspects of Cancer*; Springer: Boston, MA, USA, 2012; pp. 119–127.
102. Lazarus, R.S.; Folkman, S. *Stress, Appraisal, and Coping*; Springer Publishing Company: New York, NY, USA, 1984; ISBN 0-8261-4192-7.
103. Pugliese, E.; Mosca, O.; Paolini, D.; Mancini, F.; Puntonieri, D.; Maricchiolo, F. Families in Quarantine for COVID-19 in Italy. Resilience as a Buffer of Parental Distress and Problematic Children's Emotions and Behaviors. *Curr. Psychol.* **2022**, *42*, 20101–20113. [CrossRef] [PubMed]
104. Panisch, L.S.; LaBrenz, C.A.; Lawson, J.; Gerlach, B.; Tennant, P.S.; Nulu, S.; Faulkner, M. Relationships between Adverse Childhood Experiences and Protective Factors among Parents At-Risk for Child Maltreatment. *Child. Youth Serv. Rev.* **2020**, *110*, 104816. [CrossRef]
105. Rutter, M. Implications of Resilience Concepts for Scientific Understanding. *Ann. N. Y. Acad. Sci.* **2006**, *1094*, 1–12. [CrossRef]
106. Kiel, E.J.; Kalomiris, A.E. Current Themes in Understanding Children's Emotion Regulation as Developing from within the Parent–Child Relationship. *Curr. Opin. Psychol.* **2015**, *3*, 11–16. [CrossRef]
107. Morris, A.S.; Criss, M.M.; Silk, J.S.; Houltberg, B.J. The Impact of Parenting on Emotion Regulation during Childhood and Adolescence. *Child Dev. Perspect.* **2017**, *11*, 233–238. [CrossRef]
108. Fonagy, P.; Gergely, G.; Jurist, E.; Target, M. *Affect Regulation, Mentalization and the Development of the Self*; Routledge: London, UK, 2002.
109. Tronick, E.Z. Emotions and Emotional Communication in Infants. In *Parent-Infant Psychodynamics*; Routledge: London, UK, 2018; pp. 35–53.
110. Eisenberg, N.; Cumberland, A.; Spinrad, T.L. Parental Socialization of Emotion. *Psychol. Inq.* **1998**, *9*, 241–273. [CrossRef]
111. Cohodes, E.M.; McCauley, S.; Gee, D.G. Parental Buffering of Stress in the Time of COVID-19: Family-Level Factors May Moderate the Association between Pandemic-Related Stress and Youth Symptomatology. *Res. Child Adolesc. Psychopathol.* **2021**, *49*, 935–948. [CrossRef] [PubMed]
112. Crockenberg, S.C. Rescuing the Baby from the Bathwater: How Gender and Temperament (May) Influence How Child Care Affects Child Development. *Child Dev.* **2003**, *74*, 1034–1038. [CrossRef] [PubMed]

113. Votruba-Drzal, E.; Coley, R.L.; Maldonado-Carreño, C.; Li-Grining, C.P.; Chase-Lansdale, P.L. Child Care and the Development of Behavior Problems among Economically Disadvantaged Children in Middle Childhood. *Child Dev.* **2010**, *81*, 1460–1474. [CrossRef] [PubMed]
114. Williford, A.P.; Calkins, S.D.; Keane, S.P. Predicting Change in Parenting Stress across Early Childhood: Child and Maternal Factors. *J. Abnorm. Child Psychol.* **2007**, *35*, 251–263. [CrossRef] [PubMed]

healthcare

MDPI

Article

Vulnerability to Suicide Ideation: Comparative Study between Adolescents with and without Psychosocial Risk

Marta Brás [1,*], Patrícia Elias [2], Francisca Ferreira Cunha [1], Cátia Martins [1], Cristina Nunes [1] and Cláudia Carmo [1]

[1] Psychology Research Centre (CIP), Universidade do Algarve, Campus de Gambelas, 8005-139 Faro, Portugal; fmcunha@ualg.pt (F.F.C.); csmartins@ualg.pt (C.M.); csnunes@ualg.pt (C.N.); cgcarmo@ualg.pt (C.C.)

[2] Universidade do Algarve, Campus de Gambelas, 8005-139 Faro, Portugal; eliaspatricia@aoa.pt

* Correspondence: mbras@ualg.pt

Abstract: Adolescents are characterized as a risk group for suicide, being the fourth leading cause of death in young people. The main aim was to compare vulnerability to suicidal ideation in a sample of young people with and without psychosocial risk. The total sample consisted of 137 adolescents, aged between 10 and 19 years (M = 14.76; SD = 1.40), and it was composed of two groups—the psychosocial risk group (n = 60) and general population group (n = 77). In both groups, suicidal ideation correlated positively with negative events and negatively with self-esteem and social support satisfaction. When comparing the two groups, the psychosocial risk group presented significantly higher mean values of negative life events (mainly separations/losses and physical and sexual abuse) and significantly lower mean values of satisfaction with social support (particularly with family and social activities). It was also found that, in the psychosocial risk group, negative life events were the only significant predictors of suicidal ideation. This study allowed identifying the role of risk and protective factors in suicidal ideation, according to the psychosocial risk of adolescents. The practical implications of the findings on adolescents' mental health and the promotion of their well-being are discussed.

Keywords: adolescents; suicidal ideation; mental health; psychosocial risk; social support

Citation: Brás, M.; Elias, P.; Cunha, F.F.; Martins, C.; Nunes, C.; Carmo, C. Vulnerability to Suicide Ideation: Comparative Study between Adolescents with and without Psychosocial Risk. *Healthcare* **2023**, *11*, 2663. https://doi.org/10.3390/healthcare11192663

Academic Editor: Roberta Frontini

Received: 5 August 2023
Revised: 16 September 2023
Accepted: 29 September 2023
Published: 1 October 2023

1. Introduction

Suicide is a complex and multifaceted phenomenon, resulting from the interaction of several biopsychosocial factors [1]. The incidence of suicide attempts peaks during the mid-adolescent years, and suicide mortality is the fourth leading cause of death in young people between the ages of 10 and 24 [2]. In Portugal, a mortality rate was of 8.9% per 100,000 inhabitants in 2019, also being one of the main causes of death among young adults [3].

Suicide—death intentionally caused by the individual themselves—is the result of a suicidal process, which usually begins with suicidal ideation and can go on to suicide attempts—an intentional act with a non-fatal outcome. Suicidal ideation consists of a set of thoughts about ending one's own life. A higher frequency of suicidal ideation and the conception of a plan to carry out the act can be indicators of a higher risk of attempted suicide or suicide. For this reason, assessing the level of suicidal ideation and associated risk factors—often beginning in adolescence—is fundamental for developing prevention strategies [4].

There are distinct differences in the characteristics of suicidality between adolescents and adults [5]. Consequently, there is a pressing need to know the factors that can effectively identify young people who are at higher risk of suicide. While depression is strongly linked to suicidality among adolescents [6], it is not always present in every case [7], highlighting the complex interplay of multiple factors contributing to suicidal behavior. Being able to predict which adolescents are more likely to repeat suicidal behavior would greatly aid in establishing preventive measures and intervention strategies for suicidality in this vulnerable population [8].

Studies on suicidal ideation in adolescents emphasize that there is a positive relationship between family cohesion and support with strong social support, and that in these situations, there is less suicidal ideation [9–11]. Research on different forms of family functioning regarding suicidal adolescents describe the family's lack of ability to adapt to change and scarce problem-solving strategies due to poor intra-family communication, so the adolescent's suicidal behavior can be related to the perception of family functioning [12].

Negative life events and adversity in the family context are a type of risk factor, which includes parental separation or divorce, death of one of the parents, history of physical or sexual abuse, mental illness in the family, family history of suicidal behaviors, bullying, and alcohol or drug abuse among others. Examples of psychological risk factors include impulsivity, low self-esteem, and hopelessness [13]. Several studies suggest that negative life events are a common denominator for most people who commit suicidal acts and, in addition, predispose the development of certain characteristics, such as hopelessness [14,15].

Hopelessness is an individual risk factor referenced in several models [16,17] that makes people interpret current problems as irresolvable [18]. Also, adverse living conditions together with personal characteristics (e.g., low educational level, scarce or inadequate problem-solving strategies, impulsivity, and lack of self-control) may trigger risky family environments among families at psychosocial risk [19]. This may affect the various family members, particularly the well-being and biopsychosocial development of children and adolescents, due to the chaotic scenario and dysfunctional communication. Studies show that the smaller the displays of affection and the weak configuration of family rules, the greater the psychological stress and the decrease in problem-solving skills [20].

Adolescents from families at psychosocial risk effectively experience several negative life events and seem to have low expectations for the future, thus the contribution of these factors to suicidal ideation seems relevant to study, since suicide in adolescence is a tragic experience at the individual, family, and community levels [21]. In this sense, adolescents with psychosocial risk, caused by family dysfunction, are more vulnerable to suicidal ideation [10,22].

In an opposite direction, there are the protective factors, which reduce the risk of suicide and can be considered "insulators" against suicide, which include family support; friendships and other significant relationships' support; religious, cultural, and ethnic beliefs; community involvement; satisfactory social life; good social integration; and access to mental health services and care [23]. In terms of individual variables, reasons for living and self-esteem can function as protectors, since when they exist, even in the presence of risk factors, they lead to a lower probability for the suicidal act to occur. The satisfaction with social support, since it is negatively correlated with higher levels of suicidal ideation, also seems to work as a protective factor [18].

Studies suggest that the assessment of the probability of suicidal ideation lies in the balance between risk and protective factors [21], referring to greater or lesser vulnerability. Thus, if young people with psychosocial risk are more vulnerable, they may have higher levels of suicidal ideation than young people who do not present psychosocial risk.

In the Portuguese context, there is a lack of cross-national literature on suicidal ideation in adolescents, especially comparative studies. Studies on suicide risk mainly assess samples from the general population [18] or other specific risk characteristics (e.g., [24]), but to our knowledge, there are few comparative studies [25]. Furthermore, emphasis has been placed on the study of risk factors for suicidal ideation/suicide, to the detriment of studying protective factors [18]. There are also comparative studies that have investigated the mental health of institutionalized versus non-institutionalized adolescents, but they have not assessed the risk of suicide [26]. With this study, we aim to fill the gaps identified and contribute to the advancement of knowledge so that it can be translated into suicide prevention strategies.

The main aim of the present study was to compare the psychological factors for suicidal ideation between adolescents from a psychosocial risk group and from the general population. More specifically, we intend (a) to compare clinical antecedents and history of suicidal behaviors between psychosocial risk adolescents and adolescents in the general population; (b) to evaluate the relationship between risk and protective factors and suicidal ideation in psychosocial risk adolescents; (c) to compare the levels of risk and protective factors for suicidal ideation between the two groups of adolescents; (d) to explore the frequency and impact of negative life events (NLEs) in the two groups; and (e) to assess the direct influence of NLEs, hopelessness, self-esteem, and satisfaction with social support on suicidal ideation in psychosocial risk adolescents and adolescents in the general group.

2. Materials and Methods

2.1. Participants

A total of 137 adolescents with ages from 10 and 19 years participated (M = 14.76; SD = 1.40). The total sample was divided in the psychosocial risk group (PRG), composed of 60 participants, and the general group (GG) of 77 participants. The young people in the PRG were recruited under a social project, which exclusively covers young people from neighborhoods coming from families at psychosocial risk.

The participants in the PRG have a mean age of 13.76 years (SD = 1.95) and mainly are male (66.7%), and the GG participants have a mean age of 15.53 (SD = 0.50) and for the most part are male (53.2%). There were no significant differences between the groups in terms of gender ($\chi^2 = 2.94$, $p = 0.087$, $V = 0.15$), but the participants in the GG were significantly older than those in the PRG ($t = -6.77$, $p = 0.01$, $d = 1.34$).

2.2. Instruments

The Personal Data Questionnaire (PDQ), composed of 17 questions, gathers information regarding (a) sociodemographic information; (b) history of psychological disorders, (c) history of self-injurious behaviors and suicidal acts; and (d) history of suicidal acts of family members or close persons.

The Reasons for Living Inventory for Adolescents (RFL-A; [27,28]) assesses the reasons for living considered adaptive and protective, and how these act against suicidal behavior in young people. It consists of 32 items that evaluate five dimensions: family alliance (8 items; e.g., "Feel close to family"; $\alpha = 0.89$), suicide-related concerns (6 items; e.g., "Thought scares me"; $\alpha = 0.85$), peer acceptance and support (6 items; e.g., "Friends stand by me"; $\alpha = 0.84$), future optimism (7 items; e.g., "I like to accomplish"; $\alpha = 0.85$), and self-acceptance (6 items; e.g., "I accept myself"; $\alpha = 0.86$). The items have a self-response hypothesis according to a six-point Likert-type scale, from 1 (not at all important) to 6 (extremely important). The total scale of this instrument shows good internal consistency ($\alpha = 0.93$) and higher scores reveal higher domains' levels.

The Beck Hopelessness Scale (BHS; [29,30]) assesses the symptoms of hopelessness in relation to future events. It is composed of 20 closed response items (e.g., "My past experiences have prepared me well for my future"; $\alpha = 0.64$) of a dichotomous format (true/false). Higher values expose higher hopelessness levels.

The Self-Esteem Scale (SES; [31,32]) assesses adolescents' self-esteem in ten items (e.g., "On the whole, I am satisfied with myself"; $\alpha = 0.85$) with responses on a 4-point Likert-type scale, from 1 (strongly disagree) to 4 (strongly agree). Higher scores reveal higher levels of self-esteem.

The Negative Life Events Inventory (NLEI; [33]) assesses experienced negative experiences in terms of severity, impact, and frequency. It is composed of 25 items that evaluate four dimensions: adverse family environment (9 items; e.g., "Family conflicts"; $\alpha = 0.70$), psychological abuse (6 items; e.g., "Humiliations"; $\alpha = 0.82$), separation and loss (6 items; e.g., "permanent separations (e.g., due to death)"; $\alpha = 0.59$), and physical and sexual abuse (4 items; e.g., "Severe aggressions"; $\alpha = 0.83$). It is subdivided into response hypotheses in terms of frequency rated from 0 to 4, from 0 (never) to 4 (very often), and in terms of impact, rated from 1 to 5, with a progressive response from 1 (none) to 5 (extremely negative). The total scale internal consistency is very good (α = 0.88). Higher values expose higher domains' levels.

The Social Support Satisfaction Scale (SSSS; [34]) is a 15-item instrument that assesses the perception regarding satisfaction with social support through four dimensions: (1) satisfaction with friends (5 items; e.g., "I am satisfied with the amount of friend I have"; α = 0.83); (2) intimacy (4 items; e.g., "Sometimes I feel alone in the world and without support"; α = 0.46); (3) satisfaction with family (3 items; e.g., "I am satisfied with the way I relate with my family"; α = 0.47); and (4) satisfaction with social activities (3 items; e.g., "I miss satisfied social activities"; α = 0.66). Each item is of a self-answer based on a Likert-type scale of agreement from 1 (strongly agree) to 5 (strongly disagree) and higher scores reveal higher dimensions' levels.

The Suicidal Ideation Questionnaire (SIQ; [35,36]) for the Portuguese population aims to assess the severity of thoughts and cognitions about suicide in adolescents. It is composed of 30 items (e.g., "Thoughts of killing self"; α = 0.95) of a self-answer and relation to the frequency of thoughts/cognitions rated between 0 (I have never had this thought) and 6 (Almost every day). Higher values expose higher suicidal ideation.

2.3. Procedure

The data collection was gathered in Algarve (a region in the south of Portugal). The data of young people at psychosocial risk were collected as part of a social project whose goal was to prevent crime, promote social inclusion, and combat the trend towards social exclusion and school absenteeism. As part of this project, the teenagers attended structured activities in classrooms (extra formal curricular activity), so data collection was scheduled with the trainers and carried out while these activities were taking place. The sample of young people from the general population was collected in region secondary schools, with previous authorization from the Directorate General of Innovation and Curriculum Development of the Ministry of Education. The directors of the schools that agreed to take part in the study randomly selected classes whose students met the age criteria and organized a date for the questionnaires to be administered.

In both samples, after the formal authorizations were obtained, a request for authorization was made to the parents and an informed consent was requested from the young people themselves. The collection protocol was applied in groups, in a classroom setting for both samples, always in the presence of a researcher.

2.4. Analysis Plan

The data analysis was carried out using the Statistical Package for the Social Sciences (SPSS) statistical data processing program (version 28.0). The Cronbach alpha was computed and scores above 0.70 indicate proper reliability of the factors. Since some of the scales have fewer items, although undesirable, alpha scores between 0.60 and 0.70 can also be accepted. The statistical treatment includes Chi-Square (to compare categorical data) and comparative analyses (to determine significant differences between the mean values of each study group) for each of the variables analyzed, and Student's t-test for independent samples was performed (after the normality and homogeneity conditions were insured); Pearson's correlation analysis was performed between negative life events and suicidal ideation, in order to verify the relationship between psychological risk and protective factors and suicidal ideation, along with multiple linear regressions (to understand the direct effects of the variables on suicidal ideation). Effect size was calculated with Cramer's V (varying between 0 and 1) and Cohen' d (0.20 = small effect; 0.50 = medium effect; and 0.80 = large effect). For each of the mentioned analyses, the results are considered significant when the p value is less than 0.05 [37].

3. Results

In order to meet the objectives outlined, we first conducted a global descriptive analysis of all participants and then separately at the psychosocial risk group (PRG) and the general group (GG) levels. This descriptive analysis refers to the clinical history and suicidal behavior of the self and of family members and friends.

Through the analysis of results obtained in the total sample, it was found that 7 out of 137 participants have already presented a psychological problem (5.1%) and 13 have already received professional psychological help (9.5%). Regarding suicidal behavior, 13 out of 137 participants have already attempted the act with the aim of ending their own lives (9.5%) and 16 have already committed self-injurious acts intentionally (11.7%). In respect to family members and friends, 22 out of 137 had recorded suicide attempts by family members (16.1%) and 37 out of 137 had recorded suicide attempts by friends or close people (27.1%).

We then proceeded to analyze the same indicators in each of the groups (Table 1).

Table 1. Clinical History and Suicidal Behavior in the Psychosocial Risk Group and the General Group.

	PRG (n = 60)	GG (n = 77)	χ^2	p	V
History of psychological problem	4 (67.0%)	3 (3.9%)	0.57	0.451	0.07
Received psychological help	8 (13.3%)	5 (6.5%)	1.84	0.288	0.07
Committed acts with the aim of ending one's life	10 (16.7%)	3 (3.9%)	6.40	0.011	0.22
Self-injurious acts	10 (16.7%)	6 (7.8%)	2.58	0.109	0.14
Suicide attempts by family members	10 (16.7%)	12 (15.6%)	0.03	0.864	0.02
Suicide attempts by friends or close people	20 (33.0%)	17 (22.1%)	2.36	0.126	0.13

PRG = psychosocial risk group; GG = general group; χ^2 = statistic test; p = significance level; V = effect size.

When comparing the two groups, significant differences were found regarding acts with the aim of ending one's own life (χ^2 = 6.40, p = 0.011, Cramer's V = 0.22), which were significantly more prevalent in the PRG.

To explore the relationship between variables—reasons for living, hopelessness, self-esteem, negative life events, and satisfaction with social support—with suicidal ideation, a Pearson's correlation analysis was performed (Table 2).

Table 2. Correlations between RFL-A, BHS, SES, NLEI, and SSSS with SIQ in GRP.

	Suicide Ideation (SIQ)	
	PRG	GG
Reasons for Living (RFL-A)	−0.13	−0.43 ***
Family Alliance	−0.16	−0.28 *
Fear of Suicide	0.09	−0.40 **
Peer Acceptance and Support	−0.18	−0.24 *
Optimism about the Future	−0.03	−0.37 **
Self-Acceptance	−0.31 *	−0.22
Hopelessness (BHS)	0.21	0.61 ***
Self-esteem (SES)	−0.33 **	−0.46 ***
Negative Life Events—Total (NLE)	0.58 **	0.52 ***
Adverse Family Environment	0.57 **	0.30 **
Psychological Abuse	0.59 **	0.55 ***
Separation and Loss	0.32 *	0.37 ***
Physical or Sexual Abuse	0.33 **	0.23 *
Social Support Satisfaction Scale—Total (SSSS)	−0.39 **	−0.74 ***
Satisfaction with Friends/Acquaintances	−0.18	−0.61 ***
Satisfaction with Intimacy	−0.37 **	−0.57 ***
Satisfaction with Family	−0.32 *	−0.53 ***
Satisfaction with Social Activities	−0.29 *	−0.48 ***

* $p \leq 0.05$; ** $p \leq 0.01$; *** $p \leq 0.001$.

In the PRG, there was no significant association between reasons for living (total scale) and suicidal ideation; however, there was a negative association between the subscale of self-acceptance of the RFL-A inventory and suicidal ideation ($r = -0.31; p \leq 0.05$).

In the GG, a negative and statistically significant association was found between reasons for living (total scale) and suicidal ideation, and with all subscales, except the self-acceptance subscale ($r = -0.22, p \geq 0.05$).

Regarding self-esteem, there was a negative and significant association in both groups (PRG: $r = -0.31, p \leq 0.05$; GG: $r = -0.46, p \leq 0.001$), indicating that the more self-esteem an individual has, the lower the propensity for suicidal ideation.

The negative life events and suicidal ideation reveal positive and significant associations, in the PRG and GG groups, with higher scores in total-scale NLE (PRG: $r = 0.58$, $p \leq 0.01$; GG: $r = 0.52, p \leq 0.001$) and psychological abuse (PRG: $r = 0.59, p \leq 0.01$; GG: $r = 0.55, p \leq 0.001$), and lower correlations in separations and losses (PRG: $r = 0.32, p \leq 0.05$; GG: $r = 0.37, p \leq 0.001$) and physical or sexual abuse (PRG: $r = 0.33, p \leq 0.01$; GG: $r = 0.23$, $p \leq 0.05$). The adverse family environment subscale shows moderate correlation in the PRG ($r = 0.57; p \leq 0.01$) and low correlation in the GG ($r = 0.30; p \leq 0.01$). The greater the experience of negative life events for an individual, the greater the tendency for thoughts related to suicidal behavior.

In relation to satisfaction with social support, in the PRG, there was a negative correlation between the suicidal ideation and the total-scale SSSS ($r = -0.39; p \leq 0.01$), satisfaction with intimacy ($r = -0.37; p \leq 0.01$), satisfaction with family ($r = -0.32; p \leq 0.05$), and satisfaction with social activities ($r = -0.29; p \leq 0.05$). In the general group, there was also a negative association between satisfaction with social support and suicidal ideation, but with greater intensity in the total scale (total SSSS: $r = -0.74; p \leq 0.001$) and in the subscales (friends: $r = -0.61, p \leq 0.001$; intimacy: $r = -0.57, p \leq 0.001$; family: $r = -0.53$, $p \leq 0.001$; and social activities: $r = -0.48, p \leq 0.001$). These results suggest that with greater satisfaction with social support, there is less tendency to have suicidal thoughts.

The differences between the psychosocial risk group and the general group were analyzed (Table 3) in relation to the risk factors (i.e., negative life events and hopelessness).

Table 3. Descriptive statistics and comparison between PRG and GG of the NLEI and BHS.

	PRG (n = 60)		GG (n = 70)		t	p	d
	M	SD	M	SD			
Negative Life Events (NLEI)	1.95	1.80	1.30	1.28	2.22	0.028	0.38
Adverse Family Environment	1.78	1.85	1.23	1.30	1.95	0.053	0.34
Psychological Abuse	2.67	2.90	1.15	1.45	1.09	0.274	0.66
Separation and Loss	1.97	2.04	1.15	1.45	2.63	0.010	0.72
Physical and/or Sexual Abuse	1.48	2.42	0.68	1.46	2.22	0.027	0.39
Hopelessness (BHS)	4.04	2.67	3.83	2.75	0.44	0.654	0.08

PRG = Psychosocial Risk Group; GG = General Group; M = Mean; SD = Standard Deviation; t = Statistic Test; p = Significance Level; d = Effect Size.

The experience of negative life events (NLEI) showed significant and small effect differences at the total scale ($t_{(102.13)} = 2.22, p = 0.028, d = 0.38$), a large effect in the category of separations/losses ($t_{(102.56)} = 2.63; p = 0.010; d = 0.72$), and a small effect in the physical and sexual abuse subscale ($t_{(91.46)} = 2.22; p = 0.027; d = 0.39$), with higher mean values in the PRG ($M_{\text{NLEI}} = 1.95; SD_{\text{LEI}} = 1.80; M_{\text{Separation/Losses}} = 1.97; SD_{\text{Separation/Losses}} = 2.04;$ $M_{\text{Physical/Sexual Abuse}} = 1.48; SD_{\text{Physical/Sexual Abuse}} = 2.42$) than in the GG ($M_{\text{NLEI}} = 1.30;$ $SD_{\text{NLEI}} = 1.28; M_{\text{Separation/Losses}} = 1.15; SD_{\text{Separation/Losses}} = 1.45; M_{\text{Physical/Sexual Abuse}} = 0.68;$ $SD_{\text{Physical/Sexual Abuse}} = 1.46$).

In terms of hopelessness, the results did not reveal statistically significant differences between the groups.

As Table 4 shows, in regard to the comparison of the protective factors between the two groups, there are not significant differences at the level of the total scale of reasons for living ($t_{(112.71)}$ = 0.52; p = 0.883; d = 0.24), nor in the subscales, namely family alliance, concerns about suicide, peer acceptance, optimism for the future, and self-acceptance.

Table 4. Descriptive statistics and comparison between PRG and GG of the RFL-A, SES, and SSSS.

	PRG (n = 60)		GG (n = 70)		t	p	d
	M	SD	M	SD			
Reasons for Living Inventory (RFL-A) Total	4.61	0.83	4.59	0.70	0.14	0.883	0.24
Family Alliance	4.91	0.98	4.84	1.02	0.40	0.690	0.06
Fear of Suicide	3.47	1.57	3.61	1.46	−0.56	0.576	0.09
Peer Acceptance and Support	4.59	1.11	4.77	0.81	−1.08	0.263	0.18
Optimism about the Future	5.00	0.92	4.78	0.71	1.58	0.117	0.26
Self-Acceptance	4.94	1.04	4.85	0.85	0.54	0.588	0.09
Self-Esteem Scale (SES) Total	30.22	4.85	25.68	6.62	4.63	0.000	0.78
Social Support Satisfaction Scale (SSSS) Total	52.55	9.66	54.55	9.01	−1.24	0.215	0.21
Satisfaction with Friends/Acquaintances	20.10	4.92	19.64	4.14	0.60	0.550	0.10
Intimacy	13.76	3.31	13.08	2.27	1.36	0.175	0.20
Satisfaction with Family	9.67	1.87	11.48	3.19	−4.13	0.000	0.69
Satisfaction with Social Activities	9.02	9.72	10.35	2.32	−2.42	0.017	0.19

PRG = Psychosocial Risk Group; GG = General Group; M = Mean; SD = Standard Deviation; t = Statistic Test; p = Significance Level; d = Effect Size.

Regarding self-esteem, the results showed highly significant and large effect differences between the two groups ($t_{(134.54)}$ = 4.63; $p \leq 0.001$; d = 0.78), showing higher self-esteem in the psychosocial risk group (M = 30.22; SD = 4.85) than in the general group (M = 25.68; SD = 6.62).

In satisfaction with social support, significant and large effect differences were found between PRG and GG in relation to satisfaction with family ($t_{(126.26)} = -4.13$; $p \leq 0.001$; d = 0.69), and a small effect in the social activities ($t_{(93.39)} = -2.42$; p = 0.017; d = 0.19), with the psychosocial risk group showing lower values in both (PRG: $M_{\text{Satisfaction Family}} = 9.67$, $SD_{\text{Satisfaction Family}} = 1.87$; GG: $M_{\text{Satisfaction Family}} = 11.48$, $SD_{\text{Satisfaction Family}} = 3.19$; PRG: $M_{\text{SocialActivities}} = 9.02$, $SD_{\text{SocialActivities}} = 9.72$; GG: $M_{\text{SocialActivities}} = 10.35$, $SD_{\text{SocialActivities}} = 2.32$).

To understand the contribution of the variables to suicidal ideation, we studied the predictors of suicidal ideation, separately, in the RPG (Table 5) and GG (Table 6), using the multiple regression technique. The psychological variables that were significantly correlated with suicidal ideation were included in the model.

Table 5. Contribution of the NLEI, SES-Total, and SSSS in explaining suicidal ideation in the Psychosocial Risk Group (n = 60).

	Suicide Ideation	
Constant (39.59)		
NLEI—Total	β = 0.49 ***	
SES—Total	$\beta = -0.10$	R^2 = 0.38
SSSS—Total	$\beta = -0.15$	

β = Standardized Regression Coefficient; R^2 = Coefficient of Determination; NLEI-Total = Total Value of the Negative Life Events Inventory; SES-Total = Total Value of the Self-Esteem Scale; SSSS-Total = Total Value of the Social Support Satisfaction Scale. *** $p < 0.001$.

The analysis of the results in Table 5 shows that, in the GRP, negative life events, self-esteem, and satisfaction with social support explain 38.0% of the variance in the levels of suicidal ideation, with the contribution of negative life events being positive and quite significant ($p \leq 0.001$). Although the contribution of self-esteem and satisfaction with social support is negative, it is not significant for explaining the variance of suicidal ideation.

Table 6. Contribution of the NLIE, SES-Total, and SSSS in explaining suicidal ideation in the General Group (n = 77).

	Suicide Ideation	
Constant (84.47 ***)		
NLEI—Total	β = 0.21 ***	
SES—Total	β = −0.23 *	R^2 = 0.63
SSSS—Total	β = −0.56 **	

β = Standardized Regression Coefficient; R^2 = Coefficient of Determination; NLEI-Total = Total Value of the Negative Life Events Inventory; SES-Total = Total Value of the Self-Esteem Scale; SSSS-Total = Total Value of the Social Support Satisfaction Scale. * $p < 0.05$; ** $p < 0.01$; *** $p < 0.001$.

In GG, according to Table 6, these three factors explain 63.0% of the variance of suicidal ideation. All variables have a significant contribution, with the contribution of negative life events being positive ($\beta = 0.21, p \leq 0.001$) and that of self-esteem ($\beta = -0.23, p \leq 0.05$) and satisfaction with social support ($\beta = -0.56, p \leq 0.01$) being negative.

Through a comparative analysis between the two tables presented, it is possible to infer that, in the psychosocial risk group, negative life events seem to be the best predictor of suicidal ideation ($\beta = 0.49$), while in the general group, all three factors are important, the best predictor being satisfaction with social support. The isolated contribution of negative life events, in this group, is smaller ($\beta = 0.21$) compared to GRP.

4. Discussion

The main objective of this study was to compare the vulnerability to suicidal ideation in young people with and without psychosocial risk; thus, two samples were selected, one as a general group (GG) and the other as a psychosocial risk group (PRG), specifically collected from young people with a psychosocial risk community. The importance of this differentiation between the groups was due to previous studies indicating that the existence of greater psychosocial vulnerability may lead to greater suicidal ideation [38]. In this line of reasoning, young people from families at psychosocial risk are more likely to experience negative events in their environment and in the presence of psychological risk factors, which act as facilitators of suicidal ideation [21,26].

The present study suggests that youth at psychosocial risk committed more acts with the goal of ending their own lives than the general population group. The suicidal process involves social, psychological, and biological variables that can overcome suicidal ideation and go from cognition to the act itself, with the aim of ending one's own life [39]. Young people with a history of suicide attempts are usually characterized by poor social support, which is consistent with the results obtained, since psychosocially at-risk young people are inserted in contexts with a lack of social resources at various levels [25,38].

In the general population, as expected, we found negative correlations between suicidal ideation and the protective factors (reasons for living, self-esteem, and social support satisfaction) and positive correlations with risk factors (hopelessness and negative life events). Regarding the analysis of the association between risk and protective factors with suicidal ideation in the psychosocial risk sample, negative significant associations were found between suicidal ideation and the self-acceptance of the reasons for living, self-esteem, satisfaction with social support, and also with intimacy and family satisfaction, and positive correlations with negative life events, involving all types of adverse life events.

Self-acceptance is the only subscale of the reasons for living that is negatively associated with suicidal ideation in the PRG. This fact points, on the one hand, to the fact that in the PRG the multiple reasons for living are protective of suicidal ideation and, on the other hand, in the PGR, self-acceptance seems to be the reason more associated with suicidal ideation. These results are congruent with those of self-esteem.

Self-esteem shows a significant and negative association with suicidal ideation, that is, the higher the levels of self-esteem presented by a subject, the lower the tendency to present ideation for suicidal behavior. These data support the idea that self-esteem operates as a protective factor for suicidal ideation in this risk group [23].

A relationship was found between negative life events and suicidal ideation in the psychosocial risk group, that is, the more negative events experienced by the young person, the greater the propensity for suicidal ideation. Adverse events such as an adverse family environment and psychological abuse seem to be more impactful regarding the development of suicidal ideation.

The scientific literature suggests that the effects of social support satisfaction on the development of suicidal behavior indicate that the lower the satisfaction with social support, the greater the vulnerability for adolescents to commit suicide (e.g., [40]). The data obtained in the present study are congruent with the scientific literature, since a significant negative association was found between social support and suicidal ideation, particularly in satisfaction with intimacy in interpersonal relationships and satisfaction with family. To minimize the risk of developing suicidal behavior, it is important to have social support, such as family and friends, who are the most significant relationships for an adolescent. Thus, the less intimacy the adolescent feels with those around them, as well as the less satisfaction they feel with their family, the greater the propensity will be for thoughts related to ending their own life.

The comparative analysis indicates that risk and protective factors may be involved for suicidal ideation. Risk factors are characterized by variables that predispose the development of suicidal ideation [41] such as negative life events. In the present study, the adolescents with psychosocial risk showed higher scores regarding the presence of negative life events, compared to the general group. These data are congruent with the literature, in which youth at psychosocial risk experience many more negative life events than youth not at risk, with more frequency and greater impact [26,41], as well as in the setting of negative life events associated with psychological and sexual abuse, and related to separations and losses, which are experienced more by youth in an adverse social environment than by youth free of psychosocial risk [38,42].

In another sense, there are several protective factors that allow reducing the risk of suicide risk, acting as insulators against it, such as self-esteem [21,43], reasons for living [28], and satisfaction with social support [14,21]. According to the results obtained, at-risk adolescents showed higher self-esteem compared to not-at-risk adolescents, which contradicts the tendency for low self-esteem in this type of population [42]. This may be due to the social skills trained with a social project for over a year, which may have influenced their levels of self-esteem, since one of the project's objectives is to promote this domain.

Adverse living conditions can influence the family environment of psychosocial risk, as it affects several members of the household, particularly adolescents' development and well-being, because of a scenario characterized by the lack of family rules and dysfunctional communication [19]. This scenario of family deprivation leads them to a negative perception of the received family support [12]. This study shows agreement in that young people with psychosocial vulnerabilities show less satisfaction with social support than young people without these vulnerabilities. In the perception that young people have of their social support, dissatisfaction with family support stands out quite significantly. Thus, young people have a negative perception of the support provided by their families, and they are also dissatisfied with their participation in social activities, compared to the general group.

According to the associations obtained, there is a need to understand the effect of these variables as possible predictors of suicidal ideation, both in the psychosocial risk group and in the general group. When analyzing possible explanatory models, the model that integrated the variables negative life events, self-esteem, and satisfaction with social support explained 38% of the variance of suicidal ideation in the PRG. The contribution of negative life events proved to be positive and significant, showing greater predictive power than the remaining factors, with negative and non-significant contributions. These three factors proved to be strong predictors in the general group, explaining 63% of the levels of suicidal ideation. Although together they showed a significant contribution, satisfaction with social support had the strongest and most significant contribution.

Based on several studies, negative life events have been found to be a significant predictor for levels of suicidal ideation in youth, with a positive and significant association observed between these two variables (e.g., [44,45]). It has also been found that levels of suicidal ideation are higher the higher the frequency of adverse experiences [46].

It is noteworthy that the results show that negative life events in the psychosocial risk group are the only predictor of the development of suicidal ideation, without requiring the contribution of other variables, while in the general group, the contribution of negative life events is smaller and shared with self-esteem and satisfaction with social support.

Several limitations were found regarding data collection. One refers to participants' age, since, for intending to study youth from such a specific population (psychosocial risk), a wide range of ages was included (youth between 10 and 19 years old), although it corresponds to the adolescent age group defined by the World Health Organization. Geographic specificity was another limitation, since we only characterize a population of the Algarve region, not allowing results' generalization. The samples size was also a limitation, since it reflected in, for example, the obtained reliability scores.

The fact that the sample of the psychosocial risk group refers to young people in a social project may represent another limitation of the study, since they were being intervened at the level of prevention of unwellness. This project aimed to prevent crime and promote social inclusion, working on the social skills of adolescents through various promotional activities such as school support, dance and music workshops, and computers, promoting greater well-being. Thus, there may be a regulation of emotions, encouraging young people to perceive and view themselves and the world in a more positive way.

This study also presents relevant contributions, such as highlighting the need for further research on those who are at risk for suicidal ideation, and for having detected the existence of several associated psychological factors. For example, it is known that negative life events are an important risk factor for suicide, and more negative life events are identified in young people from families at psychosocial risk.

Also, it drew attention to the need for an intervention at the level of selective prevention, directed at this specific population, for the promotion of mental health to better ensure the well-being of the young person and promote individual strategies, and for the relationship with others in their environment. Attention was specially drawn to the promotion of positive perceptions and experiences of social support by several significant interveners (e.g., peers, parents, and teachers). Another relevant suggestion refers to the direct intervention with families of the psychosocial group, to empower their abilities to manage their adolescents' emotions and detect early eventual psychosocial and suicide risks. This type of intervention has the cross-cutting objective of increasing suicide literacy among the different stakeholders, and it is proposed that in addition to the classic face-to-face versions, digital versions could be offered [47].

Considering all the limitations and potentialities mentioned above, we suggest, in terms of research, the repetition of the study with a larger population of Portuguese adolescents and one that is more diverse (i.e., from other regions of Portugal), the extension of the study to other European adolescents using the same instrumentation, and, in terms of practical implications, more targeted programs to specific groups of greater vulnerability, namely, of psychosocial risk, in a suicide prevention direction.

5. Conclusions

This study allowed us to identify, analyze, and compare factors associated with suicidal ideation in both samples of young people with and without psychosocial risk. Thus, it was possible to understand the effect that the experience of negative life events has on suicidal ideation in young people with psychosocial risk, compared to young people in the general population. Also, it highlights relevant protection factors that can attenuate potential psychosocial risks.

Several limitations and potentialities were pointed out, reinforcing the importance of programs, at different levels of intervention, that allow for the healthy development of young people. So, it is important to continue the investigation of the predictors of suicide, considering the environment, individual characteristics, and the individual's role in society, to decrease the prevalence of suicide and associated behaviors, through its prevention and promotion of biopsychosocial well-being.

Author Contributions: Conceptualization, M.B., P.E., C.M., C.N. and C.C.; methodology, M.B., P.E., C.M. and C.N.; software, M.B., P.E. and C.C.; formal analysis, M.B., P.E., C.M., C.N. and C.C.; investigation, M.B. and P.E.; resources, M.B. and P.E.; data curation, M.B., P.E., C.M. and C.N.; writing—original draft preparation, M.B., P.E., F.F.C. and C.C.; writing—review and editing, M.B., F.F.C., C.M. and C.C.; supervision, M.B. and C.C.; project administration, M.B. and C.C.; funding acquisition, M.B., C.N. and C.C. All authors have read and agreed to the published version of the manuscript.

Funding: This research was partially funded by the FCT—Fundação para a Ciência e a Tecnologia, grant number: UIDB/PSI/04345/2020.

Institutional Review Board Statement: The study was conducted in accordance with the Declaration of Helsinki and approved by the Scientific Commission of the Psychology and Educational Sciences Department, University of Algarve, Reference No. CC/2019/32877.

Informed Consent Statement: Informed consent was obtained from all subjects involved in the study.

Data Availability Statement: The data presented in this study are available on request from the corresponding author. The data are not publicly available due to licence constraints.

Conflicts of Interest: The authors declare no conflict of interest.

References

1. Valadas, M.; Barbosa, P.; Freitas, R.; Silva, S. *Prevenção do Suicídio: Manual para Profissionais de Saúde*; Direção-Geral da Saúde: Lisboa, Portugal, 2021.
2. Suicide Worldwide in 2019: Global Health Estimates. Available online: Who.int/publications/i/item/9789240026643 (accessed on 5 May 2023).
3. Indicadores dos Objetivos de Desenvolvimento Sustentável (ODS) em Portugal—2022. Available online: https://www.ine.pt/xportal/xmain?xpid=INE&xpgid=ine_destaques&DESTAQUESdest_boui=594480276&DESTAQUESmodo=2 (accessed on 5 May 2023).
4. Direção-Geral da Saúde. *Plano Nacional de Prevenção do Suicídio 2013/2017*; Direção-Geral da Saúde: Lisboa, Portugal, 2013.
5. Parellada, M.; Saiz, P.; Moreno, D.; Vidal, J.; Llorent, C.; Alvarez, M.; García-Portilla, P.; Ruiz-Sancho, A.; Arango, C.; Bobes, J. Is attempted suicide diferente in adolescente and adults? *Psychiatry Res.* **2008**, *157*, 131–137. [CrossRef] [PubMed]
6. Goldston, D.; Daniel, S.; Erkanli, A.; Reboussin, B.; Mayfield, A.; Frazier, P.; Treadway, S. Psychiatric diagnoses as contemporaneous risk factors for suicide attempts among adolescents and young adults: Developmental changes. *J. Consult. Clin. Psychol.* **2009**, *77*, 281–290. [CrossRef] [PubMed]
7. Arria, A.; O'Grady, K.; Caldeira, K.; Vincent, K.; Wilcox, H.; Wish, E. Suicide ideation among college students: A multivariate analysis. *Arch. Suicide Res.* **2009**, *13*, 230–246. [CrossRef] [PubMed]
8. Carballo, J.; Llorent, C.; Kehrmann, L.; Flamarique, I.; Zuddas, A.; Purper-Ouakil, D.; Hoekstra, P.; Coghill, D.; Schulze, U.; Dittmann, R.; et al. Psychosocial risk factors for suicidality in children and adolescents. *Eur. Child. Adolesc. Psychiatry* **2020**, *29*, 759–776. [CrossRef] [PubMed]
9. Yang, Q.; Hu, Y.-Q.; Zeng, Z.-H.; Liu, S.-J.; Wu, T.; Zhang, G.H. The Relationship of Family Functioning and Suicidal Ideation among Adolescents: The Mediating Role of Defeat and the Moderating Role of Meaning in Life. *Int. J. Environ. Res. Public. Health* **2020**, *19*, 15895. [CrossRef]
10. Alvarez-Subiela, X.; Castellano-Tejedor, C.; Villar-Cabeza, F.; Vila-Grifoll, M.; Palao-Vidal, D. Family Factors Related to Suicidal Behavior in Adolescents. *Int. J. Environ. Res. Public. Health* **2022**, *19*, 9892. [CrossRef]
11. Gelvez-Gafaro, L.-M.; Medina-Duarte, D.-M.; Villa-Belluci, I.-F., Rivera-Porras, D.; Bonilla-Cruz, N.-J. Psychosocial risk factors associated with suicide in youth and adolescents: A systematic review. *Gad. Méd. Caracas* **2022**, *130*, S595–S617. [CrossRef]
12. Adams, D.; Overholser, J.; Lehnert, K. Perceived family functioning and adolescent suicidal behavior. *J. Am. Acad. Child. Adolesc. Psychiatry* **1994**, *33*, 498–507. [CrossRef]
13. Wang, Y.-R.; Sun, J.-W.; Lin, P.-Z.; Zhang, H.-H.; Mu, G.-X.; Cao, F.-L. Suicidality among young adults: Unique and cumulative roles of 14 different adverse childhood experiences. *Child. Abus. Negl.* **2019**, *98*, 104183. [CrossRef]
14. Puig-Amores, I.; Cuadrado-Gordillo, I.; Mart´n-Mora-Parra, G. Health Service Protection vis-à-vis the Detection of Psychosocial Risks of Suicide during the Years 2019–2021. *Healthcare* **2023**, *11*, 1505. [CrossRef]

15. Aboagye, R.; Seid, A.-A.; Hagan, J.; Frimpong, J.; Okyerem, J.; Cadri, A.; Ahinkorah, B.O. Bullying Victimization among In-School Adolescents in Ghana: Analysis of Prevalence and Correlates from the Global School-Based Health Survey. *Healthcare* **2021**, *9*, 292. [CrossRef]
16. Rush, A.; Beck, A. Cognitive therapy of depression and suicide. *Am. J. Psychoter.* **1978**, *32*, 201–219. [CrossRef] [PubMed]
17. Wenzel, A.; Beck, A. A cognitive model of suicidal behavior: Theory and treatment. *Appl. Prev. Psychol.* **2008**, *12*, 189–201. [CrossRef]
18. Brás, M.; Jesus, S.; Carmo, C. Risk and Protective Psychological Factors Associated with Suicidal Ideation in Adolescents. *Psicol. Saúde E Doenças* **2016**, *17*, 132–149. [CrossRef]
19. Willems, Y.; Li, J.B.; Hendriks, A.; Bartels, M.; Finkenauer, C. The Relationship between Family Violence and Self-Control in Adolescence: A Multi-Level Meta-Analysis. *Int. J. Environ. Res. Public. Health* **2018**, *15*, 2468. [CrossRef] [PubMed]
20. Morris, A.; Silk, J.; Steinberg, L.; Myers, S.; Robinson, L. The Role of the Family Context in the Development of Emotion Regulation. *Soc. Dev.* **2007**, *16*, 361–388. [CrossRef] [PubMed]
21. Sharaf, A.; Thompson, E.; Walsh, E. Protective effects of self-esteem and family support on suicide risk behaviors among at-risk adolescents. *J. Child. Adolesc. Psychiatr. Nurs.* **2009**, *22*, 160–168. [CrossRef] [PubMed]
22. Inderbitzen-Nolan, H.; Walters, K. Social Anxiety Scale for Adolescents: Normative data and further evidence of construct validity. *J. Clin. Child. Psychol.* **2000**, *29*, 360–371. [CrossRef]
23. World Suicide Prevention Day. Available online: https://www.who.int/campaigns/world-suicide-prevention-day/2023 (accessed on 16 May 2023).
24. Santos, J.C.; Quaresma, H.; Brás, M.; Carmo, C.; Façanha, J.; Nabais, A.; Simeão, L.; Calças, C.; Matos, E.; Coruche, I.; et al. Performing emotions and suffering. Recovery of depressive symptoms involving adolescent intervention in art and dance schools. *Eur. J. Ment. Health* **2022**, *17*, 65–77. [CrossRef]
25. Brás, M.; Abrantes, P.; Carmo, C. Ideação Suicida E Acontecimentos de Vida Negativos em Adolescentes Institucionalizados. In *International Handbook of Clinical Psychology, 1*; Buela-Casal, G., Ed.; Editorial Thomson Reuters: Granada, Spain, 2022.
26. Lemos, I.; Brás, M.; Lemos, M.; Nunes, C. Psychological Distress Symptoms and Resilience Assets in Adolescents in Residential Care. *Children* **2021**, *8*, 700. [CrossRef]
27. Osman, A.; Downs, W.; Kopper, B.; Barrios, F.; Baker, M.; Osman, J.; Besett, T.; Linehan, M. The Reasons for Living Inventory for Adolescents (RFL-A): Development and psychometric properties. *J. Clin. Psychol.* **1998**, *54*, 1063–1078. [CrossRef]
28. Brás, M.; Carmo, C.; Jesus, S. Reasons for Living Inventory for Adolescents: Psychometric Properties Among Portuguese Adolescents. *Omega* **2021**, *82*, 527–547. [CrossRef]
29. Beck, A.; Weissman, A.; Lester, D.; Trexler, L. The measurement of pessimism: The hopelessness scale. *J. Consult. Clin. Psychol.* **1974**, *42*, 861–865. [CrossRef] [PubMed]
30. Cruz, J.P. Terapia Cognitiva de Los Intentos de Suicidio: Cambiando Historias de Muerte Por Historias De Vida. Ph.D. Thesis, University of Sevilla, Sevilla, Spain, 2000.
31. Rosenberg, M. Rosenberg Self-Esteem Scale (RSES). *APA PsycTests* **1965**, *61*, 18. [CrossRef]
32. Santos, P.; Maia, J. Adaptação e análise factorial confirmatória da *Rosenberg Self-Esteem Scale* com uma amostra de adolescentes: Resultados preliminares. In *Avaliação Psicológica: Formas e Contextos*; Soares, A., Araújo, S., Caires, S., Eds.; APPORT: Braga, Portugal, 1999; Volume 3, pp. 154–196.
33. Brás, M.; Cruz, J. Inventário de Acontecimentos de Vida Negativos (IAV-N)—Construção e validação numa população adulta. In *Actas da XIII Conferência Internacional de Avaliação Psicológica: Formas e Contextos*; Noronha, A., Machado, C., Almeida, L., Gonçalves, M., Martins, S., Ramalho, V., Eds.; Psiquilíbrios: Braga, Portugal, 2008.
34. Pais-Ribeiro, J. Escala de Satisfação com o Suporte Social (ESSS). *Análise Psicol.* **1999**, *3*, 547–588.
35. Reynolds, W. *Suicidal Ideation Questionnaire: Professional Manual*; Odessa—Psychological Assessment Resources: Lutz, FL, USA, 1988.
36. Ferreira, J.; Castela, M. Questionário de Ideação Suicida (Q.I.S.). In *Testes e Provas Psicológicas em Portugal*; Simões, M., Gonçalves, M., Almeida, L., Eds.; APPORT/SHO: Braga, Portugal, 1999; pp. 123–130.
37. Tabachnick, B.G.; Fidell, L.S. *Using Multivariate Statistics*, 7th ed.; Pearson Education: New York, NY, USA, 2019.
38. Nunes, C.; Ayala-Nunes, L. Famílias em risco psicossocial: Desafios para a avaliação e intervenção. *Psicol. Crian. Adoles.* **2015**, *6*, 95–107.
39. Lopes, P.; Barreira, D.P.; Pires, A. Tentativa de suicídio na adolescência: Avaliação do efeito de género na depressão e personalidade. *Psicol. Saúde Doenças* **2001**, *2*, 47–57.
40. Esposito, C.; Spirito, A.; Boergers, J.; Donaldson, D. Affective, behavioral, and cognitive functioning in adolescents with multiple suicide attempts. *Suicide Life-Threat. Behav.* **2003**, *33*, 389–399. [CrossRef]
41. Gutierrez, P.; Osman, A. *Adolescent Suicide: An Integrated Approach to the Assessment of Risk and Protective Factors*; Northern Illinois University Press: DeKalb, IL, USA, 2008.
42. Wadsby, M.; Svedin, C.; Sydsjö, G. Children of mothers at psychosocial risk growing up: A follow up at the age of 16. *J Adolesc.* **2007**, *30*, 147–164. [CrossRef]
43. Díez, C.; Fontanil, Y.; Alonso, Y.; Ezama, E.; Gómez, L. Adolescents at Serious Psychosocial Risk: What is the Role of Additional Exposure to Violence in the Home? *J. Interpers. Violence* **2018**, *33*, 865–888. [CrossRef]

44. Yoder, K.; Hoyt, D. Family economic pressure and adolescent suicidal ideation: Application of the family stress model. *Suicide Life Threat Behav* **2005**, *35*, 251–264. [CrossRef] [PubMed]
45. Kwon, H.; Lee, J.-S.; Kim, A.R.; Hong, H.J.; Kweon, Y.-S. Risk Factors for Suicidal Ideation and Attempts in Adolescents. *Korean Acad. Child Adolesc. Psychiatry* **2018**, *29*, 114–121. [CrossRef] [PubMed]
46. Serafini, G.; Muzio, C.; Piccinini, G.; Flouri, E.; Ferrigno, G.; Pompili, M.; Girardi, P.; Amore, M. Life adversities and suicidal behavior in young individuals: A systematic review. *Eur. Child Adolesc. Psychiatry* **2015**, *24*, 1423–1446. [CrossRef] [PubMed]
47. Torok, M.; Calear, A.L.; Smart, A.; Nicolopoulos, A.; Wong, Q. Preventing adolescent suicide: A systematic review of the effectiveness and change mechanisms of suicide prevention gatekeeping training programs for teachers and parents. *J. Adolesc.* **2019**, *73*, 100–112. [CrossRef] [PubMed]

healthcare MDPI

Article

Do Emotion Regulation Strategies Mediate the Relationship of Parental Emotion Socialization with Adolescent and Emerging Adult Psychological Distress?

Liliana Bujor [1,*] and Maria Nicoleta Turliuc [2]

1 Faculty of Sciences of Education, Ştefan cel Mare University of Suceava, 720229 Suceava, Romania
2 Department of Psychology, Alexandru Ioan Cuza University, 700554 Iasi, Romania; turliuc@uaic.ro
* Correspondence: liliana.bujor@usm.ro

Abstract: A child's ability to cope with stress is shaped by experiences in a parent–child relationship. In this study, the direct effect of a parent's response to anger and happiness in childhood on adolescents' and emerging adults' psychological distress and the indirect effect through the mediating role of emotion regulation strategies—specifically, cognitive reappraisal and emotional suppression—were measured. To achieve our research aim, we tested four parallel mediation models using the bootstrapping method. A group of 497 participants aged between 14 and 35 years (M = 18.62; SD = 3.32), 66% female (n = 332) and 34% male (n = 165), completed a questionnaire comprising self-reporting measures. The results indicate direct effects between emotion socialization and distress for seven independent variables. The mother's and father's positive responses to anger and happiness are significant negative predictors of distress; the negative responses of both parents to happiness, and the mother's negative response to anger—but not the father's—are significant positive predictors of distress. The findings also provide support for the mediating role of expressive suppression and cognitive reappraisal for the mother's positive response to both anger and happiness, as well as for the mother's negative response to the child's expression of happiness. None of the father's responses—positive or negative, in relation to anger or happiness—are mediated by emotion regulation strategies in relation to distress. Our findings have practical implication for a preventative intervention program focused on the psychological growth of adolescents by adaptative emotional responses.

Keywords: parental style of emotion socializing; cognitive reappraisal; expressive suppression; psychological distress; anger; happiness

Citation: Bujor, L.; Turliuc, M.N. Do Emotion Regulation Strategies Mediate the Relationship of Parental Emotion Socialization with Adolescent and Emerging Adult Psychological Distress? *Healthcare* **2023**, *11*, 2620. https://doi.org/10.3390/healthcare11192620

Academic Editor: Roberta Frontini

Received: 4 August 2023
Revised: 5 September 2023
Accepted: 18 September 2023
Published: 25 September 2023

1. Theoretical and Conceptual Framing

Developmental studies consistently indicate that parents have a primary role in shaping a child's emotional development through their direct and indirect, verbal and nonverbal messages addressed to their children. Dealing with anger, happiness, fear or sadness are emotional and social daily lessons that put parent and child together in a positive or negative interaction with implications for their development and wellbeing.

Our conceptual framework is the Tripartite Model of the Impact of the Family on Children's Emotion Regulation and Adjustment [1]. Family context affects the development of emotion regulation in three ways: (1) observation via social modeling, (2) specific parenting practices in relation to emotions and (3) the emotional climate of the family, reflected in attachment, parenting style and marital relations. The family context has direct effects on children's adjustment (e.g., internalizing, externalizing), but much of the effects of the family context are mediated through children's emotion regulation [2].

According to the tripartite model of parental influences [1], the family context impacts emotional development through three pathways: the emotional climate, the parenting style and the emotional quality of marital relationships. Parent–child interactions with all its components (parents' reactions to the child's emotions), whether supportive (e.g., *reward*) or unsupportive (e.g., *punishment, neglect*), are reflected in their emotional life and represent an important predictor for the development of emotion regulation [3] and wellbeing [4]. Thus, parental emotion socialization is a process that helps a child to identify and appropriately express and manage their emotions, due to parental reactions to a child's emotions. Certain retrospective reports of adolescents have shown that parental socialization emotional strategies project emotional effects into adulthood. The Malatesta-Magai model of the parental style of emotion socialization [5], which defined the concepts and variables of this study, delineates five distinct strategies used by parents when it comes to emotion socialization: *rewarding (i.e., provision of comfort and empathy following children's emotion expression), punishing (i.e., discouraging or punishing expression), overriding (i.e., suggesting that others have it worse or distracting children from emotion), neglecting (i.e., ignoring emotional expression) and magnifying (i.e., parent matches the child's expression of emotion equally or with more intensity).*

From a functionalist approach, emotion socialization implies responses to concrete emotions. In this research, we will analyze anger and happiness because a number of studies have identified the existence of core emotions relevant for emotional development, frequently implied in internalization or externalization problems [6,7]. Anger is an emotion that communicates a need for limits and rules and activates a defense system. Happiness functions as a signal to engage in activities that bring personal satisfaction, promote positive relationships through emotional contagion and ensure wellbeing [7].

According to a processual model of emotion regulation [8], there are many strategies that can intervene in different moments of emotional experience: *anterior-focused*, like situation selection, situation modification, attentional deployment and cognitive change; or *response-focused*, which can be response modulation. A specific type of cognitive change is *cognitive reappraisal* (CR), and for response modulation, there is *expressive suppression* (ES). CR and ES are two strategies with multiple implications for mental health and wellbeing.

A person who activates CR tends to negotiate stressful events by interpreting them in an optimistic manner [9,10] and has a high level of life satisfaction and self-esteem, as well as a lower level of anxiety, depression or posttraumatic stress disorder [3,11,12]. ES involves the inhibition of emotion expression and leads to a series of psychological consequences, like both externalizing and internalizing problems in early childhood, through adolescence and emerging adulthood [13].

Although together, all these theories and models explain the emotional impact of parents with regard to their child's development; it is important to extend knowledge by examining the role of emotion regulation strategies, like protective factors, between parental influences and distress [14].

A principal limitation of specific studies on the emotion socialization process in relation to emotion regulation, stress and mental health is that only the mother is included in reports. The lack of inclusion of the father is a significant limitation to a deep understanding of parenting influences and effects [15], and efforts are currently proposed to evidence the implication of other caregivers, like fathers [16–20]. Another distinctive addition to the literature is our focus on discrete emotions, anger and happiness, in parents' emotion socialization. Our examination of emotion socialization relied on two composite variables, both for negative and positive parenting behaviors in relation to one negative and one positive discrete emotion (anger and happiness). In the literature, there are few studies that analyze discrete emotions (sadness and anger) in relation to parental emotion socialization [6].

The relationship between our variables were studied more in Western, individualistic cultures and less in Eastern, collectivist ones. Because of the fact that, in the last twenty years, there has been a paradigm change in Eastern culture from an authoritarian parenting style to an authoritative parenting style, which emphasizes children's wellbeing and less distress [21], it is important to understand the explanatory mechanisms between different parental styles as relates to emotion socialization and distress in an Eastern cultural context.

In accordance with these limitations and recommendations, this study expands the existing literature in three important ways: first, we integrated fathers' responses to children's emotions, obtained different analyses for both parents and highlighted the contribution of fathers to the emotion socialization process; secondly, we explored two discrete emotions for a specific understanding of the emotion socialization process; thirdly, we proposed an explanatory mechanism in the relationship between parental strategies for emotion socialization during childhood and distress in adolescence and emerging adulthood.

Because of the evidence from the literature about long-term parental influences [11,22], we decided to analyze longer periods after childhood, in particular adolescence and emerging adulthood (a period that is neither adolescence nor young adulthood, from 18 to 25 years and normative in adulthood but not having entered a phase concerned with enduring responsibilities) [23].

The purpose of this study is to have a general view of the relation between maternal and paternal emotion socialization of anger and happiness in the childhood period and distress in adolescence and emerging adulthood.

2. Problem Statement

2.1. Parental Emotion Socialization and Its Emotional Consequences

Significant correlations between negative emotion socialization and internalization issues are a constant in several studies; thus, sadness or fear and punishment or neglect were associated with high levels of psychological distress in adulthood [7,24,25]. Punishment of positive emotions correlates with high levels of distress, while reward is associated with lower levels of distress [22].

Although the topic of emotion socialization is important and relevant in multiple areas of psychology, few studies have examined the socialization process of specific negative (e.g., fear, anger) or positive emotions (e.g., happiness) as separate influences stemming from both the mother and the father [4]. Furthermore, there is relatively extensive research on negative emotions and a lack of research on positive socialization emotions [22].

There are a few studies regarding emotion socialization as separate influences from the mother and the father [26]. Although there are concordant findings suggesting that a mother's focus and implication is deeper in relation to their child's emotions than the father's [6,13,25,27], the data regarding the long-term implications of the mother and father's emotional behavior produced mixed results. A meta-analysis highlighted that paternal psychopathology is more related to children's emotional and behavioral problems than maternal psychopathology [28], and paternal emotion socialization is more consistently related to the psychopathology of daughters [22]. A father's response to their child's emotions has a powerful relation to the child's emotional skills [27]. More precisely, a father's acceptance attitude towards their child's sadness and anger at five years old is associated with better social skills at eight years old [29]. Based on this finding, we formulated the first objective of this research: to analyze the relation between anger and happiness socialization in childhood and their effects on adolescents and emerging adults' distress by conducting a separate analysis for both the mother and the father.

2.2. Emotion Regulation Strategies as Mediators

Recent research [3,13,30,31] investigated the mediating role of emotion regulation strategies between parental responses to a child's emotions and emotional consequences in adolescence and adulthood, but there is a lack of evidence concerning specific analyses, like separate investigations for mothers and fathers in the case of specific emotions (e.g., anger, fear, happiness, sadness). For example, in a family with different maternal and paternal nonconsensual parental responses to a specific emotion, it is difficult to build coherent emotional behavior and adaptative emotion regulation strategies [13]. The quality of parent–child interactions has profound implications for the expression and regulation of emotions that can become a mediating variable between parental influences and distress or wellbeing [13,32]. In this context, recent research has shown interest in studying responsible mechanisms when it comes to the relation between parental influences and emotional development [3] and suggests the role of emotion regulation as a mediating variable be studied. Summarizing these findings, we established the second objective: to analyze the relation between maternal and paternal emotion socialization in childhood and their effects on adolescent and emerging adult distress, taking into account the mediational role of both parents' cognitive reappraisal and expressive suppression as emotion regulation strategies.

3. This Study

Due to the impact of emotional experiences during childhood on mental health mboxciteB3-healthcare-2569186,B13-healthcare-2569186,B33-healthcare-2569186, it is useful to investigate the mediator's role of emotion regulation between emotional experiences during childhood and emotional life during adolescence or early adulthood. Based on the tripartite model of family relationships [1], related with the Malatesta-Magai model of the parental strategies of emotion socialization [5], a functionalist approach of emotions and the processual model of emotion regulation [8], we tested four mediation models in order to answer the question of whether emotion regulation strategies can mediate positive and negative parental impacts in childhood—separate for the mother and father—regarding distress in adolescence and emerging adulthood in relation to two distinct emotions: anger and happiness.

In our research, family context was represented by parental practices of emotion socialization in childhood that was then related to adolescent adjustment as measured by the level of distress, like internalizing difficulty, via emotion regulation strategies (cognitive reappraisal and emotion suppression). Each of these concepts was integrated in a distinct theoretical model; parental emotion socialization was related with The Malatesta-Magai Model of the Parental Style of Emotion Socialization [5], and emotion regulation was explained from a Processual Model of Emotion Regulation perspective [8]. This conceptual framework, globally and sequentially presented, was analyzed from a functionalist approach that implies responses to concrete emotions (e.g., happiness, anger). Together, this conceptual framework and this theoretical model became measures in our research investigation: The Emotion as a Child Scale—EAC, Version 2 [7] and The Emotion Regulation Questionnaire—ERQ [8].

Therefore, the following hypotheses were formulated:

Hypothesis 1. *The relation between negative anger socialization (mother and father) and distress is mediated by emotion regulation (expressive suppression, cognitive reappraisal).*

Hypothesis 2. *The relation between positive anger socialization (mother and father) and distress is mediated by emotion regulation (expressive suppression, cognitive reappraisal).*

Hypothesis 3. *The relation between negative happiness socialization (mother and father) and distress is mediated by emotion regulation (expressive suppression, cognitive reappraisal).*

Hypothesis 4. *The relation between positive happiness socialization (mother and father) and distress is mediated by emotion regulation (expressive suppression, cognitive reappraisal).*

4. Materials and Methods

4.1. Participants

Initially, 525 participants accepted our invitation to fill out the research questionnaire. By controlling the variable *type* of *family origin*, we only chose the questionnaires from respondents who come from intact families. We excluded 28 questionnaires from participants who reported having one biological parent and one step-parent or as belonging to a single-parent family. The final sample consisted of 497 participants, aged between 14 and 25 years (M = 18.62; SD = 3.32), of whom 53% were adolescents, 47%—emerging adults, 66%—female (N = 332) and 34%—male (N = 165). The sample is composed of students from Stefan cel Mare University of Suceava (55%) as well as high school students (45%) from several national state colleges (Table 1).

Table 1. Sample by gender, age, and school level.

		No	Percent
Gender	Male	165	33%
	Female	332	67%
Age	Adolescent	261	53%
	Emerging adult	236	47%
School level	Higher Secondary	222	45%
	University	275	55%
Total Sample Size		497	

4.2. Procedures

First, the study protocol was approved by the Ethics Committee of Alexandru Ioan Cuza University (1013/17.05.2022). Two high schools agreed to take part in the study and to inform the classes of students aged between 14 and 18 years and one university with students aged between 19 and 25 years. Second, all the participants received and signed their informed consent. Then, the participants filled out the questionnaire, which included three scales and several sociodemographic items (*gender, age, school level, family type*). The data were collected using self-reporting scales, applied in pencil-paper format, in different educational contexts: at courses, seminars and classes and in the presence of one of the research team members. Time for the administration of the questions was 25–30 min for all the questionnaires. To avoid social desirability, the questionnaires were anonymous (except for the participants who wanted personal results).

4.3. Measures

4.3.1. Parental Emotion Socialization

Emotion as a Child Scale—EAC (Version 2) [7] was measured in the following way: For each scale, the participants recalled parental responses (separately for the mother and father) to their positive (e.g., happiness) or negative (e.g., anger) emotions during their childhood period. The instrument had 15 items, evaluated on a Likert Scale in five steps from 1 (*not at all*) to 5 (*very much*), for each analyzed emotion and the following five parental styles: Reward (item: *Helped me to deal with the issue*), Punish (item: *Gave me a disgusted look*), Override (item: *Bought me something I liked*), Neglect (item: *Ignored me*) and Magnify (item: *Got anxious herself/himself*). Due to data reduction strategies, we computed and used two summary indexes: positive parental emotion socialization (Reward scale) and negative parental emotion socialization (Neglect and Punishment scales). Factor analyses with the negative emotion scales in this study demonstrated that Punishment and Neglect are the most representative for negative parental emotion socialization styles. In this study, Cronbach's alphas were between 0.70 and 0.89 for all dimensions.

4.3.2. Emotion Regulation

The Emotion Regulation Questionnaire—ERQ, [8] had 10 items and measured cognitive reappraisal (item: *When I want to feel more positive emotions, I change the way I'm thinking about the situation*) and expressive suppression (item: *When I am feeling negative emotions, I make sure not to express them*). Answers were scored on a 7-point Likert Scale from 1 (*strongly disagree*) to 7 (*strongly agree*). The cognitive reappraisal subscale had an adequate internal consistency with a Cronbach's alpha = 0.76, and for expressive suppression, we had a Cronbach's alpha = 0.75.

4.3.3. Psychological Distress

The Profile of Emotional Distress—PED, [34] is a 26-item scale that measured dysfunctional negative emotions and functional negative emotions in the *fear (e.g., Anxious, Panicked)* and *sadness/depression (e.g., Sad, Hopeless)* categories. The scale was designed in 2005, starting from the Profile of Mood Disorders, a Short Version [35]. The scale allowed for the calculation of a general distress score by adding item scores evaluated by the Likert Scale from 1 (*not at all*) to 5 (*extremely*). The Psychological Distress Scale had an adequate internal consistency with a Cronbach's alpha = 0.95.

4.4. Data Analyses

To conduct our analyses, we used a version 2.3.16 JOMOVI GLM Mediation Model. We calculated both the direct and indirect effects of positive and negative parental emotion socialization (mother/father; anger/happiness) on psychological distress through emotion regulation strategies (cognitive reappraisal and expressive suppression). This was achieved by testing the independent variables (anger positive socialization by the mother, anger positive socialization by the father, anger negative socialization by the mother, anger negative socialization by the mother, happiness positive socialization by the mother, happiness positive socialization by the father, happiness negative socialization by the mother and happiness negative socialization by the father), dependent variables (psychological distress) and mediators (cognitive reappraisal and expressive suppression) in four parallel mediation models, while checking for key background variables (sex, age and family structure). We used 5000 bootstrapped samples, and the biases were corrected at 95% confidence intervals (CI) for each indirect effect, where the significance of indirect effect path was indicated when the confidence interval did not contain zero ($p < 0.05$). Bootstrapping is a resampling method that constructs a confidence interval around the examined indirect effect and provides a more accurate estimate of indirect effects independently via sample distribution (normal or not) [36,37].

5. Results

Descriptive statistics (means, standard deviation, minimum, maximum, Skewness and Kurtosis) are presented in Table 2.

Table 2. Descriptive statistics.

	M	*SD*	Min	Max	Skew	Kurt
Anger_P_M (Anger_positive_mother)	10.66	2.59	3	15	−0.65	0.49
Anger_P_F (Anger_positive_father)	9.23	3.10	3	15	−0.26	−0.62
Anger_N_M (Anger_negative_mother)	6.05	1.87	3	13	0.55	0.22
Anger_N_F (Anger_negative_father)	6.16	1.97	3	14.5	0.62	0.17
Happiness_P_M (Happiness_positive_mother)	12.43	2.37	3	15	−1.26	1.95
Happiness_P_F (Happiness_positive_ father)	11.06	2.85	3	15	−0.71	0.26
Happiness_N_M (Happiness_negative_mother)	4.59	1.83	3	14.5	1.52	2.56
Happiness_N_F (Happiness_negative_father)	5.02	1.80	3	12	0.91	0.38
Cognitive reappraisal (CR)	29.13	5.81	7	42	−0.47	0.38
Expressive suppression (ES)	14.49	4.78	4	27	0.24	−0.35
Distress	56.08	19.65	26	128	0.93	0.54

M = mean; *SD* = standard deviation; Min = minimum; Max = maximum; Skew = skewness; Positive is the Reward (mother/father, anger/happiness) measured from 1 (*not at all*) to 5 (*very much*). Negative is the mean between Punishment and Neglect, ranging from 1 (*not at all*) to 5 (*very much*) (mother/father, anger/happiness). Cognitive reappraisal and expressive suppression ranges are from 1 (*strongly disagree*) to 7 (*strongly agree*). Psychological distress ranges from 1 (*not at all*) to 5 (*extremely*).

Bivariate correlations among the main constructs are reported in Table 3. All positive answers by the mother and father for anger and happiness have significant and negative correlations with psychological distress. Negative emotion socialization has significant and positive correlations with psychological distress. Paternal reward of anger does not have a correlation with expressive suppression, and paternal negative socialization of anger does not have a significant correlation with cognitive reappraisal.

Table 3. Correlations among the study variables regarding parent socialization emotions and emotional consequences.

	1	2	3	4	5	6	7	8	9	10
1. Anger P_M										
2. Anger P_F	0.53 **									
3. Happiness P_M	0.54 **	0.25 **								
4. Happiness P_F	0.35 **	0.63 **	0.47 **							
5. Anger N_M	−0.35 **	−0.20 **	−0.33 **	−0.20 **						
6. Anger N_F	−0.23 **	−0.33 **	−0.21 **	−0.32 **	0.71 **					
7. Happiness N_M	−0.35 **	−0.13 **	−0.55 **	−0.25 **	0.59 **	0.45 **				
8. Happiness N_F	−0.26 **	−0.35 **	−0.39 **	−0.52 **	0.48 **	0.62 **	0.67 **			
9. CR	0.24 **	0.09 *	0.22 **	0.10 *	−0.11 *	−0.07	−0.19 **	−0.11 *		
10. ES	−0.11 **	−0.01	−0.22 **	−0.14 **	0.18 **	0.12 **	0.20 **	0.19 **	0.08	
11. Distress	−0.21 **	−0.17 **	−0.20 **	−0.20 **	0.31 **	0.25 **	0.30 **	0.34 **	−0.11 *	0.19 **

** $p < 0.01$, * $p < 0.05$; Anger P_M = Anger Positive response from the Mother; Anger P_F = Anger Positive response from the Father; Happiness P_M = Happiness Positive response from the Mother; Happiness P_F = Happiness Positive response from the Father; Anger N_M = Anger Negative response from the Mother; Anger P_F = Anger Positive response from the Father; Happiness P_M = Happiness Positive response from the Mother; Happiness P_F = Happiness Positive response from the Father; CR = Cognitive Reappraisal; ES = Expressive Suppression.

According to our research in the analysis of the relation between parental emotion socialization in childhood and its effects in adolescence and emerging adulthood with regard to distress, and taking into account a separate analysis for the mother and father as well as specific emotions (anger and happiness), we have significant results (Table 4).

As we expected, the coefficients for the direct effect show that anger positive socialization (rewarding) is negatively associated with distress for the mother (b = −0.83, $p < 0.05$) and the father (b = −0.68, $p < 0.05$). A negative socialization of anger is a significant predictor for distress in relation to the mother's response (b = 0.91, $p < 0.001$) but not the father's.

In relation to happiness, the father's positive (b = −0.85, $p < 0.05$) and negative (b = 0.65, $p < 0.05$) responses, and the mother's negative (b = 0.54, $p < 0.05$) responses are significant predictors for distress.

The parental response is significant, not for distress, but for emotion regulation strategies too. Both cognitive reappraisals and expressive suppression are predicted just from the mother's response. Anger positive socialization (b = 0.56, $p < 0.001$) is a significant predictor for cognitive reappraisal, while happiness positive (b = 0.53, $p < 0.001$) and negative (b = −0.29, $p < 0.001$) responses are predictors for cognitive reappraisal. Expressive suppression is predicted from both the mother's positive response for anger (b = −0.28, $p < 0.01$) and happiness (b = −0.38, $p < 0.001$) and negative responses for anger (b = 0.11, $p < 0.01$) and happiness (b = 0.14, $p < 0.01$).

Path Model of Anger. We studied the mediating effects of cognitive reappraisal and expressive suppression between anger socialization and distress (Figures 1 and 2).

Table 4. The findings from the parallel mediation models (unstandardized).

Independent Measures (IV)	Dependent Measure (DV)	Cognitive Reappraisal (M_1)											
		Total Effect		Direct Effect		IV → M_1		M_1 → DV		Indirect Effect		95% CI	
		C		*c′*		*a1*		*b1*		*a1* × *b1*			
		b	SE	b	SE	B	SE	b	SE	b	SE	BootLLCI	BootULCI
Anger_P_M	Distress	−1.26 **	0.38	−0.83 *	0.38	0.56 ***	0.11	−0.37 **	0.14	−0.21 *	0.09	**−0.39**	**−0.02**
Anger_P_F	Distress	−0.58 *	0.31	−0.68 *	0.31	−0.00	0.09	−0.37 **	0.14	0.00	0.03	−3.43	0.06
Anger_N_M	Distress	1.01 ***	0.18	0.91 ***	0.18	−0.07	0.05	−0.44 **	0.13	0.03	0.02	−0.01	0.08
Anger_N_F	Distress	−0.10	0.17	−0.10	0.17	0.03	0.05	0.44 **	0.13	−0.01	0.02	−0.06	0.03
Happiness_P_M	Distress	−1.19 **	0.40	−0.73 *	0.40	0.53 ***	0.11	−0.37 **	0.14	−0.20 *	0.09	**−0.37**	**−0.02**
Happiness_P_F	Distress	−0.90 **	0.33	−0.85 **	0.32	0.05	0.09	−0.37 **	0.14	−0.02	0.03	−0.09	0.05
Happiness_N_M	Distress	0.71 ***	0.21	0.54 **	0.21	−0.29 ***	0.06	−0.33 **	0.14	0.09 *	0.04	**0.006**	**0.19**
Happiness_N_F	Distress	0.65 **	0.20	0.65 **	0.20	0.10	0.06	−0.33 **	0.14	−0.03	0.02	−0.08	0.01

Independent Measures (IV)	Dependent Measure (DV)	Expressive Suppression (M_2)											
		Total Effect		Direct Effect		IV → M_2		M_2 → DV		Indirect Effect		95% CI	
		C		*c′*		*a1*		*b1*		*a2* × *b2*			
		b	SE	b	SE	B	SE	b	SE	b	SE	BootLLCI	BootULCI
Anger_P_M	Distress	−1.26 **	0.38	−0.83 *	0.38	−0.28 **	0.09	0.74 ***	0.17	−0.21 **	0.08	**−0.30**	**−0.04**
Anger_P_F	Distress	−0.58 *	0.31	−0.68 *	0.31	0.12	0.07	0.74 ***	0.17	0.09	0.06	−0.02	0.21
Anger_N_M	Distress	1.01 ***	0.18	0.91 ***	0.18	0.11 **	0.04	0.59 ***	0.17	0.07 *	0.03	**0.003**	**0.13**
Anger_N_F	Distress	−0.10	0.17	−0.10	0.17	0.02	0.04	0.59 ***	0.17	0.01	0.02	−0.03	0.06
Happiness_P_M	Distress	−1.19 **	0.40	−0.73 *	0.40	−0.38 ***	0.09	0.65 ***	0.17	−0.25 **	0.09	**−0.43**	**−0.06**
Happiness_P_F	Distress	−0.90 **	0.33	−0.85 **	0.32	−0.04	0.08	0.65 ***	0.17	−0.03	0.05	−0.13	0.07
Happiness_N_M	Distress	0.71 ***	0.21	0.54 **	0.21	0.14 **	0.05	0.51 **	0.17	0.07 *	0.03	**8.53×10^{-4}**	**0.14**
Happiness_N_F	Distress	0.65 **	0.20	0.65 **	0.20	0.07	0.05	0.51 **	0.17	0.03	0.02	−0.02	0.09

* $p < 0.05$; ** $p < 0.01$; *** $p < 0.001$. Anger P_M = Anger Positive response from the Mother; Anger P_F = Anger Positive response from the Father; Happiness P_M = Happiness Positive response from the Mother; Happiness P_F = Happiness Positive response from the Father; Anger N_M = Anger Negative response from the Mother; Anger P_F = Anger Positive response from the Father; Happiness P_M = Happiness Positive response from the Mother; Happiness P_F = Happiness Positive response from the Father; CR = Cognitive Reappraisal; ES = Expressive Suppression. Bolded values do not include zero, indicating a significant indirect effect.

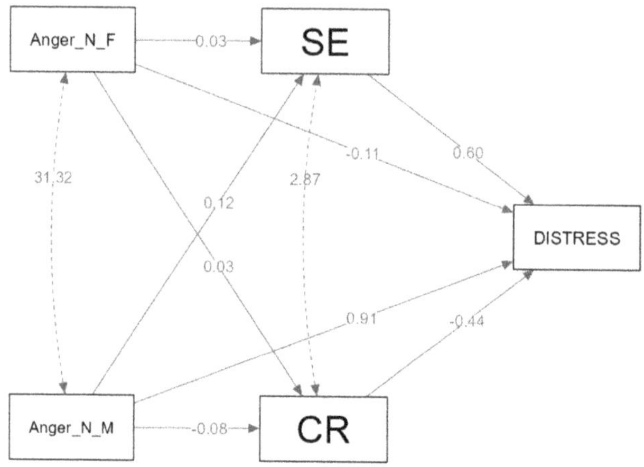

Figure 1. The mediating effect of expressive suppression and cognitive reappraisal between negative anger socialization and distress.

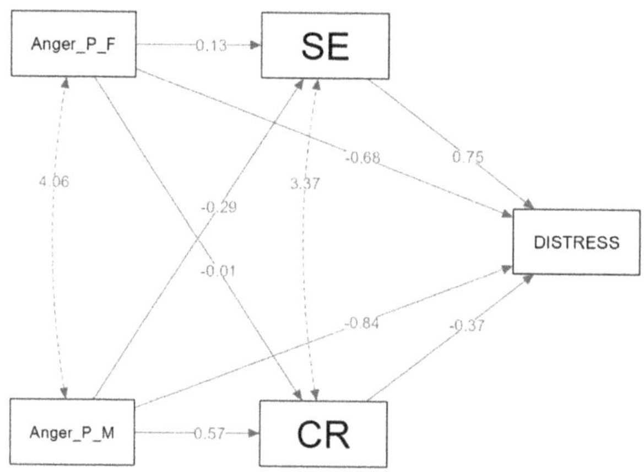

Figure 2. The mediating effect of expressive suppression and cognitive reappraisal in positive anger socialization and distress.

Additionally, we investigated emotion regulation mediating effects between parental emotion socialization and psychological distress.

The relation between the negative emotion socialization of anger and distress is mediated by emotion regulation strategies (expressive suppression, cognitive reappraisal). *Hypothesis 1* is partially confirmed. From all four paths analyzed, we found one mediation in the relation between the maternal negative socialization of anger and distress, occurring through expressive suppression. From our parallel mediation model (Figure 1), which has no supportive emotion socialization relating to anger IV, one of them does not meet the statistical assumptions [36,37] in the model regarding negative anger socialization from the father; IV does not predict M_1 (cognitive reappraisal) and M_2 (expressive suppression). The results from our parallel mediation analysis indicate that the maternal negative socialization of anger is indirectly related to psychological distress through its relationship with expressive suppression. In a parallel mediation model, a 95% bias-corrected confidence interval based on 5000 bootstrap samples was indicated as an indirect effect of expressive suppression between the mother's negative response to anger ($b = 0.07$, $SE = 0.03$), CI (0.003 to 0.13) and psychological distress. By contrast, the indirect effects of cognitive reappraisal included zero (−0.01 to 0.08). The relation between the positive emotion socialization of anger (rewarding response) and distress is mediated by emotion regulation strategies (expressive suppression, cognitive reappraisal). *Hypothesis 2* is partially confirmed. From all four paths analyzed, we found two mediations in the relation between the maternal positive socialization of anger and distress, occurring through expressive suppression and cognitive reappraisal. The relation between the father's emotional response to anger and distress is not mediated by emotion regulation strategies. The model (Figure 2) meets the statistical conditions to conduct parallel mediation models. Our results indicate two significant indirect effects. The maternal reward of anger is indirectly related to psychological distress through cognitive reappraisal (b = −0.21, SE = 0.09), CI (−0.39 to −0.02) and expressive suppression (b = −0.21, SE = 0.08), CI (−0.30 to −0.04). We can therefore say, with 95% confidence, that the indirect effect is negative in all these cases. In this model, we do not have any indirect effects of emotion regulation strategies between the father's response and distress.

Path Model of Happiness. We studied the mediating effects of cognitive reappraisal and expressive suppression between happiness socialization and distress (Figures 3 and 4).

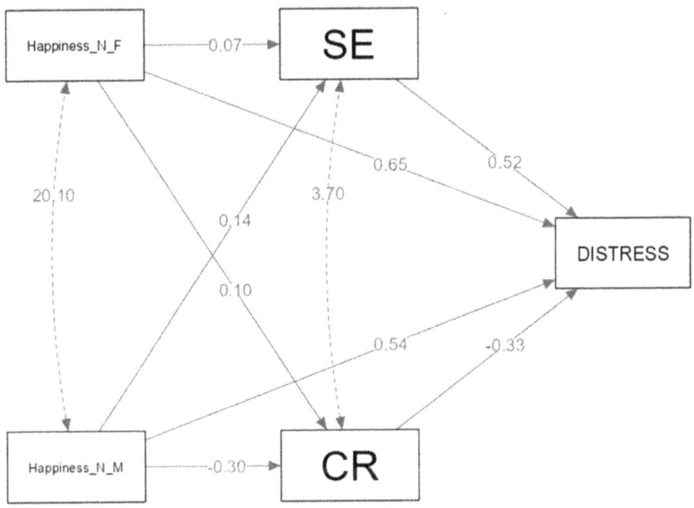

Figure 3. The mediating effect of expressive suppression and cognitive reappraisal between negative happiness socialization and distress.

The relation between negative parental emotion socialization of happiness (punishment and neglect) and distress is mediated by emotion regulation strategies (expressive suppression, cognitive reappraisal). *Hypothesis 3* is partially confirmed. From all four paths analyzed, we found two mediations in the relation between the maternal negative socialization of happiness and distress, occurring through expressive suppression and cognitive reappraisal. Fathers' negative responses to happiness are directly related with adolescent distress. From the two parallel mediation models we used (Figure 3), one of them does not meet the statistical assumptions of developing parallel mediations, like the IV unsupportive emotion socialization of happiness; in the model with the paternal negative socialization of happiness, IV did not predict M_1 (cognitive reappraisal) and M_2 (expressive suppression). We found two significant indirect effects of cognitive reappraisal (b = 0.09, SE = 0.04), CI (0.006 to 0.19) and expressive suppression (b = 0.07, SE = 0.03), CI (8.53×10^4 to 0.14) between the mother's response and distress.

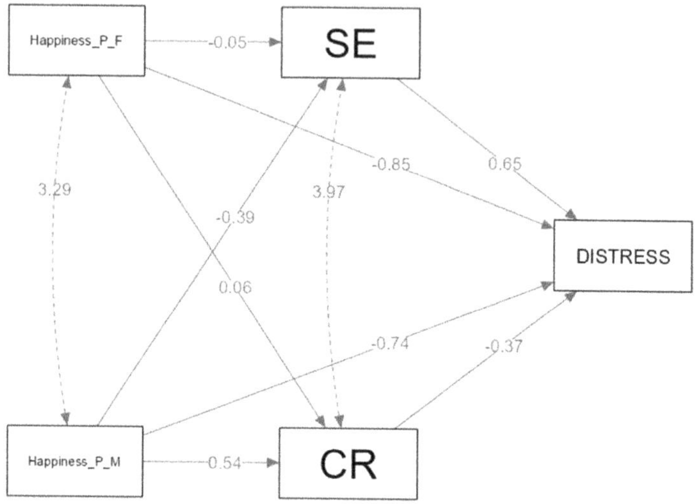

Figure 4. The mediating effect of expressive suppression and cognitive reappraisal between positive happiness socialization and distress.

The relation between the positive emotion socialization of happiness and distress is mediated by emotion regulation strategies (expressive suppression, cognitive reappraisal). *Hypothesis 4* is partially confirmed. From all four paths analyzed, we found two mediations in the relation between the maternal positive socialization of happiness and distress, occurring through expressive suppression and cognitive reappraisal. Fathers' positive responses to happiness are directly related with adolescent distress. In the model, we have nonsignificant relations between the father's response in relation to M_1 (cognitive reappraisal) and M_2 (expressive suppression). The model has two significant indirect effects of cognitive reappraisal (b = −0.20, SE = 0.09), CI (−0.37 to −0.02) and expressive suppression (b = −0.25, SE = 0.09), CI (−0.043 to −0.06) between the mother's socialization of happiness and distress.

6. Discussion

This study examined the mechanisms underlying the association between parental emotion socialization during childhood and adolescents'—as well as emerging adults'—psychological distress. The results show that not only does emotion socialization have a direct and significant effect on distress, but there are also mechanisms, like emotion regulation strategies, that mediate the relation between parental responses to emotions during the childhood period and adolescents'/emerging adults' distress.

Our first significant finding is in accordance with the tripartite model of parental influences [1], which emphasizes family context impact on emotional development through three pathways: the parenting style, the emotional climate and the emotional quality of marital relationships. In our research, the results validate a path model of anger and happiness, which states that a parent's emotion socialization style and supportive (rewarding) or unsupportive (punishment and neglecting) behavior has a significant influence on a child's emotional development. When a parent reacts to the anger or happiness of their child in a positive or negative way, he/she creates predictive relations with emotion regulation and distress. Parents' reactions shape, over time, the ability to deal with emotions from childhood to adolescence and emerging adulthood [13]; these findings are consistent with previous studies [24,25,38]. Unsupportive and cold parental behavior is related to nonadaptive emotion regulation development, even when temperamental dispositions are positive [32]. Emotion regulation abilities and healthy emotional development is significantly better when children receive a high level of positive parenting [39].

According to recent research [22], our results confirm the importance of both positive and negative emotion socialization strategies for concrete emotions (e.g., anger and happiness) by the same number of predictive relationships for supportive and unsupportive strategies.

As such, a second important idea is that positive parenting, although less researched, takes places in the furnishing of individual or interpersonal resources throughout adolescence and emerging adulthood, which are used to regulate emotional experiences and to protect emotional disorders like depression, anxiety and post-traumatic stress disorder [40], in order to grow a sense of personal value and even marital satisfaction [41,42]. Recent neuroimage studies have reflected the connection between positive parent emotion socialization and emotion regulatory brain networks, especially in the primary regions of the prefrontal cortex [43].

A third important idea to emphasize is that maternal influence is more present and more evident in the outcome of children in the literature [44–46] and in our research. We found predictive relationships for only the mother in relation to emotion regulation strategies and distress. The father's emotional response is a predictive factor for distress in relation to concrete emotions, especially happiness. Our results are in accordance with the findings from the literature, which indicate that fathers show more happiness and a greater variety of positive and negative emotions than mothers [45]. Perhaps this is due to the fact that fathers have a stronger role when it comes to play and recreational activities, in contrast to mothers, who spend a lot of time engaged in caregiver activities [47]. But, at the same time, the father retains many stereotypical norms of emotion socialization [29], a greater influence in their daughters' psychopathology [22] and even a long-term influence [13]. Therefore, fathers and mothers have differentiated and specific contributions to the emotional growth of their children [22,28], and this can be an argument for the design of parenting courses that can be projected to take into account gender differences. From an emotion regulation theoretical perspective, one of the key findings of this study is the statistical evidence and explanatory mechanisms of emotion regulation strategies, like protective factors between parental influences and distress.

The fourth idea of this investigation is that cognitive reappraisal and expressive suppression are emotion regulation strategies, present as mediators between both supportive and unsupportive emotion socialization strategies. A rewarding response of the mother, when it comes to a child's expression toward anger and happiness, is mediated by expressive suppression and cognitive reappraisal in four mediation paths. A negative response of the mother to their child's anger and happiness is indirect, related to distress by expressive suppression and cognitive reappraisal in three model paths.

These results are concordant with a recent study that identifies indirect pathways from parental over-control to major depressive disorders, general anxiety disorders, suicidal thoughts and self-harm via expressive suppression [33]. Concerning cognitive reappraisal, similar research [13] reported, as an unanticipated finding, that neither conflict between offspring and the mother nor conflict between offspring and the father was related to their cognitive reappraisal as emerging adults. Despite this, it is important to note that the impact of parental influences loses its power in emotional disorder issues (e.g., distress, general anxiety disorders or suicidal thoughts) when emotion regulation strategies are mediators [33]. Understanding early emotional experiences is critical for maintaining a lifespan perspective on healthy development, but early experiences per se might not be essential when it comes to answering proximal questions about adolescent, emerging adult and adult emotional functioning [48].

Our results add to evidence in the recent literature on emotion socialization [22], which state that parental emotion socialization is indirectly associated with adolescent and emerging adult distress through emotional processes, specifically through emotion regulation strategies. These results are all the more significant, as there are not many analyses in the literature concerning the father–child relationship [44], and because there is evidence demonstrating that different personal choices can transform initial emotional experiences with caregivers and give them a new and assumed direction.

This study supported the Tripartite Model of the Impact of the Family on Children's Emotion Regulation and Adjustment [1]. From this theoretical framework, validated in our research, the results are significant in relation to preventative intervention programs for the psychological growth of adolescents. From the perspective of significant relations between parental emotion socialization in a child, adolescent and emerging adult's emotion regulation and distress, it is evident that emotion socialization parenting programs represent an effective method for the prevention of adolescent difficulties, especially related to emotional responses in a social context. If parents improve their emotion socialization abilities as relates to specific emotions, this will be related to child emotion regulation and psychological wellbeing in turn [49]. Also, it is important to evidence that the parental socialization of emotions has significant indirect influence on an adolescent's distress, especially as concerns the mother's response. Of more practical importance is the relation between emotion socialization and distress in the proximal influence of an adolescent's ER. Given the relation between parental emotion socialization and distress, which is mediated by an adolescent's emotion regulation, an increase in ER abilities could be a protective factor in relation to a dysfunctional family context [50].

7. Limitation and Future Directions

There are some limitations that give us a realistic view and open new directions. First, we have collected data from the self-report only, and thus can carry the risk of mono-method bias. For the future, this bias should be considered by including assessments from parents. Second, the data were collected retrospectively, by measuring past emotional memories that could have been affected by forgetting or even by more positive current attitudes. Therefore, conducting a longitudinal investigation constitutes a difficulty for future work. At the same time, there are authors who consider [51] self-reporting measures of emotion socialization as being the single way of collecting data about parental responses to negative emotions in most cases. Concerning this tendency to express a positive attitude, adolescents tend to appreciate parental emotion socialization more favorably, even idealistically, from a desire to avoid negative emotions associated with perceived relationships with parents [52]. Third, concerning the group of subjects, we studied a large group, who were balanced from the perspective of age but unbalanced by gender grouping (girls predominantly numerically) and not representative of most adolescents and emerging adults. For future research, we intend to expand the sample size and the age group of both pre-adolescents and adults, in order to have continuous perspectives of emotion socialization, especially because maturity brings distance and more objectivity, implicitly in recognition of negative aspects [52].

8. Conclusions

The mother's and father's positive responses to anger and happiness are significant negative predictors of distress; the negative responses of both parents to happiness and the mother's negative response to anger—but not the father's—are significant positive predictors of distress. The findings also provide support for the mediating role of expressive suppression and cognitive reappraisal for the mother's positive response to both anger and happiness, and also for the mother's negative response to the child's expression of happiness. None of the father's responses—positive or negative, in relation to anger or happiness—are mediated by emotion regulation strategies in relation to distress. The findings have some important theoretical and clinical implications for distressed adolescents and emerging adults.

Author Contributions: Conceptualization, M.N.T.; Methodology, L.B.; Formal analysis, L.B.; Resources, M.N.T.; Writing—Original draft, L.B.; Supervision, M.N.T. All authors have read and agreed to the published version of the manuscript.

Funding: This research received no external funding.

Institutional Review Board Statement: The study protocol was approved by the Ethics Committee of Alexandru Ioan Cuza University (1013/17.05.2022).

Informed Consent Statement: Informed consent was obtained from all subjects involved in the study.

Data Availability Statement: The data presented in this study are available on request from the corresponding author. The data are not publicly available due to ethical issues.

Conflicts of Interest: The authors declare no conflict of interest.

References

1. Morris, A.S.; Silk, J.S.; Steinberg, L.; Myers, S.S.; Robinson, L.R. The Role of the Family Context in the Development of Emotion Regulation. *Soc. Dev.* **2007**, *16*, 361–388. [CrossRef] [PubMed]
2. Eisenberg, N.; Morris, A.S. Children's Emotion-Related Regulation. *Adv. Child Dev. Behav.* **2002**, *30*, 189–229. [PubMed]
3. Kullik, A.; Petermann, F. Attachment to Parents and Peers as a Risk Factor for Adolescent Depressive Disorders: The Mediating Role of Emotion Regulation. *Child Psychiatry Hum. Dev.* **2013**, *44*, 537–548. [CrossRef] [PubMed]
4. Root, A.E.; Rasmussen, K.E. Maternal Emotion Socialization: The Contribution of Inhibited Behaviour and Mothers' Dissatisfaction with the Parent–Child Relationship. *Infant Child Dev.* **2017**, *26*, e1955. [CrossRef]
5. Malatesta-Magai, C. Emotional Socialization: Its Role in Personality and Developmental Psychopathology. *Intern. Extern. Expr. Dysfunct.* **1991**, *2*, 203.
6. Sanders, W.; Zeman, J.; Poon, J.; Miller, R. Child Regulation of Negative Emotions and Depressive Symptoms: The Moderating Role of Parental Emotion Socialization. *J. Child Fam. Stud.* **2015**, *24*, 402–415. [CrossRef]
7. Klimes-Dougan, B.; Brand, A.E.; Zahn-Waxler, C.; Usher, B.; Hastings, P.D.; Kendziora, K.; Garside, R.B. Parental Emotion Socialization in Adolescence: Differences in Sex, Age and Problem Status. *Soc. Dev.* **2007**, *16*, 326–342. [CrossRef]
8. Gross, J.J. The Emerging Field of Emotion Regulation: An Integrative Review. *Rev. Gen. Psychol.* **1998**, *2*, 271–299. [CrossRef]
9. John, O.P.; Gross, J.J. Healthy and Unhealthy Emotion Regulation: Personality Processes, Individual Differences, and Life Span Development. *J. Personal.* **2004**, *72*, 1301–1334. [CrossRef]
10. Haga, S.M.; Kraft, P.; Corby, E.-K. Emotion Regulation: Antecedents and Well-Being Outcomes of Cognitive Reappraisal and Expressive Suppression in Cross-Cultural Samples. *J. Happiness Stud.* **2009**, *10*, 271–291. [CrossRef]
11. Zimmer-Gembeck, M.J.; Rudolph, J.; Kerin, J.; Bohadana-Brown, G. Parent Emotional Regulation: A Meta-Analytic Review of Its Association with Parenting and Child Adjustment. *Int. J. Behav. Dev.* **2022**, *46*, 63–82. [CrossRef]
12. Miklósi, M.; Martos, T.; Szabó, M.; Kocsis-Bogár, K.; Forintos, D. Cognitive Emotion Regulation and Stress: A Multiple Mediation Approach. *Transl. Neurosci.* **2014**, *5*, 64–71. [CrossRef]
13. Cheung, R.Y.M.; Leung, M.C.; Chan, K.K.S.; Lam, C.B. Effects of Mother-Offspring and Father-Offspring Dynamics on Emerging Adults' Adjustment: The Mediating Role of Emotion Regulation. *PLoS ONE* **2019**, *14*, e0212331. [CrossRef] [PubMed]
14. Cloitre, M.; Khan, C.; Mackintosh, M.-A.; Garvert, D.W.; Henn-Haase, C.M.; Falvey, E.C.; Saito, J. Emotion Regulation Mediates the Relationship between ACES and Physical and Mental Health. *Psychol. Trauma Theory Res. Pract. Policy* **2019**, *11*, 82. [CrossRef] [PubMed]
15. Barker, B.; Iles, J.E.; Ramchandani, P.G. Fathers, Fathering and Child Psychopathology. *Curr. Opin. Psychol.* **2017**, *15*, 87–92. [CrossRef] [PubMed]
16. Byrd-Craven, J.; Auer, B.J.; Granger, D.A.; Massey, A.R. The Father–Daughter Dance: The Relationship between Father–Daughter Relationship Quality and Daughters' Stress Response. *J. Fam. Psychol.* **2012**, *26*, 87–94. [CrossRef] [PubMed]
17. Godleski, S.A.; Eiden, R.D.; Shisler, S.; Livingston, J.A. Parent Socialization of Emotion in a High-Risk Sample. *Dev. Psychol.* **2020**, *56*, 489. [CrossRef] [PubMed]
18. Lunkenheimer, E.; Hamby, C.M.; Lobo, F.M.; Cole, P.M.; Olson, S.L. The Role of Dynamic, Dyadic Parent–Child Processes in Parental Socialization of Emotion. *Dev. Psychol.* **2020**, *56*, 566. [CrossRef]
19. Arikan, G.; Kumru, A. A Person-Based Approach to Emotion Socialization in Toddlerhood: Individual Differences in Maternal Emotion Regulation, Mental-Health and Parental Sense of Competence. *Sci. Rep.* **2023**, *13*, 13606. [CrossRef]
20. Burniston, A.B.; Chan, C.P.; Vicman, J.M.; Smiley, P.A.; Doan, S.N. Maternal and Paternal Emotion Socialization and Children's Physiological Stress Regulation. *J. Child Fam. Stud.* **2023**, *32*, 2099–2112. [CrossRef]
21. Turliuc, M.N.; Marici, M. What Do Romanian Parents and Adolescents Have Conflicts About? *Rev. Cercet. Si Interv. Soc.* **2013**, *42*, 28–49.
22. Ramakrishnan, J.L.; Garside, R.B.; Labella, M.H.; Klimes-Dougan, B. Parent Socialization of Positive and Negative Emotions: Implications for Emotional Functioning, Life Satisfaction, and Distress. *J. Child Fam. Stud.* **2019**, *28*, 3455–3466. [CrossRef]
23. Arnett, J.J. Emerging Adulthood: A Theory of Development from the Late Teens through the Twenties. *Am. Psychol.* **2000**, *55*, 469–480. [CrossRef] [PubMed]
24. Morris, A.S.; Criss, M.M.; Silk, J.S.; Houltberg, B.J. The Impact of Parenting on Emotion Regulation during Childhood and Adolescence. *Child Dev. Perspect.* **2017**, *11*, 233–238. [CrossRef]
25. Brand, A.E.; Klimes-Dougan, B. Emotion Socialization in Adolescence: The Roles of Mothers and Fathers. *New Dir. Child Adolesc. Dev.* **2010**, *2010*, 85–100. [CrossRef] [PubMed]

26. Jespersen, J.E.; Hardy, N.R.; Morris, A.S. Parent and Peer Emotion Responsivity Styles: An Extension of Gottman's Emotion Socialization Parenting Typologies. *Children* **2021**, *8*, 319. [CrossRef] [PubMed]
27. Rodas, N.V.; Chavira, D.A.; Baker, B.L. Emotion Socialization and Internalizing Behavior Problems in Diverse Youth: A Bidirectional Relationship across Childhood. *Res. Dev. Disabil.* **2017**, *62*, 15–25. [CrossRef]
28. Connell, A.M.; Goodman, S.H. The Association between Psychopathology in Fathers versus Mothers and Children's Internalizing and Externalizing Behavior Problems: A Meta-Analysis. *Psychol. Bull.* **2002**, *128*, 746–773. [CrossRef]
29. Cassano, M.; Perry-Parrish, C.; Zeman, J. Influence of Gender on Parental Socialization of Children's Sadness Regulation. *Soc. Dev.* **2007**, *16*, 210–231. [CrossRef]
30. Bertie, L.-A.; Johnston, K.; Lill, S. Parental Emotion Socialisation of Young Children and the Mediating Role of Emotion Regulation. *Aust. J. Psychol.* **2021**, *73*, 293–305. [CrossRef]
31. Scott, S.A.; Hakim-Larson, J. Temperament, Emotion Regulation, and Emotion-Related Parenting: Maternal Emotion Socialization during Early Childhood. *J. Child Fam. Stud.* **2021**, *30*, 2353–2366. [CrossRef]
32. Kochanska, G.; Boldt, L.J.; Goffin, K.C. Early Relational Experience: A Foundation for the Unfolding Dynamics of Parent–Child Socialization. *Child Dev. Perspect.* **2019**, *13*, 41–47. [CrossRef] [PubMed]
33. McLafferty, M.; Bunting, B.P.; Armour, C.; Lapsley, C.; Ennis, E.; Murray, E.; O'Neill, S.M. The Mediating Role of Emotion Regulation Strategies on Psychopathology and Suicidal Behaviour Following Negative Childhood Experiences. *Child. Youth Serv. Rev.* **2020**, *116*, 105212. [CrossRef]
34. Opriş, D.; Macavei, B. The Distinction between Functional and Dysfunctional Negative Emotions; An Empirical Analysis. *J. Cogn. Behav. Psychother.* **2005**, *5*, 181–195.
35. Dilorenzo, T.A.; Bovbjerg, D.H.; Montgomery, G.H.; Valdimarsdottir, H.; Jacobsen, P.B. The Application of a Shortened Version of the Profile of Mood States in a Sample of Breast Cancer Chemotherapy Patients. *Br. J. Health Psychol.* **1999**, *4*, 315–325. [CrossRef]
36. Hayes, A.F.; Preacher, K.J. Statistical Mediation Analysis with a Multicategorical Independent Variable. *Br. J. Math. Stat. Psychol.* **2014**, *67*, 451–470. [CrossRef] [PubMed]
37. Kane, L.; Ashbaugh, A.R. Simple and Parallel Mediation: A Tutorial Exploring Anxiety Sensitivity, Sensation Seeking, and Gender. *TQMP* **2017**, *13*, 148–165. [CrossRef]
38. Garside, R.B.; Klimes-Dougan, B. Socialization of Discrete Negative Emotions: Gender Differences and Links with Psychological Distress. *Sex Roles* **2002**, *47*, 115–128. [CrossRef]
39. Yagmurlu, B.; Altan, O. Maternal Socialization and Child Temperament as Predictors of Emotion Regulation in Turkish Preschoolers. *Infant Child Dev. Int. J. Res. Pract.* **2010**, *19*, 275–296. [CrossRef]
40. Zhou, X.; Zhen, R.; Wu, X. How Does Parental Attachment Contribute to Post-Traumatic Growth among Adolescents Following an Earthquake? Testing a Multiple Mediation Model. *Eur. J. Psychotraumatology* **2019**, *10*, 1605280. [CrossRef]
41. Grossmann, K.; Grossmann, K.E.; Fremmer-Bombik, E.; Kindler, H.; Scheuerer-Englisch, H.; Zimmermann, P. The Uniqueness of the Child–Father Attachment Relationship: Fathers' Sensitive and Challenging Play as a Pivotal Variable in a 16-year Longitudinal Study. *Soc. Dev.* **2002**, *11*, 301–337. [CrossRef]
42. Flouri, E.; Sarmadi, Z.; Francesconi, M. Paternal Psychological Distress and Child Problem Behavior from Early Childhood to Middle Adolescence. *J. Am. Acad. Child Adolesc. Psychiatry* **2019**, *58*, 453–458. [CrossRef] [PubMed]
43. Kerr, K.L.; Ratliff, E.L.; Cosgrove, K.T.; Bodurka, J.; Morris, A.S.; Kyle Simmons, W. Parental Influences on Neural Mechanisms Underlying Emotion Regulation. *Trends Neurosci. Educ.* **2019**, *16*, 100118. [CrossRef] [PubMed]
44. Bariola, E.; Gullone, E.; Hughes, E.K. Child and Adolescent Emotion Regulation: The Role of Parental Emotion Regulation and Expression. *Clin. Child Fam. Psychol. Rev.* **2011**, *14*, 198–212. [CrossRef] [PubMed]
45. Denham, S.A.; Bassett, H.H.; Wyatt, T.M. Gender Differences in the Socialization of Preschoolers' Emotional Competence. *New Dir. Child Adolesc. Dev.* **2010**, *2010*, 29–49. [CrossRef] [PubMed]
46. Fivush, R.; Brotman, M.A.; Buckner, J.P.; Goodman, S.H. Gender Differences in Parent–Child Emotion Narratives. *Sex Roles* **2000**, *42*, 233–253. [CrossRef]
47. Lamb, M.E.; Lewis, C. Father-Child Relationships. *Handb. Father Involv. Multidiscip. Perspect.* **2013**, *2*, 119–135.
48. Low, R.S.; Overall, N.C.; Hammond, M.D.; Girme, Y.U. Emotional Suppression during Personal Goal Pursuit Impedes Goal Strivings and Achievement. *Emotion* **2017**, *17*, 208. [CrossRef]
49. England-Mason, G.; Gonzalez, A. Intervening to Shape Children's Emotion Regulation: A Review of Emotion Socialization Parenting Programs for Young Children. *Emotion* **2020**, *20*, 98. [CrossRef]
50. Fainsilber Katz, L.; Stettler, N.; Gurtovenko, K. Traumatic Stress Symptoms in Children Exposed to Intimate Partner Violence: The Role of Parent Emotion Socialization and Children's Emotion Regulation Abilities: Traumatic Stress and Emotion Socialization. *Soc. Dev.* **2016**, *25*, 47–65. [CrossRef]
51. Eisenberg, N. Findings, Issues, and New Directions for Research on Emotion Socialization. *Dev. Psychol.* **2020**, *56*, 664. [CrossRef]
52. Consedine, N.S.; Magai, C.; King, A.R. Deconstructing Positive Affect in Later Life: A Differential Functionalist Analysis of Joy and Interest. *Int. J. Aging Hum. Dev.* **2004**, *58*, 49–68. [CrossRef]

healthcare

MDPI

Article

Identifying Social Determinants and Measuring Socioeconomic Inequalities in the Use of Four Different Mental Health Services by Australian Adolescents Aged 13–17 Years: Results from a Nationwide Study

Md Irteja Islam [1,2,3,*], Shumona Sharmin Salam [4], Enamul Kabir [3] and Rasheda Khanam [2]

1 Sydney School of Public Health, Faculty of Medicine and Health, The University of Sydney, Camperdown, NSW 2006, Australia
2 Centre for Health Research and School of Business, Faculty of Business, Education, Law and Arts, University of Southern Queensland, Toowoomba, QLD 4350, Australia; rasheda.khanam@usq.edu.au
3 School of Mathematics, Physics and Computing, Faculty of Health, Engineering and Sciences, University of Southern Queensland, Toowoomba, QLD 4350, Australia; enamul.kabir@usq.edu.au
4 Bristol Medical School (PHS), The University of Bristol, Bristol BS8 1QU, UK; shumona.salam@bristol.ac.uk
* Correspondence: m.i.islam@sydney.edu.au

Abstract: Aim: In this study, we aimed to identify the determinants of four different forms of mental health service usage (general health services, school counselling, telephone, and online services), and the number of mental health services accessed (single and multiple) by Australian adolescents aged 13–17 years. We also measured socioeconomic inequality in mental health services' usage following the concentration index approach within the same sample. Subject and Methods: The data came from the nationwide cross-sectional survey, Young Minds Matter (YMM): the second Australian Child and Adolescent Survey of Mental Health and Wellbeing. Random effect models were used to identify the factors associated with four different mental health services and the number of services accessed. Further, the Erreygers' corrected concentration indices for binary variables were used to quantify the socioeconomic inequality in each mental health service. The four services were the general health service (GP, specialist, psychiatrist, psychologist, hospital including emergency), school services, telephone counselling and online services. Results: Overall, 31.9% of the total analytical sample (n = 2268) aged 13–17 years old visited at least one service, with 21.9% accessing a single service and 10% accessing multiple services. The highest percentage of adolescents used online services (20.1%), followed by general mental health services (18.3%), while school services (2.4%) were the least used service. Age, gender, family type and family cohesion statistically significantly increased the use of general health and multiple mental health service usage ($p < 0.05$). Area of residence was also found to be a significant factor for online service use. The concentration indices (CIs) were -0.073 ($p < 0.001$) and -0.032 ($p < 0.001$) for health and telephone services, respectively, which implies pro-rich socio-economic inequality. Conclusion: Adolescents from low-income families frequently used general mental health services and telephone services compared to those who belonged to high-income families. The study concluded that if we want to increase adolescents' usage of mental health services, we need to tailor our approaches to their socioeconomic backgrounds. In addition, from a policy standpoint, a multi-sectoral strategy is needed to address the factors related to mental health services to reduce inequity in service utilisation.

Keywords: mental health services; social determinants; socioeconomic inequality; concentration index; adolescents; Australia

check for updates

Citation: Islam, M.I.; Salam, S.S.; Kabir, E.; Khanam, R. Identifying Social Determinants and Measuring Socioeconomic Inequalities in the Use of Four Different Mental Health Services by Australian Adolescents Aged 13–17 Years: Results from a Nationwide Study. *Healthcare* **2023**, *11*, 2537. https://doi.org/10.3390/healthcare11182537

Academic Editor: Roberta Frontini

Received: 24 July 2023
Revised: 4 September 2023
Accepted: 12 September 2023
Published: 14 September 2023

1. Introduction

Adolescent mental health is a global concern with evidence indicating an inverse relationship between socioeconomic background and mental health problems [1]: socioeconomically disadvantaged adolescents are two to three times more likely to develop mental health problems [2–4]. These inequalities are driven by complex and interrelated factors. Several studies over the years have indicated that the selection and causation effects are not mutually exclusive; rather these processes a cycle of deprivation and mental health problems that persists across generations [3,5]. Irrespective of socioeconomic status, adolescents should have access to and receive mental health services according to their needs. Studies, however, also reveal significant variations in the utilisation of mental health services among individuals, including adolescents, by their socioeconomic status (SES), the environments in which they live, and their capability to access available services [5–9].

Estimates from national surveys in Australia show that about 14% of adolescents suffer from mild to severe mental health disorders, the most common ones being attention-deficit-hyperactivity disorder and anxiety disorder [10,11]. Despite the availability of effective services delivered by the mixed public-private health system, a concerning proportion of adolescents in the country have unmet mental health needs and remain untreated [12] (Sheppard, Deane et al., 2018). Only 65% of adolescents aged 12–17 years old with a mental disorder in the past year sought care or spoke to a health professional about their symptoms [13]. Among the different kinds of available services, health professionals and online services were accessed more frequently, followed by school and telephone services [13,14].

The most common socio-demographic factors that influence mental health service utilisation among adolescents, identified across Australia and other developed nations, include gender [15–17], age [16,18], household/parental income [17], parental education and employment [14], location and ethnicity/immigration status [19,20]. Moreover, Vu, Biswas et al. [14] and Radez, Reardon et al. [21] revealed differences in access to services based on family types with children from blended, step-, and sole-parent households compared to original-parent households being more likely to use any type of mental health services. However, the majority of the previous research has been focused on overall service usage by adolescents and limited research investigates the impact of individual and family-related factors on each available service and the number of services accessed by adolescents aged 13–17 years.

Furthermore, regardless of the high number of adolescents with unmet needs in Australia, we found the body of research on socioeconomic inequality in mental health services' use in adolescents, especially using advanced analytical approaches such as concentration indices, to be scarce. A recent study by Bartram and Stewart [22], using nationally representative data among adults in Australia, found the utilisation of psychologist services to be more concentrated at higher income levels (i.e., pro-rich) and the distribution of unmet needs for psychotherapy (as a negative indicator of access) to be more concentrated at lower income levels (i.e., pro-poor) despite expanded public insurance coverage.

In this paper, we used the corrected Erreygers' concentration index approach to measure socioeconomic inequality in each mental health service and identified the determinants of four different mental health services and the number of mental health services accessed by adolescents aged 13–17 years. We believe that the exploration of service use in a more sophisticated way will provide a greater understanding of the relationship between SES and mental health service use in adolescents.

2. Subjects and Methodology

2.1. Data Source and Sample Size

This study is based on a de-identified secondary dataset available from the Young Minds Matter (YMM) nationwide survey conducted between May 2013 and April 2014, which supplies the most reliable and comprehensive source of data till date on mental health and well-being among Australian children and adolescents [23]. The YMM is cross-sectional in design and follows a multi-stage, area-based random sampling technique to represent a sample of households across the country [10,24]. In total, 6310 parents of children aged 4–17 years (55% of eligible households) willingly completed a structured computer-based survey questionnaire via face-to-face interview. In addition, a tab-based, self-reported questionnaire was completed privately at home for 2967 children aged 11–17 years (89% of eligible households) to gather information on the health risk behaviours in the past 12 months before the survey. All the study participants provided written informed consent before data collection. For households with more than one qualifying child, the sample included one child. The sample excluded the most remote areas, homeless adolescents and adolescents living in residential care and families that could not supply an interview in the English language. Out of the sampled adolescents, only those aged between 13 and 17 years were considered for this paper (n = 2268), as the self-reported child data on service use were strictly limited to 13–17-year-olds [10,24].

The YMM was conducted by the Telethon Kids Institute, the University of Western Australia in partnership with Roy Morgan Research, and the Australian Government Department of Health. Ethics was obtained through the Human Research Ethics Committees (HREC) of the University of Western Australia and the Australian Government Department of Health (RA/4/1/9197, Project 17/2012). In addition, the authorship team obtained ethics approval from the HREC of the University of Southern Queensland for further research using YMM data (HREC Approval No. H16REA205). More detail about the YMM study design and data collection procedure can be found elsewhere [24].

2.2. Outcome Variables

Mental health service accessed by adolescents aged 13–17 years was considered as the outcome variable. Both parent data and self-reported child data provided information on the utilisation of the following services: (i) health services—any mental health-related services provided by the general medical practitioners, family physicians, paediatricians, psychiatrists, psychologists, psychotherapists, mental health counsellors, nurses and social workers, mental health support centres such as headspace centres and community clinics; (ii) school services—counselling service provided to a child at any school or in an educational institute; (iii) telephone service—when a child receives psychological counselling support over the phone; (iv) online services [13]. In the analysis, both parent data and self-reported child data were combined to create a dichotomous variable for each service and responses were included 'Yes' (coded as 1) and 'No' (coded as 0). Moreover, a new categorical variable was created as 'number of services accessed' with children who did not access any services (coded as 0), accessed a single service (coded as 1), and accessed multiple (two or more) services (coded as 2).

2.3. Explanatory Variables

Sociodemographic covariates included the age of the child (continuous variable), gender (boys and girls), country of birth (overseas and Australia), place of residence (regional/remote and major cities), education of parents (Year 10/11, diploma and bachelor), employment of parents (unemployed and employed), family type (original parents and others included step, blended, sole or foster parents), family cohesion (good and poor). Family cohesion variable was measured by the item: 'How the family members get along with each other?', using a Likert scale of very good, good, fair, poor, and very poor. Response options, 'very good' or 'good' were categorised as 'Good' (coded as 1), and responses 'fair', 'poor' and 'very poor' were categorised as 'Poor' (coded as 0). The equivalised household income quintiles were calculated by using an equivalence factor based on the 'Modified OECD' equivalence scale [25]. The equivalised household income quintiles were Q1: poorest, Q2: 2nd poorest, Q3: middle, Q4: 2nd richest and Q5: richest.

2.4. Statistical Analysis

The sociodemographic characteristics of the sample (n = 2268) were described using frequencies and percentages. Random effect logistic models were used to examine the association between each sociodemographic characteristic and mental health services. Factors yielding a p-value of less than 0.05 in the unadjusted models were included in the adjusted models. To measure socioeconomic inequality in the use of mental health services, concentration indices (CIs) were computed for each outcome variable. The value of CI is a summary measure of socio-economic inequality that ranges between +1 and −1 (i.e., $-1 \leq CI \leq 1$), where a value of 0 (zero) shows no inequality. A positive value of the CI suggests inequality concentrated among the richest while the negative value indicates the disproportionate concentration amongst the poorest. The larger the absolute value of the CI, the greater the extent of inequality [26–28].

However, in the case of binary outcomes (e.g., whether a child accessed mental health services or not), CI values differ with the upper and lowest limits [26], as their mean varies over time and populations, which can lead to unreliable comparisons of inequalities [29,30]. Typically, two potential approaches are used to deal with this kind of issue: (i) the Wagstaff approach—standardising CIs by dividing with one minus the means of mental health services variables [27], and (ii) the corrected Erreygers' approach—adjusting CIs by multiplying it by four times with the means of mental health services variables [30]. In the present study, the latter approach was used which satisfied all four properties of the rank-dependent variable of inequalities [31]. All analyses were performed in Stata software version 14.1.

3. Results

Table 1 portrays sample characteristics. The mean age of the study sample was 15.4 (SD = 1.38), more than half were boys (51.9%), the majority of the sample was from Australia (85.1%) and almost two-thirds (64.7%) were living in major cities. A higher percentage of adolescents had educated parents (68.2%, diploma and above), and employed parents (76.3%). About 41% of adolescents belonged to a blended family type, and around 81% reported good family cohesion. Most of the adolescents were from middle- to high-income households (62%, combination of quintile 1, quintile 2 and quintile 3).

Figure 1 illustrates the percentage distribution of the use of mental health services by Australian adolescents aged 13–17 years. Out of the four services, online services (20.1%) were preferable, and school services (2.4%) were the least popular service among adolescents, while approximately 18.3% of adolescents used general health services and 3.5% used telephone counselling services. Figure 2 shows that about nearly 22% of the sample accessed single services and 10.0% used two or more mental health services.

Figure 2 shows that about nearly 22% of the sample accessed single services and 10.0% used two or more mental health services.

Adjusted random effects model in Table 2 reveals children with increased age (aOR: 1.10, 95% CI 1.01–1.19), being girls (aOR: 1.67, 95% CI 1.34–2.08), being born in Australia (aOR: 1.65, 95% CI 1.16–2.35), living in a blended family (aOR: 1.72, 95% CI 1.36–2.18), and children with poor family cohesion (aOR: 1.31, 95% CI 0.99–1.71) were more likely to use general health services compared to their respective counterparts. Table 2 also shows that no factors were significantly associated with school services, while being girls (aOR: 2.29, 95% CI 1.41–3.73), and blended-family types (aOR: 2.36, 95% CI 1.46–3.78) were significantly associated with the higher use of telephone counselling services compared to boys and original-family type, respectively. The adjusted model for online services in Table 2 also demonstrates that children with increased age (aOR: 1.15, 95% CI 1.06–1.25), being girls (aOR: 2.38, 95% CI 1.90–2.99), living in major cities (aOR: 1.31, 95% CI 1.00–1.71), and children with educated parents (Diploma, aOR: 1.34, 95% CI 1.01–1.77; Bachelor, aOR: 1.37, 95% CI 1.02–1.84) were more likely to increase the probability of using online services than their respective counterparts.

Table 1. Sample characteristics.

Characteristics	*n*	%
Age	Mean = 15.42, SD = 1.38	
Gender		
Boys	1177	51.9
Girls	1091	48.1
Country of Birth		
Overseas	339	14.9
Australia	1929	85.1
Place of residence		
Regional/remote	801	35.3
Major cities	1467	64.7
Parental education		
Year 10/11	722	31.8
Diploma	819	36.1
Bachelor	727	32.1
Parental employment		
Employed	1730	76.3
Unemployed	538	23.7
Family type		
Original	1339	59.0
Blended and others	929	41.0
Family cohesion		
Good	1853	81.7
Poor	415	18.3
Household income quintile		
Q1 (0–20%)	402	17.2
Q2 (20–40%)	473	20.9
Q3 (40–60%)	400	17.6
Q4 (60–80%)	543	23.9
Q5 (80–100%)	450	19.8

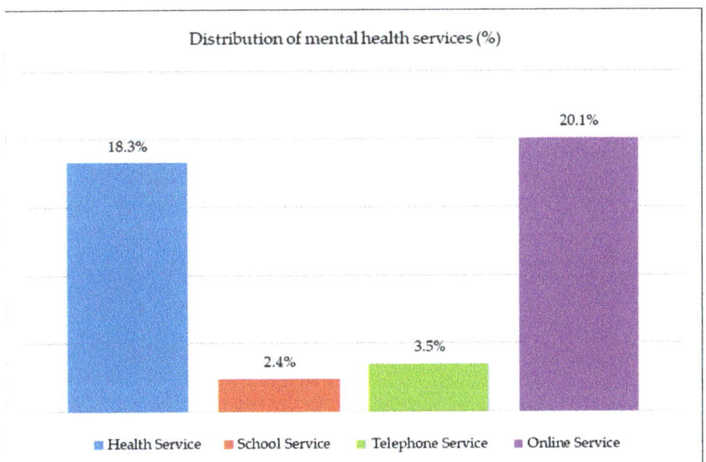

Notes:
- Health service: When children recieved any services from private, hospital, CAMHS, public mental health, headspace centre, community and/or any health professional in last 12 months;
- School service: When children accessed any mental health related counselling services in the school or in any educational institute in the past 12 months;
- Telephone service: When children recieved any service through phone or mobile in the previous 12 months;
- Online service: When children used online services to recieve mental health support or counselling or to participae in a personalised assessment program in the past 12 months;
**The 'Don't know' responses were omitted.

Figure 1. Distribution of four different mental health services.

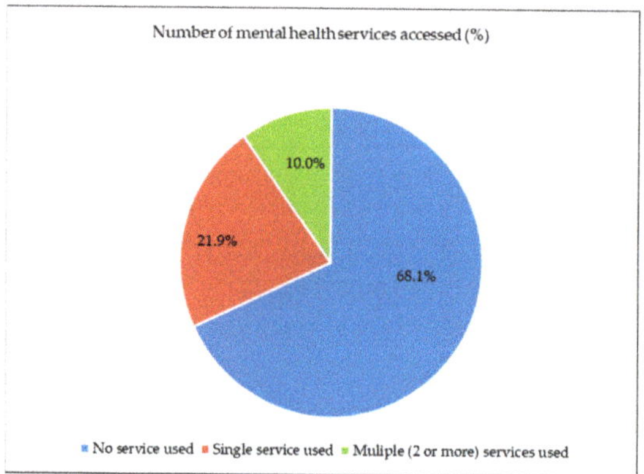

Figure 2. Percentages of the number of mental health services accessed.

Table 2. Determinants of each mental health services (n = 2268).

	Health Service		School Service		Telephone Service		Online Service	
	Unadjusted OR (95% CI)	Adjusted OR (95% OR)	Unadjusted OR (95% CI)	Adjusted OR (95% OR)	Unadjusted OR (95% CI)	Adjusted OR (95% OR)	Unadjusted OR (95% CI)	Adjusted OR (95% OR)
Age	1.11 ** (1.02–1.20)	1.10 * (1.01–1.19)	0.78 * (0.64–0.94)	-	1.02 (0.86–1.21)	-	1.15 *** (1.06–1.25)	1.15 ** (1.06–1.25)
Gender								
Boys	Ref	Ref	Ref	-	Ref	Ref	Ref	Ref
Girls	1.68 *** (1.35–2.09)	1.67 *** (1.34–2.08)	1.51 (0.87–2.62)		2.34 ** (1.44–3.80)	2.29 ** (1.41–3.73)	2.41 *** (1.93–3.02)	2.38 *** (1.90–2.99)
Country of birth								
Overseas	Ref	Ref	Ref	-	Ref	-	Ref	-
Australia	1.71 ** (1.20–2.41)	1.65 ** (1.16–2.35)	0.91 (0.43–1.91)		1.40 (0.68–2.87)		0.89 (0.67–1.21)	
Place of residence								
Regional/remote	Ref	-	Ref	-	Ref	-	Ref	Ref
Major cities	1.10 (0.86–1.39)		1.35 (0.72–2.52)		1.21 (0.72–1.99)		1.41 ** (1.09–1.83)	1.31 * (1.00–1.71)
Parental education								
Year 10/11	Ref	-	Ref	-	Ref	-	Ref	Ref
Diploma	1.02 (0.78–1.32)		1.03 (0.52–2.05)		0.94 (0.55–1.61)		1.34 (1.02–1.76)	1.34 (1.01–1.77)
Bachelor	0.93 (0.71–1.22)		1.22 (0.62–2.42)		0.77 (0.43–1.39)		1.40 (1.07–1.85)	1.37 (1.02–1.84)
Parental employment								
Unemployed	Ref	Ref	Ref	-	Ref	Ref	Ref	-
Employed	0.61 *** (0.48–0.78)	0.71 * (0.55–0.92)	0.88 (0.47–1.66)		0.53 * (0.33–0.86)	0.61 * (0.37–0.98)	1.07 (0.83–1.39)	
Family type								
Original	Ref	Ref	Ref	-	Ref	Ref	Ref	-
Blended and others	1.97 *** (1.58–2.44)	1.72 *** (1.36–2.18)	1.58 (0.91–2.75)		2.51 *** (1.57–4.02)	2.36 *** (1.46–3.78)	1.06 (0.85–1.32)	
Family cohesion								
Good	Ref	Ref	Ref	-	Ref	-	Ref	-
Poor	1.36 * (1.04–1.78)	1.31 * (0.99–1.71)	1.59 (0.84–2.99)		1.35 (0.78–2.34)		1.13 (0.85–1.49)	
Household income quintile								
Q1 (0–20%)	Ref	Ref	Ref	-	Ref	-	Ref	Ref
Q2 (20–40%)	0.79 (0.57–1.08)	1.01 (0.72–1.41)	0.93 (0.36–2.34)		0.84 (0.45–1.56)		1.62 (1.12–2.32)	1.59 (1.09–2.31)
Q3 (40–60%)	0.52 *** (0.36–0.75)	0.73 (0.49–1.09)	1.22 (0.49–3.03)		0.53 (0.25–1.10)		1.53 (1.05–2.24)	1.40 (0.95–2.06)
Q4 (60–80%)	0.53 *** (0.38–0.73)	0.80 (0.55–1.16)	1.07 (0.44–2.57)		0.52 (0.26–1.01)		1.16 (0.81–1.67)	1.08 (0.74–1.58)
Q5 (80–100%)	0.58 ** (0.41–0.82)	0.90 (0.61–1.32)	1.15 (0.47–2.84)		0.31 ** (0.13–0.71)		1.58 ** (1.09–2.29)	1.37 (0.93–2.03)

Notes: CI = confidence interval. Level of significance considered: $p < 0.05$ *, $p < 0.01$ **, $p < 0.001$ ***.

Table 3 depicts the factors associated with single- and multiple-service usage by the sample population. Girls and children living in a blended family or with stepparents significantly increases the likelihood of using both single and multiple mental health services compared to boys and those who were living in the original family or with biological parents, respectively. In addition, the increased age of the study child and poor family cohesion were also found to be significantly associated with the higher use of multiple services compared to their counterparts.

Table 3. Factors associated with the number of mental health service accessed.

	Single Service Accessed		Multiple (Two or More) Services Accessed	
	Unadjusted OR (95% CI)	Adjusted OR (95% OR)	Unadjusted OR (95% CI)	Adjusted OR (95% OR)
Age	1.04 (0.97–1.12)	-	1.15 * (1.03–1.28)	1.13 * (1.01–1.27)
Gender				
Boys	Ref	Ref	Ref	Ref
Girls	1.38 ** (1.13–1.68)	1.37 ** (1.12–1.68)	2.72 *** (2.00–3.69)	2.67 *** (1.95–3.63)
Country of birth				
Overseas	Ref	-	Ref	-
Australia	1.19 (0.89–1.59)		1.11 (0.73–1.68)	
Place of residence				
Regional/remote	Ref	-	Ref	Ref
Major cities	1.08 (0.87–1.33)		1.43 * (1.01–2.02)	1.36 (0.96–1.94)
Parental education				
Year 10/11	Ref		Ref	
Diploma	1.02 (0.81–1.31)	-	1.21 (0.85–1.73)	-
Bachelor	0.98 (0.76–1.26)		1.21 (0.84–1.75)	
Parental employment				
Unemployed	Ref	-	Ref	-
Employed	0.81 (0.64–1.02)		0.78 (0.56–1.08)	
Family type				
Original	Ref	Ref	Ref	Ref
Blended and others	1.27 * (1.04–1.55)	1.26 * (1.03–1.55)	1.63 ** (1.22–2.18)	1.59 ** (1.18–2.14)
Family cohesion				
Good	Ref	-	Ref	Ref
Poor	0.93 (0.71–1.21)		1.53 * (1.08–2.17)	1.51 * (1.06–2.16)
Household income quintile				
Q1 (0–20%)	Ref		Ref	
Q2 (20–40%)	0.92 (0.67–1.26)		1.14 (0.73–1.78)	
Q3 (40–60%)	0.85 (0.61–1.18)	-	0.84 (0.51–1.37)	-
Q4 (60–80%)	0.71 (0.51–0.96)		0.79 (0.50–1.26)	
Q5 (80–100%)	0.81 (0.59–1.12)		1.00 (0.62–1.59)	

Notes: CI = confidence interval. Level of significance considered: $p < 0.05$ *, $p < 0.01$ **, $p < 0.001$ ***.

The concentration indices (CIs) for four mental health services in Table 4 suggests that adolescents from economically worse-off households were more likely to use general health services (CI = −0.073, $p < 0.001$) and telephone counselling services (CI = −0.032, $p < 0.001$) than those who were economically better off.

Table 4. Inequalities in the utilisation of mental health services among Australian adolescents.

Services	Concentration Index (CI)	Standard Error (CI)	p-Value
By each service			
Health service	−0.073	0.018	<0.001
School service	0.005	0.008	0.474
Telephone service	−0.032	0.009	0.002
Online services	0.017	0.019	0.363

Notes: The corrected Erreygers' concentration index (CI) was used.

4. Discussion

The Australian Government has made substantial investments in implementing extensive interventions aimed at delivering mental health services to mitigate mental health issues and their associated consequences among adolescents [32]. The impetus behind this initiative stemmed from the observation that a significant number of adolescents do not receive timely mental health care owing to a lack of services or access restrictions [11,33–35]. The current study sheds light on the key determinants of four different mental health services (general health service, school service, telephone service and online services), the factors associated with the number of mental health services accessed (single and multiple), and the socioeconomic inequalities in the usage of four different mental health services by Australian adolescents aged 13–17 years. Overall, this study revealed that older age groups, being a girl, living in major cities, being a child from a step/blended families or a child with poor family cohesion are factors that significantly increased use of mental health services compared to their counterparts, and socioeconomic inequalities exist in the use of general mental health services and telehealth services.

Despite previous research [36,37] showing a decline in overall mental health service use from mid-adolescence (14–15 years), this study found that the use of general mental health, online, and multiple mental health services increased with the higher age of study compared to younger ones. This is maybe because the older ones have internet access, and have a better idea about the service availability compared to the younger age group [14]. This study also indicates that the age of study was not significantly associated with school services and telephone services, maybe due to social stigma and embarrassment, as reported in previous studies [21].

Moreover, this study found that girls were more likely than boys to use mental health services (general health, telephone, online, single and/or multiple services) except school services. As reported in the published literature, this is maybe due to genetic and biological factors. For instance, research suggests that possibly due to hormonal fluctuations during the menstrual cycles, girls experience mood swings and eventually may develop anxiety/depression and seek mental health services [38–40].

Moreover, along with other studies [21,41–43], this study also revealed that children from step/blended families and children with poor family cohesion were more likely to use health, telephone and multiple mental health services compared to their counterparts. There is a possibility that adolescents belonging to these families may encounter an increased likelihood of mental health disorders, leading them to be more inclined towards seeking assistance compared to those residing with their biological families or families characterised by strong cohesion.

Our study also found that adolescents living in major cities used more online services than those who were living in regional/remote areas. This could primarily be because adolescents living in major cities had more access to modern hi-tech devices such as smartphones, iPad/tabs, and laptops with very good internet connections for their personal use than adolescents living in regional/remote areas [44–47].

Furthermore, the findings of the study revealed the existence of socioeconomic inequalities in general mental health and telehealth services usage within the same sample. In this study, we measured the equivalised household income-based socioeconomic inequalities by adopting the concentration index (CI) approach, which assisted us in gaining a deeper understanding of the underlying causes of socioeconomic inequalities in mental health services utilisation in our communities, which is essential from policy perspectives [48]. Evidence suggests that income-based health-related inequalities in Australia are both considerable and persistent [49]; as a result, the Government of Australia launched a country-wide programme (i.e., Better Access to Mental Health Care) in 2006 [22,50]. Consistent with previous studies from other developed countries including the USA, the UK and Australia [48,51–54], the results indicate pro-rich (in health and telephone services) inequalities in the utilisation of mental health services in Australia; however, the extent of inequality found was small.

Although the current study did not estimate the prevalence of mental health problems in the sample by socioeconomic status, an earlier study reported that children and adolescents from poorer families usually live in harmful conditions of abuse, crime, social strife, civil unrest, homelessness, and unemployment which places them at a higher risk for psychological distress and mental illnesses. Moreover, research suggests poor neighbourhoods also seem to have much greater effects on mental illnesses than well-to-do families [49]. Another study conducted in Spain reported that under-15-year-old adolescents from lower socioeconomic status accessed more mental health services compared to children belonging to higher socioeconomic families [42], while a population-based cohort study in Denmark claimed that people from low-income backgrounds accessed fewer mental healthcare services compared to high-income ones [55]. A study from Australia, on the other hand, reported that respondents from low-income backgrounds were more likely to use health services (e.g., general practitioners), but were less likely to use other healthcare services for preventive purposes such as mental health counselling for self-harm/suicidality, pap-smear, mammography for breast cancer, etc. [50].

There are several policy implications of this study, which can be contextualised nationally and globally. For example, public health researchers and policymakers should address inequality in mental health services' use among children and adolescents as it is a matter of concern that, although Better Access was launched in 2006, inequality persists in Australia. In addition, Government policy should be structured in such a way that children and adolescents can obtain adequate psychological counselling support online, particularly focusing on those from lower socioeconomic backgrounds. Moreover, since this study has found some socioeconomic factors that affect mental health service utilisation among adolescents, it would be worthwhile to conduct an inequality analysis to track down the progress toward equality in service use.

Although this study has used the latest child and adolescent mental health survey data in Australia, this study also has some limitations. First, the main outcome of this study, access to mental health services, is likely to be subject to recall bias and social desirability bias as the YMM study used self-reported child- and parent-reported information. Additionally, causal interpretations were not possible due to the cross-sectional study design. Further, as this study only covers adolescents aged 13–17 years, the study findings may not be generalisable for other age groups such as children aged less than 13 years, young adults, and adults, who make up a significant proportion of the Australian population. Moreover, this study lacks information on the distribution of mental health service use among the indigenous and refugee populations, which might have additional policy implications. Furthermore, since the data were collected using a computer-based questionnaire, access to technology and self-completion of the questionnaire might be an issue for participants from disadvantaged groups, which may under/overestimate the findings.

5. Conclusions

The study revealed age, gender, family type and family cohesion were the key determinants of general mental health-, online-, and multiple mental health-service usage. Further, when compared to adolescents from higher socioeconomic backgrounds, those from lower socioeconomic backgrounds were more likely to make use of general mental health services and telephone services in Australia, implying pro-rich inequalities even though the magnitude of inequality was small. The study also found that targeting interventions specifically for low-income adolescent populations can be the most effective way to improve their use of mental health care services. In addition, from a policy perspective, a tailored as well as holistic approach is required to widen the knowledge about the determinants and inequalities of mental health services.

These findings will help in guiding mental health planners and policymakers in developing effective mental health services that can be accessed and used by all those who need them the most.

Author Contributions: M.I.I.: conceptualisation, methodology, resources, software, data curation, formal analysis, validation, visualisation, investigation, writing—original draft, writing—review and editing; S.S.S.: writing—original draft, writing—review and editing; E.K.: supervision, writing—review and editing; R.K.: resources, supervision, project administration, writing—review and editing. All authors have read and agreed to the published version of the manuscript.

Funding: This research received no external funding.

Institutional Review Board Statement: Ethics for the Young Minds Matter (YMM) study was obtained from the Human Research Ethics Committee of the Australian Government Department of Health (Project 17/2012) and the University of Western Australia (RA/4/1/9197). Further, the authorship team obtained ethical approval from the Human Research Ethics Committee of the University of Southern Queensland (Approval No. H16REA205) for using the YMM survey datasets.

Informed Consent Statement: All study participants signed written informed consent forms (available at https://youngmindsmatter.telethonkids.org.au/for-researchers/) before participating in the study.

Data Availability Statement: Young Minds Matter (YMM) survey datasets are available on request at the Australian Data Archive (ADA) repository. For detailed information about the application for the YMM data, please visit https://dataverse.ada.edu.au/.

Acknowledgments: The authors would like to thank the Telethon Kids Institute, The University of Western Australia, Roy Morgan Research, the Australian Government Department of Health for conducting the survey, and the Australian Data Archive for providing access to YMM survey data.

Conflicts of Interest: The authors have no conflict of interest.

References

1. Parra-Mujica, F.; Johnson, E.; Reed, H.; Cookson, R.; Johnson, M. Understanding the relationship between income and mental health among 16- to 24-year-olds: Analysis of 10 waves (2009–2020) of Understanding Society to enable modelling of income interventions. *PLoS ONE* **2023**, *18*, e0279845. [CrossRef] [PubMed]
2. Ravens-Sieberer, U.; Wille, N.; Erhart, M.; Nickel, J.; Richter, M.; Suhrcke, M. Socioeconomic inequalities in mental health among adolescents in Europe. *Soc. Cohes. Ment. Well Being Among Adolesc.* **2008**, 26–42. Available online: https://www.semanticscholar.org/paper/Socioeconomic-inequalities-in-mental-health-among-Ravens-Sieberer-Wille/6108a54c5faac9ff62a32f535f8917e465817a4d (accessed on 28 August 2023).
3. Reiss, F. Socioeconomic inequalities and mental health problems in children and adolescents: A systematic review. *Soc. Sci. Med.* **2013**, *90*, 24–31. [CrossRef]
4. Weinberg, D.; Stevens, G.W.; Duinhof, E.L.; Finkenauer, C. Adolescent Socioeconomic Status and Mental Health Inequalities in the Netherlands, 2001–2017. *Int. J. Environ. Res. Public Health* **2019**, *16*, 3605. [CrossRef]
5. Amaddeo, F.; Jones, J. What is the impact of socio-economic inequalities on the use of mental health services? *Epidemiol. Psychiatr. Sci.* **2007**, *16*, 16–19. [CrossRef]
6. Lin, E.; Goering, P.; Offord, D.R.; Campbell, D.; Boyle, M.H. The use of mental health services in Ontario: Epidemiologic findings. *Can. J. Psychiatry* **1996**, *41*, 572–577. [CrossRef]
7. Tello, J.E.; Jones, J.; Bonizzato, P.; Mazzi, M.; Amaddeo, F.; Tansella, M. A census-based socio-economic status (SES) index as a tool to examine the relationship between mental health services use and deprivation. *Soc. Sci. Med.* **2005**, *61*, 2096–2105. [CrossRef]
8. Alegría, M.; Green, J.G.; McLaughlin, K.A.; Loder, S. *Disparities in Child and Adolescent Mental Health and Mental Health Services in the US*; William T. Grant Foundation: New York, NY, USA, 2015.
9. Dey, M.; Jorm, A.F. Social determinants of mental health service utilization in Switzerland. *Int. J. Public Health* **2017**, *62*, 85–93. [CrossRef] [PubMed]

10. Lawrence, D.; Hafekost, J.; Johnson, S.E.; Saw, S.; Buckingham, W.J.; Sawyer, M.G.; Ainley, J.; Zubrick, S.R. Key findings from the second Australian child and adolescent survey of mental health and wellbeing. *Aust. N. Z. J. Psychiatry* **2016**, *50*, 876–886. [CrossRef] [PubMed]
11. Islam, M.I.; Yunus, F.M.; Isha, S.N.; Kabir, E.; Khanam, R.; Martiniuk, A. The gap between perceived mental health needs and actual service utilization in Australian adolescents. *Sci. Rep.* **2022**, *12*, 5430. [CrossRef]
12. Sheppard, R.; Deane, F.P.; Ciarrochi, J. Unmet need for professional mental health care among adolescents with high psychological distress. *Aust. N. Z. J. Psychiatry* **2018**, *52*, 59–67. [CrossRef] [PubMed]
13. Johnson, S.E.; Lawrence, D.; Hafekost, J.; Saw, S.; Buckingham, W.J.; Sawyer, M.; Ainley, J.; Zubrick, S.R. Service use by Australian children for emotional and behavioural problems: Findings from the second Australian Child and Adolescent Survey of Mental Health and Wellbeing. *Aust. N. Z. J. Psychiatry* **2016**, *50*, 887–898. [CrossRef] [PubMed]
14. Vu, X.B.B.; Biswas, R.K.; Khanam, R.; Rahman, M. Mental health service use in Australia: The role of family structure and socio-economic status. *Child. Youth Serv. Rev.* **2018**, *93*, 378–389. [CrossRef]
15. Bergeron, E.; Poirier, L.R.; Fournier, L.; Roberge, P.; Barrette, G. Determinants of service use among young Canadians with mental disorders. *Can. J. Psychiatry* **2005**, *50*, 629–636. [CrossRef] [PubMed]
16. Sawyer, M.G.; Miller-Lewis, L.R.; Clark, J.J. The mental health of 13–17 year-olds in Australia: Findings from the national survey of mental health and well-being. *J. Youth Adolesc.* **2007**, *36*, 185–194. [CrossRef]
17. Cheung, A.; Dewa, C.; Cairney, J.; Veldhuizen, S.; Schaffer, A. Factors associated with use of mental health services for depressed and/or suicidal youth aged 15–24. *Community Ment. Health J.* **2009**, *45*, 300–306. [CrossRef] [PubMed]
18. Zahner, G.E.; Daskalakis, C. Factors associated with mental health, general health, and school-based service use for child psychopathology. *Am. J. Public Health* **1997**, *87*, 1440–1448. [CrossRef] [PubMed]
19. Cuffe, S.P.; Waller, J.L.; Addy, C.L.; McKeown, R.E.; Jackson, K.L.; Moloo, J.; Garrison, C.Z. A longitudinal study of adolescent mental health service use. *J. Behav. Health Serv. Res.* **2001**, *28*, 1–11. [CrossRef]
20. John, F. Ethnic and gender disparities in needed adolescent mental health care. *J. Health Care Poor Underserved* **2011**, *22*, 101.
21. Radez, J.; Reardon, T.; Creswell, C.; Lawrence, P.J.; Evdoka-Burton, G.; Waite, P. Why do children and adolescents (not) seek and access professional help for their mental health problems? A systematic review of quantitative and qualitative studies. *Eur. Child Adolesc. Psychiatry* **2021**, *30*, 183–211. [CrossRef]
22. Bartram, M.; Stewart, J.M. Income-based inequities in access to psychotherapy and other mental health services in Canada and Australia. *Health Policy* **2019**, *123*, 45–50. [CrossRef]
23. Telethon Kids Institute. Young Minds Matter. 2023. Available online: https://youngmindsmatter.telethonkids.org.au/about-young-minds-matter/ (accessed on 28 August 2023).
24. Hafekost, J.; Lawrence, D.; Boterhoven de Haan, K.; Johnson, S.E.; Saw, S.; Buckingham, W.J.; Sawyer, M.G.; Ainley, J.; Zubrick, S.R. Methodology of young minds matter: The second Australian child and adolescent survey of mental health and wellbeing. *Aust. N. Z. J. Psychiatry* **2016**, *50*, 866–875. [CrossRef] [PubMed]
25. Zubrick, S.; Lawrence, D.; Sawyer, M.; Ainley, J. Young Minds Matter: The Second Australian Child and Adolescent Survey of Mental Health and Wellbeing, 2013–2014. ADA Dataverse. 2013. Available online: https://dataverse.ada.edu.au/dataset.xhtml?persistentId=doi:10.4225/87/LCVEU3 (accessed on 28 February 2021). [CrossRef]
26. Wagstaff, A.; Van Doorslaer, E.; Paci, P. On the measurement of horizontal inequity in the delivery of health care. *J. Health Econ.* **1991**, *10*, 169–205. [CrossRef] [PubMed]
27. Wagstaff, A. The bounds of the concentration index when the variable of interest is binary, with an application to immunization inequality. *Health Econ.* **2005**, *14*, 429–432. [CrossRef]
28. Van Doorslaer, E.; O'Donnell, O. Measurement and Explanation of Inequality in Health and Health Care in Low-Income Settings. In *Health Inequality and Development*; Palgrave Macmillan: London, UK, 2011; pp. 20–44.
29. Erreygers, G. Can a single indicator measure both attainment and shortfall inequality? *J. Health Econ.* **2009**, *28*, 885–893. [CrossRef]
30. Erreygers, G. Correcting the concentration index. *J. Health Econ.* **2009**, *28*, 504–515. [CrossRef] [PubMed]
31. Kjellsson, G.; Gerdtham, U.-G. Gerdtham On correcting the concentration index for binary variables. *J. Health Econ.* **2013**, *32*, 659–670. [CrossRef] [PubMed]
32. AIHW. Australia's Mental Health System. 2023. Available online: https://www.aihw.gov.au/mental-health/overview/australias-mental-health-services (accessed on 28 August 2023).
33. Stephan, S.H.; Weist, M.; Kataoka, S.; Adelsheim, S.; Mills, C. Transformation of children's mental health services: The role of school mental health. *Psychiatr. Serv.* **2007**, *58*, 1330–1338. [CrossRef]
34. McGrath, P.J.; Lingley-Pottie, P.; Thurston, C.; MacLean, C.; Cunningham, C.; Waschbusch, D.A.; Watters, C.; Stewart, S.; Bagnell, A.; Santor, S.; et al. Telephone-based mental health interventions for child disruptive behavior or anxiety disorders: Randomized trials and overall analysis. *J. Am. Acad. Child Adolesc. Psychiatry* **2011**, *50*, 1162–1172. [CrossRef]
35. Islam, M.I.; Kabir, E.; Khanam, R. Suicidality, mental disorder and the utilization of mental health services among Australian adolescents. *Child. Youth Serv. Rev.* **2020**, *111*, 104821. [CrossRef]
36. Ringeisen, H.; Miller, S.; Munoz, B.; Rohloff, H.; Hedden, S.L.; Colpe, L.J. Mental health service use in adolescence: Findings from the National Survey on Drug Use and Health. *Psychiatr. Serv.* **2016**, *67*, 787–789. [CrossRef] [PubMed]
37. Papachristou, E.; Flouri, E. Distinct developmental trajectories of internalising and externalising symptoms in childhood: Links with mental health and risky behaviours in early adolescence. *J. Affect. Disord.* **2020**, *276*, 1052–1060. [CrossRef]

38. Gouwy, A.; Christiaens, W.; Bracke, P. Mental health services use in the general Belgian population: Estimating the impact of mental health and social determinants. *Arch Public Health* **2008**, *66*, 50–68.
39. Pattyn, E.; Verhaeghe, M.; Bracke, P. The gender gap in mental health service use. *Soc. Psychiatry Psychiatr. Epidemiol.* **2015**, *50*, 1089–1095. [CrossRef]
40. Jiang, W.; Ji, M.; Chi, X.; Sun, X. Relationship between adverse childhood experiences and mental health in Chinese adolescents: Differences among girls and boys. *Children* **2022**, *9*, 689. [CrossRef]
41. Brydsten, A.; Hammarström, A.; San Sebastian, M. Health inequalities between employed and unemployed in northern Sweden: A decomposition analysis of social determinants for mental health. *Int. J. Equity Health* **2018**, *17*, 59. [CrossRef] [PubMed]
42. García-Altés, A.; Ruiz-Muñoz, D.; Colls, C.; Mias, M.; Bassols, N.M. Socioeconomic inequalities in health and the use of healthcare services in Catalonia: Analysis of the individual data of 7.5 million residents. *J. Epidemiol. Community Health* **2018**, *72*, 871–879. [CrossRef]
43. Reiss, F.; Meyrose, A.K.; Otto, C.; Lampert, T.; Klasen, F.; Ravens-Sieberer, U. Socioeconomic status, stressful life situations and mental health problems in children and adolescents: Results of the German BELLA cohort-study. *PLoS ONE* **2019**, *14*, e0213700. [CrossRef]
44. Rideout, V.; Katz, V.S. *Opportunity for All? Technology and Learning in Lower-Income Families*; Joan Ganz Cooney Center at Sesame Workshop: New York, NY, USA, 2016.
45. Livingstone, S.; Nandi, A.; Banaji, S.; Stoilova, M. *Young Adolescents and Digital Media: Uses, Risks and Opportunities in Low- and Middle-Income Countries: A Rapid Evidence Review*; Gage: London, UK, 2017.
46. Greenberg, A.J.; Haney, D.; Blake, K.D.; Moser, R.P.; Hesse, B.W. Differences in access to and use of electronic personal health information between rural and urban residents in the United States. *J. Rural Health* **2018**, *34*, s30–s38. [CrossRef]
47. Palozzi, G.; Schettini, I.; Chirico, A. Enhancing the sustainable goal of access to healthcare: Findings from a literature review on telemedicine employment in rural areas. *Sustainability* **2020**, *12*, 3318. [CrossRef]
48. Morasae, E.K.; Forouzan, A.S.; Majdzadeh, R.; Asadi-Lari, M.; Noorbala, A.A.; Hosseinpoor, A.R. Understanding determinants of socioeconomic inequality in mental health in Iran's capital, Tehran: A concentration index decomposition approach. *Int. J. Equity Health* **2012**, *11*, 18. [CrossRef]
49. Isaacs, A.N.; Enticott, J.; Meadows, G.; Inder, B. Lower income levels in Australia are strongly associated with elevated psychological distress: Implications for healthcare and other policy areas. *Front. Psychiatry* **2018**, *9*, 536. [CrossRef]
50. Turrell, G.; Stanley, L.; De Looper, M.; Oldenburg, B. *Health Inequalities in Australia: Morbidity, Health Behaviours, Risk Factors and Health Service Use*; Australian Institute of Health and Welfare: Canbera, Australia, 2006.
51. Hong, J.; Knapp, M.; McGuire, A. Income-related inequalities in the prevalence of depression and suicidal behaviour: A 10-year trend following economic crisis. *World Psychiatry* **2011**, *10*, 40. [CrossRef]
52. Gornick, J.C.; Milanovic, B. Income inequality in the United States in cross-national perspective: Redistribution revisited. *LIS Cent. Res. Brief* **2015**, *1*, 1–7.
53. Garratt, E.A.; Chandola, T.; Purdam, K.; Wood, A.M. The interactive role of income (material position) and income rank (psychosocial position) in psychological distress: A 9-year longitudinal study of 30,000 UK parents. *Soc. Psychiatry Psychiatr. Epidemiol.* **2016**, *51*, 1361–1372. [CrossRef] [PubMed]
54. Pulok, M.H.; van Gool, K.; Hall, J. Horizontal inequity in the utilisation of healthcare services in Australia. *Health Policy* **2020**, *124*, 1263–1271. [CrossRef] [PubMed]
55. Packness, A.; Waldorff, F.B.; Christensen, R.D.; Hastrup, L.H.; Simonsen, E.; Vestergaard, M.; Halling, A. Impact of socioeconomic position and distance on mental health care utilization: A nationwide Danish follow-up study. *Soc. Psychiatry Psychiatr. Epidemiol.* **2017**, *52*, 1405–1413. [CrossRef]

healthcare

MDPI

Article

Knowledge about COVID-19 between Children and Adolescents with and without High Intellectual Abilities

Gabriela López-Aymes [1,*], María de los Dolores Valadez Sierra [2,*], África Borges [3], Grecia Emilia Ortiz Coronel [2], Juan Francisco Flores-Bravo [2], Celia Josefina Rodríguez-Cervantes [4] and Norma A. Ruvalcaba-Romero [2]

1 Transdisciplinary Research Center in Psychology, Autonomous University of the State of Morelos, Cuernavaca 62350, Mexico

2 Institute of Psychology and Special Education, Department of Applied Psychology, University Center for Health Sciences, University of Guadalajara, Guadalajara 44340, Mexico; grecia.ortiz5850@academicos.udg.mx (G.E.O.C.); juan.flores8719@academicos.udg.mx (J.F.F.-B.); norma.ruvalcaba@academicos.udg.mx (N.A.R.-R.)

3 Department of Clinical Psychology, Psychobiology and Methodology, University of La Laguna, 38200 San Cristóbal de La Laguna, Spain; aborges@ull.edu.es

4 National System for Integral Family Development, Tlajomulco de Zúñiga 45640, Mexico; celiajo_1@hotmail.com

* Correspondence: gabriela.lopez@uaem.mx (G.L.-A.); dolores.valadez@academicos.udg.mx (M.d.l.D.V.S.)

Abstract: Among the characteristics within people with high intellectual abilities, some that stand out are a better handling of information, asynchronous development, high awareness, and sensibility. Therefore, our goal was to learn if, due to these characteristics, the children and adolescents with high intellectual abilities have a better understanding and comprehension about COVID-19 compared to those with average intellectual abilities. A qualitative study was conducted at the beginning of the lockdown with 649 children with and without high intellectual abilities. An online questionnaire was used and three open questions were analyzed with the ALCESTE software. The results showed that both groups had a similar handling of the information regarding COVID-19. Despite this, in the high ability group there is a greater social concern, which coincides with some characteristics associated with a more developed moral conscience. The results are then discussed in terms of the importance of designing actions that allow us to adequately follow the control and intervention strategies, as well as to propose improvements in the communication of relevant information before diverse crises to which the child population may be exposed.

Keywords: knowledge; COVID-19; children; adolescents; gifted people

Citation: López-Aymes, G.; Valadez Sierra, M.d.l.D.; Borges, Á.; Ortiz Coronel, G.E.; Flores-Bravo, J.F.; Rodríguez-Cervantes, C.J.; Ruvalcaba-Romero, N.A. Knowledge about COVID-19 between Children and Adolescents with and without High Intellectual Abilities. *Healthcare* **2023**, *11*, 2408. https://doi.org/10.3390/healthcare11172408

Academic Editor: Walter R. Schumm

Received: 11 June 2023
Revised: 21 August 2023
Accepted: 22 August 2023
Published: 28 August 2023

1. Introduction

The year 2020 has been marked forever in the memory of humanity. The COVID-19 pandemic, which was declared by the World Health Organization [WHO] on 11 March 2020 [1], spread over five continents, paralyzing some of the essential functions and activities of individuals and disrupting daily life, including education. By the 25th epidemiological week, more than two million cumulative cases of infections were reported in Mexico, including deaths associated with the clinical diagnosis of COVID-19, so pandemic control measures had to be prolonged for a long time [2]. The COVID-19 pandemic caused the closure of all facilities, causing people to stay in their homes [3]. Among the prevention measures that were implemented at the national level based on WHO recommendations were constant hand washing, sneezing etiquette, avoiding touching eyes, nose, and mouth, using masks, healthy distancing, staying at home, sanitization, and isolation; in addition, community control filters were installed. In this way, the reopening of activities was carried out in a gradual, orderly and cautious manner, in order to control the transmission of the SARS-CoV-2 virus [4]. The lockdown had an impact in Mexico, increasing social vulnerability. For example, the education system was affected by a prolonged closure of its facilities and a move to virtual or distance education (from March 2020 to September 2021), which is likely to cause pre-existing inequalities to widen [5]. The pandemic provided a new opportunity for the use of digital media. During the lockdown, digital media consumption increased by 65–75% in many countries around the world [6]. However, the overabundance of information on this phenomenon, whether accurate or false, known as infodemics, provoked various behaviors from the population, ranging from compliance with protective measures dictated by the government, to xenophobic events, aggressions against health personnel, and denial of the disease [7]. This of course led to difficulties in finding reliable information [8], and misinformation about COVID-19 has claimed lives around the world [9].

Although children and adolescents have not been the most affected groups in terms of health by the virus, they are a vulnerable group since the measures taken by the government have altered their life and their habits [10,11]. A survey conducted by the United Nations Children's Fund (UNICEF) highlights that the collateral effects of the lockdown on children included individual factors (nutrition, physical and mental health), as well as context factors (education, protection, leisure and recreation), because children have been exposed to adverse conditions like mistreatment, violence, abuse, or exploitation. Moreover, they have been continuously exposed to information from their primary sources like parents and traditional and social media [1]. However, the consequences of the lockdown on both children and young people have yet to be studied, so more research is needed. According to the "Web of the Science", accessed in January 2022, only 1093 out of 138,399 articles addressed emotions (0.78%), of which only 110 addressed children; three of these focused on children with special educational needs and only one on children with high intellectual abilities. Most of these studies were parental reports of their children, in agreement with what Martiny et al. [12] pointed out, that empirical research on children's perception, its restrictions, and the effect of the pandemic on their wellbeing is still scarce.

Given the lack of knowledge of the health risk associated with COVID-19, there were multiple perceptions on how to face it; the most evidence on risk perception comes from research in previous pandemics, especially the H1N1 Swine Flu in 2009, the Ebola outbreak, as well as the SARS and the Avian Flu epidemics [13]. In the case of COVID-19, the perception can be shaped by media pressure or life experience, but in this case, there was no previous experience of the same magnitude [14]. It is important to know the perception of adults and their self-care practices within their parenting role, as they are the decision makers at home and if their knowledge is mistaken, the health of the young population will be at risk [7,15,16].

The knowledge and perceptions from children and adolescents regarding COVID-19 are important because it is known that the perception they have of the restrictions will have an impact on their wellbeing [12]. Jiao et al. [17] mention that in order to give appropriate attention to children and adolescents' emotions, it is important to know and understand first their reactions and emotions. Bonoti et al. [18] state that it is fundamental to know how children understand COVID-19 in order to develop targeted campaigns focused on their protection.

In the research by Idoiaga et al. [19], the authors identified the social and emotional representations from kids regarding COVID-19 through an analysis of their answers with the Reinet method using Iramuteq software for lexical analysis; this method is based on the premise that all discourses are expressed through groups of words that can be organized relationally. From this approach, the situations, thoughts, and emotions present in the lexical worlds or social representations shared by school children in schools in a region of northern Spain were examined [19]. The researchers identified that although the children represent COVID-19 as a harming "bug", they also acknowledge the battle of the physicians against it. Regarding their emotions, concern and fear were observed on the one hand, and safety and joy of being with their families on the other hand. These results demonstrate the need to address the effects of the pandemic on children.

In the study conducted by Cauberghe et al. [20] on children during the COVID-19 lockdown, it was found that the period of confinement and the threat of the disease caused concern, such as getting sick from the virus; as for the educational context, they expressed concerns related to the lack of school content, that is, the absence or insufficiency of educational subjects that allow for the fulfillment of the curriculum, as well as the delay in planning.

Regarding the knowledge that children have about COVID-19, it has been found that they identify the causes and symptoms of COVID-19, as well as the importance of precautionary measures [18].

In a study carried out in Spain, which sought to find out how children were experiencing the lockdown, in which 425 children and adolescents between 8 and 17 participated, resilience was present in these children, but at a high cost in terms of emotions and reactions to the pandemic [21]. In another study carried out by 47 organizations related to social work with children in Central America and Mexico, it was found that COVID-19 caused them sadness, worry, and fear [22]. These results are consistent with those obtained in other studies conducted with children [23–25].

Few studies have been conducted with children with special needs, among which the following stand out: those conducted with children and adolescents with attention-deficit/hyperactivity disorder [26–28], autistic spectrum disorder [29,30], or with high intellectual abilities [31], among other needs. Regarding children and adolescents with high intellectual abilities, Amend et al. [32] mention that due to their characteristics, they may experience anxiety or intense emotions when facing COVID-19. These characteristics, such as asynchronous development and high perception and sensitivity, can intensify their reactions to events and, combined with external factors, can jeopardize their social and emotional well-being [33,34]. It is true that they can cognitively process information about COVID-19, but for some, their emotional or social skills may not be as mature. When exposed to inaccurate information or media, high-ability children may imagine situations that are more frightening than reality [33]. A study by Valadez et al. [25] found that there were no significant differences in reactions and emotions to COVID-19 during the first months of lockdown between children and adolescents with high intellectual abilities, and those in a community sample. Duraku and Hoxha [35], on the other hand, found a negative impact on the psychological well-being of children with high intellectual abilities, in the face of social isolation and school closures due to COVID-19.

Given these characteristics associated with people with high intellectual abilities, we are wondering whether students with high intellectual abilities have a greater knowledge and understanding of this new virus compared to students of average abilities; in addition, we are interested in knowing if there are differences in the perception of the consequences of the disease and self-care behaviors, compared to students without these characteristics.

Therefore, the objective of this research is to analyze the knowledge about COVID-19 among children and adolescents with and without high intellectual abilities, and to compare if there are differences between these groups, since these factors allow us to adequately follow the control and intervention strategies, as well as to propose improvements in the communication of relevant information before diverse crises to which the child population may be exposed.

2. Materials and Methods

2.1. Participants

A convenience sampling procedure was used to determine the sample. It consisted of 649 children between 5 and 14 years of age (mean = 9.6, SD = 2.6). A total of 319 belonged to the population with high intellectual abilities (115 girls and 204 boys) and 330 belonged to the community sample (155 girls and 175 boys). Most of them were from Mexico (624), and the rest from Spain (20) and the United States (2). In the case of children between 5 and 7 years of age who had not acquired reading skills, they could rely on their parents for reading the items. Table 1 shows the characteristics of the participants.

Table 1. Characteristics of participants.

Type of Group	Sex		Age	Country	Type of School	
	Male	Female			Public	Private
High intellectual abilities	204	115	Media = 8.94	Mexico, Spain	190	129
Average intellectual abilities	175	155	Media = 9.04	Mexico, Spain, USA	168	162

2.2. *Instruments*

An instrument of 7 open-ended questions was designed, distributed in two sections, namely:

(1) General data, where age, sex, type of school attended, participation in psychoeducational intervention programs, and place of residence are explored.
(2) Knowledge and attitudes towards the health contingency caused by COVID-19. The items that compose the questionnaire are described in Table 2.

Table 2. Questions used to determine the knowledge and attitudes of children and adolescents regarding the COVID-19 lockdown.

Item	Description
1	I believe that the Coronavirus (COVID-19) is...
2	I know that Coronavirus (COVID-19) is transmitted by...
3	I understand that I should stay home because...
4	My favorite thing about staying at home during these days is...
5	What bothers me most about staying at home during these days is...
6	I have learned that I can take care of myself by...
7	My parents think that the Coronavirus (COVID-19) is...

In this study, only the first three items of the instrument were considered, since these are the ones that refer to knowledge about the COVID-19 pandemic.

2.3. *Procedure*

The research group carried out this study, which is part of a more comprehensive project about emotions and reactions to the COVID-19 lockdown of children and adolescents with and without high intellectual abilities. The instrument was administered through Google Forms and distributed to parents through social media networks (Facebook and Whatsapp), at the beginning of the lockdown (May–June 2020). The instructions were addressed to the children, and parents could help write the answers, respecting what the children themselves said.

In the case of the group of children with high intellectual abilities, associations working with children with these characteristics were contacted and invited to participate in the study. Parents in both groups were asked to ensure that the children did not consult any sources to answer the questions.

A qualitative methodology was used; the sample is non-probabilistic, by convenience, collected by snowball.

This study was conducted ethically according to the principles of the Declaration of Helsinki. The questionnaire began with informed consent, where parents were notified of the objective of the study and other ethical details such as the confidentiality of the data; after this information, they were asked to give or withhold their consent for children and adolescents to participate in the study. The confidentiality of the data was guaranteed, with no records allowing individual identification of the research participants.

In addition, the ethics committee of the University of Guadalajara was asked for its approval to carry out the research, which was obtained through certification and registration number CI-03820.

2.4. Data Analysis

For the qualitative analysis of the responses, the The Analyse Lexicale par Contexte d'un Ensemble de Segments de Texte [ALCESTE] software [36] was used, where the essential information is extracted and the words are grouped by association and proximity, thus differentiating the lexical world [37]. This methodology considers the simultaneous presence of several words in the same sentence. Consequently, classes are identified as semantic fields present in the discourse, represented in dendograms, which are generated by the software [37]. The researcher defines and names each class that makes up the dendogram according to the words that were grouped by the software in each of them.

The purpose of this methodology is to recognize and measure the most robust parts of a piece of writing. The software employs a statistical approach that classifies text sets by means of the chi-square test. It also performs a correspondence factor analysis process. This approach centers on the statistical organization of word sequences that form the sentences within a written composition. It takes into account the simultaneous appearance of various words (nouns, adjectives, and verbs), omitting the analysis of prepositions or conjunctions, among other elements. The objective is to differentiate the most significant lexical groupings.

This methodology has been used in other qualitative studies involving a population with high intellectual ability [25,31].

3. Results

The results are presented below based on the answers given to the questions used to find out the knowledge and attitudes of children and adolescents regarding the COVID-19 lockdown.

3.1. I Believe That the Coronavirus (COVID-19) Is...

The analysis for the group of high-intellectual-ability students shows four classes ("Disease", "Dangerous virus", "Possibility of contagion", and "Virus"), with an average processing relevance, explaining 64% of the answers given. It reveals a tree-like relationship, since the first class "disease" connects with the second one "dangerous virus", and this one with classes 3 "possibility of contagion" and 4 "virus", which are linked, the latter class being the most relevant. The combination of these classes indicates that students with high intellectual abilities recognize the coronavirus as a disease caused by a dangerous and easily transmissible virus (see Figure 1).

Table 3 shows the content of the phrases that make up each class, indicating the word with the highest χ^2.

Table 3. Classes. How children with high intellectual abilities define COVID-19.

High Intellectual Abilities					
Class	**Phrases**	**UCE**	**%**	χ^2	**Word**
1	**It is a disease**	60	30.15		Disease
	It is a serious disease.			7	
	It is a serious disease that spreads fast.			7	
	It is a serious disease that can kill you and you can get severe aches. It is like a flu, but stronger.			7	

Table 3. *Cont.*

High Intellectual Abilities					
Class	**Phrases**	**UCE**	**%**	χ^2	**Word**
2	**Dangerous virus**	**24**	**12.06**		**Danger**
	Dangerous and very bad			25	
	It is very bad and has killed many people.			25	
	It is a dangerous virus that is killing many people.			11	
3	**Chance of infection**	**16**	**8.04**		**Person**
	A virus that rapidly and easily infects many people. It is in many countries. Some of the people from infected countries are traveling to Mexico.			30	
	We are not infected so we have to stop doing inappropriate things that aren't useful and do as much as possible to stay at home and cheer everyone else in our houses and others for a more positive COVID-19			26	
	A virus that kills people and if you don't wash your hands you can get infected.			16	
4	**Virus**	**99**	**49.75%**		**Virus**
	A virus transmitted by an animal			4	
	An exaggerated virus that spreads all over the world and we can overcome.			4	
	It is a virus that became a pandemic a few days ago.			4	

Note: The words in bold correspond to the words with the highest frequency in the analyses of each classe. The words highlighted in colour correspond to examples of the most frequent words in each classe, according to the Dendogram. Words in red correspond to Classe 1; words in blue correspond to Classe 2; words in green correspond to Classe 3; words in brown correspond to Classe 4.

Figure 1. Dendogram showing how children with high intellectual abilities define COVID-19.

The group of children and adolescents without high intellectual abilities show three classes, with a weak processing relevance, explaining 53% of the answers given. The class 1 "Disease" links with classes 2 "virus" and 3 "A virus that affects people". The most representative is the second class, which groups 54.95% of the text (see Figure 2). In Table 4 is shown the content of the sentences that make up each class, indicating the word with the highest χ^2.

No significant differences are observed in the two samples. Although the responses of the participants with high intellectual abilities are more varied when explaining why the disease occurs, by including one more class, the explanations of both groups are similar: speaking of disease, produced by a virus, which affects people, explained in more or less detail. The different class in the sample with high intellectual abilities points out one of the aspects of this disease, its contagiousness.

Figure 2. Dendogram showing how children with average intellectual abilities define COVID-19.

Table 4. Classes. How children with average intellectual abilities define COVID-19.

	Average Intellectual Abilities				
Class	**Phrases**	**UCE**	**%**	χ^2	**Words**
1	**It is a disease**	**58**	**33.92**		**Disease**
	A very contagious disease and if it's not taken care of can be serious			14	
	It is a disease that can cause you to die			8	
	A very ugly disease because it is a disease that can kill people.			7	

Table 4. *Cont.*

Class	Phrases	UCE	%	χ^2	Words
	Average Intellectual Abilities				
2	**Virus**	**94**	**54.97**		**Virus**
	It is a virus that developed in China			5	
	A chinese virus			5	
	The Coronavirus is a virus			3	
3	**a virus that affects people**	**19**	**11.11**		**Person**
	A virus that affects elderly persons, people with lung problems, diabetes, children's immune system prevents them from becoming infected. The infected are traveling to Mexico			10	
	a dangerous virus that not only affects health but also affects the population's economy and sanity.			10	
	a virus that is not very dangerous because it has become weaker as it comes from other countries and affects the lungs of the elderly.			8	

Note: The words in bold correspond to the denomination of each of the classes. Also, the words highlighted in colour correspond to examples of the most frequent words in each Classe, according to the Dendogram. Words in red correspond to Classe 1; words in blue correspond to Classe 2; words in green correspond to Classe 3.

3.2. I Know That the Coronavirus (COVID-19) Is Transmitted by…

The analysis in the group with high intellectual abilities shows differences in the explanations provided, since the responses are grouped into five classes. The relevance of the process is weak, although it allows 58% of the answers to be ordered. The first class, "Physical contact", is linked to the classes that come together in pairs: 4 "Infection by contact" and 5 "Person-to-person transmission", as well as 2 "Infection through areas on the face" and 3 "Airborne infection". These classes refer to the form of infection by the type, while the first ones refer to the person who can infect. The most representative class is 3, which accounts for 26.52% of the text units analyzed (see Figure 3).

Table 5 shows the content of the phrases that make up each class, indicating the word with the highest χ^2.

Table 5. Classes. How children with high intellectual abilities perceive that the coronavirus (COVID-19) is transmitted.

Class	Phrases	UCE	%	χ^2	Word
	High Intellectual Abilities				
1	**Physical contact**	**34**	**18.78**		**Physical**
	Physical contact and respiratory tract			23	
	Bats, physical contact, pangolin.			16	
	By physical contact			16	
2	**Infection through areas on the face**	**30**	**16.57**		**Nose**
	If a person has coronavirus and meets someone else, being very close, he can get it through the eyes, nose, ears or mouth.			23	
	Eyes, mouth, nose.			21	
	Flush mouth, nose, eyes, bruises It is ending that is killing a lot of people			21	

Table 5. *Cont.*

	High Intellectual Abilities				
Class	**Phrases**	**UCE**	**%**	χ^2	**Word**
3	**Airborne infection**	**48**	**26.52**		**Infection**
	The saliva, airborne because it is alive for a while.			14	
	An airborne virus transmitted by infected things.			13	
	Through the saliva and the sight I heard that on the internet.			11	
4	**Infection by contact**	**36**	**19.89**		**Coughing**
	Handshake, kissing or by not covering properly while sneezing or coughing.			16	
	Handshake and touching			10	
	Not washing the hands and sneezing			10	
5	**Person-to-person transmission**	**33**	**18.24**		**Being**
	By the body of other infected persons.			14	
	With people that travel around the world, if he is sick and you touch him			14	
	When an infected person doesn't take precautionary measures and somebody is in front of the infected when coughing or sneezing and the other person touches his face, he gets infected and so on.			13	

Note: The words in bold correspond to the denomination of each of the classes. Also, the words highlighted in colour correspond to examples of the most frequent words in each Classe, according to the Dendogram. Words in red correspond to Classe 1; words in blue correspond to Classe 2; words in green correspond to Classe 3, words in brown correspond to Classe 4, words in pink correspond to Classe 5.

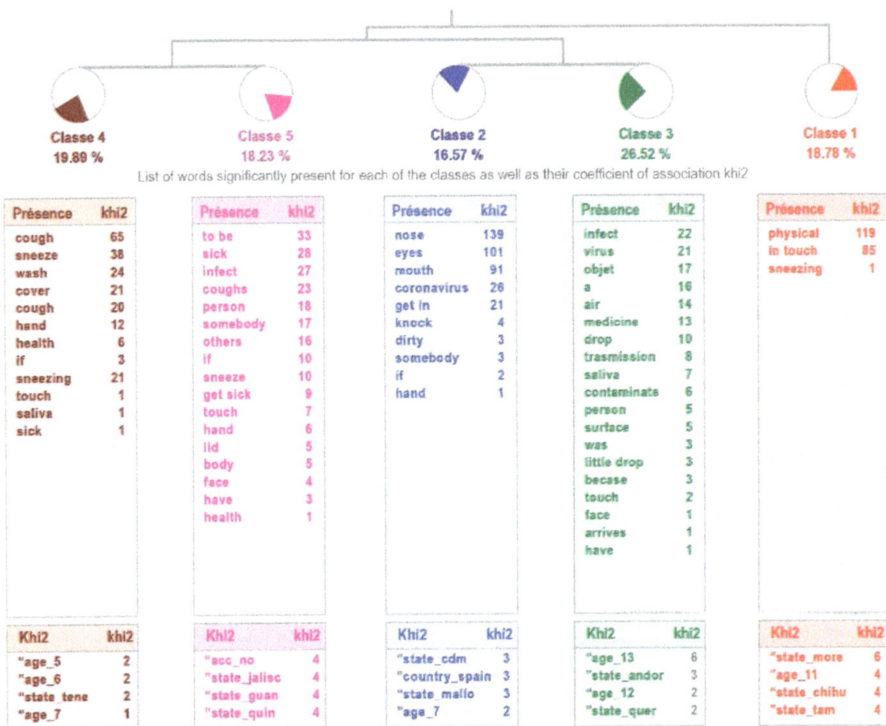

Figure 3. Dendogram showing how children with high intellectual abilities perceive that the coronavirus (COVID-19) is transmitted.

For the sample of the children without high intellectual abilities, the analysis of the way in which the disease is transmitted also results in five classes, although the arrangement differs from the previous one, with different groupings: class 1 "Infection through areas on the face" links with class 2 "Physical contact", which connects with class 3 "Airborne transmission"; this is related to the tandem formed by classes 4 "Person-to-person transmission" and 5 "Infection by mucus", which talk about the way it is transmitted. The relevance of the treatment is weak, explaining 54% of text units. The most representative class is 3, grouping 52 text units, that is, 29.55% of them (see Figure 4).

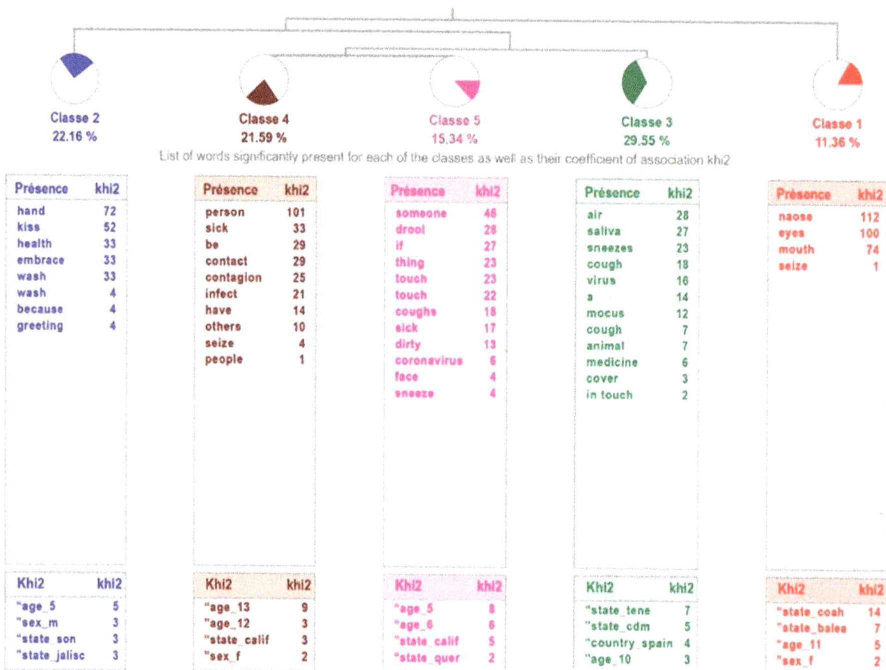

Figure 4. Dendogram showing how children with average intellectual abilities perceive that the coronavirus (COVID-19) is transmitted.

Table 6 shows the content of the phrases that make up each class, indicating the word with the highest χ^2.

Although the structure differs in both samples, the contents are very similar. Evidently, the pandemic has led to important knowledge of its characteristics and means of transmission, even in the young population.

Table 6. Classes. How children with average intellectual abilities perceive that the coronavirus (COVID-19) is transmitted.

	Average Intellectual Abilities				
Class	Phrases	UCE	%	χ^2	Word
1	**Infection through areas on the face**	**20**	**11.36**		**Nose**
	respiratory tract, eyes, mouth.			35	
	mucous membranes, eyes, mouth and nose			26	
	Eyes, nose and mouth			26	

Table 6. *Cont.*

Average Intellectual Abilities					
Class	**Phrases**	**UCE**	**%**	χ^2	**Word**
2	**Physical contact**	**39**	**22.16**		**Hand**
	By kissing, hugging and shaking hands			23	
	Kissing, hugging without washing the hands			23	
	Shaking hands, Kiss, hugs			23	
3	**Airborne transmission**	**52**	**29.55**		**Air**
	it is an airborne virus.			13	
	The air a virus			10	
	Coughing and sneezing.			7	
4	**Person-to-person transmission**	**38**	**21.59**		**Person**
	By being in touch with people that are infected.			12	
	Sick people infect others.			12	
	By being in touch with an infected person.			12	
5	**Infection by mucus**	**27**	**15.34**		**Someone**
	If you are dirty or someone sneezes or coughs in front of you.			25	
	If I touch or suck on something or if someone sick sneezes.			25	
	If someone sneezes or coughs, the Coronavirus Chief jumps and gets to the other person.			19	

Note: The words in bold correspond to the denomination of each of the classes. Also, the words highlighted in colour correspond to examples of the most frequent words in each Classe, according to the Dendogram. Words in red correspond to Classe 1; words in blue correspond to Classe 2; words in green correspond to Classe 3, words in brown correspond to Classe 4, words in pink correspond to Classe 5.

3.3. *I Understand That I Should Stay at Home Because...*

Among all the questions analyzed, in the case of students with high intellectual abilities, this is the one with the weakest treatment relevance, as it classifies 42% of the text units. It generates three classes, the most representative being the first one, "Avoid infection", which groups 44.27% of the classified text units. This links to the union between classes 2 "Getting infected" and 3 "Getting sick with Coronavirus". The sample considers that they should stay at home either to avoid spreading the disease (more social sense) or, from a more personal perspective, to prevent infection or not catching the disease (see Figure 5).

Table 7 shows the content of the phrases that make up each class, indicating the word with the highest χ^2.

Table 7. Classes. Why children with high intellectual abilities perceive that they should stay at home.

High Intellectual Abilities					
Class	**Phrases**	**UCE**	**%**	χ^2	**Word**
1	**Avoid infection**	**58**	**44.27**		**Avoid**
	To avoid spreading the virus.			12	
	This way I avoid spreading the virus.			12	
	It is the best way of not spreading the virus.			8	

Table 7. *Cont.*

	High Intellectual Abilities				
Class	**Phrases**	**UCE**	**%**	χ^2	**Word**
2	**Getting infected**	**40**	**30.53**		**Because**
	Because if I go out I will get infected.			5	
	nothing may happen to me if I get infected, but then I become a carrier and I can infect my family.			5	
	Because if I go out I could get infected.			5	
3	**Getting sick with Coronavirus**	**33**	**25.19**		**Get sick**
	I could get sick with the coronavirus COVID-19.			15	
	If you go out, the Coronavirus you get sick. And you can spread it to the others. It starts with one and then breaks in halves			11	
	Because of Coronavirus if we go out we can get sick.			9	

Note: The words in bold correspond to the denomination of each of the classes. Also, the words highlighted in colour correspond to examples of the most frequent words in each Classe, according to the Dendogram. Words in red correspond to Classe 1; words in blue correspond to Classe 2; words in green correspond to Classe 3.

Figure 5. Dendogram showing why children with high intellectual abilities perceive that they should stay at home.

In the sample of students without high intellectual abilities, the responses show greater dispersion, since they are grouped into six classes, but with a treatment relevance that is also weak, although a little higher with 48% of the text units. Class 1 “Avoid infection” connects with the two links, the one between classes 2 "No getting infected and infect others", 3 "So that they do not infect me", and 4 "Fear to contagion", which raises concerns about the risk of spreading the coronavirus to themselves and others, as well as the one between classes 5 "Avoiding infected people" and 6 "Coronavirus infection", the combination related to prevention (see Figure 6).

Figure 6. Dendogram showing why children with average intellectual abilities perceive that they should stay at home.

Table 8 shows the content of the phrases that make up each class, indicating the word with the highest χ^2.

Table 8. Classes. Why children with average intellectual abilities perceive that they should stay at home.

Average Intellectual Abilities					
Class	**Phrases**	**UCE**	**%**	**χ^2**	**Word**
	Avoid infection	**17**	**10.97**		**Contagion**
1	Physical contact and respiratory tract			17	
	This reduces the risk of spreading the virus, slows down and avoids overloading the country's health care system.			17	
	I must avoid contagion			17	

Table 8. *Cont.*

Class	Phrases	UCE	%	χ^2	Word
	Average Intellectual Abilities				
2	**Not getting infected and infect others**	**21**	**13.55**		**Family**
	Yes, my safety and the ones that I live with my family			21	
	So as not to get infected or infect others.			21	
	Otherwise, I can infect others.			21	
3	**So that they do not infect me**	**42**	**27.10**		**If**
	Because if I go out someone can get me infected.			7	
	Because if we go out someone sick can get us infected			7	
	If I go out someone could get me infected.			5	
4	**Fear to contagion**	**22**	**14.19**		**A**
	I should not get the virus because it can be fatal.			30	
	if I catch the virus I could pass it to my parents and we would have a serious problem.			21	
	it is a very contagious virus.			12	
5	**Avoiding infected people**	**32**	**20.65**		**Person**
	because we don't have to have contact with other people who could be infected.			18	
	I can get infected by being with other people			17	
	because being in contact with many people makes you more likely to get sick.			11	
6	**Coronavirus infection**	**21**	**13.54**		**Coronavirus**
	I can get coronavirus and die.			35	
	because I can get coronavirus and I can die I have toys.			10	
	because I can't go out because I get coronavirus.			10	

Note: The words in bold correspond to the denomination of each of the classes. Also, the words highlighted in colour correspond to examples of the most frequent words in each Classe, according to the Dendogram. Words in red correspond to Classe 1; words in blue correspond to Classe 2; words in green correspond to Classe 3, words in brown correspond to Classe 4, words in pink correspond to Classe 5, words in cyan correspond to Classe 6.

The main difference between the two samples is that while the fears of the average-capability participants have a personal perspective (fear of getting sick or infected) and cause them to stay at home, the participants with high intellectual abilities show a more social perspective, which is the fear of infecting others.

4. Discussion

The goal of this study was to analyze the knowledge that children and adolescents with and without high intellectual abilities have about the COVID-19 pandemic, examining if there are differences between the two groups, with the intention of assessing whether the lockdown measures might be perceived differently based on their available information.

Regarding the first question ("I believe that the Coronavirus [COVID-19] is…"), which refers to what they understand about the disease, there is clearly good information about it, since they not only know that it is a disease, but that it is caused by a virus. What was found in this study shows that children with and without high intellectual abilities have received information in such a way that they can give a definition about COVID-19, which matches the one provided by the WHO [1]. This demonstrates the great impact that the disease has had on the population, even in children and adolescents, who provided reliable information about COVID-19.

It is inferred that there has been an impact of the information given to the population, as the UNICEF study [38] suggests, which also agrees with the explanation of Dalton et al. [39]: Children and adolescents have gathered information from different sources, which are not limited to their families, but also include the media and social media. It is also important that there are differences between the two samples, for example, the social vision or interest of the students with high intellectual abilities, that is, concern for the speed of contagion worldwide, which corresponds to what Amend et al. [32] mentioned regarding the high emotional perception of this group, in addition to the ability for reasoning and understanding of the phenomenon in this case, COVID-19, and a highly developed social vision.

Regarding the knowledge that children and adolescents with and without high intellectual abilities have about COVID-19, analyzed through the incomplete sentence "I know that the Coronavirus (COVID-19) is transmitted by...", they respond that it is transmitted by physical contact, touching the face, through the air, by contact with other people, and from person to person. It can be inferred, as previously mentioned, that the information received and internalized by children and adolescents with and without high intellectual abilities through the different media is in line with that disseminated worldwide or responds to the global reality, as already reported by the WHO [1]. On this point, the means of transmission also correspond to what was reported by Colomé-Hidalgo et al. [40] in adults, regarding the study carried out with the Dominican population, which reflected an acceptable level of knowledge in accordance with the local reality. Similar results were found with adults in Mexico [7,16] and Colombia [41]. In other words, the child and teenage populations, with and without high intellectual abilities, are aware of the means of transmission of COVID-19. Once again, this fact shows the great impact that the disease has had on the population, even on the youngest, who have internalized where the risk factors for transmission are.

Finally, in relation to the understanding of the need to stay at home, as a measure of confinement under the statement "I understand that I must stay at home because..." that children and adolescents with and without high intellectual abilities expressed, the main explanation was to avoid contagion, as a result of the dissemination of information by the WHO [42], as mentioned in the studies conducted by UNICEF [38]. The differences between the groups relate to the social awareness possessed by the children with high intellectual abilities, corresponding to what was described by Albes et al. [43]. These children present a high moral sense of right and wrong, fair and unfair, what should be, and the implications that some facts have on the individual and social level.

When faced with a new disease such as COVID-19, we observed that both samples handle almost similar information. However, it is important to highlight the social component that stands out in the responses of children and adolescents with high intellectual abilities, reflecting their social sensitivity [33], which is a characteristic of this population, evident on health issues, such as this one. One of the differentiating characteristics between the two groups was in the type of grouping of the classes in the dendograms; for example, in the average ability group, there was more dispersion of the responses, increasing the number of classes.

Children and adolescents have been exposed to numerous sources of information: the media, social media, and of course, their parents or guardians. Likewise, they perceive in adults the concerns and reactions to the crises generated by COVID-19, and they are the ones shaping coping strategies. Therefore, it is important to protect children's mental health by promoting adequate communication about the disease and its consequences [14,39].

One of the limitations of this study is that, since the questionnaire was applied online, there is no certainty that the parents did not influence the responses of the children and adolescents. Nevertheless, this study has allowed us to deepen the knowledge that both populations (children and adolescents with and without high intellectual abilities) have regarding COVID-19, at a time when the characteristics of the disease, as well as the strategies for dealing with it, were just being learned. Regardless of their intellectual capability, both populations have similar knowledge in general, the most important difference being, however, the social interest shown by students with high intellectual abilities.

Finally, at the national level, as of June 2020, statistics showed that 65% of households were highly concerned about the health consequences of the virus; the reduction in the purchasing power of families affected their ability to access sufficient and nutritious food in some households (42% of households with children are food-insecure in Mexico). This shows that families with children face greater pressure during the pandemic. In terms of education, by the end of the 2019–2020 school year, nine out of ten children were able to continue their education during the lockdown period, and in households with fewer resources, two out of ten were unable to continue their education [44].

Actions in favor of health and physical and emotional well-being that governments, schools, and families carry out will be crucial for mitigating the impact of the pandemic on children and adolescents, regardless of their intellectual capability [25].

5. Conclusions

Although children and adolescents with and without high intellectual abilities received information about COVID, their interpretation was similar, according to what was found in this study. Despite this, children and adolescents with high intellectual ability had a greater vision of the health problem, being aware of the global population impact, given their ability to generalize, as well as showing social sensitivity, with concerns about the impact of the pandemic. It is important to consider these differences in regards to emotional support in situations of great impact in terms of health. On the other hand, improving the manner in which information is disseminated across diverse media platforms to mitigate heightened apprehension in times of uncertainty is important, as witnessed during the COVID-19 pandemic.

Author Contributions: Conceptualization, G.L.-A., M.d.l.D.V.S., G.E.O.C., J.F.F.-B. and N.A.R.-R.; methodology, M.d.l.D.V.S., Á.B. and C.J.R.-C.; formal analysis, G.E.O.C. and Á.B.; investigation, G.L.-A., M.d.l.D.V.S., Á.B., G.E.O.C., G.E.O.C. and J.F.F.-B.; data curation, M.d.l.D.V.S. and Á.B.; writing—original draft preparation, G.L.-A., M.d.l.D.V.S. and G.E.O.C.; writing—review and editing, all authors; visualization, all autors; supervision, M.d.l.D.V.S. and G.L.-A.; project administration, M.d.l.D.V.S. and G.L.-A. All authors have read and agreed to the published version of the manuscript.

Funding: This research received no external funding.

Institutional Review Board Statement: The study was conducted in accordance with the guidelines of the Declaration of Helsinki. The information will be used for strictly academic and research purposes as stipulated in the current Organic Law 3/2018, of 5 December, on Personal Data Protection and guarantee of digital rights (BOE no. 294 of 6 December). The Ethics Committee of the Centro Universitario de Ciencias de la Salud de la Universidad de Guadalajara has approved this proposal, with the code CONBIOÉTICA-14-CEI-002-20191003, on 6 July 2020.

Informed Consent Statement: Informed consent was obtained from all subjects involved in the study.

Data Availability Statement: Data can be requested from the corresponding author.

Acknowledgments: We thank all the participants in this study and their families.

Conflicts of Interest: The authors declare no conflict of interest.

References

1. World Health Organization (WHO). Monitoring the COVID-19 Epidemic in the Context of Widespread Local Transmission. Available online: https://www.thelancet.com/action/showPdf?pii=S2213-2600%2820%2930162-4 (accessed on 9 August 2023).
2. Dirección General de Epidemiología. Available online: https://www.gob.mx/cms/uploads/attachment/file/648004/Informe_COVID-19_2021.06.21.pdf (accessed on 9 August 2023).
3. Nicola, M.; Alsafi, Z.; Sohrabi, C.; Kerwan, A.; Al-Jabir, A.; Losifidis, C.; Agha, M.; Agha, R. The socio-economic implications of the coronavirus and COVID-19 pandemic. *Inter. J. Surg.* **2020**, *78*, 185–193. [CrossRef]
4. Instituto Nacional de los Pueblos Indígenas. Available online: https://coronavirus.gob.mx/wp-content/uploads/2020/10/ABC-de-la-COVID-19-ebook-Bertha-Dimas-Huacuz-INPI-2020.pdf (accessed on 13 June 2022).

5. Organization for Economic Co-Operation and Development [OECD]. Available online: https://read.oecd-ilibrary.org/economics/estudios-economicos-de-la-ocde-mexico-2022_8b913f19-es#page18 (accessed on 13 June 2022).
6. Casero-Ripollés, A. Impact of COVID-19 on the media system. Communicative and democratic consequences of news consumption during the outbreak. *Prof. Inf.* **2020**, *29*, e290223. [CrossRef]
7. Moro, C.S.; Jiménez, P.A.; Hernández, M.Y.; Barba, M.D.L.P. Aplicación de los conocimientos científicos y la prevención de COVID-19 en México en tiempos de la posverdad. *Prism. Soc. Rev. Investig. Soc.* **2020**, *31*, 82–109. Available online: https://revistaprismasocial.es/article/view/3904 (accessed on 9 August 2023).
8. Pan American Health Organization [PAHO]. Understanding the Infodemic and Misinformation in the Fight against COVID-19. 2020. Available online: https://iris.paho.org/handle/10665.2/52052 (accessed on 9 August 2023).
9. British Broadcasting Corporation. 'Hundreds Dead' Because of COVID-19 Misinformation. Available online: https://www.bbc.com/news/world-53755067 (accessed on 9 August 2023).
10. Arévalo, H.; Urina, M.; Santacruz, J.C. Impacto del aislamiento preventivo obligatorio en la actividad física diaria y en el peso de los niños durante la pandemia por SARS-CoV-2. *Surcolomb J. Cardiol.* **2020**, *27*, 589–596. [CrossRef]
11. Child Trends. Resources for Supporting Children's Emotional Well-Being during the COVID-19 Pandemic. Available online: https://www.childtrends.org/publications/resources-for-supporting-childrens-emotional-well-being-during-the-covid-19-pandemic (accessed on 9 August 2023).
12. Martiny, S.; Thorsteinsen, K.; Parks-Stamm, E.; Olsen, M.; Kvalø, M. Children's Well-being during the COVID-19 pandemic: Relationships with attitudes, family structure, and mothers' Well-being. *Eur. J. Dev. Psychol.* **2021**, *1*, 711–731. [CrossRef]
13. Pan American Health Organization (PHO) Communicating the Risks to Health Posed by COVID-19 Is Key to Protecting Populations and Mitigating Spread. Available online: https://www3.paho.org/hq/index.php?option=com_content&view=article&id=15751:communicating-the-risks-to-health-posed-by-covid-19-is-key-to-protecting-populations-and-mitigating-spread&Itemid=1926&lang=es (accessed on 9 August 2023).
14. Gómez-Luna, L.M.; Guasch-Hechavarría, F.; García-González, A.; Muñoz-Padilla, A.; Moya-Gómez, A.; Savón-Vaciano, Y. Un análisis de la percepción del riesgo ante la COVID-19. *Sci. Yours PC.* **2020**, *1*, 1–24.
15. Case, A.; Paxson, C. Parental behavior and child health. *Health Aff.* **2002**, *21*, 164–178. [CrossRef]
16. Gaona-Pineda, E.B.; Mundo-Rosas, V.; Méndez-Gómez-Humarán, I.; Gómez-Acosta, L.M.; Ávila-Arcos, M.A.; Cuevas-Nasu, L.; Shamah-Levy, T. Vulnerabilidad, Conocimiento Sobre Medidas de Mitigación y Exposición Ante COVID-19 en Adultos de México: Resultados de la ENSARS-CoV-2. *Salud Publica Mex.* 2020, pp. 1–20. Available online: https://saludpublica.mx/index.php/spm/article/view/11875 (accessed on 9 August 2023).
17. Jiao, W.; Wang, L.; Liu, J.; Fang, S.; Jiao, F.; Mantovani, M. Behavioral and emotional disorders in children during the COVID-19 epidemic. *J. Pediatric.* **2020**, *211*, 264–266. [CrossRef] [PubMed]
18. Bonoti, F.; Christidou, V.; Papadopoulou, P. Children's conceptions of coronavirus. *Public Underst. Sci.* **2022**, *31*, 35–52. [CrossRef]
19. Idoiaga, N.; Berasategi, N.; Eiguren, A.; Picaza, M. Exploring Children's Social and Emotional Representations of the COVID-19 Pandemic. *Front. Psychol.* **2020**, *11*, 1952. [CrossRef]
20. Cauberghe, V.; De Jans, S.; Hudders, L.; Vanwesenbeeck, I. Children's resilience during COVID-19 confinement. A child's perspective-Which general and media coping strategies are useful? *J. Commun. Psychol.* **2021**, *53*, 1503–1520. [CrossRef] [PubMed]
21. Martínez, M.; Rodríguez, I.; Velásquez, G. *¿Cómo Vive la Situación de Confinamiento Niñas, Niños y Adolescentes?* Infancia confinada y Enclave de Evaluación: Madrid, España, 2020; pp. 1–128.
22. Terre des Hommes. Apoyo a la Niñez. Available online: https://tdh-latinoamerica.de/?p=4670. (accessed on 6 May 2022).
23. Cabana, J.; Pedra, C.; Ciruzzi, M.S.; Garategary, M.; Cutri, A.; Lorenzo, C. Percepciones y sentimientos de niños argentinos frente a la cuarentena COVID-19. *Arc. Argent Pediatr.* **2021**, *119*, S107–S122.
24. Erades, N.; Morales, A. Impacto psicológico del confinamiento por la COVID-19 en niños españoles: Un estudio transversal. *Rev. Psicol. Clínica Con Niños Adolesc.* **2020**, *7*, 27–34. [CrossRef]
25. Valadez, M.D.; López-Aymes, G.; Ruvalcaba, N.A.; Flores, F.; Ortiz, G.E.; Rodríguez, C.; Borges, A. Emotions and reactions to the confinement by COVID-19 of children and adolescents with high abilities and community samples: A mixed methods research study. *Front. Psychol.* **2020**, *11*, 2881. [CrossRef] [PubMed]
26. De Alba-Villegas, E.; Castro-Gámez, T.; Corona-Padilla, S.; González-Suarez, H.; Valadez, M.D. Comparación de la calidad de vida en niños con trastorno por déficit de la atención e hiperactividad y niños con altas capacidades ante el confinamiento por COVID-19. *Talincrea* **2021**, *7*, 52–58.
27. Navarro, I.; Real, M.; Juárez, R.; Costa, B.; Sánchez, M.; Lavigne, R. Consequences of Confinement due to COVID-19 in Spain on Anxiety, sleep and executive functioning of children and adolescents with ADHD. *Sustainability* **2021**, *13*, 2487. [CrossRef]
28. Zhang, J.; Shuai, L.; Yu, H.; Wang, Z.; Qiu, M.; Lu, L.; Cao, X.; Xia, W.; Wang, Y.; Chen, R. Acute stress, behavioural symptoms and mood states among school-age children with attention-deficit/hyperactive disorder during the COVID-19 outbreak. *Asian J. Psychiatr.* **2020**, *51*, 102077. [CrossRef]
29. Amorim, R.; Catarino, S.; Miragaia, P.; Ferreras, C.; Viana, V.; Guardiano, M. Impacto de la COVID-19 en niños con trastorno del espectro autista. *J. Neurol.* **2020**, *71*, 285–291. [CrossRef]
30. Baweja, R.; Brown, S.L.; Edwards, E.M.; Murray, M.J. COVID-19 Pandemic and Impact on Patients with Autism Spectrum Disorder. *J. Autism Dev. Disord.* **2021**, *52*, 473–482. [CrossRef]

31. López-Aymes, G.; Valadez, M.D.; Rodríguez-Naveiras, E.; Castellanos-Simons, D.; Aguirre, T.; Borges, Á. A Mixed Methods Research Study of Parental Perception of Physical Activity and Quality of Life of Children Under Home Lock Down in the COVID-19 Pandemic. *Front. Psychol.* **2021**, *12*, 649481. [CrossRef]
32. Amend, E.R.; Koehler, J.; Peters, M.P.; Joerg, M.; Nilles, K. Supporting Your Gifted Child during COVID-19 & Other Crises by Developmental Stage. NAGC: Washington, DC, USA, 2020. Available online: https://www.gadoe.org/Curriculum-Instruction-and-Assessment/Curriculum-and-Instruction/Documents/Gifted%20Education/Supporting%20your%20gifted%20child%20during%20COVID-19.pdf (accessed on 6 May 2022).
33. Cross, J.R.; Cross, T.L. Clinical and mental health issues in counseling the gifted individual. *J. Couns. Dev.* **2015**, *93*, 163–172. [CrossRef]
34. Hsin-Jen, C.; Ching-Chih, K. Overexcitabilities: Empirical studies and application. *Learn. Individ. Differ.* **2013**, *23*, 53–63.
35. Duraku, H.Z.; Hoxha, N. The impact of COVID-19, school closure, and social isolation on gifted students' wellbeing and attitudes toward remote (online) learning. In *Impact of the COVID-19 Pandemic on Education and Wellbeing. Implications for Practice and Lessons for the Future*; Mala, M., Jemini-Gashi, L., Eds.; University of Prishtina "Hasan Psishtina": Pristina, Albania, 2021; Volume 1, pp. 17–45.
36. Reinert, M. *Alceste Users' Manual*; Image: Touluse, Francia, 2012; pp. 1–46.
37. De Alba, M. El método ALCESTE y su aplicación al estudio de las representaciones sociales del espacio urbano: El caso de la ciudad de México. *Papers Soc. Represent.* **2004**, *13*, 1.1–1.20.
38. Fondo de las Naciones Unidas para la Infancia (UNICEF). Available online: https://www.unicef.org/argentina/media/8056/file/Covid19-EncuestaRapida-InformeEducacion.pdf (accessed on 5 May 2022).
39. Dalton, L.; Rapa, E.; Stein, A. Protecting the psychological health of children through effective communication about COVID-19. *Lancet Child Adolesc. Health* **2020**, *4*, 346–347. [CrossRef]
40. Colomé-Hidalgo, M.; Herrera, D.A.; Méndez, R.; Torres, Z.L.; Méndez, M.; Japa, J.; Sosa, C. Conocimiento y percepciones que los adultos tienen del COVID-19 en República Dominicana. *Sci. Health* **2020**, *5*, 27–42.
41. Rivera-Diaz, A.; Rubiano-Daza, H.; Quintero-Quimbaya, J.C.; Hoyos-Armero, D.P.; Herrera-Ramírez, C.; Rivera-Ospitia SMOrtiz, C.P. Conocimiento preventivo y su práctica entre la población de Colombia hacia la enfermedad por Coronavirus (COVID-19): Una perspectiva de género. *Rev. Colomb. Cienc. Quím. Farm.* **2020**, *49*, 776–789.
42. World Health Organization (WHO). Five Steps to Kicking Out Coronavirus. Available online: https://www.fifa.com/news/five-steps-to-kicking-out-coronavirus (accessed on 9 August 2023).
43. Albes, C.; Aretxaga, L.; Etxebarria, I.; Galende, I.; Santamaría, A.; Uriarte, B.; Vigo, P. *Orientaciones Educativas. Alumnado con Altas Capacidades Intelectuales*, 1st ed.; Eusko Jaurlaritzaren Argitalpen Zerbitzu Nagusia: País Vasco, España, 2013; pp. 30–43.
44. United Nations International Children's Emergency Fund (UNICEF). Genera Ciudad de México Datos Sobre COVID-19 y los Impactos en la Infancia. Available online: https://www.unicef.org/mexico/comunicados-prensa/genera-ciudad-de-m%C3%A9xico-datos-sobre-covid-19-y-los-impactos-en-la-infancia#:~:text=Comunicado%20de%20prensa-,Genera%20Ciudad%20de%20M%C3%A9xico%20datos%20sobre%20COVID%2D19,los%20impactos%20en%20la%20infancia&text=La%20reducci%C3%B3n%20en%20los%20ingresos,(6%20de%20cada%2010) (accessed on 9 August 2023).

healthcare

MDPI

Article

Young People and the Future: School Students' Concerns and Hopes for the Future after One Year of COVID-19 in Austria—Findings of a Mixed-Methods Pilot Study

Sonja Fehkührer [1], Elke Humer [1,2], Stefan Kaltschik [1], Christoph Pieh [1], Thomas Probst [1], Gertraud Diestler [3] and Andrea Jesser [1,*]

1 Department for Psychosomatic Medicine and Psychotherapy, University of Continuing Education Krems, 3500 Krems, Austria; sonja.fehkuehrer@edu.donau-uni.ac.at (S.F.); elke.humer@donau-uni.ac.at (E.H.); stefan.kaltschik@outlook.com (S.K.); christoph.pieh@donau-uni.ac.at (C.P.); thomas.probst@donau-uni.ac.at (T.P.)

2 Faculty of Psychotherapy Science, Sigmund Freud University Vienna, 1020 Vienna, Austria

3 Österreichischer Arbeitskreis für Gruppentherapie und Gruppendynamik, Fachsektion Integrative Gestalt Therapy Vienna, 1080 Vienna, Austria; g.diestler@gmx.at

* Correspondence: andrea.jesser@donau-uni.ac.at

Abstract: The COVID-19 pandemic resulted in enormous changes in everyday life and numerous burdens for adolescents. This pilot study focused on how young people look to the future in the face of these burdens. Responses to two open-ended questions on concerns and hopes for the future that were part of a larger online survey on the mental health of school students in Austria were analyzed using qualitative content analysis. Subsequently, differences in the experiences of boys and girls, young people with and without a migration background and psychologically stressed and non-stressed young people were examined by applying a mixed-methods approach. Data collection took place from 3 February to 28 February 2021. From a total survey sample of 3052 adolescents aged 14–20, a representative sample according to gender and migration background ($N = 500$) was drawn. Qualitative content analysis revealed several areas of concern about the future, including school-related concerns, concerns about the further development of the pandemic and the associated restrictions, concerns related to a lack of locus of control, health-related concerns and concerns about social relationships. The analysis also indicated young people's greatest hopes for the future, such as hopes related to further pandemic development, hopes regarding major life goals, school, social relationships and health. Young people's experiences differ according to gender, migration background and the extent of psychological distress. This study contributes to research on the psychological well-being of adolescents during the pandemic and provides important insights into the subjective experience of young people. It aims to gain a more comprehensive understanding of the concerns and hopes for the future of young people in a time marked by various challenges. The results of the study should be used to develop ideas for measures, such as the expansion of school psychological services and low-threshold support services for students, such as school social work and counseling.

Keywords: adolescents; COVID-19; concerns about the future; hopes for the future; qualitative research; mixed-methods research

Citation: Fehkührer, S.; Humer, E.; Kaltschik, S.; Pieh, C.; Probst, T.; Diestler, G.; Jesser, A. Young People and the Future: School Students' Concerns and Hopes for the Future after One Year of COVID-19 in Austria—Findings of a Mixed-Methods Pilot Study. *Healthcare* **2023**, *11*, 2242. https://doi.org/10.3390/healthcare11162242

Academic Editors: Tao-Hsin Tung and Roberta Frontini

Received: 20 June 2023
Revised: 21 July 2023
Accepted: 4 August 2023
Published: 9 August 2023

1. Introduction

Adolescence is a stage of development characterized by many changes, both physical and psychological. During this time, adolescents are exposed to new and complex social situations, such as peer pressure, romantic relationships and academic stress, which can contribute to psychological distress. All of these factors combined make adolescence a vulnerable stage for mental health [1,2].

The circumstances of the COVID-19 pandemic further contributed to the deterioration in the mental well-being of children and adolescents [1,3,4]. Internationally, a high prevalence of psychological distress could be observed in adolescents during the COVID-19 pandemic, including increased depressive, anxiety, stress and post-traumatic symptomatology [1–13]. Younger age, female gender and migration background are risk factors for increased psychological distress [1,5,9,13–16].

Not only did young people's psychological distress increase significantly during the pandemic, but so did their concerns for the future [17,18]. Concerns and fears were identified in different areas of life.

The fear of contracting the virus, as well as the fear of infecting loved ones, was frequently addressed by children and adolescents surveyed during the pandemic [19–24]. Sarkadi et al. [17] found that 60% of the children and adolescents surveyed in Sweden worried that they or their relatives would contract the virus or die as a result. Moreover, 15% of the children and adolescents worried that no cure would be found for the coronavirus. They also expressed fears that the pandemic might be unstoppable and remain for a long time, worsening lives [17,25–27]. Similar results were found in other studies [19,28].

Measures and restrictions to contain the coronavirus were accompanied by great uncertainty among children and adolescents. In a study by Hoffmann et al. [29], the young Danish research participants were most concerned about the return to daily life. Moreover, 71% of the German children and adolescents surveyed by Ravens-Sieberer et al. [30] felt burdened by restrictions on contact with friends and family as well as restrictions on leisure activities. This was supported by the results of other studies [18,25,26,29,31,32].

Another area of concern about the future was identified by several studies and addressed the impact of COVID-19 on school performance. Students were concerned about the inability to meet school requirements and having difficulty graduating from high school or transitioning to college [2,18,23–26,31,33–36]. Based on a qualitative research design, Jesser et al. [37] found that school-related concerns associated with distance learning were expressed by 63% of Austrian school students surveyed in February 2021. In a German study by Ravens-Sieberer et al. [30], 65% of the surveyed students perceived school and learning as more stressful compared to before the pandemic. In a study by Lehmann et al. [22], 63% of respondents reported learning less during the pandemic.

Concerns about the future were also reported about an uncertain future in the wake of the COVID-19 pandemic [26,28,37]. In a study by Duby et al. [19], female respondents expressed that their dreams and hopes for the future had been shattered. In their view, the pandemic had changed the world. In an Austrian study by Jesser et al. [37], survey participants addressed their fear of lack of prospects, hopelessness and fear of making the wrong decisions. Lehmann et al. [22] showed that 19% of Norwegian adolescents surveyed in mid-May 2020 feared a more difficult future due to the pandemic. This was particularly true for older adolescents (16–19 years). Among other things, the young people were concerned about their future education, career path and career opportunities, and about not being able to achieve their career aspirations in the future. They also addressed challenges in finding a job [25,26,31,37]. Adolescents, particularly those already living in socioeconomically disadvantaged families, were also found to be concerned about their families' financial circumstances [18,23,25,28,29].

Another concern about the future raised by the adolescent participants in Sarkadi et al.'s study [17] was the feared impact of the COVID-19 pandemic on democracy. It was also found that young people's trust in politicians was decreasing due to their management decisions during the pandemic.

Several studies have found differences in COVID-19-related concerns about the future between boys and girls and between young people with and without a migration background. Young women and adolescents with migration backgrounds were generally more likely to be concerned than male students [26,28,36,38,39].

Most studies looking at the impact of the COVID-19 pandemic on young people's concerns and hopes for the future have used quantitative research designs. Few studies have focused on the subjective accounts of adolescents in the wake of the pandemic. This pilot study aimed to gain a deeper insight and understanding of Austrian school students' concerns and hopes for the future. Open-ended questions were used to encourage free narratives from young people and to get a picture of the range of subjective concerns and hopes for the future that young people are experiencing as the pandemic progresses. The online survey format and sampling design aimed to ensure that we reached many diverse young people, giving a representative picture of their concerns and hopes for the future. Differences in concerns and hopes for the future according to gender, migration background and level of psychological distress were also explored.

This pilot study contributes findings from Austria to the existing knowledge base. The open-ended qualitative approach allowed for a broad view of self-reported concerns and hopes for the future, while the subsequent mixed-methods analysis complemented the findings by looking at differences between genders, young people with and without a migration background, and mentally distressed and non-distressed young people. The findings and lessons learned from our pilot study are intended to form the basis for further in-depth qualitative research in the future.

2. Materials and Methods

2.1. Research Design

We conducted a cross-sectional online survey between 3 February and 28 February 2021, among 14- to 20-year-old students. The study was part of a larger study in which the current psychological state of adolescent students, as well as their concerns and hopes for the future, were surveyed. We obtained approval from the ethics committee for this study (protocol code EK GZ 41/2018–2021).

The study was carried out using Research Electronic Data Capture (REDCap) [40,41]. and comprised 67 items. While most items were to be answered using rating scales, four open-ended questions provided school students with options to express their thoughts in their own words. Questions addressed respondents' current concerns, their concerns and hopes for the future, and helpful coping strategies. Quantitative results have already been published [42,43], as well as the results of the two open-ended questions related to current concerns and helpful coping strategies [37].

The study was conducted as an exploratory sequential mixed-methods design. To shed more light on young people's concerns and hopes for the future, we investigated the following two open-ended questions: (1) What is your greatest concern when you think about the future? (2) What do you hope for most when you think about the future? The results of the qualitative analysis informed the quantitative analysis, which explored differences in the categories of concerns and hopes for the future according to gender, migration background and level of psychological distress.

2.2. COVID-19-Related Situation in Austrian Schools during the Period of Study Implementation

When the survey was launched on 3 February 2021, a third lockdown was in place in Austria [44]. As in the previous lockdowns, people were no longer allowed to enter public spaces except to cover their basic needs. All non-essential shops as well as all facilities such as cafés, restaurants, public baths and other sports facilities were closed, and cultural and sports events were canceled. There were strict contact restrictions and curfews that largely brought public life to a standstill. Schools and universities were closed and switched to distance learning. Mouth-nose protection had to be worn in public places, shops and on public transport [45]. After the end of the lockdown on 7 February 2021, schools were reopened in a shift system to minimize the number of students in attendance [46]. The school-leaving examination, the final examination in the Austrian education system, taken by students at the end of their secondary education, was postponed by three weeks to give them more time to prepare. Due to the difference in conditions between distance learning and classroom teaching, the examination content was decreased by 33% [47].

2.3. Selection of the Sample

The Department of Psychosomatic Medicine and Psychotherapy at the University of Continuing Education Krems conducted the online study with support from the Federal Ministry of Education, Science, and Research. Secondary school students were made aware of the online survey through social media channels maintained by the university. Participation was voluntary and without incentives. Participants were asked to agree to the privacy policy as well as to confirm their age of 14 years or older.

The total sample of N = 3052 was representative of Austria by region, but not by gender and migration background. The average age of the participants was M = 16.47 (SD = 1.44) years. Here, 70.1% of the sample were female, 28.1% male and 1.8% non-binary. Furthermore, 16.6% of them had a migration background. Based on data from Statistics Austria [48] a representative sample of 500 adolescents was stratified and proportionally weighted by gender and migration background, as numerous studies have demonstrated that adolescent mental health is significantly moderated by these two variables [1,5,9,15,16]. Furthermore, only participants who answered both questions were selected.

2.4. Data Analysis

2.4.1. Qualitative Data Analysis

The data were subjected to a conventional qualitative content analysis approach [49] and analyzed within an iterative framework for qualitative data analysis [50]. To increase transparency [51] and to facilitate discussion and revision of categories within the research team, we used the software Atlas.ti 23 [52]. In the first step, all responses in the sample were read carefully by one coder (SF). Individual responses to open-ended questions ranged from single words to entire paragraphs. In the process of reading, she composed the first list of inductive categories. In the next step, these categories were sorted thematically and assigned to main categories at a higher level of abstraction. The resulting preliminary category system was iteratively discussed and revised by the research team. Subsequently, SF coded the entire data material using the category system. In some cases, additional inductive categories were added. Text passages that could not be clearly assigned were discussed with the research team. After coding all the data, the category system was reviewed by the research team. The focus was on checking categories for their distinctiveness, evaluating the assignment of subcategories to higher-level main categories and merging smaller categories into more abstract categories.

Finally, the analysis resulted in 11 main categories and 40 subcategories for concerns about the future and 11 main categories and 42 subcategories for hopes for the future.

2.4.2. Quantitative and Mixed-Methods Analysis

Following qualitative analysis, we examined differences based on gender, migration background and the degree of psychological distress using a mixed-methods approach. Mixed-methods analysis was carried out with SPSS version 26 (IBM Corp, Armonk, NY, USA). Chi-squared tests (χ^2) or Fisher's exact tests were used to examine:

1. Differences in the proportion of female and male school students reporting in main or subcategories of concerns about the future and hopes for the future.
2. Differences in the proportion of school students with or without migration background in reports in main or subcategories of concerns about the future and hopes for the future.
3. Differences in the proportion of school students with or without psychological distress in reports in main or subcategories of concerns about the future and hopes for the future.

The significance level for all tests was set at 5%. All tests were performed two-tailed. For the analyses of differences in students with or without psychological distress students were categorized into those exceeding the cut-offs for clinically relevant symptoms of depression, anxiety, or insomnia vs. those scoring below the cut-offs for clinically relevant symptoms of depression, anxiety and insomnia. Detailed information on the assessment of symptoms of depression, anxiety and insomnia and the cut-offs applied is provided in our companion paper [42].

3. Results

3.1. Sample Description

The sample of 500 participants consists of 50% (n = 250) female (compared to 49% in the general population of 15–29 years old females in Austria) and 50% male school students. Of the participants, 30.8% (n = 154) had a migration background (compared to 28% of the general population aged 15–29 in Austria). The average age of the participants was M = 16.50 (SD = 1.50) years. Further sample characteristics are summarized in Supplementary Table S1.

3.2. Qualitative Results

3.2.1. Concerns about the Future

In the following, we report the results related to the first question: "What is your greatest concern when you think about the future?" The results are presented in Figure 1 and Supplementary Table S2 and are now described in more detail.

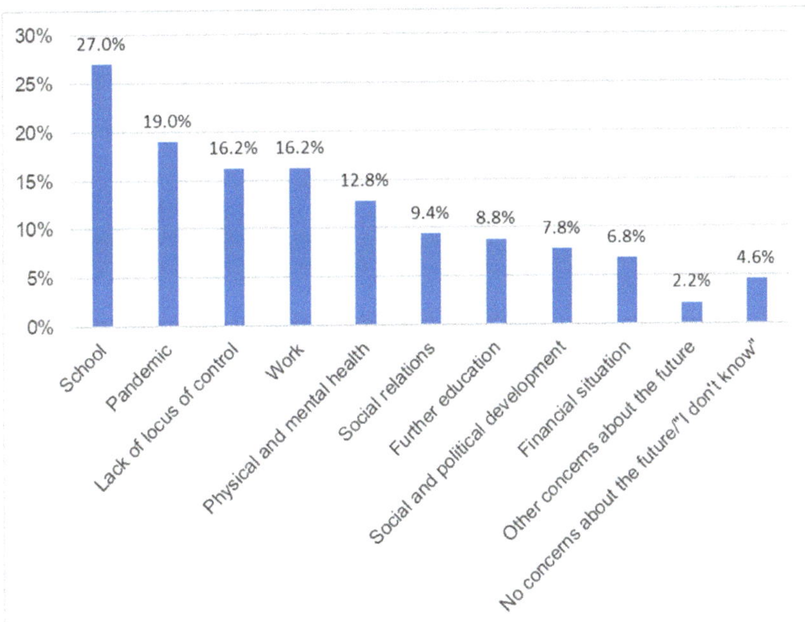

Figure 1. The greatest concerns about the future. The percentages of respondents reporting each main category of concerns about the future that emerged from the data for question 1: "What is your greatest concern when you think about the future?"

School-Related Concerns about the Future

With n 135 (27.0%) mentions, school related concerns about the future are the largest category. It consists of four subcategories.

Most respondents, n = 66 (13.2%), expressed their fear of not being able to graduate from school or having difficulties with the school-leaving examination. N = 55 (11.0%) expressed concerns about their future academic performance. They worried about not achieving learning objectives due to COVID-19 measures, such as distance learning. N = 13 (2.6%) mentioned concerns about the future regarding school in general, without elaborating on what these concerns related to. N = 8 (1.6%) expressed concerns related to the future organization of the school. They were worried about the continuation of distance learning, of being taught in alternating groups (shift system) and about the school closing again. On the other hand, respondents were also concerned about the reopening of schools.

Pandemic-Related Concerns about the Future

$N = 95$ (19.0%) respondents mentioned concerns about the future which were related to the COVID-19 pandemic. The main category comprises four subcategories.

The largest subcategory, addressed by $n = 43$ (8.6%), includes concerns related to the further development of the pandemic. Respondents mainly expressed concerns that the situation might worsen or that the pandemic might never end. Further $n = 32$ (6.4%) respondents uttered concerns about pandemic-related restrictions, e.g., the continuation of the restriction to enter public spaces, contact restrictions, limited opportunities to travel and the burden of wearing masks. $N = 26$ (5.2%) expressed concern about whether it will ever be possible to return to normal life as it was before the pandemic. Finally, $n = 8$ (1.6%) raised the issue of vaccination, expressing both concerns that not enough people would be vaccinated and fear that possible compulsory vaccination would come with greater restrictions for the unvaccinated.

Concerns about a Lack of Locus of Control in the Future

$N = 81$ (16.2%) respondents expressed concern about having no or insufficient power to shape their own lives and pursue their goals in the future. We have subsumed five subcategories under the more abstract main category "lack of locus of control".

$N = 56$ (11.2%) respondents referred to their fears of failure, fears of not achieving their goals, of making the wrong decisions, or of disappointing themselves and their families. $N = 14$ (2.8%) expressed uncertainty about their future. $N = 9$ (1.8%) showed a pessimistic attitude toward the future in the form of hopelessness, resignation or negative thinking about the future. $N = 8$ (1.6%) stated that they had no life plan of their own. $N = 2$ (0.4%) were worried about not being able to live independently in the future.

Work-Related Concerns about the Future

$N = 81$ (16.2%) respondents expressed concerns regarding their future work situation. We subsumed four subcategories.

$N = 34$ (6.8%) were concerned about not being able to find a job that they like and that offers good working conditions. Respondents indicated that they were concerned about not being able to pursue their "dream job". $N = 28$ (5.6%) expressed concern about not being able to find a job at all, partly due to the more difficult conditions caused by the pandemic. $N = 16$ (3.2%) reported uncertainty about their future career after leaving school. $N = 7$ (1.4%) mentioned concerns about the future in relation to work, without going into detail.

Concerns about the Future Related to Physical and Mental Health

Another category, mentioned by $n = 64$ (12.8%), summarizes concerns related to physical and mental health in the future. Responses were assigned to four subcategories.

Several respondents, ($n = 31$, 6.2%), described concerns about their mental health, including fears that mental health problems might resurface or worsen. Respondents also expressed concern that missing out on adolescence due to the pandemic would have a negative long-term impact on their mental health. Further $n = 18$ (3.6%) raised concerns about being unhappy and joyless in the future. $N = 13$ (2.6%) were concerned about becoming physically ill or even dying. $N = 7$ (1.4%) worried about the mental or physical well-being of others.

Concerns about the Future Related to Social Relationships

$N = 47$ (9.4%) respondents expressed concerns about their social relationships in the future.

The subcategories illustrate that n = 37 (7.4%) were afraid of being alone, of not making friends or of losing important family members or friends. N = 7 (1.4%) expressed concerns about conflicts in their family of origin. N = 6 (1.2%) were worried about their relationship—that it would end or that they would not find a partner or the right partner. N = 3 (0.6%) were worried that they would not be able to start a family in the future.

Concerns about the Future Regarding Further Education

Concerns about the future in relation to further education were named by n = 44 (8.8%). Four subcategories were defined.

N = 17 (3.4%) expressed uncertainty about their further education after leaving school, e.g., whether or not to study or which subject to study. N = 11 (2.2%) were worried about their academic performance at university. Respondents were concerned about having educational deficits caused by the pandemic, which could affect their academic success. N = 10 (2.0%) reported concerns regarding their chances of being accepted into a university or not being able to study abroad due to travel restrictions. N = 6 (1.2%) mentioned concerns about the future in relation to their studies, without going into more detail.

Concerns about the Future Related to Social and Political Developments

Another category mentioned by n = 39 (7.8%) respondents, summarizes concerns about future social and political developments. Respondents were assigned to four subcategories.

N = 16 (3.2%) were concerned about climate change. N = 14 (2.8%) referred to the political situation. N = 14 (2.8%) were concerned about the further development of the current economic and financial crisis and n = 4 (0.8%) expressed concerns about possible further pandemics and the occurrence of other disasters.

Further Concerns about the Future

N = 34 (6.8%) addressed their financial situation as a concern about the future. N = 11 (2.2%) expressed other concerns, e.g., concerns about compulsory military service or about the coming out. N = 23 (4.6%) stated that they were not worried about the future or that they did not think about the future or could not say anything about it ("I don't know").

3.2.2. Hopes for the Future

In the following section, we report the results of the second open-ended question: "What do you hope for most when you think about the future?" The results are illustrated in Figure 2 and Supplementary Table S3. They are described in detail below.

Pandemic-Related Hopes for the Future

Most hopes for the future (n = 181, 36.2%) are directly related to the COVID-19 pandemic. Within the main category, five subcategories were formed.

The largest subcategory, with n = 92 (18.4%) mentions, relates to the desire to return to normality and life as it was before the pandemic.

N = 69 (13.8%) related their hopes to the end of the measures. N = 55 (11.0%) wanted the COVID-19 pandemic to end. They wished for the pandemic to be brought under control or for the coronavirus to be defeated. N = 7 (1.4%) wanted a higher vaccination rate. N = 4 (0.8%) wanted reassurance—more knowledge about what will happen next or a fixed date when the lockdown will end.

Hopes for the Future Regarding Major Life Goals

The second largest category of hopes for the future, with n = 142 (28.4%) mentions, relates to various general life goals young people want to achieve. Five subcategories were defined.

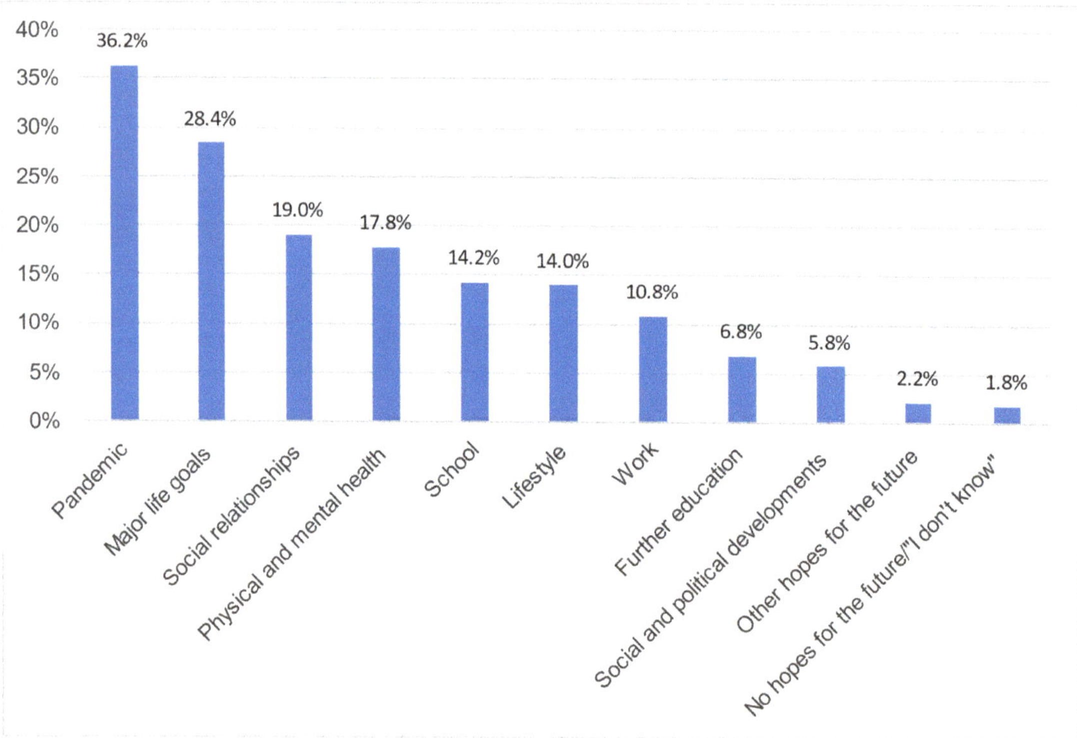

Figure 2. Greatest hopes for the future. The percentages of respondents reporting each main category of hopes for the future that emerged from the data for question 2: "What do you hope for most when you think about the future?"

Most respondents (n = 83, 16.6%) wanted to be satisfied with their lives. They hoped for a good life, using adjectives such as "happy" (respondent 3046), "cheerful" (respondent 2316), "lighthearted" (respondent 968) and "satisfying" (respondent 1837). N = 40 (8.0%) expressed a desire for self-actualization. Respondents wished for success. Others wanted to make the right choices about their lives, realize their dreams and achieve their goals for the future. N = 14 (2.8%) wanted autonomy, i.e., an independent, self-determined way of life. Respondents expressed this as follows: "to be self-reliant" (respondent 826), "to be able to lead a self-determined life" (respondent 1639) or "to be independent of others" (respondent 2714). N = 11 (2.2%) reported hopes for the future that were subsumed under the category "personal strength". The following hopes were expressed: "courage" (respondent 2389), "hope" (respondent 2389), "confidence" (respondent 3052) and "self-confidence and strength" (respondent 1098). N = 5 (1.0%) expressed a desire for a life full of experiences and a lot of impressions.

Hopes for the Future Relating to Social Relationships

Another category, comprising four subcategories, summarizes hopes for the future relating to social relationships (n = 95, 19.0%).

N = 52 (10.4%) expressed the wish to have more contact with their friends in the future, to continue to have good friends or to make new friends. N = 30 (6.0%) expressed the wish to start their own family or to live in a happy family with their children. N = 17 (3.4%) wished to be loved, to find or keep a partner, to have a fulfilling relationship or to marry their current partner. N = 12 (2.4%) wished for more contact with their family of origin or for greater family cohesion or the resolution of family conflicts.

Health-Related Hopes for the Future

N = 89 (17.8%) respondents expressed hopes for the future related to health, which were classified into five subcategories.

N = 34 (6.8%) expressed a desire for well-being, e.g., rest, relaxation, less stress and freedom of worry. *N* = 32 (6.4%) wished for physical health or a long life. *N* = 16 (3.2%) wished for the health and well-being of others, especially their loved ones and friends. A further *n* = 11 (2.2%) expressed a desire to improve their fitness or lose weight in the future. *N* = 6 (1.2%) wanted to maintain or regain their mental health.

School-Related Hopes for the Future

N = 71 (14.2%) respondents expressed hopes for the future regarding their school situation. Four subcategories were formed.

Several respondents (*n* = 34, 6.8%) wanted to complete their school-leaving examinations or graduate successfully from secondary school. *N* = 18 (3.6%) referred to their future school performance, expressing a desire to get good or better grades, to pass exams and thus pass the current school year. *N* = 18 (3.6%) commented on school organization and wished for a return to normal school attendance. Only a few expressed the opposite wish, that schools would remain closed and that there would be no exams, or that school would continue to be run in shifts *n* = 8 (1.6%) expressed the wish to have less stress at school and more free time in the future.

Hopes for the Future Related to Lifestyle

Another category summarizes hopes for the future related to lifestyle (*n* = 70, 14.0%). We differentiated five subcategories.

Several respondents within this main category (*n* = 38, 7.6%) wanted to be financially secure and to have no financial problems *n* = 17 (3.4%) wanted to travel, see the world, move abroad to live, study or work, or return to their home country in the future. *N* = 9 (1.8%) referred to their future living situation, mainly expressing a desire to live in a house in the future. *N* = 6 (1.2%) wished for a secure future or stability, without elaborating on what this meant to them. *N* = 6 (1.2%) expressed a desire to get a driving license or own a car.

Work-Related Hopes for the Future

N = 54 (10.8%) expressed hopes regarding their future work situation.

Several respondents (*n* = 43, 8.6%) wanted a good job that they enjoyed, with good working conditions and a good salary. *N* = 6 (1.2%) wanted to find a job at all and *n* = 5 (1.0%) wanted to be professionally successful and have a career.

Hopes for the Future Regarding Further Education

N = 34 (6.8%) respondents stated hopes for the future regarding their further education.

N = 17 (3.4%) expressed general hopes regarding their further education, such as getting a place at university. *N* = 12 (2.4%) expressed hopes about their future careers, such as finding a suitable career for themselves. *N* = 5 (1.0%) expressed the wish that they would do well in their studies.

Hopes for the Future Related to Social and Political Developments

Another category including five subcategories describes hopes related to future social and political developments (*n* = 29, 5.8%).

Concerning social developments, *n* = 16 (3.2%) expressed hopes for global cooperation, social cohesion or world peace. *N* = 6 (1.2%) referred to political development, wishing for better government, communism or less right-thinking people. *N* = 6 (1.2%) referred to climate change and expressed the hope that people would recognize the urgency of the issue and act. *N* = 2 (0.4%) wished for economic growth. Further *n* = 2 (0.4%) wished for an end to new pandemics or other crises.

Other Hopes for the Future

N = 11 (2.2%) expressed other, sometimes less differentiated wishes, such as that many or all things should change. Two respondents said that they would like to belong to the opposite sex in the future without suffering negative consequences. N = 9 (1.8%) stated that they had no wishes for the future or were unable to express any wishes for the future and answered, "I don't know".

3.3. *Quantitative and Mixed-Methods Results*

3.3.1. Differences According to Gender

The calculated Chi-squared tests, depicted in Supplementary Table S4, showed significant gender differences related to concerns and hopes for the future in both main and subcategories. Female respondents predominantly described themselves as more concerned about the future than male respondents. The pandemic-related concern about whether it will ever be possible to return to a normal life, as well as concerns with regard to their chances of accessing university, were mentioned more frequently by female respondents. Lack of locus of control (main category) and fear of failure, physical and mental health concerns (main category), and the associated subcategories of concerns regarding mental health and becoming unhappy in the future were also mentioned more often by female respondents.

In comparison, male respondents stated more frequently concerns about social and political developments (main category) or not having any concerns, compared to female respondents.

3.3.2. Differences According to Migration Background

The statistically significant differences in the main and subcategories according to migration background in relation to mentioned concerns and hopes for the future are presented in Supplementary Table S5.

In comparison to the other two characteristics, gender and degree of psychological distress, fewer statistically significant differences were found. Respondents with a migration background described concerns related to a lack of locus of control (main category) and fear of failure to a greater extent, compared to respondents without a migration background.

On the other hand, respondents without a migration background described a higher degree of pandemic-related concerns about the future (main category) and pandemic-related hopes for the future (main category), particularly the desire for an end to pandemic-related measures. Concerns about the future related to social and political developments were also more often reported among respondents without a migration background. Respondents with a migration background expressed a higher degree of hopes for the health of others, especially their family and friends.

3.3.3. Differences According to the Degree of Psychological Distress

The statistically significant differences in the main and subcategories according to the degree of psychological distress are presented in Supplementary Table S6.

In our study, a correlation was found between a higher degree of psychological distress and concerns about the future related to school (main category), especially the concern of not passing the school-leaving examination. Health-related concerns about the future (main category), especially fear of future psychological distress, were also more often expressed by psychologically distressed respondents. Additionally, fear of failure was associated with higher psychological distress. Psychologically distressed adolescents expressed major life goals (main category) more frequently and wished for life satisfaction.

The group of psychologically unstressed respondents expressed concerns about the future related to the vaccination for protection against COVID-19 more often than distressed respondents. They also expressed hopes about future social developments more frequently. This group also more often reported not being concerned about the future.

4. Discussion

The present study explored school students' concerns and hopes for the future after the first year of the pandemic. In addition, the study investigated whether there were differences regarding expressed concerns about and hopes for the future based on gender, migration background and mental health, as often found in the literature [1,5,9,13–16].

4.1. School-Related Concerns and Hopes for the Future

We found that the most common area of concern regarding the future was related to school (27%). The findings illustrate how much young people's mental well-being depends on academic performance and the learning environment, with individual differences also evident.

Our findings are comparable to other studies. Internationally, adolescents expressed significant concerns about the impact of the pandemic on school attendance and academic performance [22,25,31,32,35–37,53]. Compared to our study, Riiser et al. [54] found in a qualitative study with Norwegian adolescents aged 16–18, that the constant change between different forms of teaching and the lack of continuity harmed students' work habits, motivation, learning progress and learning outcomes. School-related worries were also identified as a risk factor and a strong predictor of psychological distress among adolescents [53,55]. However, other studies have also shown that some students experienced positive effects from the pandemic-related changes in the education system. While 46% of students surveyed in the Swiss Corona Stress Study reported feeling burdened by distance learning, 41% of respondents reported experiencing relief as a result [53]. In addition, the complex demands of personal life were simplified by measures such as contact restrictions, which make it easier for adolescents to concentrate on schoolwork [56].

School-related hopes for the future were mentioned less frequently (14%) than would be expected given the prevalence of school-related concerns. It may be that school students associated their worries about school with the pandemic and its restrictions. This would explain the frequency of pandemic-related hopes for the future (36%). As with concerns about the future, some adolescents expressed a wish for schools to remain closed in the future. Other studies with children and adolescents also indicated improved well-being for some of them during lockdowns [57,58]. Students reported observing progress in self-organization, independent learning and computer skills [59].

4.2. Pandemic-Related Concerns and Hopes for the Future

Another relevant aspect of our study relates to school students' concerns about the future regarding the COVID-19 pandemic. Concerns mainly revolved around the further development of the pandemic and that the pandemic-related restrictions might continue.

Similar results were found by Magson et al. [60]. Young people were more concerned about government restrictions to contain the virus than about the virus itself. Concerns about when life will return to normal are also reflected in another study from Austria [27] and in international comparisons [19,29].

4.3. Concerns about the Lack of Locus of Control and Hopes Related to Major Life Goals

Another central theme of our study is young people's sense of locus of control. Internal locus of control is defined as the belief that the outcome of life events depends on one's actions and external locus of control is the belief that chance and powerful others control one's life [61]. Research findings during the COVID-19 pandemic in adults suggest that an internal locus of control contributed to a reduction in pandemic-related psychological distress, whereas an external locus of control increased pandemic-related psychological distress [29,61–63]. In their study of adults, Würtzen et al. [64] showed that internal locus of control decreased during the pandemic, especially in younger adults (18–24 years).

In our study, young people also described a lack of internal locus of control and, in particular, a fear of failure. Their concerns can be linked to hopes for the future that relate to young people's major life goals, such as the desire for life satisfaction, self-actualization and autonomy. The high frequency of these categories should be seen in the context of decreased life satisfaction among young people during the pandemic [60,65–67]. Fear of failure has been found to be associated with lower life satisfaction [68,69]. On the other hand, students who felt more competent and supported in their autonomy reported higher well-being [59].

4.4. Physical and Mental Health-Related Concerns and Hopes for the Future

An issue that has already received considerable attention in previous research is the concern about contracting COVID-19 in the future or the possibility of close family members contracting the disease. Both aspects were mentioned by only a few adolescents in our study. Other studies have also shown that young people have little fear of contracting COVID-19 themselves [22,24,25,29,31], which may be explained by the lower burden of COVID-19 symptoms in children and adolescents [70].

In our study, health-related concerns about the future focused mainly on the concern that one's mental well-being might (again) deteriorate. Young people's health-related hopes for the future were also mainly related to their psychological well-being. This is consistent with research showing a significant impact of the pandemic on young people's mental well-being and an increase in mental health concerns [17,25,42,54,71–73].

4.5. Concerns and Hopes Related to Social Relationships

Another aspect of young people's lives that has been strongly affected by COVID-19 measures is their friendships [25,27,29,60,74]. In our study, young people expressed concerns about the future regarding their social relationships. Being with friends is significantly related to adolescents' well-being and quality of life [59,75–78]. Spatial distance and social deprivation can have profound psychological effects [60,79–82]. While it is plausible to assume that adolescents' extensive use of social media could mitigate the potentially harmful effects of physical distancing, research shows that adolescents perceived social media use during the pandemic as insufficient compensation for meeting friends in real life [54]. A high level of online contact even promoted depressive symptoms [18,24].

4.6. Differences According to Gender

In terms of gender differences, female respondents expressed more concerns, which is consistent with the results of many other studies [21,22,24,32,36,38]. Girls were more concerned about the difficulty of returning to normal life and were more likely to express a desire to return to pre-pandemic life. This suggests that female respondents generally felt more burdened by the pandemic measures, which is consistent with other studies [83] and may indicate that female adolescents rely more on face-to-face contact than male adolescents [84]. Female respondents were also more likely to fear failure, which is in line with other studies [68,85]. At the same time, they were more likely to express a desire for a happy life in the future. This seems plausible in light of recent research indicating lower life satisfaction among female respondents [65,68,86]. Female respondents were more likely to report health-related concerns about the future. Similar findings were observed in the recent study by Hawke et al. [71] on health issues and health-related concerns during the COVID-19 pandemic. Moreover, numerous studies have already demonstrated higher levels of psychological distress among female adolescents during the COVID-19 pandemic [39,73,87–90]. One of the possible reasons for this may be that males are less likely to vocalize their problems to adhere to the traditional male gender role of projecting strength [91].

4.7. Differences According to Migration Background

In terms of migration background, pandemic-related concerns were more likely to be expressed by respondents without a migration background. In particular, the wish for the measures to be discontinued stood out. It may be the case that, due to their generally higher socio-economic status [92], young people without a migration background were more involved in social and cultural activities before the pandemic and therefore experienced the restrictions on freedom as more burdensome than young people with a migration background. On the other hand, respondents with a migration background were more likely to express concerns about the future addressing a lack of internal locus of control, particularly fear of failure. There is also evidence in the research literature of a general, pandemic-independent association between migration background and external locus of control [93].

4.8. Differences According to the Degree of Psychological Distress

Due to the association between pandemic-related concerns and psychological distress in numerous studies [21,24,60,71,86], this aspect was also investigated in our study. Rodríguez-Cano et al. [24] found an association between depressive symptoms and worries about school, financial situation and COVID-19 infection in their study. Similar results were reported by Kim et al. [21]. In our study, psychologically distressed adolescents were also more likely to express school-related concerns. Psychologically distressed adolescents were more likely to report major life goals as hopes for the future, especially life satisfaction. As higher levels of psychological distress are associated with lower quality of life [24,60], it is understandable that psychologically distressed adolescents are more likely to long for a satisfying life.

4.9. Implications

The results of this study suggest an increased need for counseling, support and assistance for adolescent school students, and the need to critically examine school-based measures for pandemic containment in the future. The study by Kaltschik et al. [87] demonstrates that even after the end of the COVID-19 pandemic, there is still a need for support among adolescent students, as they showed poorer mental well-being in spring 2022 compared to February 2021. Despite an increase in the demand for help among young people with mental distress [90], young Austrians have shown a reluctance to access professional support services [37]. Therefore, support services for young people should be designed to be easily accessible, with schools being a suitable setting for such support. Services such as the school psychological service and school social work, which are currently only available sporadically or with limited hours [94–96], should be expanded and made available in all schools. Outpatient counseling and psychotherapy services, for which young people currently have to wait several months [97], need to be expanded to serve more young people than is currently possible. To make these services accessible to socially disadvantaged young people, an increased number of free counseling hours should be made available at a regional level. As some students benefited from the pandemic-related changes to their daily lives, it is important to consider not only the negative effects of COVID-19 on the mental health and well-being of children and adolescents but also to include the perspective of young people and their families who have benefited from the changes brought about by the lockdown, particularly in the educational domain.

4.10. Limitations

This study has several limitations. The first and most important limitation is that the study was conducted based on an online survey. Although the young people were given the opportunity to express their subjective experiences in their own words in the free text boxes, the responses give only a limited picture of the reality of the school students' lives. The richness of detail that could be generated, for example, by qualitative in-depth interviews, which deepen the narratives and place them in relevant contexts, is not possible with this type of research. However, as a pilot study, our research can provide indications as to which issues could be explored in more depth in a further qualitative interview study.

The online survey format also meant that school students' responses varied in detail, from very brief keyword responses to more substantial and differentiated responses. It is possible that the willingness to answer could be increased by incentives. In addition, the research questions were very broad and non-specific and did not refer to any time frame. As a result, young people's responses covered a wide range of life domains and periods, from the near future to the next stages of their lives. Specifying a timeframe when formulating the open-ended questions would narrow down the young people's responses.

Secondly, our sample ensures a representative selection in terms of gender and migration background. However, other factors, such as age and socioeconomic status, also have an impact on the well-being and mental health of adolescents [36,98]. The subjective socioeconomic status is, for example, associated with subjective well-being, mental health and self-rated health during adolescence [99,100]. Unfortunately, no information on the socioeconomic background was collected in the present study, which should be considered in future studies to avoid bias.

Thirdly, the concerns about and hopes for the future expressed by the young people in our sample cannot be attributed solely to the pandemic, as other factors such as family problems, personal illnesses, etc., may contribute to individual deterioration in mental well-being.

5. Conclusions

The findings of our pilot study add to our understanding of what young people are facing at a time of major change and provide insights into their concerns and hopes for the future one year after the beginning of the pandemic. The findings show that young people have concerns about the future in many areas of their lives, which society must address if we are to take young people's fears and needs seriously. The findings of this pilot study help to raise awareness of the concerns of school students in Austria and can serve as a basis for further in-depth qualitative research.

Supplementary Materials: The following supporting information can be downloaded at: https://www.mdpi.com/article/10.3390/healthcare11162242/s1, Table S1: Study sample characteristics (N = 500); Table S2: The greatest concerns about the future. The percentages of respondents reporting each main category (in bold) and subcategory of concerns about the future that emerged from the data for question 1: "What is your greatest concern when you think about the future?"; Table S3: The greatest hopes for the future. The percentages of respondents reporting each main category (in bold) and subcategory of concerns about the hopes for the future that emerged from the data for question 2: "What do you hope for most when you think about the future?"; Table S4: Proportion of female and male students differing in reportings in main or subcategories of (1) Concerns about the future and (2) Hopes for the future (N = 500); Table S5: Proportion of students with and without migration background differing in reportings in main or subcategories of (1) Concerns about the future and (2) Hopes for the future (N = 500); Table S6: Proportion of students with and without psychological distress differing in reportings in main or subcategories of (1) Concerns about the future and (2) Hopes for the future (N = 500).

Author Contributions: Conceptualization, C.P., E.H. and A.J.; methodology, E.H. and A.J.; software, S.F., A.J. and E.H.; validation, A.J. and E.H.; formal analysis, S.F., A.J., E.H. and S.K.; data curation, E.H.; writing—original draft preparation, S.F., A.J. and E.H.; writing—review and editing, S.K., C.P., T.P. and G.D.; visualization, S.F.; supervision, A.J. and E.H.; project administration, E.H. All authors have read and agreed to the published version of the manuscript.

Funding: This research received no external funding.

Institutional Review Board Statement: The study was conducted following the Declaration of Helsinki and approved by the Ethics Committee and the data protection officer of the University for Continuing Education Krems (EK GZ 41/2018–2021).

Informed Consent Statement: Informed consent was obtained from all subjects involved in the study.

Data Availability Statement: The raw data supporting the conclusions of this article will be made available by the authors upon reasonable request after signing a confidentiality agreement.

Acknowledgments: Open Access Funding by the University for Continuing Education Krems.

Conflicts of Interest: The authors declare no conflict of interest.

References

1. Racine, N.; McArthur, B.A.; Cooke, J.E.; Eirich, R.; Zhu, J.; Madigan, S. Global prevalence of depressive and anxiety symptoms in children and adolescents during COVID-19: A meta-analysis. *JAMA Pediatr.* **2021**, *175*, 1142–1150. [CrossRef] [PubMed]
2. Samji, H.; Wu, J.; Ladak, A.; Vossen, C.; Stewart, E.; Dove, N.; Long, D.; Snell, G. Review: Mental health impacts of the COVID-19 pandemic on children and youth—A systemic review. *Child Adolesc. Ment. Health* **2021**, *27*, 173–189. [CrossRef] [PubMed]
3. Meherali, S.; Punjani, N.; Louie-Poon, S.; Rahim, K.A.; Das, J.K.; Salam, R.A.; Lassi, Z.S. Mental health of children and adolescents amidst COVID-19 and past pandemics: A rapid systematic review. *Int. J. Environ. Res. Public Health* **2021**, *18*, 3432. [CrossRef] [PubMed]
4. Viner, R.; Russell, S.; Saulle, R.; Croker, H.; Stansfield, C.; Packer, J.; Nicholls, D.; Goddings, A.L.; Bonell, C.; Hudson, L.; et al. School closures during social lockdown and mental health, health behaviors, and well-being among children and adolescents during the first COVID-19 wave: A systematic review. *JAMA Pediatr.* **2022**, *176*, 400–409. [CrossRef]
5. Alamolhoda, S.H.; Zare, E.; HakimZadeh, A.; Zalpour, A.; Vakili, F.; Mohammadi Chermahini, R.; Ebadifard, R.; Masoumi, M.; Khaleghi, N.; Nasiri, M. Adolescent mental health during covid-19 pandemics: A systematic review. *Int. J. Adolesc. Med. Health* **2022**, *35*, 41–60. [CrossRef]
6. Harrison, L.; Carducci, B.; Klein, J.D.; Bhutta, Z.A. Indirect effects of COVID-19 on child and adolescent mental health: An overview of systematic review. *BMJ Glob. Health* **2022**, *7*, e010713. [CrossRef]
7. Irwin, M.; Lazarevic, B.; Soled, D.; Adesman, A. The COVID-19 pandemic and its potential enduring impact on children. *Curr. Opin. Pediatr.* **2022**, *34*, 107–115. [CrossRef]
8. Jones, E.A.K.; Mitra, A.K.; Bhuijan, A.R. Impact of COVID-19 on mental health in adolescents: A systematic review. *Int. J. Environ. Res. Public Health* **2021**, *18*, 2470. [CrossRef] [PubMed]
9. Panchal, U.; Salazar de Pablo, G.; Franco, M.; Moreno, C.; Parellada, M.; Arango, C.; Fusar-Poli, P. The impact of COVID-19 lockdown on child and adolescent mental health: Systematic review. *Eur. Child Adolesc. Psychiatry* **2021**, *32*, 1151–1177. [CrossRef] [PubMed]
10. Ramaiya, A.; Chandra-Mouli, V.; Both, R.; Gottert, A.; Guglielmi, S.; Beckwith, S.; Li, M.; Blum, R.W. Assessing the health, social, educational and economic impact of the COVID-19 pandemic on adolescents in low- and middle-income countries: A rapid review of the literature. *Sex. Reprod. Health Matters* **2023**, *31*, 2187170. [CrossRef]
11. Schlack, R.; Neuperdt, L.; Junker, S.; Eicher, S.; Hölling, H.; Thom, J.; Ravens-Sieberer, U.; Beyer, A.K. Changes in mental health in the German child and adolescent population during the COVID-19 pandemic—Results of a rapid review. *J. Health Monit.* **2023**, *8* (Suppl. 1), 2–72. [CrossRef] [PubMed]
12. Theberath, M.; Bauer, D.; Chen, W.; Salinas, M.; Mohabbat, A.B.; Yang, J.; Chon, T.Y.; Bauer, B.A.; Wahner-Roedler, D.L. Effects of COVID-19 pandemic on mental health of children and adolescents: A systematic review of survey studies. *SAGE Open Med.* **2022**, *10*, 1–14. [CrossRef] [PubMed]
13. Wolf, K.; Schmitz, J. Scoping review: Longitudinal effects of the COVID-19 pandemic on child and adolescent mental health. *Eur. Child Adolesc. Psychiatry* 2023, *advance online publication*. [CrossRef] [PubMed]
14. Deng, J.; Zhou, F.; Hou, W.; Heybati, K.; Lohit, S.; Abbas, U.; Silver, Z.; Wong, C.Y.; Chang, O.; Huang, E.; et al. Prevalence of mental health symptoms in children and adolescents during the COVID-19 pandemic: A meta-analysis. *Ann. N. Y. Acad. Sci.* **2023**, *1520*, 53–73. [CrossRef]
15. Ma, L.; Mazidi, M.; Li, K.; Li, X.; Chen, S.; Kirwan, R.; Zhou, H.; Yan, N.; Rahman, A.; Wang, W.; et al. Prevalence of mental health problems among children and adolescents during the COVID-19 pandemic: A systematic review and meta-analysis. *J. Affect. Disord.* **2021**, *293*, 78–89. [CrossRef]
16. Manchia, M.; Gathier, A.W.; Yapici-Eser, H.; Schmidt, M.V.; de Quervain, D.; van Amelsvoort, T.; Bisson, J.I.; Cryan, J.F.; Howes, O.D.; Pinto, L.; et al. The impact of the prolonged COVID-19 pandemic on stress resilience and mental health: A critical review across waves. *Eur. Neuropsychopharmacol.* **2022**, *55*, 22–83. [CrossRef]
17. Sarkadi, A.; Sahlin Torp, L.; Pérez-Aronsson, A.; Warner, G. Children's expressions of worry during the COVID-19 pandemic in Sweden. *J. Pediatr. Psychol.* **2021**, *46*, 939–949. [CrossRef]
18. Ellis, W.E.; Dumas, T.M.; Forbes, L.M. Physically isolated but socially connected: Psychological adjustment and stress among adolescents during the initial COVID-19 crisis. *Can. J. Behav. Sci.* **2020**, *52*, 177–187. [CrossRef]
19. Duby, Z.; Bunce, B.; Fowler, C.; Bergh, K.; Jonas, K.; Dietrich, J.J.; Govindasamy, D.; Kuo, C.; Mathews, C. Intersections between COVID-19 and socio-economic mental health stressors in the lives of South African adolescent girls and young women. *Child. Adolesc. Psychiatry Ment. Health* **2022**, *16*, 23. [CrossRef]
20. Hsieh, W.-J.; Powell, T.; Tan, K.; Chen, J.-H. Kidcope and the COVID-19 pandemic: Understanding high school students' coping and emotional well-being. *Int. J. Environ. Res. Public Health* **2021**, *18*, 10207. [CrossRef]
21. Kim, H.; Jhon, M.; Kim, J.W.; Kang, H.J.; Ryu, S.; Kim, J.M.; Lee, J.Y.; Kim, S.W. Factors associated with depression and anxiety in Korean adolescents during the COVID-19 pandemic. *Psychiatry Investig.* **2022**, *19*, 551–561. [CrossRef] [PubMed]
22. Lehmann, S.; Skogen, J.C.; Haug, E.; Maeland, S.; Fadnes, L.T.; Sandal, G.M.; Hysing, M.; Bjørknes, R. Perceived consequences and worries among youth in Norway during the COVID-19 pandemic lockdown. *Scand. J. Public Health* **2021**, *49*, 755–765. [CrossRef] [PubMed]
23. Luthar, S.S.; Ebbert, A.M.; Kumar, N.L. Risk and resilience during COVID-19: A new study in the Zigler paradigm of developmental science. *Dev. Psychopathol.* **2021**, *33*, 565–580. [CrossRef] [PubMed]

24. Rodríguez-Cano, R.; Cortés-Garcia, L.; Ulset, V.S.; von Soest, T. Worries about COVID-19 and adolescents' mental health and life satisfaction: The role of sociodemographics and social support. *Front. Pediatr.* **2022**, *10*, 847434. [CrossRef] [PubMed]
25. Bjørknes, R.; Mjeldheim Sandal, G.; Mæland, S.; Haug, E.; Lehmann, S. 'We are unlikely to return to the same world, and I do not want it to destroy my future.' Young people's worries through the outbreak of the COVID-19 pandemic. *Child. Fam. Soc. Work* **2021**, *27*, 246–253. [CrossRef]
26. Kästner, A.; Lücker, P.; Hannich, A.; Schmeyers, L.; Lücker, J.; Hoffmann, W. COVID-19-related future anxiety is associated with the health-related quality of life in school-aged children and adolescents—A cross-sectional study. *Front. Public Health* **2022**, *10*, 1003876. [CrossRef] [PubMed]
27. Eigl, E.S.; Widauer, S.S.; Schabus, M. Burdens and psychosocial consequences of the COVID-19 pandemic for Austrian children and adolescents. *Front. Psychol.* **2022**, *13*, 971241. [CrossRef]
28. Hagquist, C. Worry and psychosomatic problems among adolescents in Sweden in the wake of the COVID-19 pandemic: Unequal patterns among sociodemographic groups? *J. Adolesc. Health* **2023**, *72*, 688–695. [CrossRef]
29. Hoffmann, S.H.; Pisinger, V.S.C.; Rosing, J.A.; Tolstrup, J.S. Symptoms of distress among young Danes during the national lockdown in May 2020. *Eur. Child Adolesc. Psychiatry* **2021**, *32*, 611–620. [CrossRef]
30. Ravens-Sieberer, U.; Kaman, A.; Otto, C.; Adedeji, A.; Devine, J.; Erhart, M.; Napp, A.K.; Becker, M.; Blanck-Stellmacher, U.; Löffler, C.; et al. Mental health and quality of life in children and adolescents during the COVID-19 pandemic-results of the Copsy Study. *Dtsch. Arztebl. Int.* **2020**, *117*, 828–829. [CrossRef]
31. Scott, S.R.; Rivera, K.M.; Rushing, E.; Manczak, E.M.; Rozek, C.S.; Doom, J.R. "I hate this": A qualitative analysis of adolescents' self-reported challenges during the COVID-19 pandemic. *J. Adolesc. Health* **2021**, *68*, 262–269. [CrossRef]
32. Shukla, M.; Pandey, R.; Singh, T.; Riddleston, L.; Hutchinson, T.; Kumari, V.; Lau, J.Y.F. The effect of COVID-19 and related lockdown phases on young peoples' worries and emotions: Novel data from India. *Front. Public Health* **2021**, *9*, 645183. [CrossRef] [PubMed]
33. Koly, K.N.; Islam, M.S.; Potenza, M.N.; Mahumud, R.A.; Islam, M.S.; Uddin, M.S.; Sarwar, M.A.H.; Begum, F.; Reidpath, D.D. Psychosocial health of school-going adolescents during the COVID-19 pandemic: Findings from a nationwide survey in Bangladesh. *PLoS ONE* **2023**, *18*, e0283374. [CrossRef]
34. Larcher, V.; Dittborn, M.; Linthicum, J.; Sutton, A.; Brierley, J.; Payne, C.; Hardy, H.; GOSH Young People's Forum. Young people's views on their role in the COVID-19 pandemic and society's recovery from it. *Arch. Dis. Child.* **2020**, *105*, 1192–1196. [CrossRef]
35. Lessard, L.M.; Puhl, R.M. Adolescent academic worries amid COVID-19 and perspectives on pandemic-related changes in teacher and peer relations. *Sch. Psychol.* **2021**, *36*, 285–292. [CrossRef]
36. Muñoz-Fernández, N.; Rodríguez-Meirinhos, A. Adolescents' concerns, routines, peer activities, frustration, and optimism in the time of COVID-19 confinement in Spain. *J. Clin. Med.* **2021**, *10*, 798. [CrossRef]
37. Jesser, A.; Schaffler, Y.; Gächter, A.; Dale, R.; Humer, E.; Pieh, C. School students' concerns and support after one year of COVID-19 in Austria: A qualitative study using content analysis. *Healthcare* **2022**, *10*, 1334. [CrossRef]
38. Ciudad-Fernández, V.; Schoeps, K.; Montoya-Castilla, I. Emotional state, life satisfaction and worries regarding COVID-19 in Spanish and Chilean adolescents during spring 2020. *Scand. J. Child. Adolesc. Psychiatr. Psychol.* **2022**, *10*, 144–152. [CrossRef] [PubMed]
39. Engel de Abreu, P.M.J.; Neumann, S.; Wealer, C.; Abreu, N.; Coutinho Macedo, E.; Kirsch, C. Subjective well-being of adolescents in Luxembourg, Germany, and Brazil during the COVID-19 pandemic. *J. Adolesc. Health* **2021**, *69*, 211–218. [CrossRef] [PubMed]
40. Harris, P.A.; Taylor, R.; Minor, B.L.; Elliott, V.; Fernandez, M.; O'Neal, L.; McLeod, L.; Delacqua, G.; Delacqua, F.; Kirby, J.; et al. The REDCap consortium: Building an international community of software platform partners. *J. Biomed. Inform.* **2019**, *95*, 103208. [CrossRef]
41. Harries, P.A.; Taylor, R.; Thielke, R.; Payne, J.; Gonzalez, N.; Conde, J.G. Research electronic data capture (REDCap)—A metadata-driven methodology and workflow process for providing translational research informatics support. *J. Biomed. Inform.* **2009**, *42*, 377–381. [CrossRef] [PubMed]
42. Pieh, C.; Plener, P.L.; Probst, T.; Dale, R.; Humer, E. Assessment of mental health of high school students during social distancing and remote schooling during the COVID-19 pandemic in Austria. *JAMA Netw. Open* **2021**, *4*, e2114866. [CrossRef] [PubMed]
43. Pieh, C.; Dale, R.; Plener, P.L.; Humer, E.; Probst, T. Stress levels in high-school students after a semester of home-schooling. *Eur. Child Adolesc. Psychiatry* **2022**, *31*, 1849–1857. [CrossRef]
44. Pollak, M.; Kowarz, N.; Partheymüller, J. Blog 100—Chronologie zur Corona-Krise in Österreich—Teil 4: Erneute Lockdowns, Massentests und der Beginn der Impfkampagne. Universität Wien, 2021. Available online: www.univie.ac.at (accessed on 12 March 2023).
45. Pollak, M.; Kowarz, N.; Partheymüller, J. Blog 51—Chronologie zur Corona-Krise in Österreich—Teil 1: Vorgeschichte, der Weg in den Lockdown, die akute Phase und wirtschaftliche Folgen. Universität Wien, 2020. Available online: www.uni-vie.ac.at (accessed on 12 March 2023).
46. ORF. Dritter Lockdown mit Test als Türöffner. 2020. Available online: https://orf.at/stories/3194349/ (accessed on 3 August 2023).
47. Neubauer. Zentralmatura 2021 wird auf 20. Mai verschoben. Wiener Zeitung. 2020. Available online: https://www.wienerzeitung.at/nachrichten/politik/oesterreich/2083835-AHS-Direktoren-gegen-Notamputation-der-Matura.html (accessed on 12 March 2023).

48. Statistics Austria. Bevölkerung mit Migrationshintergrund im Überblick (Jahresdurchschnitt 2020). Statistics Austria, 2021. Available online: https://www.statistik.at/wcm/idc/idcplg?IdcService=GET_NATIVE_FILE&RevisionSelectionMethod=LatestReleased&dDocName=033240 (accessed on 24 April 2023).
49. Hsieh, H.F.; Shannon, S.E. Three approaches to qualitative content analysis. *Qual. Health Res.* **2005**, *15*, 1277–1288. [CrossRef] [PubMed]
50. Srivastava, P.; Hopwood, N. A practical iterative framework for qualitative data analysis. *Int. J. Qual. Methods* **2009**, *8*, 76–84. [CrossRef]
51. Woods, M.; Paulus, T.; Atkins, D.P.; Macklin, R. Advancing Qualitative Research Using Qualitative Data Analysis Software (QDAS)? Reviewing Potential Versus Practice in Published Studies using ATLAS.ti and NVivo, 1994–2013. *Soc. Sci. Comput. Rev.* **2016**, *34*, 597–617. [CrossRef]
52. Atlas.ti. ATLAS.ti: The Qualitative Data Analysis & Research Software (Version 23) [Computer Software]. 2023. Available online: https://atlasti.com/de (accessed on 3 August 2023).
53. de Quervain, D.; Coynel, D.; Aerni, A.; Amini, E.; Bentz, D.; Freytag, V.; Gerhards, C.; Papassotiropoulos, A.; Schicktanz, N.; Schlitt, T.; et al. Swiss Corona Stress Study: Survey in high school students, March 2021. *OSF Prepr.* **2021**. [CrossRef]
54. Riiser, K.; Richardsen, K.R.; Haraldstad, K.; Helseth, S.; Torbjørnsen, A. "It's hard to keep a distance when you're with someone you really care about"—A qualitative study of adolescents' pandemic-related health literacy and how COVID-19 affects their lives. *PLoS ONE* **2022**, *17*, e0266510. [CrossRef]
55. Dändliker, L.; Brünecke, I.; Citterio, P.; Lochmatter, F.; Buchmann, M.; Grütter, J. Educational concerns, health concerns and mental health during early COVID-19 school closures: The role of perceived support by teachers, family, and friends. *Front. Psychol.* **2022**, *12*, 733683. [CrossRef]
56. Andresen, S.; Lips, A.; Möller, R.; Rusack, T.; Schröer, W.; Thomas, S.; Wilmes, J. *Das Leben von Jungen Menschen in der Corona-Pandemie: Erfahrungen, Sorgen, Bedarfe*; Bertelsmann Stiftung: Gütersloh, Germany, 2020. [CrossRef]
57. Bruining, H.; Bartels, M.; Polderman, T.J.C.; Popma, A. COVID-19 and child and adolescent psychiatry: An unexpected blessing for part of our population? *Eur. Child Adolesc. Psychiatry* **2021**, *30*, 1139–1140. [CrossRef]
58. Verheyden, C.; Van Holen, F.; West, D.; Vanderfaeillie, J. Psychosocial well-being of Flemish foster children residing in their foster homes during the COVID-19 lockdown. *Child. Youth Serv. Rev.* **2022**, *139*, 106535. [CrossRef] [PubMed]
59. Schober, B.; Lüftenegger, M.; Spiel, C. Lernen unter COVID-19-Bedingungen. Zwischenbericht. Fakultät für Psychologie, Universität Wien, 2021. Available online: https://lernencovid19.univie.ac.at/fileadmin/user_upload/p_lernencovid19/Zwischenbericht_Befragung_5_final_Update_09_07.pdf (accessed on 3 August 2023).
60. Magson, N.R.; Freeman, J.Y.A.; Rapee, R.M.; Richardson, C.E.; Oar, E.L.; Fardouly, J. Risk and protective factors for prospective changes in adolescent mental health during the COVID-19 pandemic. *J. Youth Adolesc.* **2021**, *50*, 44–57. [CrossRef] [PubMed]
61. Krampe, H.; Danbolt, L.J.; Haver, A.; Stålsett, G.; Schnell, T. Locus of control moderates the association of COVID-19 stress and general mental distress: Results of a Norwegian and a German-speaking cross-sectional survey. *BMC Psychiatry* **2021**, *21*, 437. [CrossRef]
62. Flesia, L.; Monaro, M.; Mazza, C.; Fietta, V.; Colicino, E.; Segatto, B.; Roma, P. Predicting perceived stress related to the COVID-19 outbreak through stable psychological traits and machine learning models. *J. Clin. Med.* **2020**, *9*, 3350. [CrossRef]
63. Mori, M.; Seko, T.; Ogawa, S. Association of social capital and locus of control with perceived health during the COVID-19 pandemic in Japan. *Int. J. Environ. Res. Public Health* **2020**, *19*, 9415. [CrossRef]
64. Würtzen, H.; Clausen, L.H.; Andersen, P.B.; Santini, Z.I.; Erkmen, J.; Pedersen, H.F. Mental well-being, health, and locus of control in Danish adults before and during COVID-19. *Acta Neuropsychiatr.* **2022**, *34*, 93–98. [CrossRef] [PubMed]
65. Mikkelsen, H.T.; Skarstein, S.; Helseth, S.; Småstuen, M.C.; Haraldstad, K.; Rohde, G. Health-related quality of life, health literacy and COVID-19-related worries of 16- to 17-year-old adolescents and parents one year into the pandemic: A cross-sectional study. *BMC Public Health* **2022**, *22*, 1321. [CrossRef]
66. Myhr, A.; Naper, L.R.; Samarawickrema, I.; Vesterbekkmo, R.K. Impact of COVID-19 pandemic lockdown on mental well-being of Norwegian adolescents during the first wave—Socioeconomic position and gender differences. *Front. Public Health* **2021**, *9*, 717747. [CrossRef]
67. Soest, T.V.; Bakken, A.; Pedersen, W.; Sletten, M.A. Life satisfaction among adolescents before and during the COVID-19 pandemic. Livstilfredshet blant ungdom før og under covid-19-pandemien. *Tidsskrift Den Nor. Laegeforening Tidsskr. Prakt. Med. Ny Raekke* **2020**, *140*, 10. [CrossRef]
68. Eriksson, K.; Strimling, P. Gender differences in competitiveness and fear of failure help explain why girls have lower life satisfaction than boys in gender equal countries. *Front. Psychol.* **2023**, *14*, 1131837. [CrossRef]
69. Govorova, E.; Benítez, I.; Muñiz, J. Predicting Student Well-Being. Network Analysis Based on PISA 2018. *Int. J. Environ. Res. Public Health* **2020**, *17*, 4014. [CrossRef] [PubMed]
70. Izquierdo-Pujol, J.; Moron-Lopez, S.; Dalmau, J.; Gonzalez-Aumatell, A.; Carreras-Abad, C.; Mendez, M.; Rodrigo, C.; Martinez-Picado, J. Post COVID-19 condition in children and adolescents: An emerging problem. *Front. Pediatr.* **2022**, *10*, 894204. [CrossRef] [PubMed]
71. Hawke, L.D.; Szatmari, P.; Cleverley, K.; Courtney, D.; Cheung, A.; Voineskos, A.N.; Henderson, J. Youth in a pandemic: A longitudinal examination of youth mental health and substance use concerns during COVID-19. *BMJ Open* **2021**, *11*, e049209. [CrossRef] [PubMed]

72. Marciano, L.; Viswanath, K.; Morese, R.; Camerini, A.L. Screen time and adolescents' mental health before and after the COVID-19 lockdown in Switzerland: A natural experiment. *Front. Psychiatry* **2022**, *13*, 981881. [CrossRef]
73. Pieh, C.; Plener, P.L.; Probst, T.; Dale, R.; Humer, E. Mental health in adolescents during COVID-19-related social distancing and home-schooling. *SSRN Electr. J.* **2021**. [CrossRef]
74. Kung, C.S.J.; Kunz, J.S.; Shields, M.A. COVID-19 lockdowns and changes in loneliness among young people in the U.K. *Soc. Sci. Med.* **2023**, *320*, 115692. [CrossRef]
75. Farrell, A.H.; Vitoroulis, I.; Eriksson, M.; Vaillancourt, T. Loneliness and Well-Being in Children and Adolescents during the COVID-19 Pandemic: A Systematic Review. *Children* **2023**, *10*, 279. [CrossRef]
76. Halldorsdottir, T.; Thorisdottir, I.E.; Meyers, C.C.A.; Asgeirsdottir, B.B.; Kristjansson, A.L.; Valdimarsdottir, H.B.; Allegrante, J.P.; Sigfusdottir, I.D. Adolescent well-being amid the COVID-19 pandemic: Are girls struggling more than boys? *JCPP Adv.* **2021**, *1*, e12027. [CrossRef]
77. Helseth, S.; Misvaer, N. Adolescents' perceptions of quality of life: What it is and what matters. *J. Clin. Nurs.* **2010**, *19*, 1454–1461. [CrossRef]
78. Pepe, A.; Farina, E. A mixed-method study on adolescents' well-being during the COVID-19 syndemic emergency. *Sci. Rep.* **2023**, *13*, 871. [CrossRef]
79. Houghton, S.; Kyron, M.; Hunter, S.C.; Lawrence, D.; Hattie, J.; Carroll, A.; Zadow, C. Adolescents' longitudinal trajectories of mental health and loneliness: The impact of COVID-19 school closures. *J. Adolesc.* **2022**, *94*, 191–205. [CrossRef]
80. Loades, M.E.; Chatburn, E.; Higson-Sweeney, N.; Reynolds, S.; Shafran, R.; Brigden, A.; Linney, C.; McManus, M.N.; Borwick, C.; Crawley, E. Rapid systematic review: The impact of social isolation and loneliness on the mental health of children and adolescents in the context of COVID-19. *J. Am. Acad. Child Adolesc. Psychiatry* **2020**, *59*, 1218–1239.e3. [CrossRef]
81. Postigo-Zegarra, S.; Julián, M.; Schoeps, K.; Montoya-Castilla, I. Psychological adjustment of Spanish adolescents and their parents during COVID-19 lockdown: A mixed method approach. *PLoS ONE* **2021**, *16*, e0255149. [CrossRef] [PubMed]
82. Sawyer, S.M.; Azzopardi, P.S.; Wickremarathne, D.; Patton, G.C. The age of adolescence. *Lancet Child Adolesc. Health* **2018**, *2*, 223–228. [CrossRef] [PubMed]
83. Kerekes, N.; Bador, K.; Sfendla, A.; Belaatar, M.; Mzadi, A.E.; Jovic, V.; Damjanovic, R.; Erlandsson, M.; Nguyen, H.T.M.; Nguyen, N.T.A.; et al. Changes in adolescents' psychosocial functioning and well-being as a consequence of long-term COVID-19 restrictions. *Int. J. Environ. Res. Public Health* **2021**, *18*, 8755. [CrossRef]
84. Thorisdottir, I.E.; Agustsson, G.; Oskarsdottir, S.Y.; Kristjansson, A.L.; Asgeirsdottir, B.B.; Sigfusdottir, I.D.; Valdimarsdottir, H.B.; Allegrante, J.P.; Halldorsdottir, T. Effect of the COVID-19 pandemic on adolescent mental health and substance use up to March, 2022, in Iceland: A repeated, cross-sectional, population-based study. *Lancet Child Adolesc. Health* **2023**, *7*, 347–357. [CrossRef]
85. Borgonovi, F.; Han, S.W. Gender disparities in fear of failure among 15-year-old students: The role of gender inequality, the organisation of schooling and economic conditions. *J. Adolesc.* **2021**, *86*, 28–39. [CrossRef]
86. Schoeps, K.; Tamarit, A.; De la Barrera, U.; Lacomba-Trejo, L.; Montoya-Castilla, I.; Del Rosario, C.; Coello, F.; Herrera, S.; Trujillo, Á.; Riveros Munevar, F.; et al. Social and Psychological Effects of COVID-19 Pandemic on Adolescents' and Young Adults' Mental Health: A Cross-Cultural Mediation Study. *Psychol. Rep.* 2022, *advance online publication*. [CrossRef]
87. Kaltschik, S.; Pieh, C.; Dale, R.; Probst, T.; Pammer, B.; Humer, E. Assessment of the long-term mental health effects on Austrian students after COVID-19 restrictions. *Int. J. Environ. Res. Public Health* **2022**, *19*, 13110. [CrossRef] [PubMed]
88. Dale, R.; Jesser, A.; O'Rourke, T.; Probst, T.; Humer, E.; Pieh, C. Mental health burden of high school students 1.5 years after the beginning of the COVID-19 pandemic in Austria. *Eur. Child Adolesc. Psychiatry* **2023**, *32*, 1015–1024. [CrossRef]
89. Dale, R.; Jesser, A.; Pieh, C.; O'Rourke, T.; Probst, T.; Humer, E. Mental health burden of high school students, and suggestions for psychosocial support, 1,5 years into the COVID-19 pandemic in Austria. *Eur. Child Adolesc. Psychiatry* **2022**, *32*, 1015–1024. [CrossRef] [PubMed]
90. Haider, K.; Humer, E.; Weber, M.; Pieh, C.; Ghorab, T.; Dale, R.; Dinhof, C.; Gächter, A.; Probst, T.; Jesser, A. An assessment of Austrian school students' mental health and their wish for support: A mixed methods approach. *Int. J. Environ. Res. Public Health* **2023**, *20*, 4749. [CrossRef] [PubMed]
91. Yousaf, O.; Grunfeld, E.A.; Hunter, M.S. A systematic review of the factors associated with delays in medical and psychological help-seeking among men. *Health Psychol. Rev.* **2015**, *9*, 264–276. [CrossRef]
92. Household Income. Available online: http://www.statistik.at/web_en/statistics/PeopleSociety/social_statistics/household_income/index.html (accessed on 22 May 2023).
93. Xiong, M.; Johnson, W. Perceived discrimination and relative deprivation in Chinese migrant adolescents: The mediating effect of locus of control and moderating effect of duration since migration. *Child Adolesc. Psychiatry Ment. Health* **2022**, *16*, 1. [CrossRef]
94. Kinder- und Jugendanwaltschaft Österreichs. *Recht auf Psychische Gesundheit: Verbesserung der Psychosozialen und Psychotherapeutischen Versorgung für Kinder und Jugendliche*; Kinder- und Jugendanwaltschaft Österreichs: Vienna, Austria, 2022. Available online: https://www.tirol.gv.at/fileadmin/themen/gesellschaft-soziales/kinder-und-jugendanwaltschaft/downloads/oeffentlichkeitsarbeit/psychosoziale_versorgung_positionspapier_2022.pdf (accessed on 22 May 2023).
95. Kurier. *Psychotherapeuten wollen regelmäßig an die Schulen*; Kurier: Vienna, Austria, 2021. Available online: https://kurier.at/politik/inland/psychotherapeuten-wollen-regelmaessig-an-die-schulen/401394435 (accessed on 22 May 2023).
96. Plener, P.; Klier, C.M.; Thun-Hohenstein, L.; Sevecke, K. Psychische Versorgung von Kindern und Jugendlichen in Österreich neu aufstellen: Dringender Handlungsbedarf besteht JETZT! *Neuropsychiatr* **2021**, *35*, 213–215. [CrossRef]

97. Burgenland.ORF.at. Psychotherapie auf Krankenschein: Lange Wartezeiten. Available online: Hppts://burgenland.orf.at/stories/3123255 (accessed on 22 May 2023).
98. Brettschneider, A.-K.; Hölling, H.; Schlack, R.; Ellert, U. Psychische Gesundheit von Jugendlichen in Deutschland. Ein Vergleich nach Migrationshintergrund und Herkunftsland. *Bundesgesundheitsbl* **2015**, *58*, 474–489. [CrossRef]
99. Quon, E.C.; McGrath, J.J. Subjective socioeconomic status and adolescent health: A meta-analysis. *Health Psychol.* **2014**, *33*, 433–447. [CrossRef] [PubMed]
100. Tan, J.J.X.; Kraus, M.W.; Carpenter, N.C.; Adler, N.E. The association between objective and subjective socioeconomic status and subjective well-being: A meta-analytic review. *Psychol. Bull.* **2020**, *146*, 970–1020. [CrossRef]

healthcare

MDPI

Article

Changes in Physical Activity and Depression among Korean Adolescents Due to COVID-19: Using Data from the 17th (2021) Korea Youth Risk Behavior Survey

Yong-Sook Eo [1] and Myo-Sung Kim [2,*]

1 College of Nursing, Dongguk University, Gyeongju 38066, Republic of Korea
2 Department of Nursing, Dong-Eui University, Busan 47340, Republic of Korea
* Correspondence: myosg@deu.ac.kr; Tel.: +82-51-890-2862

Abstract: This study aimed to identify changes in the health behavior and mental health of adolescents due to coronavirus disease 2019 (COVID-19) and the characteristics related to changes in physical activity and depression among health behavior changes. Data were extracted from the 17th Korea Youth Risk Behavior Web-based Survey of 54,835 adolescents. We classified the adolescents into three groups according to changes in physical activity and depression: no change, increased, or decreased. Independent variables included changes in health behavior due to COVID-19, demographic characteristics, health-related behavior, and mental health. Data were analyzed using the $\chi 2$-test and multiple logistic regressions using the SPSS Statistics 27 program. Changes in physical activity and depression showing negative changes due to the pandemic were related to factors such as having breakfast, current smoking, current drinking, stress, loneliness, despair, suicidal ideation, suicide plans, and suicide attempts. The related factors differed between the increased and decreased groups. The results of this study confirm that it is necessary to develop programs to promote the health of youth by considering the factors that affect physical activity and depression, which in turn influences the status of their health.

Keywords: adolescents; COVID-19; health behavior; mental health; physical activity

check for updates

Citation: Eo, Y.-S.; Kim, M.-S. Changes in Physical Activity and Depression among Korean Adolescents Due to COVID-19: Using Data from the 17th (2021) Korea Youth Risk Behavior Survey. *Healthcare* **2023**, *11*, 517. https://doi.org/10.3390/healthcare11040517

Academic Editor: Roberta Frontini

Received: 10 January 2023
Revised: 31 January 2023
Accepted: 8 February 2023
Published: 9 February 2023

1. Introduction

Since its first outbreak in 2019, coronavirus disease 2019 (COVID-19) emerged as a global pandemic and it continues to this day owing to the occurrence of new mutations [1]. Due to the severity of the pandemic, Korea implemented social distancing rules—the opening of schools was postponed for health and safety reasons, daily school activities were suspended due to remote learning, and overall time spent at home increased. As a result of these adjustments, teenagers experienced physical and psychological changes in daily life [2,3]. It has been shown that COVID-19 affects the school lives of adolescents as well as their psychological, emotional, health, and physical development [4]. In addition, these effects show differential effects on gender, age, region, and family background [4,5].

Several studies around the world also have found that the COVID-19 pandemic has not only impacted children's and adolescents' physical health but also their mental health and well-being. An Italian study of children and adolescents aged 6–18 years found that 61.3% of participants were more concerned about the future, 46% reported sleep difficulties, and 72.8% reported experiencing more attention difficulty than before the pandemic [6]. Another study in Germany showed that children and adolescents felt sadder and less well during this period than children and adolescents before the pandemic [7]. Their findings also indicated that well-being and sadness were positively associated with physical activities. Similar results were also found in a Canadian study on children aged 9–15 that 37.6% of participants felt bored, and 31% of them were more worried than before the pandemic in 2020 [8].

A key indicator of adolescent health development is physical activity—it affects lifelong health, including physical health (such as obesity and physical strength) and mental health (such as anxiety and depression) [9,10]. Previous studies have shown that the pandemic reduced the time spent engaging in physical activity among adolescents due to school closures and home confinement [11–14]. In addition, due to prolonged lockdowns causing higher levels of stress, children and adolescents experienced depression, anxiety, and fearful emotions, which increased the uptake of mental health counseling [15]. Physical activity is correlated with psychological health and can improve mental health [16]. According to a scoping review of adult and child studies on changes in physical activity during the pandemic, changes in physical activity levels were the most evaluated results, followed by a relation between physical and mental health issues [14]. However, studies investigating the factors that affect the positive or negative changes in physical activity and depression caused by COVID-19 are insufficient. More attention should be paid to adolescent activities and depression.

Therefore, the aims of this study are as follows:

1. To look at the changes in physical activity and depression in adolescents due to the pandemic.
2. To investigate characteristics related to changes in physical activity and depression among the changes in health behaviors.

2. Materials and Methods

2.1. Study Design

This study employed a descriptive correlation methodology, using raw data from the 17th Korea Youth Risk Behavior Web-based Survey (KYRBS), which was conducted in 2021.

2.2. Participants

The KYRBS is a nationally representative survey and is conducted annually to understand the current status of the health behaviors of adolescents. The questionnaires of the survey are focused on health status and health behaviors of adolescents and include potential health risks issues such as smoking, drinking, physical activity, eating habits, obesity, mental health, sexual behavior, internet and mobile use, drugs, and mental health

The data of 54,835 participants were used in the study by excluding 13 participants who did not respond to items concerning changes in physical activity due to COVID-19. Data were collected using a unique anonymous participant number and anonymity and confidentiality were maintained throughout data collection. Consent was obtained from all participants at the time of data collection.

2.3. Measures

2.3.1. Changes in Health Behavior Due to COVID-19

Changes in health behavior due to COVID-19 were classified into five categories from greatly increased to greatly decreased when compared to the pre-pandemic period for a total of five areas (physical activity, having breakfast, drinking, smoking, and depression). These were recategorized as "greatly increased" and "increased" in the "increased group", "decreased" and "greatly decreased" in the "decreased group", and "no change" in the "no change group".

2.3.2. Demographic and Sociological Characteristics

The demographic characteristics of the subjects were analyzed based on gender, school level, residence area, changes in economic status due to COVID-19, whether participants were living with family, and subjective health status. Gender was categorized as "male" and "female", school level was "middle school" and "high school", and residence area was categorized as "large cities (metropolitan cities with a population of more than 500,000)" and "small and medium-sized cities or below with a total population of less than 500,000 or around 100,000". Changes in economic status were categorized as "difficulty" and "no change" and whether participants were living with a family member was categorized as "living together" and "not living together". For subjective health status, participants were asked "how do you rate your health?". Responses of "very healthy", "healthy", "normally healthy" were classified as "healthy", and "unhealthy" and "very unhealthy" were classified as "unhealthy".

2.3.3. Health-Related Behavior

Having breakfast, smoking, and drinking were used as health-related behavior variables. For having breakfast variables, the question "In the last 7 days, how many days did you eat breakfast (excluding milk or juice only)?" was used. Having breakfast more than 6 days a week was categorized as having breakfast regularly and having breakfast 5 days or less per week was classified as "not having breakfast regularly". For currently smoking variables, the question "In the past 30 days, how many days have you smoked at least one regular cigarette?" was used. "No" was recorded as "non-smoking" and "more than 1–2 days a month" was recorded as "smoking". For currently drinking variables, the question "How many days have you had at least one drink in the last 30 days?" was used. "No" was recorded as "not drinking" and "More than 1–2 days a month" was recorded as "drinking". For physical activity, participants were asked "In the last seven days, how many days did you spend more than 60 min a day on physical activities where your heart rate increased, or you were out of breath?". Responses of "5 days a week or more" was classified as "yes" and "4 days a week or less" was classified as "no"

2.3.4. Mental Health

For mental health variables, stress, loneliness, despair, suicidal ideation, suicide plans, and suicide attempts were used. For stress, the question "How much stress do you normally feel?" was used, from "Not at all" to "Feel a little" to "no", and "Feel a lot" to "Feel very much" to "yes". For loneliness, the question "How often have you felt lonely in the past 12 months?" was used. "I felt lonely at all or almost never" was recorded as "no" and "sometimes, often, always felt lonely" was recorded as "yes". For feelings of despair, the question "Have you ever felt sadness or despair enough to stop your daily life for 2 weeks in the last 12 months?" was used. It was categorized as "no" and "yes". For suicidal ideation, the question, "Have you seriously thought of suicide in the past 12 months?" was used. It was categorized as "no" and "yes". For the suicide plan, the question "Have you made a specific plan to commit suicide in the past 12 months?" was used. It was categorized as "no" and "yes". Finally, for suicide attempts, the question "Have you attempted suicide in the past 12 months?" was used. It was categorized as "no" and "yes".

2.4. Data Collection

The KYRBS has been published annually since 2005 to identify the status and trends of Korean adolescent health behaviors. The 17th KYRBS is an anonymous, self-reported, online survey of middle and high school students. The sampling process was conducted during the stages of population stratification, sampling distribution, and sampling. Accordingly, the population was divided into 117 strata, using the stratification variables of 39 regional groups and school levels (middle school, general high school, and specialized high school) across the country. The sample number of schools was distributed by applying the proportional distribution method so that the population composition ratio and sample composition ratio for each stratification variable matched for each of the 400 middle and high schools. For the sampling unit, a phylogenetic sampling method was used with the school as the primary sampling unit and a randomly selected class as the secondary sampling unit. Prior to data collection, sample schools and classes were selected, and student status was registered. The teachers in charge of survey support at the sample school were selected and trained. They explained the purpose of the survey to the participants who submitted written consent. All students in the sample class were surveyed excluding long-term absentees, differently abled students who could not participate in the survey on their own, and students with reading disabilities. The survey was conducted by completing a pre-set online survey using a school computer or mobile device (tablet, personal computer, smartphone). The survey took between 45 and 50 min.

2.5. Statistical Analysis

To explore the characteristics of the multiple-sample design, multiple-sample design data analysis was used by stratifying multistage probability sampling of the raw KYRBS data. IBM SPSS Statistics 27.0 program (IBM Corp., Armonk, NY, USA) was used to reflect the integrated layer (Strata), cluster variable (Cluster), weight (W), and finite population correction coefficient (FPC), which were present in the raw data and analyzed.

First, the demographic characteristics, health-related behaviors, and mental health of adolescents were analyzed by frequency (applied sample size) and percentage (applied weighted value).

Second, changes in health-related behaviors and mental health due to COVID-19 were analyzed using frequency (applied sample size) and percentage (applied weighted value).

Third, differences between physical activity and depression caused by COVID-19 according to the demographic, health-related behavioral, and mental health characteristics of adolescents were analyzed using a composite sample Rao–Scott $\chi2$-test.

Fourth, to analyze the effect of changes in physical activity due to COVID-19, multiple logistic regression analysis was conducted on the group without changes in physical activity and depression as the reference group, and the increased and decreased groups were the comparison group.

3. Results

3.1. Participant Characteristics

The KYRBS research subjects were Korean middle and high school students and a total of 800 schools—400 middle schools and 400 high schools—were enrolled. The total number of subjects recruited was 59,066, from 796 schools (399 middle schools, 397 high schools), and 54,848 students participated in the survey. The teachers in charge of survey support had a large workload, and there was reduced access to the computer room due to COVID-19; therefore, the participation rate based on the number of students was 92.9%.

Table 1 shows the demographic characteristics, health-related behaviors, and mental health characteristics of participants. The gender distribution of the participants was 51.7% male and 48.3% female. At the school level, 51.0% were in middle school, 49.0% were in high school, 58.1% were in small and medium cities, and 41.9% were in large (metropolitan) cities. Regarding changes in economic conditions due to COVID-19, 70.1% of respondents said there was no change, and 29.9% said that their family economics were more difficult than before. Of the participants, 96.2% lived with their family members, while 3.8% did not live with their family or parents. Regarding subjective health status, 90.8% of participants saw themselves as healthy, while 9.2% felt unhealthy. As for currently physical activity, 14.6% of respondents were spending more than 5 days a week on physical activities, while 85.4% were spending less than that.

As for the health-related behavioral characteristics of participants, 64.8% of participants had breakfast less than five days a week, 4.5% of the participants were currently smoking, and 10.8% were currently drinking alcohol.

The results for the mental health characteristics of participants showed that 38.8% were stressed, 52.3% felt lonely, 26.8% felt hopeless, 12.7% had suicidal thoughts, 4.0% had a specific suicide plan, and 2.2% had attempted suicide.

Table 1. Participants' characteristics (*n* = 54,835).

Characteristics	Categories	*n* (%)
Gender	Male	28,393 (51.7)
	Female	26,442 (48.3)
School type	Middle school	30,006 (51.0)
	High school	24,829 (49.0)
Region of residence	M-S and rural city	30,978 (58.1)
	Metropolitan	23,857 (41.9)
Economic change with COVID-19	None	38,128 (70.1)
	Yes	16,707 (29.9)
Reside with family	No	2421 (3.8)
	Yes	52,414 (96.2)
Subjective health status	Unhealthy	5020 (9.2)
	Healthy	49,815 (90.8)
Current physical activity	None	46,486 (85.4)
	Yes	8349 (14.6)
Eat breakfast	No	35,649 (64.8)
	Yes	19,186 (35.2)
Current Smoking	None	52,428 (95.5)
	Yes	2407 (4.5)
Current drinking	None	49,012 (89.2)
	Yes	5822 (10.8)
Stress	None	33,593 (61.2)
	Yes	21,242 (38.8)
Loneliness	None	26,315 (47.7)
	Yes	28,520 (52.3)
Despair	None	40,148 (73.2)
	Yes	14,687 (26.8)
Suicidal ideation	None	47,880 (87.3)
	Yes	6955 (12.7)
Suicidal plan	None	52,630 (96.0)
	Yes	2205 (4.0)
Suicidal attempt	None	53,590 (97.8)
	Yes	1245 (2.2)

M-S = medium- and small-sized; *n* (%) = *n*: unweighted; %: weighted.

3.2. Changes in Health-Related Behavior and Mental Health Due to COVID-19

Table 2 shows changes in health-related behaviors and mental health caused by COVID-19. During COVID-19, 19.4% of participants increased their physical activity while 49.1% of them had decreased physical activity. Compared to before COVID-19, the group which increased its behavior missed breakfast more by 14.3%, drank more by 2.8%, smoked more by 1%, or felt depressed more by 36.9%. Meanwhile, the group who decreased their behavior did so by missing breakfast less by 13.1%, consuming alcohol less by 15%, smoking less by 15%, or feeling depressed less by 9.7%.

Table 2. Changes in health-related behavior and mental health due to COVID-19 (*n* = 54,835).

Variables	Categories	*n* (%)
	Increased change	11,094 (19.4)
Physical activity	No change	17,740 (31.5)
	Decreased change	26,001 (49.1)
	Increased change	7912 (14.3)
Missing breakfast	No change	39,791 (72.6)
	Decreased change	7132 (13.1)
	Increased change	1518 (2.8)
Drinking	No change	44,659 (82.1)
	Decreased change	8425 (15.0)
	Increased change	527 (1.0)
Smoking	No change	45,078 (83.9)
	Decreased change	8330 (15.0)
	Increased change	19,730 (36.9)
Depression	No change	29,562 (53.4)
	Decreased change	5543 (9.7)

n (%) = *n*: unweighted; %: weighted.

3.3. Differences between Physical Activity and Depression Caused by COVID-19 According to the Characteristics of Adolescents

Table 3 shows the differences between physical activity and depression caused by COVID-19 according to the characteristics of adolescents. There was a statistically significant difference in physical activity in the following characteristics: gender (χ^2 = 1667.922, p < 0.001), school level (χ^2 = 368.963, p < 0.001), residence area (χ^2 = 48.187, p < 0.001), changes in economic status due to COVID-19 (χ^2 = 160.760, p < 0.001), subjective health status (χ^2 = 402.359, p < 0.001), having breakfast (χ^2 = 19.917, p < 0.001), current smoking (χ^2 = 177.256, p < 0.001), current drinking (χ^2 = 144.934, p < 0.001), stress (χ^2 = 309.900, p < 0.001), loneliness (χ^2 = 460.128 p < 0.001), despair (χ^2 = 108.957, p < 0.001), suicidal ideation (χ^2 = 114.371, p < 0.001), suicide plan (χ^2 = 41.676, p < 0.001), and suicide attempts (χ^2 = 15.851, p = 0.001).

Table 3. Participants' characteristics, health-related behaviors, mental health, and relationship to COVID-19 physical activity change and depression change (n = 54,835).

Variables	Categories	Physical Activity				Depression			
		No Change (n = 17,740) n (%)	Increase Group (n = 11,094) n (%)	Decrease Group (n = 26,001) n (%)	χ^2 (p)	No Change (n = 29,562) n (%)	Increase Group (n = 19,730) n (%)	Decrease Group (n = 5543) n (%)	χ^2 (p)
Gender	Male	9375 (53.3)	7492 (67.6)	11,526 (44.4)	1667.922 (<0.001)	16,962 (57.5)	7679 (39.3)	3752 (66.9)	2135.019 (<0.001)
	Female	8365 (46.7)	3602 (32.4)	14,475 (55.6)		12,051 (42.5)	12,051 (60.7)	1791 (33.1)	
School type	Middle school	9355 (48.3)	7030 (59.3)	13,621 (49.4)	368.963 (<0.001)	16,169 (50.8)	10,221 (48.4)	3616 (61.6)	292.314 (<0.001)
	High school	8385 (51.7)	4064 (40.7)	12,380 (50.6)		13,393 (49.2)	9509 (51.6)	1927 (38.4)	
Region of residence	M-S & rural city	10,303 (59.3)	6515 (59.8)	14,160 (56.6)	48.187 (<0.001)	16,669 (57.8)	11,105 (58.2)	3204 (59.1)	3.203 (0.843)
	Metropolitan	7437 (40.7)	4579 (40.2)	11,841 (43.4)		12,893 (42.2)	8625 (41.8)	2339 (40.9)	
Economic change with COVID-19	None	12,970 (73.6)	7398 (67.1)	17,760 (69.1)	160.760 (<0.001)	21,867 (74.5)	12,537 (64.4)	3724 (67.7)	593.554 (<0.001)
	Yes	4770 (26.4)	3696 (32.9)	8241 (30.9)		7695 (25.5)	7193 (35.6)	1819 (32.3)	
Reside with family	No	779 (3.8)	532 (4.4)	1110 (3.6)	13.999 (0.053)	28,440 (96.7)	18,663 (95.3)	5311 (96.6)	66.680 (<0.001)
	Yes	16,961 (96.2)	10,562 (95.6)	24,891 (96.4)		1122 (3.3)	1067 (4.7)	232 (3.4)	
Subjective health status	Unhealthy	1365 (7.6)	637 (5.7)	3018 (11.7)	402.359 (<0.001)	27,696 (93.6)	16,953 (86.0)	5166 (92.9)	853.635 (<0.001)
	Healthy	16,375 (92.4)	10,457 (94.3)	22,983 (88.3)		1866 (6.4)	2777 (14.0)	377 (7.1)	
Eat breakfast	No	11,734 (66.0)	7235 (65.1)	16,680 (63.9)	19.917 (<0.001)	18,711 (63.0)	13,231 (66.8)	3707 (67.3)	88.202 (<0.001)
	Yes	6006 (34.0)	3859 (34.9)	9321 (36.1)		10,851 (37.0)	6499 (33.2)	1836 (32.7)	
Current Smoking	None	16,872 (94.9)	10,443 (93.7)	25,113 (96.6)	177.256 (<0.001)	28,393 (95.9)	18,741 (95.0)	5294 (95.4)	24.927 (<0.001)
	Yes	868 (5.1)	651 (6.3)	888 (3.4)		1169 (4.1)	989 (5.0)	249 (4.6)	
Current drinking	None	15,820 (88.9)	9626 (86.4)	23,566 (90.6)	144.934 (<0.001)	26,769 (90.4)	17,268 (87.5)	4975 (89.5)	107.126 (<0.001)
	Yes	1920 (11.1)	1468 (13.6)	2434 (9.4)		2793 (9.6)	2461 (12.5)	568 (10.5)	
Stress	None	11,595 (65.4)	7039 (63.7)	14,959 (57.6)	309.900 (<0.001)	7669 (25.7)	11,974 (60.2)	1599 (28.9)	6234.939 (<0.001)
	Yes	6145 (34.6)	4055 (36.3)	11,042 (42.4)		21,893 (74.3)	7756 (39.8)	3944 (71.1)	
Loneliness	None	9539 (53.6)	5526 (49.2)	11,250 (43.3)	460.128 (<0.001)	18,557 (62.8)	4222 (21.9)	3536 (62.7)	8564.969 (<0.001)
	Yes	8201 (46.4)	5568 (50.8)	14,751 (56.7)		11,005 (38.0)	15,508 (78.1)	2007 (37.3)	

Table 3. *Cont.*

Variables	Categories	Physical Activity				Depression			
		No Change (n = 17,740) n (%)	Increase Group (n = 11,094) n (%)	Decrease Group (n = 26,001) n (%)	χ^2 (p)	No Change (n = 29,562) n (%)	Increase Group (n = 19,730) n (%)	Decrease Group (n = 5543) n (%)	χ^2 (p)
Despair	None	13,527 (76.0)	7878 (71.0)	18,743 (72.3)	108.957 (<0.001)	24,826 (84.0)	10,806 (55.4)	4516 (81.3)	5194.104 (<0.001)
	Yes	4213 (24.0)	3216 (29.0)	7258 (27.7)		4736 (16.0)	8924 (44.6)	1027 (18.7)	
Suicidal ideation	None	15,865 (89.4)	9683 (87.2)	22,332 (86.0)	114.371 (<0.001)	27,871 (94.4)	14,858 (75.7)	5151 (92.3)	3881.061 (<0.001)
	Yes	1875 (10.6)	1411 (12.8)	3669 (14.0)		1691 (5.6)	4872 (24.3)	392 (7.7)	
Suicidal plan	None	17,145 (96.6)	10,561 (95.0)	24,924 (95.9)	41.676 (<0.001)	29,016 (98.1)	18,242 (92.6)	5372 (96.8)	941.879 (<0.001)
	Yes	595 (3.4)	533 (5.0)	1077 (4.1)		546 (1.9)	1488 (7.4)	171 (3.2)	
Suicidal attempt	None	17,367 (97.9)	10,796 (97.3)	25,427 (97.9)	15.851 (0.001)	29,281 (99.1)	18,853 (95.7)	5456 (98.4)	646.924 (<0.001)
	Yes	373 (2.1)	298 (2.7)	574 (2.1)		281 (0.1)	877 (4.3)	87 (1.6)	

M-S = medium- and small sized; n (%) = n: unweighted; %: weighted.

Among the various characteristics of adolescents, depression showed statistically significant differences in all characteristics except residence area. In other words, there was a significant difference in gender (χ^2 = 2135.019, p < 0.001), school level (χ^2 = 292.314, p < 0.001), change in economic status due to COVID-19 (χ^2 = 593.554, p < 0.001), living with family (χ^2 = 66.680, p < 0.001), subjective health status (χ^2 = 853.635, p < 0.001), having breakfast (χ^2 = 88.202, p < 0.001), current smoking (χ^2 = 24.927, p < 0.001), current drinking (χ^2 = 107.126, p < 0.001), stress (χ^2 = 6234.939, p < 0.001), loneliness (χ^2 = 8564.969 p < 0.001), despair (χ^2 = 5194.104, p < 0.001), suicidal ideation (χ^2 = 3881.061, p < 0.001), suicide plan (χ^2 = 941.879, p < 0.001), and suicide attempts (χ^2 = 646.924, p < 0.001).

3.4. Factors Affecting Changes in Physical Activity and Depression Due to COVID-19

Before conducting logistic regression analysis, we examined the confounding variables that affect physical activity and depression due to COVID-19. These variables were gender, school of type, region of residence, change in economic status due to COVID-19, reside with family, and subjective health status. After controlling these variables and using "no change" in physical activity and depression as the reference group, the factors affecting changes in physical activity and depression due to COVID-19 are shown in Table 4.

The number of adolescents with increased physical activity compared to before COVID-19 were lower in having breakfast (aOR = 0.93), currently drinking (aOR = 0.85), loneliness (aOR = 0.90), despair (aOR = 0.82), and suicidal plan (aOR = 0.76) than those who reported no change. Compared to the pre-pandemic, adolescents whose physical activity decreased were higher in current smoking (aOR = 1.53), current drinking (aOR = 1.15), stressed (aOR = 1.24), and attempted suicide (aOR = 1.33) than those who reported no change. On the other hand, adolescents whose physical activity decreased were lower in having breakfast (aOR = 0.90), loneliness (aOR = 0.70), and suicidal ideation (aOR = 0.83).

Compared to the pre-pandemic, adolescents with increased rates of depression were higher among students who were currently smoking (aOR = 1.31) and experiencing stress (aOR = 2.38). On the other hand, loneliness (aOR = 0.27), despair (aOR = 0.56), suicidal ideation (aOR = 0.49), and attempted suicide (aOR = 0.84) had lower indications of depression. Compared to the pre-pandemic period, the group with reduced depression was higher among those having regular breakfast (aOR = 1.19), stressed adolescents (aOR = 1.12), and those who experienced loneliness (aOR = 1.09). On the other hand, it was found to be lower among students in feeling despair (aOR= 0.90) and experiencing suicide plans (aOR = 0.73).

Table 4. Multinomial logistic regression for predictors of COVID-19 exchange physical activity and depression among adolescents (n = 54,835).

Variables	Physical Activity				Depression			
	Increase Group (n = 11,094)		Decrease Group (n = 26,001)		Increase Group (n = 19,730)		Decrease Group (n = 5543)	
	aOR (95% CI)	p	aOR (95% CI)	p	aOR (95% CI)	p	aOR (95% CI)	p
Eat breakfast	0.93 (0.88, 0.98)	0.005	0.90 (0.86, 0.93)	<0.001	0.99 (0.95, 1.03)	0.645	1.19 (1.11, 1.27)	<0.001
Current smoking	0.93 (0.83, 1.05)	0.265	1.53 (1.38, 1.71)	<0.001	1.31 (1.18, 1.46)	<0.001	0.98 (0.83, 1.17)	0.833
Current drinking	0.85 (0.78, 0.92)	<0.001	1.15 (1.07, 1.24)	<0.001	1.01 (0.94, 1.08)	0.837	0.95 (0.86, 1.06)	0.394
Stress	0.95 (0.90, 1.01)	0.093	1.24 (1.18, 1.30)	<0.001	2.38 (2.28, 2.49)	<0.001	1.12 (1.04, 1.20)	0.003
Loneliness	0.90 (0.85, 0.95)	<0.001	0.70 (0.67, 0.73)	<0.001	0.27 (0.25, 0.28)	<0.001	1.09 (1.02, 1.16)	0.013
Despair	0.82 (0.77, 0.88)	<0.001	1.03 (0.98, 1.09)	0.246	0.56 (0.53, 0.58)	<0.001	0.90 (0.83, 0.97)	0.009
Suicidal ideation	0.99 (0.90, 1.09)	0.870	0.83 (0.76, 0.89)	<0.001	0.49 (0.45, 0.53)	<0.001	0.88 (0.77, 1.01)	0.064
Suicidal plan	0.76 (0.66, 0.88)	0.001	1.00 (0.89, 1.14)	0.948	1.04 (0.90, 1.20)	0.610	0.73 (0.59, 0.90)	0.003
Suicidal attempt	1.09 (0.90, 1.32)	0.369	1.33 (1.19, 1.62)	<0.001	0.84 (0.71, 0.99)	0.042	0.82 (0.63, 1.08)	0.156

Notes. The reference group was adolescents who reported no change; aOR = adjusted odds ratio, CI = 95% confidence interval.

4. Discussion

This study used raw data from the 17th KYRBS to identify changes in adolescents' health behaviors due to COVID-19 and analyzed the characteristics related to changes in physical activity and depression among these changes in health behaviors. It was found that drinking and smoking among adolescents before and after the pandemic showed a positive change, with the decreased group (15% each) being higher than the increased group (drinking 2.8%, smoking 1%). Not having breakfast remained at similar levels for both the decreased group (13.1%) and increased group (14.3%), but physical activity was higher in the decreased group (49.1%) than in the increased group (19.4%), and the rate of experiencing depression was higher in the increased group (36.9%) than in the decreased group (9.7%). This indicates that COVID-19 is associated with a decrease in physical activity and an increase in depression among adolescents. The decrease in drinking and smoking in adolescents is consistent with the results of the National Survey on Drug Use and Health (NSDUH) conducted among US adolescents (12–17 years old), which shows the current smoking rate (from 2.3% in 2019 to 1.4% in 2020) and the current drinking rate (from 9.4% in 2019 to 8.2% in 2020) were decreased [17].

Many previous studies have reported an increase in sedentary activity time and a decrease in physical activity time [11–14,18,19] and various psychological problems, including depression and anxiety during the pandemic [19,20]. These changes in adolescent health behavior were related to social distancing according to the rules during the pandemic, namely suspension of daily educational activities, such as postponement of school openings, remote classes, home confinement, and reduction of interaction outside the home [16,18,21]. In the case of adolescents, school life and interaction with peers are important factors that positively affect various social, physiological, and psychological adaptations [22]. A study of adolescents in southern China conducted immediately after schools reopened found that those with higher levels of physical activity were less likely to show symptoms of depression, compared to those with lower levels of physical activity [23]. Although the WHO recommends vigorous physical activity of about 60 min a day in adolescence, 81% of adolescents aged 11 to 17 worldwide lack physical activity [24]. In the case of Korean adolescents, only 13.9% of adolescents participated in physical activity for at least 60 min a day 5 days a week, which was among the lowest in the world before the pandemic [25,26]. As this lack of physical activity has worsened during the pandemic [22], it is necessary to prepare various ways to promote youth physical activity post-pandemic.

In this study, the result shows that the group with changes in physical activity due to COVID-19 was 68.5% which is more than twice as high as the group without change (31.5%), and the group with reduced physical activity was more than the increased group. The group with depression changes due to the pandemic was 46.6% which is lower than the group without change (53.4%), and the group with increased depression was higher than the reduced group. In addition, the factors affecting the increasing and decreasing groups of physical activity and depression were different. Among health-related behaviors, having regular breakfast was associated with a decrease in depression; current smoking was associated with a decrease in physical activity but an increase in depression; and current drinking was associated with a decrease in physical activity. Among the mental health characteristics, it was confirmed that stress was associated with a decrease in physical activity and an increase in depression. In addition, it was found that loneliness was associated with a decrease in depression while suicide attempt was associated with a decrease in physical activity. Considering these variables, it is important to find a way to improve the physical and mental health of adolescents during the pandemic period.

Compared to the group with no change in having breakfast, the group with increased physical activity had breakfast 0.93 times less, the group with reduced physical activity had it 0.90 times less, and the group with reduced depression had it 1.19 times more. Current smoking was 1.53 times higher in the decreased physical activity group and 1.31 times higher in the increased depression group. Current drinking was 0.85 times lower in the increased physical activity group and 1.15 times higher in the decreased physical activity group.

This differs from a study [21] that found irregular breakfast as a factor related to obesity and depression in adolescents during the pandemic and current smoking and current drinking as factors related to the experience of depression. School meals were stopped when school was suspended due to the pandemic, and local care services weakened, and this resulted in children missing meals at an increased rate, and they experienced a care gap [27,28] and the obesity level of children and adolescents worsened. When indices of metabolic syndromes, such as cholesterol and triglycerides, are elevated [4] it may affect physical health; therefore, it is necessary to manage the diet of adolescents who are at risk of under-nutrition. In addition, looking at the modifiable risk and protective factors of adolescents identified in previous studies, physical activity and a healthy diet reduced depression [29], having a daily breakfast was significantly associated with better mental health outcomes [30], and high alcohol consumption and smoking were associated with higher levels of depression [29–32]. To reduce the deterioration of dietary life indicators, the increase in obesity rate, and depression in adolescents before and after the pandemic, it is necessary to continuously evaluate the impact of lifestyle changes related to the pandemic and create an educational environment to promote health of youth.

Compared to the group with no change in stress, the reduced physical activity group was 1.24 times more stressed, the increased depression group was 2.38 times more stressed, and the reduced depression group was 1.12 times more stressed among all groups. This is similar to a study [32] in which participants who reported negative changes in physical activity had higher levels of stress symptoms. Likewise, it was similar to another study [21], where stress perception was found to be a factor related to the experience of depression. In addition, pandemic-related stress has been reported to have a significant effect on physical activity levels and depression [25].

Compared to the group with no change in the pandemic, the number of adolescents who experienced loneliness was 0.90 times lower in the increased physical activity group, 0.70 times lower in the decreased physical activity group, 0.27 times lower in the increased depression group, and 1.09 times higher in the decreased depression group. Compared to the group with no change, the number of adolescents who experienced despair was 0.82 times lower in the increased physical activity group, 0.56 times lower in the increased depression group, and 0.90 times lower in the depression decreased group. In previous studies, social isolation was found to increase loneliness in some people, and it was associated with increased depression and suicidal thoughts [33,34]. In addition, the duration of loneliness showed a stronger correlation with mental health symptoms than the intensity of loneliness [34]. In particular, the severance of interpersonal relationships has a great influence on psychological changes in adolescents. A decrease in social interaction is a major risk factor for mental health, and disconnection from social relationships, that is, loneliness, negatively affects the physical and mental health of adolescents [35]. Therefore, it is necessary to provide preventive support and early intervention, where possible, during social isolation, including forced isolation, and mitigation of mental health problems.

The frequency of suicidal ideation, suicide plans, and suicide attempts were significantly higher among the decreased physical activity and increased depression groups than in the other groups. However, as shown in the multiple logistic regression analysis, the number of adolescents having suicidal thoughts was 0.83 times lower in the decreased physical activity group and 0.49 times lower in the increased depression group, respectively, compared to the group with no change before and after COVID-19. The number of adolescents with experience of suicide planning were 0.76 times lower in the physical activity increased group and 0.73 times lower in the depression decreased group, respectively. The number of adolescents who had attempted suicide were found to be 1.33 times higher in the decreased physical activity group, confirming an association between suicide attempts and reduced physical activity. In a meta-analysis of suicidal behavior during the pandemic [36], when compared with the event rates in pre-pandemic studies, suicidal ideation (4.68%), suicide attempts (4.68%), and self-harm (9.63%) increased during the pandemic, and it differed according to age (younger people), gender (women), and geopolitics (individuals from democratic countries). However, in a study investigating the association between the pandemic and suicide-related behavior among Korean adolescents, there were fewer suicide-related behaviors, including suicidal thoughts, suicide plans, and suicide attempts, in the 2020 study than in the 2019 study [37]. Previous studies have reported a decrease in suicides since the start of the pandemic [38], and rates of suicidal ideation and attempts in pediatric emergency departments were higher for several months in 2020 compared to 2019, but this was due to COVID-19-related stress, which coincided with the period when the community response was high [39]. As such, the rate of suicide-related behaviors may vary depending on the stage of the pandemic. Therefore, it is necessary to identify the trend of suicidal behavior during the pandemic, the long-term mental health, and economic impact of the pandemic, and increase preparedness to respond to changes in the situation. In addition, there are many studies examining the relationship between depression and suicide-related behaviors, but they do not pay attention to the relationship between changes in physical activity levels and suicide attempts. Therefore, it is necessary to investigate the relationship between physical activity and suicide-related behaviors.

Demographic variables that showed statistical differences in physical activity and depression could act as confounding variables, so they were controlled for multiple logistic regression analysis. Among these variables, we found that changes in economic status due to COVID-19 and subjective health status affect changes in physical activity and depression in adolescents and show a similar pattern of increase or decrease. However, it was confirmed that the increase or decrease in physical activity or depression showed distinctly different patterns according to gender and school level. In other words, the group that showed an increase in physical activity and a decrease in depression had a high proportion of male and middle school students, while the opposite patterns were found in female and high school students.

Studies conducted during the pandemic have analyzed the relationship between physical activity and gender [11,40]. A study that analyzed the level and characteristics of moderate-to-vigorous physical activity (MVPA), according to gender and number of school physical activities for middle school students during the pandemic found that female students' physical activity levels were lower than those of male students [22]. Although it was relatively low, it has been reported that the decrease in physical activity in men was greater than that in women. International studies that longitudinally analyzed the level of physical activity before and during the pandemic also reported that the decrease in physical activity in men during the pandemic was greater than that in women [11,40].

Research has suggested that female adolescents perform light exercise, such as home training, to control their increased weight during the pandemic [41]. In COVID-19, it has been reported that stress is higher among those who perform a high level of low-intensity physical activity [25]; therefore, it is necessary to plan a physical activity program suitable for these activity differences (intensity and duration) according to gender. In addition, previous studies have shown that male students have higher levels of loneliness, anxiety, and depression due to COVID-19 than female students [25], which is in contrast with the results of this study. There is a suggestion that male students who participate in competitive activities suffer from negative psychological states due to the restrictions on physical activities [42]. However, for female students, who have lower levels of stress, loneliness, anxiety, and depression, there is a possibility that they are satisfied with light and enjoyable sports or activities during remote learning. Thus, to increase positive psychological factors, it is necessary to consider gender and the level of physical activity.

A previous study found that 17-year-old high school students had significantly lower levels of physical activity than 13-year-old or 15-year-old middle school students [43]. However, Choi et al. showed that the change in physical activity practice rate between the first and second years of the pandemic increased again for middle school students (1.5%p) and among female students increased only in middle school students (0.7%p). In the case of the depression rate during the pandemic, it decreased by (−2.2%p, −1.0%p) for female middle and high school students but increased among male and female middle school students (3.9%p, 2.0%p) [21]. In addition to the school level, the timing of the survey and the gender of the participants have an impact on results; thus, it is necessary to consider gender, school level, and the timing of the survey in future research.

The strength of this study is that it analyzes data on changes in physical activity and depression in adolescents and the factors that are associated with those changes. In particular, this study shows a difference in the factors that may associate with the increase and decrease of physical activity and depression. This needs to be considered when planning a program to promote physical activity and reduce depression among adolescents after the pandemic. As for the limitation of this study, it used secondary data and subjective indicators in relation to the changes in health behaviors rather than objective indicators of physical activity or depression. Therefore, this must be taken into consideration when interpreting the results. In addition, there is a limit to generalizing to other Asian adolescents as country-specific response guidelines in the pandemic situation may have different results on adolescents' physical activity or depression.

5. Conclusions

This study observed positive changes in drinking and smoking among adolescents before and after the pandemic, with a larger number of adolescents in the decreased group rather than in the increased group. However, there were many negative changes related to physical activity and depression in the decreased and increased groups, respectively. The changes in physical activity and depression, which showed negative changes due to COVID-19, were related to complex factors such as health-related behaviors and mental health, and it was found that the related factors differed depending on whether the group behavior increased or decreased. As revealed in the results of this study, it is necessary to develop an educational environment and program for youth health promotion by considering factors affecting physical activity and depression. It is also necessary to develop strategies and programs for promotion of physical activity in anticipation of future disruptions resulting from the pandemic.

Author Contributions: Conceptualization, Y.-S.E. and M.-S.K.; methodology, Y.-S.E. and M.-S.K.; validation, Y.-S.E. and M.-S.K.; writing—original draft preparation, Y.-S.E. and M.-S.K.; writing—review and editing, Y.-S.E. and M.-S.K. All authors have read and agreed to the published version of the manuscript.

Funding: This research received no external funding.

Institutional Review Board Statement: The study was conducted in accordance with the Declaration of Helsinki and approved by the Ethics Committee of Korea Disease Control and Prevention Agency (National approval statistics number 117058 and 1 August 2022).

Informed Consent Statement: Subject consent was waived due to the use of secondary data for this study.

Data Availability Statement: No new data were created or analyzed in this study. Data sharing is not applicable to this article.

Conflicts of Interest: The authors declare no conflict of interest.

References

1. World Health Organization (WHO). COVID-19 Explorer. Available online: https://worldhealthorg.shinyapps.io/covid (accessed on 15 October 2022).
2. Korea Disease Control and Prevention Agency. Guidelines to Prevent the Spread of COVID-19. Available online: https://www.kdca.go.kr/board/boardApi.es-mid=a20507050000&bid=0080 (accessed on 15 October 2022).
3. Ministry of Education. 2020 Education Response to COVID-19. 9 May 2021. Available online: https://moe.go.kr/sn3hcv/doc.html?fn=0a9e0f4cfad737d1ecbb33690e7ec29c&rs=/upload/synap/202301 (accessed on 15 October 2022).
4. Kim, S.E.; Park, C.H. 2021 Korea Children and Youth Panel Survey: Data Analysis Report—COVID-19 and Changes in Youth Life and Psychology. In *Research Report*; Report No.: 21-R13-1; Korea National Youth Policy Institute: Sejong, Korea, 2021.
5. Dallolio, L.; Marini, S.; Masini, A.; Toselli, S.; Stagni, R.; Bisi, M.C.; Gori, D.; Tessari, A.; Sansavini, A.; Lanari, M.; et al. The impact of COVID-19 on physical activity behaviour in Italian primary school children: A comparison before and during pandemic considering gender differences. *BMC Public Health* **2022**, *22*, 52. [CrossRef]
6. Salussolia, A.; Lenzi, J.; Montalti, M.; Rallo, F.; Paternò, M.; Agosta, M.; Resi, D.; Stillo, M.; Guaraldi, F.; Gori, D.; et al. Physical Well-Being of Children and Adolescents during the SARS-CoV-2 Pandemic: Findings from the "Come te la Passi?" Cross-sectional survey in Bologna, Italy. *Children* **2022**, *9*, 1950. [CrossRef] [PubMed]
7. Braksiek, M.; Lindemann, U.; Pahmeier, I. Physical activity and stress of children and adolescents during the COVID-19 Pandemic in Germany—A cross-sectional study in rural Areas. *Int. J. Environ. Res. Public Health* **2022**, *19*, 8274. [CrossRef]
8. Mitra, R.; Waygood, E.O.D.; Fullan, J. Subjective well-being of Canadian children and youth during the COVID-19 pandemic: The role of the social and physical environment and healthy movement behaviours. *Prev. Med. Rep.* **2021**, *23*, 101404. [CrossRef]
9. Bailey, R. Physical education and sport in schools: A review of benefits and outcomes. *J. Sch. Health* **2006**, *76*, 397–401. [CrossRef]
10. Telama, R.; Yang, X.; Viikari, J.; Välimäki, I.; Wanne, O.; Raitakari, O. Physical activity from childhood to adulthood: A 21-year tracking study. *Am. J. Prev. Med.* **2005**, *28*, 267–273. [CrossRef] [PubMed]
11. Elnaggar, R.K.; Alqahtani, B.A.; Mahmoud, W.S.; Elfakharany, M.S. Physical activity in adolescents during the social distancing policies of the COVID-19 pandemic. *Asia Pac. J. Public Health* **2020**, *32*, 491–494. [CrossRef] [PubMed]
12. Xiang, M.; Zhang, Z.; Kuwahara, K. Impact of COVID-19 pandemic on children and adolescents' lifestyle behavior larger than expected. *Prog. Cardiovasc. Dis.* **2020**, *63*, 531–532. [CrossRef]
13. Stockwell, S.; Trott, M.; Tully, M.; Shin, J.; Barnett, Y.; Butler, L.; McDermott, D.; Schuch, F.; Smith, L. Changes in physical activity and sedentary behaviours from before to during the COVID-19 pandemic lockdown: A systematic review. *BMJ Open Sport Exerc. Med.* **2021**, *7*, e000960. [CrossRef]
14. Caputo, E.L.; Reichert, F.F. Studies of physical activity and COVID-19 during the pandemic: A scoping review. *J. Phys. Act. Health* **2020**, *17*, 1275–1284. [CrossRef]
15. Korea Disease Control and Prevention Agency. Status of COVID-19 outbreaks in the Republic of Korea (Regular Briefing. 29 April 2020). Available online: https://ncov.kdca.go.kr/tcmBoardView.do?brdId=&brdGubun=&dataGubun=&ncvContSeq=354119&contSeq=354119&board_id=140&gubun=BDJ# (accessed on 15 October 2022).
16. Okuyama, J.; Seto, S.; Fukuda, Y.; Funakoshi, S.; Amae, S.; Onobe, J.; Izumi, S.; Ito, K.; Imamura, F. Mental health and physical activity among children and adolescents during the COVID-19 pandemic. *Tohoku J. Exp. Med.* **2021**, *253*, 203–215. [CrossRef] [PubMed]
17. Substance Abuse and Mental Health Services Administration. Key Substance Use and Mental Health Indicators in the United States: Results from the 2020 National Survey on Drug Use and Health. 14 February 2022. Available online: https://www.samhsa.gov/data/report/2020-nsduh-annual-national-report (accessed on 15 October 2022).
18. Guan, H.; Okely, A.D.; Aguilar-Farias, N.; Del Pozo Cruz, B.; Draper, C.E.; El Hamdouchi, A.; Florindo, A.A.; Jáuregui, A.; Katzmarzyk, P.T.; Kontsevaya, A.; et al. Promoting healthy movement behaviours among children during the COVID-19 pandemic. *Lancet Child Adolesc. Health* **2020**, *4*, 416–418. [CrossRef] [PubMed]
19. Maugeri, G.; Castrogiovanni, P.; Battaglia, G.; Pippi, R.; D'Agata, V.; Palma, A.; Rosa, M.D.; Musumeci, G. The impact of physical activity on psychological health during Covid-19 pandemic in Italy. *Heliyon* **2020**, *6*, e04315. [CrossRef] [PubMed]
20. Jiao, W.Y.; Wang, L.N.; Liu, J.; Fang, S.F.; Jiao, F.Y.; Pettoello-Mantovani, M.; Somekh, E. Behavioral and emotional disorders in children during the COVID-19 epidemic. *J. Pediatr.* **2020**, *221*, 264–266.e1. [CrossRef]
21. Choi, S.H.; Kim, Y.H.; Yang, J.E.; Oh, K.W. Changes in youth health behavior before and after the COVID-19 pandemic. In *Issues Report*; Report No.: 11-1790387-000384-01; Korea Disease Control and Prevention Agency: Osong, Korea, 2022.
22. Lee, G. The necessity of youth physical activity and role and task of school physical education in COVID-19. *Korean J. Sport Pedagog.* **2021**, *28*, 175–198. [CrossRef]

23. Lu, C.; Chi, X.; Liang, K.; Chen, S.-T.; Huang, L.; Guo, T.; Jiao, C.; Yu, Q.; Veronese, N.; Soares, F.C.; et al. Moving more and sitting less as healthy lifestyle behaviors are protective factors for insomnia, depression, and anxiety among adolescents during the COVID-19 pandemic. *Psychol. Res. Behav. Manag.* **2020**, *13*, 1223–1233. [CrossRef]
24. Guthold, R.; Stevens, G.A.; Riley, L.M.; Bull, F.C. Worldwide trends in insufficient physical activity from 2001 to 2016: A pooled analysis of 358 population-based surveys with 1.9 million participants. *Lancet Glob. Health* **2018**, *6*, e1077–e1086. [CrossRef]
25. Jang, J.-Y. Relationships of adolescents' stress and psychological state by gender and physical activity level during the early COVID-19 crisis. *Korean J. Growth Dev.* **2021**, *29*, 181–187. [CrossRef]
26. Tremblay, M.S.; Barnes, J.D.; González, S.A.; Katzmarzyk, P.T.; Onywera, V.O.; Reilly, J.J.; Tomkinson, G.R. Global matrix 2.0: Report card grades on the physical activity of children and youth comparing 38 countries. *J. Phys. Act. Health* **2016**, *13*, S343–S366. [CrossRef]
27. Shon, J.H. Korea's Education System After COVID-19. *New Radic. Rev.* **2020**, *84*, 74–93.
28. Kim, S.S.; Cho, S.Y.; Lee, J.A. What will society do ensure child rights in the post-COVID-19 era? *J. Child. Rights* **2020**, *24*, 409–438. [CrossRef]
29. Cairns, K.E.; Yap, M.B.H.; Pilkington, P.D.; Jorm, A.F. Risk and protective factors for depression that adolescents can modify: A systematic review and meta-analysis of longitudinal studies. *J. Affect. Disord.* **2014**, *169*, 61–75. [CrossRef] [PubMed]
30. Maenhout, L.; Peuters, C.; Cardon, G.; Compernolle, S.; Crombez, G.; DeSmet, A. The association of healthy lifestyle behaviors with mental health indicators among adolescents of different family affluence in Belgium. *BMC Public Health* **2020**, *20*, 958. [CrossRef]
31. Chaiton, M.O.; Cohen, J.E.; O'Loughlin, J.; Rehm, J. A systematic review of longitudinal studies on the association between depression and smoking in adolescents. *BMC Public Health* **2009**, *9*, 356. [CrossRef]
32. Stanton, R.; To, Q.G.; Khalesi, S.; Williams, S.L.; Alley, S.J.; Thwaite, T.L.; Fenning, A.S.; Vandelanotte, C. Depression, anxiety and stress during COVID-19: Associations with changes in physical activity, sleep, tobacco and alcohol use in Australian adults. *Int. J. Environ. Res. Public Health* **2020**, *17*, 4065. [CrossRef]
33. Killgore, W.D.S.; Cloonan, S.A.; Taylor, E.C.; Dailey, N.S. Loneliness: A signature mental health concern in the era of COVID-19. *Psychiatry Res.* **2020**, *290*, 113117. [CrossRef]
34. Loades, M.E.; Chatburn, E.; Higson-Sweeney, N.; Reynolds, S.; Shafran, R.; Brigden, A.; Linney, C.; McManus, M.N.; Borwick, C.; Crawley, E. Rapid systematic review: The impact of social isolation and loneliness on the mental health of children and adolescents in the context of COVID-19. *J. Am. Acad. Child Adolesc. Psychiatry* **2020**, *59*, 1218–1239.e3. [CrossRef]
35. Cacioppo, S.; Grippo, A.J.; London, S.; Goossens, L.; Cacioppo, J.T. Loneliness: Clinical import and interventions. *Perspect. Psychol. Sci.* **2015**, *10*, 238–249. [CrossRef]
36. Dubé, J.P.; Smith, M.M.; Sherry, S.B.; Hewitt, P.L.; Stewart, S.H. Suicide behaviors during the COVID-19 pandemic: A meta-analysis of 54 studies. *Psychiatry Res.* **2021**, *301*, 113998. [CrossRef]
37. Kim, S.Y.; Kim, H.-R.; Park, B.; Choi, H.G. Comparison of stress and suicide-related behaviors among Korean youths before and during the COVID-19 pandemic. *JAMA Netw. Open* **2021**, *4*, e2136137. [CrossRef]
38. Pirkis, J.; John, A.; Shin, S.; DelPozo-Banos, M.; Arya, V.; Analuisa-Aguilar, P.; Appleby, L.; Arensman, E.; Bantjes, J.; Baran, A.; et al. Suicide trends in the early months of the COVID-19 pandemic: An interrupted time-series analysis of preliminary data from 21 countries. *Lancet Psychiatry* **2021**, *8*, 579–588. [CrossRef] [PubMed]
39. Hill, R.M.; Rufino, K.; Kurian, S.; Saxena, J.; Saxena, K.; Williams, L. Suicide ideation and attempts in a pediatric emergency department before and during COVID-19. *Pediatrics* **2021**, *147*, e2020029280. [CrossRef] [PubMed]
40. García-Tascón, M.; Sahelices-Pinto, C.; Mendaña-Cuervo, C.; Magaz-González, A.M. The impact of the COVID-19 confinement on the habits of PA practice according to gender (male/female): Spanish case. *Int. J. Environ. Res. Public Health* **2020**, *17*, 6961. [CrossRef]
41. Kwon, B.; Choi, S. An exploration of adolescents' daily lives during the COVID-19 pandemic: A photovoice study. *Fam. Environ. Res.* **2022**, *60*, 211–230. [CrossRef]
42. Metsäpelto, R.-L.; Pulkkinen, L. Socioemotional behavior and school achievement in relation to extracurricular activity participation in middle childhood. *Scand. J. Educ. Res.* **2012**, *56*, 167–182. [CrossRef]
43. Suh, D.-H.; Nam, S.-M.; Um, H.-S.; Kim, M.-J. Physical activity and psychological state of adolescents experiencing the spread of coronavirus disease 19 (COVID-19). *Korean J. Growth Dev.* **2022**, *30*, 207–218. [CrossRef]

healthcare

MDPI

Article

Academic Helplessness and Life Satisfaction in Korean Adolescents: The Moderated Mediation Effects of Leisure Time Physical Activity

Mihye Kim [1], Kyulee Shin [2,*] and Sanghyun Park [3]

1 Institute of Sports Science, Seoul National University of Science & Technology, Seoul 01811, Republic of Korea
2 Department of Sports Sciences, Seoul National University of Science & Technology, Seoul 01811, Republic of Korea
3 Department of Sport for All, Korea National Open University, Seoul 03087, Republic of Korea
* Correspondence: kyuleeshin@seoultech.ac.kr

Abstract: This study examined whether depression mediates a relationship between academic helplessness and life satisfaction and whether the mediating effect differs depending on participation in leisure time physical activity (LTPA) from a sample of 2384 middle school students in South Korea. Identifying these factors could help in developing intervention strategies for promoting life satisfaction. Structural equation modeling analyses were employed to understand how various factors influence adolescents' life satisfaction. First, the effect of academic helplessness on life satisfaction was mediated by depression. Second, the mediating effect of depression was moderated according to participation in LTPA: the size of the negative mediating effect of depression on the relationship between academic helplessness and life satisfaction was reduced in the LTPA group compared to the non-LTPA group. The current findings suggest that encouraging engagement in physical activity may be a crucial vehicle for affecting academic helplessness, depression, and life satisfaction among early adolescents. Implications and future directions are discussed.

Keywords: leisure time physical activity; academic helplessness; learned helplessness; depression; life satisfaction; adolescents

Citation: Kim, M.; Shin, K.; Park, S. Academic Helplessness and Life Satisfaction in Korean Adolescents: The Moderated Mediation Effects of Leisure Time Physical Activity. *Healthcare* **2023**, *11*, 298. https://doi.org/10.3390/healthcare11030298

Academic Editor: Roberta Frontini

Received: 20 December 2022
Revised: 6 January 2023
Accepted: 17 January 2023
Published: 18 January 2023

1. Introduction

The overall life satisfaction of adolescents continues to decline [1]. East Asian adolescents, in particular, exhibited lower levels of life satisfaction than their North American and European counterparts [2]. Previous studies suggested that academic pressure contributed to adolescents' low life satisfaction in East Asia [3,4]. Despite the economic expansion, East Asian nations such as Korea, China, and Hong Kong continue to retain competitive education systems [5]. These nations have a social atmosphere emphasizing academic work, and graduating from prestigious universities is a prerequisite for good jobs, high wages, and high social status [6,7]. Consequently, not only parents but also students themselves have high academic expectations and study-related stress [8,9].

Academic stress among East Asian adolescents has reached a level that requires professional treatment and support and has morphed into "learned helplessness" [10,11]. It falls well beyond the simple dimension of tension or anxiety. Learned helplessness is a concept proposed in 1967 by Martin Seligman and Obermeyer in animal experiments. The dogs of the experimental group learned that they could not stop receiving an electric shock no matter what they tried. As a result, they did not try to escape when they were shocked, but only whined. These subjects were considered to have acquired learned helplessness [12]. Learned helplessness is defined as a psychological phenomenon in which one continuously faces a painful and uncontrollable situation and despairs instead of avoiding or overcoming it, even though one can avoid or overcome it with one's own ability [13].

Over the past decade, research on the learned helplessness of Korean teenagers has been widely documented [14,15]. In the past, most high school students were prone to extreme academic stress. They attended private academies and institutes after their regular school hours and on weekends to maintain their studies and rank among classmates [16,17]. Unfortunately, this "education fever" has now spread to middle school students. As expected, these young adolescents have a very difficult time dealing with this increased pressure and lack of leisure time at such a tender age [18–20]. Meanwhile, when Koreans enter middle school, the number of their physical education classes decreases. The seventh and eighth graders have three per week, and the ninth graders have two. This is due to an increase in mandatory academic and elective classes [21]. Despite the decrease in physical activity opportunities for middle school students, unfortunately, Korean parents do not enroll these children in outside physical extra-curricular activities such as community sports. At this age, their college admission is more valued [22].

Unsatisfied test results and test anxiety may lead to learned helplessness in a school setting, according to research findings. Adolescents' test anxiety was positively associated with learned helplessness in school [23]. Early adolescents' low subjective satisfaction with academic achievement directly affected academic helplessness [24]. Elkadri [25] also found that parents' and teachers' pressure regarding academic achievement was associated with adolescents' learned helplessness.

Accordingly, Korean scholar Bak and his colleagues developed an academic helplessness scale based on Martin Seligman's theory of learned helplessness [26]. While Seligman's learned helplessness is a question about the overall characteristics of human psychology, academic helplessness is limited to academic situations (e.g., exams, classes, etc.). Therefore, in order to specifically demonstrate the characteristics of helplessness in academic situations, separate verification is necessary because the measurement range is different for learned helplessness as opposed to academic helplessness. Specifically, it is needed to identify the relationships between academic helplessness, depression, and life satisfaction. Depression is a common symptom of learned helplessness [27] and is a strong representative factor that lowers adolescents' life satisfaction [28]. Therefore, it is reasonable to assume that depression may play a mediating role between learned helpless and life satisfaction. Previous research has examined associations between learned helplessness and life satisfaction [29], between learned helplessness and depression [27], and between depression and life satisfaction [28], respectively; however, these three factors have not been examined jointly in previous research.

To treat learned helplessness, it is vital to eliminate the habit of negative thinking and to enhance the learned helplessness defense mechanisms. For instance, cognitive-behavioral therapy [30] and emotional support from parents or instructors are beneficial [31]. Also, it has been said that reaching small, attainable goals is a good way to boost protective factors like self-efficacy [32]. Specifically, physical exercise is widely recognized as an essential way to strengthen protective qualities such as self-efficacy [33]. In addition, recent research indicated that during the COVID-19 pandemic, those who participated in leisure-time physical exercises had considerably lower levels of learned helplessness than those who did not [34]. These findings imply that physical exercise may prevent or moderate the development of learned helplessness.

Therefore, based on previous studies, we hypothesized: (1) depression mediates the relationship between academic helplessness and life satisfaction; (2) participation in LTPA moderates the mediation effect of depression between academic helplessness and life satisfaction.

1.1. Depression as a Mediator in the Academic Helplessness–Life Satisfaction Relationship

Academic helplessness is a concept of learned helplessness in academic situations based on the learned helplessness theory presented by Seligman in 1976 [35]. Academic helplessness occurs after students repeatedly experience stressful situations. When students regularly perform poorly on exams even after studying hard, they start to believe that they are incapable of success, so they give up trying [26].

Unlike elementary school students, East Asian middle school students experience higher academic stress due to the region's scholastic ranking system; absolute grading is no longer used [36,37]. In addition to an increase in the amount of studying and academic evaluation changes, high parental academic pressure has also been found to be a strong influencer on academic helplessness among Asian middle school students [37,38].

A typical symptom of learned helplessness is depression [27]. As a result of academic helplessness, students may experience a feeling of out of control and depression [39]. In other words, learned helplessness is closely related to low self-esteem [40], and low self-esteem predicts depression [41]. Therefore, learned helplessness should be identified early.

Depression increased due to academic helplessness may also affect adolescents' life satisfaction [42]. Depression is well-known to negatively affect adolescents' life satisfaction [28]. Previous studies have reported that academic helplessness and life satisfaction have a negative correlation [43,44]. While previous studies have examined associations between academic helplessness, depression, and life satisfaction separately, collaborative relationships between academic helplessness, depression, and life satisfaction have not been researched. Therefore, we hypothesized that depression would mediate relationships between academic helplessness and life satisfaction.

1.2. LTPA as a Moderator in the Academic Helplessness, Depression and Life Satisfaction Relationship

Previous studies suggested that LTPA participation can affect learned helplessness (reference). Buffart et al. [45] concluded that exercise participation increases the subject's mastery of the activity and alleviates learned helplessness through self-efficacy. Mastery is having control over the forces that affect one's life, and improving mastery through exercise can help improve cognitive distortions caused by repeated failure experiences [45,46].

Physical activities in adolescents help prevent and reduce the incidence of depressive symptoms [47]. Hrafnkelsdottir et al. (2018) reported that more frequent vigorous physical activities in adolescents lowed the risk of depressive symptoms, low self-esteem, and life dissatisfaction [48]. McMahon et al. (2017) also showed that more frequent physical activities and participation in leisure sports led to a lower level of depressive symptoms and greater well-being in adolescents [49].

2. Materials and Methods

2.1. Participants

The purpose of this study was two-fold. First, the structural relationship between adolescents' academic helplessness, depression, and life satisfaction was analyzed using the Korea Children and Youth Panel Survey 2018 (KCYPS 2018). Second, the differential effects of LTPA participation in this structural relationship were also analyzed.

To obtain a representative sample, KCYPS 2018 applied a stratified sampling method. Face-to-face surveys using tablet PCs were conducted. The data consisted of seventh-grade middle schoolers (13-year-olds). In total, 2384 data points were analyzed. Initially, there were 2590 surveys, but 206 were incomplete and were thus excluded. The demographic characteristics of participants classified by gender are shown in Table 1, since there is no meaningful difference in the mean of the three variables (academic helplessness, depression, and life satisfaction) by gender.

2.2. Measures

2.2.1. Academic Helplessness

Academic Helplessness Scale by Bak et al. [26] was used. This scale was developed based on Seligman's Learned Helplessness theory and related studies [12,50]. This particular scale, unlike general learned helplessness scales that are used to measure adults in general situations [50], focuses on students' learned helplessness in academic situations [26].

Academic helplessness occurs after a student repeatedly experiences a stressful situation. When students regularly perform poorly on exams even after studying hard, they start to believe that they are incapable of success, so they give up trying. This scale consists of 16 items under four sub-factors including lack of locus of control, lack of academic motivation, lack of positive affect, and lack of active engagement. Lack of locus of control means that it is difficult to believe that one's attitude and effort can achieve positive results. Lack of academic motivation means that the motivation to control the process and results related to academic achievement in a positive direction is low. Lack of positive affect means that as a result of academic helplessness, students experience emotions such as loss of pleasure and depression. Lack of active engagement means that dependent and passive behaviors appear in academic situations [26]. The scale is a 4-point Likert scale ranging from 1 = not true at all to 4 = very true. Higher scores indicated a higher likelihood of academic helplessness. Sample questions from the academic helplessness scale include, "No matter how hard I try, my grades will not improve", "I have no motivation to study", "I am losing interested in studies", "I don't concentrate on studying even during an exam period".

Table 1. Characteristics of participants.

Variables		Male (n = 1278)		Female (n = 1106)	
		n	%	n	%
Age (years)	12	6	0.5	3	0.3
	13	1259	98.5	1086	98.2
	14	13	1.0	17	1.5
Subjective health	very unhealthy	10	0.8	10	0.8
	unhealthy	100	7.8	91	8.2
	healthy	667	52.2	636	57.5
	very healthy	501	39.2	369	33.5
Leisure Time Physical Activity (LTPA)	none	320	25.0	572	51.7
	1 h	341	26.7	280	25.3
	2 h	246	19.2	136	12.3
	3 h	120	9.4	63	5.7
	4 h and more	251	19.6	55	5.0
Variables		**Mean (SD)**		**Mean (SD)**	
Academic helplessness		1.966 (0.507)		1.954 (0.519)	
Depression		1.733 (0.580)		1.857 (0.624)	
Life satisfaction		2.652 (0.556)		2.598 (0.538)	

2.2.2. Depression

Kim, Kim, and Won's (1984) Depression Scale was used [51]. This scale has ten items in the Symptom Checklist-90-Revised (SCL-90-R), developed by Derogatis (1977) [52]. Sample questions from the academic helplessness scale include, "I have a lot of worries", "I often blame myself when things go wrong", "I feel lonely". The scale is a 4-point Likert type scale ranging from 1 = not true at all to 4 = very true. Higher scores indicated a higher likelihood of depression.

2.2.3. Leisure Time Physical Activity

Leisure Time Physical Activity (LTPA) was measured using a questionnaire asking about one's duration of exercise that produced sweat during the previous week. Students answered on a 5-point Likert scale for this item (0 = not at all to 4 = 4 h or more). This questionnaire has been proven valid by its frequent use in the literature, such as the National Medical Checkup Questionnaire [53], the International Physical Activity Questionnaire [54], and the Student Physical Activity Measurement Sheet [55].

2.2.4. Life Satisfaction

Life Satisfaction was measured with a Korean version of the Satisfaction with Life Satisfaction (SWLS) developed by Diener et al. [56]. It contained five items, including, "In general, my life is close to my ideal", "The circumstances of my life are very good", and "I am satisfied with my life". Measurements were made on a 4-point Likert scale (1 = strongly disagree to 4 = strongly agree).

2.3. Analysis

A confirmation factor analysis (CFA) was performed to verify the relationship between the observed variables and the basic structure in the measurement model. To be specific, a two-step approach by Anderson and Gerbing (1988) was applied [57]. We first evaluated a measurement model through CFA and then evaluated a research model through a structural equation model (SEM). In this process, academic helplessness was combined into four parceled variables based on the user guide of KCYPS 2018. To evaluate measurement and structural models, we used multiple indexes, such as chi-square, the Steiger-Lind Root Mean Square Error of Approximation (RMSEA), the Tucker-Lewis index (TLI), and the comparative fit index (CFI). Composite reliability (CR) and average variance extracted (AVE) were calculated for the components of each measurement scale to verify convergent validity, discriminant validity, and reliability. Lastly, structural equation modeling was carried out to test the proposed two hypotheses.

3. Results

3.1. Descriptive Statistics

Our measurement model was evaluated by CFA using AMOS 24.0. The results revealed a suitable fit to the data (χ^2 = 1455.362, df = 149, p = 0.000, TLI = 0.925, CFI = 0.941, RMSEA = 0.058), as shown in Table 2.

Table 2. Confirmatory factor analysis for measurement model.

	λ	AVE	CR
Academic helplessness		0.569	0.839
Lack of locus of control.	0.607		
Lack of academic motivation.	0.799		
Lack of positive affect.	0.818		
Lack of active engagement.	0.775		
Depression		0.526	0.917
I feel down.	0.689		
I feel unfortunate or sad, and depressed.	0.791		
I have a lot of worries.	0.630		
I feel like I want to die.	0.690		
I cry often.	0.661		
I often blame myself when things go wrong.	0.709		
I feel lonely.	0.762		
I lack interest in everything.	0.747		
I don't think I have a bright future.	0.751		
I find everything difficult.	0.801		
Life satisfaction		0.494	0.828
In general, my life is close to my ideal.	0.670		
The circumstances of my life are very good.	0.780		
I am satisfied with my life.	0.788		
I've accomplished something important to me.	0.665		
If I could live my life again, I wouldn't change a thing.	0.590		

Chi-square = 1455.362, df = 149, p = 0.000, TLI = 0.925, CFI = 0.941, RMSEA = 0.058.

Basically, convergent validity was evaluated by the criteria recommended by Fornell and Larcker [58]. The CRs and AVEs for each latent variable should exceed the thresholds of 0.7 and 0.5, respectively. The result of our study showed that the CRs ranged from 0.839 to 0.828, and AVEs ranged from 0.494 to 0.569. It means that the AVE of life satisfaction had a lower value than the criteria. However, the value of 0.4 is acceptable because if the AVE value is less than 0.5 but the composite reliability is higher than 0.6, the convergent validity of the construct is acceptable [58]. In the case of discriminant validity, it is acceptable if the square root of AVE for each latent variable exceeds all correlation coefficients among the latent variables. As shown in Table 3, the minimum value of the square root of AVEs was 0.702. Discriminant validity was also achieved because this value was higher than the maximum value of the correlation coefficient ($r = 0.545$).

Table 3. Correlation matrix for all measurement variables.

	Academic Helplessness	Depression	Life Satisfaction
Academic helplessness	(0.754)		
Depression	0.545 ***	(0.725)	
Life satisfaction	−0.351 ***	−0.465 ***	(0.702)

Note. Square root of AVEs is in parentheses. *** $p < 0.001$

3.2. *Testing the Moderated Mediating Models*

Based on a measurement model which proved validity and reliability, SEM was conducted to test the hypothetical causal relationships among the three latent variables. The result revealed that the structural model was acceptable ($\chi^2 = 1455.362$, $df = 149$, $p = 0.000$, TLI = 0.925, CFI = 941, RMSEA = 0.058). The results of the research hypothesis are shown in Table 4. According to Table 4, three paths among academic helplessness, depression, and life satisfaction were significant. Specifically, academic helplessness had a positive influence on depression ($b = 0.834$, $p < 0.001$), depression had a negative influence on life satisfaction ($b = -0.322$, $p < 0.001$), and academic helplessness influenced life satisfaction negatively ($b = -0.176$, $p < 0.001$).

Table 4. Hypotheses testing using bootstrapping method.

Path	b	SE	*t*	*p*
Variable relationships				
Academic helplessness → depression	0.834	0.043	19.426	<0.001
Depression → life satisfaction	−0.322	0.024	−13.35	<0.001
Academic helplessness → life satisfaction	−0.176	0.035	−5.018	<0.001
Hypotheses 1. Mediation effects of depression				
Academic helplessness → depression → life satisfaction	−0.269	0.024	−11.033	<0.001
Hypotheses 2. Moderated mediation effects				
Mediation effect of depression in non-LTPA group (a)	−0.360	0.050	−7.125	<0.001
Mediation effect of depression in LTPA group (b)	−0.227	0.020	−7.985	<0.001
Moderated mediation effects (a–b)	−0.133	0.064	2.078	0.037

In order to statistically test Hypothesis 1, the mediation effect of depression between academic helplessness and life satisfaction was performed using the bootstrapping method. As a result, depression had a significant mediation effect between academic helplessness and life satisfaction ($b = -0.269$, $p < 0.001$).

Also, as a result of analyzing whether these mediation effects differed depending on participation in LTPA, the mediation effect of depression in the non-LTPA group ($b = -0.360$, $p < 0.001$) was greater than the mediation effect of depression in the LTPA group ($b = -0.227$, $p < 0.001$). Then, to statistically test Hypothesis 2, we used the 'MyModMed' package of AMOS to test whether the mediation effect of each model had a significant difference (moderated mediation effect). As a result, a significant difference was found. The mediation effect of the LTPA group was less than that of the non-LTPA group. It means that LTPA participation of adolescents contributed to lowering the negative effect of academic helplessness.

4. Discussion

This study sought to identify whether depression mediates the relationship between academic helplessness and life satisfaction of middle school students, and whether this mediating effect is moderated by participation in LTPA.

First, it was shown that academic helplessness not only negatively impacted life satisfaction directly but also negatively impacted life satisfaction via depression. In other words, it may be said that middle school students' academic helplessness had a detrimental impact on their depression levels, which lowered their degree of life satisfaction. According to these results, academic helplessness may have a significant role in determining the level of life satisfaction experienced by students through either direct or indirect pathways.

The findings of this research have implications for clinical practice. It is important that the goal of reducing depressive symptoms be included in school-based intervention programs designed for middle school students with academic helplessness. Previous research on learned helplessness has shown that it is strongly associated with reactive depression [59,60].

Unlike endogenous depression, reactive depression is a temporary symptom of depression due to a relatively specific stress event [61,62]. Therefore, middle school students can improve depressive symptoms by improving their sense of accomplishment or self-efficacy. Encouraging participation in their favorite extracurricular and school activities or participation in physical activities with parents, family, and peers might assist [63].

Second, it was found that the mediating effect of depression on the relationship between middle school students' academic helplessness and life satisfaction differed according to the presence or absence of participation in LTPA. The mediating effect of depression on the link between academic helplessness and life satisfaction was less in the group that did physical activities in their free time than in the group that did not. These findings are consistent with previous studies [64,65] that middle school students' participation in physical activities is a key factor in depression. In addition, Bélair et al. (2018) reported that inactive adolescents were more likely to be depressed and anxious as opposed to physically active adolescents [66]. The results of this study also concluded that, like previous studies, middle school students participating in physical activities were less stressed [67] and had higher life satisfaction [68].

Based on prior research, it is reasonable to speculate how LTPA influences academic helplessness. Participation in LTPA is a crucial means of experiencing positive emotions among adolescents [69]. According to Fredrickson's broaden and build theory of positive emotions, the experience of positive emotions contributes not only to feeling good but also to reducing negative thinking (e.g., I won't be able to do well) by promoting positive automatic thinking [70]. Positive emotions, according to Fredrickson, help reduce depression and increase life satisfaction by expanding the momentary thought-action repertoire [71].

In addition, LTPA improves self-efficacy which is a protective factor for learned helplessness and depression [72]. Prior literature reported that people who experienced learned helplessness could overcome this by trying to achieve small goals frequently in lieu of feeling overwhelmed by larger or occasional ones [73]. Additionally, the support of significant others in their every life of their accomplishment is vital. Therefore, we present that small goals and tasks offered throughout physical activity can help build mastery and self-control, reduce academic helplessness, and increase East Asian adolescents' life satisfaction [45,74]. For example, instead of a student's initial tennis lessons' goals being to collect points successfully, the student must first learn how much force to apply to one's swing to hit the ball over the net without going out of bounds. Once this is mastered, the student can progress to more advanced skills and strokes, eventually winning a match.

5. Conclusions

One of the primary implications of this study is that LTPA can be a major resolution to alleviate adolescents' depression due to high academic helplessness and can increase life satisfaction. Therefore, it is necessary to increase LTPA participation among adolescents who experience academic helplessness. However, considering Trout and Graber's (2009) research that showed difficult tasks in physical activities and physical education class situations, mastery-oriented tasks should be provided as an opportunity to achieve small goals [75].

Second, teenagers in East Asian countries often start private education to prepare for college entrance exams in earnest after graduating from elementary school [5]. Therefore, due to this extreme pressure, parents cannot simply be suggested to enroll their children in physical activities. In this regard, policy alternatives such as expanding physical education classes in schools and restricting operating hours of private education on weekends should be enacted.

There are a few limitations of this study. First, demographic and sociological factors (such as parenting and teachers' support) were not controlled. In future studies, such variables need to be considered. Second, the level of LTPA engagement was measured by a single scale (the duration of participating in LTPA). The scale needs to be specified into sub-types, such as the types of physical activity participation (competitive activities or non-competitive cooperative activities) in future studies. Despite such limitations, this study is meaningful in that it suggested specific treatments for East Asian adolescents, considering this population's relatively low level of life satisfaction. In addition, using national-level data, the empirical basis for participation in physical activities was presented as a means of preventing and treating academic helplessness, depression, and low life satisfaction.

In conclusion, depression mediates the relationship between academic helplessness and life satisfaction among adolescents. Clinical assessment and treatment should include goals to reduce depressive symptoms in middle school students with academic helplessness. Furthermore, participation in LTPA moderates the mediation effect of depression between academic helplessness and life satisfaction. Encouraging engagement in physical activities may be a crucial vehicle for adolescents with academic helplessness.

Author Contributions: Conceptualization, M.K. and K.S.; Methodology, S.P.; Validation, S.P.; Formal analysis, S.P.; Data curation, S.P.; Writing—original draft preparation, M.K. and K.S.; Writing—review and editing, M.K. and K.S.; Supervision, M.K. and K.S.; All authors have read and agreed to the published version of the manuscript.

Funding: This research received no external funding.

Institutional Review Board Statement: The study was approved by the Institutional Review Board of Seoul National University of Science & Technology (IRB approval no. 2022-0013). This study used data collected on Seventh graders by KCYPS. To access this data, go to https://www.nypi.re.kr/archive/mps/program/examinDataCode?menuId=MENU00226&firstCategory=1&secondCategory=3&schType=0&schText= (accessed on 5 December 2022).

Informed Consent Statement: Informed consent was obtained from all individual participants included in the study.

Data Availability Statement: Data is available upon request at https://www.nypi.re.kr/archive/mps (accessed on 22 October 2022).

Conflicts of Interest: The authors declare no conflict of interest.

References

1. OECD. *PISA 2018 Results (Volume III): Students' Well-Being*; OECD Publishing: Paris, France, 2019.
2. Marquez, J.; Long, E. A global decline in adolescents' subjective well-being: A comparative study exploring patterns of change in the life satisfaction of 15-year-old students in 46 countries. *Child Indic. Res.* **2021**, *14*, 1251–1292. [CrossRef] [PubMed]
3. Yoo, C.; Kahng, S.K.; Kim, H. The trajectory of life satisfaction and its associated factors among adolescents in South Korea. *Asia Pac. J. Soc. Work Dev.* **2017**, *27*, 1–12. [CrossRef]
4. Rappleye, J.; Komatsu, H.; Uchida, Y.; Krys, K.; Markus, H. 'Better policies for better lives'?: Constructive critique of the OECD's (mis) measure of student well-being. *J. Educ. Policy.* **2020**, *35*, 258–282. [CrossRef]
5. Ng, Y.K. The East-Asian happiness gap: Causes and implications. In *Happiness—Concept, Measurement and Promotion*; Springer: Singapore, 2022; pp. 133–143.
6. Chen, Y.; Huang, R.; Lu, Y.; Zhang, K. Education fever in China: Children's academic performance and parents' life satisfaction. *J. Happiness Stud.* **2021**, *22*, 927–954. [CrossRef]
7. Kim, J.; Bang, H. Education fever: Korean parents' aspirations for their children's schooling and future career. *Pedagog. Cult. Soc.* **2017**, *25*, 207–224. [CrossRef]
8. Ma, Y.; Siu, A.; Tse, W.S. The role of high parental expectations in adolescents' academic performance and depression in Hong Kong. *J. Fam. Issues* **2018**, *39*, 2505–2522. [CrossRef]
9. Shin, D.J.; Lee, H.J.; Ha, J.E.; Park, J.H.; Son, E.; Bong, M. Why aren't Korean students happy?: Tracing back to the sources of their academic distress 1. In *Asian Education Miracles*; Routledge: London, UK, 2018; pp. 124–138.
10. Chao, T.Y.; Sung, Y.T. An investigation of the reasons for test anxiety, time spent studying, and achievement among adolescents in Taiwan. *Asia Pac. J. Educ.* **2019**, *39*, 469–484. [CrossRef]

11. Yi, H.S.; Na, W. How are maths-anxious students identified and what are the key predictors of maths anxiety? Insights gained from PISA results for Korean adolescents. *Asia Pac. J. Educ.* **2020**, *40*, 247–262.
12. Seligman, M.E.; Maier, S. Failure to escape traumatic shock. *J. Exp. Psychol.* **1967**, *74*, 1–9. [CrossRef]
13. Nolen-Hoeksema, S.; Girgus, J.S.; Seligman, M.E. Learned helplessness in children: A longitudinal study of depression, achievement, and explanatory style. *J. Personal. Soc. Psychol.* **1986**, *51*, 435–442. [CrossRef]
14. No, U.; Song, J.; Woo, Y. Latent transition analysis of middle school students' academic helplessness: Changes across grade levels. *Korea Educ. Rev.* **2022**, *28*, 67–90. [CrossRef]
15. Woo, Y., No, U. Latent profiles of middle school students' learned helplessness: Testing the Effect of determinants and differences in cognition, emotion, and behaviors. *Korea Educ. Rev.* **2021**, *27*, 281–304. [CrossRef]
16. Cheong, Y.; Yang, M. A study on the profile analysis of self-regulated learning with Korean high school students. *Korean J. Sch. Psychol.* **2014**, *11*, 499–518.
17. Moon, E.; Bae, J. The structural relationships among history of academic achievement, social-motivational variables, and learned helplessness: A comparison of boy and girl high school students. *Korean J. Educ. Psychol.* **2010**, *24*, 183–205.
18. Cho, H. Influence of guardian expectations on middle school students' academic self-concept: Mediating effects of academic engagement and learned helplessness. *Korean Educ. Res. J.* **2020**, *41*, 51–73.
19. Kim, J. Latent Profiles of Middle School Students' Academic Helplessness: Predictor and Verification of Difference in Academic and Emotional. *Korean J. Youth Stud.* **2022**, *29*, 25–50. [CrossRef]
20. Kim, J.; Han, H.; Pare, E.; Kang, M. The serial multiple mediating effects of social withdrawal and smartphone dependency and the Influence of negative parenting attitude on adolescents' academic helplessness. *Fam. Environ. Res.* **2021**, *58*, 601–611. [CrossRef]
21. Kim, S.H.; Park, J.J. A case study on operation procedures and obstructive factors of physical activity programs in the free semester in middle schools. *J. Educ. Cult.* **2019**, *25*, 575–594.
22. Lee, S.E.; Hong, W.P. Curriculum flexibility in Korean middle school: Current situations and future tasks. *J. Curric. Stud.* **2020**, *38*, 5–32. [CrossRef]
23. Raufelder, D.; Regner, N.; Wood, M.A. Test anxiety and learned helplessness is moderated by student perceptions of teacher motivational support. *Educ. Psychol.* **2018**, *38*, 54–74. [CrossRef]
24. Kwon, E. The mediating effect of grit between academic achievement satisfaction and academic helplessness of middle school students. *J. Digit. Converg.* **2021**, *19*, 247–252.
25. Elkadri, H. Learned Helplessness, an Exploratory Study in Underachieving Adolescents. Ph.D. Thesis, The British University in Dubai, Academic City, Dubai, 2016.
26. Bak, B.G.; Roh, S.U.; Kim, J.A.; Hwang, J.S. Development and validation of the academic helplessness scale. *Korean J. Child Educ.* **2015**, *24*, 5–29. [CrossRef]
27. Valås, H. Learned helplessness and psychological adjustment: Effects of age, gender and academic achievement. *Scandinavian. J. Educ. Res. Sci.* **2001**, *45*, 71–90. [CrossRef]
28. Stankov, L. Depression and life satisfaction among European and Confucian adolescents. *Psychol. Assess.* **2013**, *25*, 1220–1234. [CrossRef] [PubMed]
29. Choi, H. The Effect of Smartphone Dependency on Life Satisfaction of Middle School Students: The Mediating Effect of Academic Helplessness. *J. Humanit. Soc. Sci.* **2021**, *12*, 1725–1740.
30. Cemalcilar, Z.; Canbeyli, R.; Sunar, D. Learned helplessness, therapy, and personality traits: An experimental study. *J. Soc. Psychol.* **2003**, *143*, 65–81. [CrossRef]
31. Jose, P.E.; Bellamy, M.A. Relationships of parents' theories of intelligence with children's persistence/learned helplessness: A cross-cultural comparison. *J. Cross Cult. Psychol.* **2012**, *43*, 999–1018. [CrossRef]
32. Trindade, I.A.; Mendes, A.L.; Ferreira, N.B. The moderating effect of psychological flexibility on the link between learned helplessness and depression symptomatology: A preliminary study. *J. Context. Behav. Sci.* **2020**, *15*, 68–72. [CrossRef]
33. Clevinger, K.; Petrie, T.; Martin, S.; Greenleaf, C. The relationship of sport involvement and gender to physical fitness, self-efficacy, and self-concept in middle school students. *Phys. Educ.* **2020**, *77*, 154–172. [CrossRef]
34. Bas, M.; Kucuk, K.; Kabak, S. A study on learned helplessness and life satisfaction of women who play sports and who don't play sports. *Ambient. Sci.* **2020**, *7*, 185–188. [CrossRef]
35. Maier, S.F.; Seligman, M.E. Learned helplessness: Theory and evidence. *J. Exp. Psychol. Gen.* **1976**, *105*, 3–46. [CrossRef]
36. You., S. Student Expectations and Perceptions of the Transition from Elementary to Middle School. *J. Elem. Educ.* **2007**, *20*, 355–374.
37. Li, W.; Li, Y. An Analysis on Social and Cultural Background of the Resistance for China's Education Reform and Academic Pressure. *Int. Educ. Stud.* **2010**, *3*, 211–215. [CrossRef]
38. Kim, Y.; Kwak, K.; Lee, S. Does optimism moderate parental achievement pressure and academic stress in Korean children? *Curr. Psychol.* **2016**, *35*, 39–43. [CrossRef]
39. Ghasemi, F.; Karimi, M.N. Learned helplessness in public middle schools: The effects of an intervention program based on motivational strategies. *Middle Sch. J.* **2021**, *52*, 23–32. [CrossRef]
40. Jiang, S.; Ren, Q.; Jiang, C.; Wang, L. Academic stress and depression of Chinese adolescents in junior high schools: Moderated mediation model of school burnout and self-esteem. *J. Affect. Disord.* **2021**, *295*, 384–389. [CrossRef]

41. Orth, U.; Robins, R.W.; Roberts, B.W. Low self-esteem prospectively predicts depression in adolescence and young adulthood. *J. Personal. Soc. Psychol.* **2008**, *95*, 695–708. [CrossRef]
42. Aziz, S.; Tariq, N. Depression, anxiety, and stress in relation to life satisfaction and academic performance of adolescents. *Pak. J. Physiol.* **2019**, *15*, 52–55.
43. Ma, E.T.; Kim, C.K. A Structural Relationship Analysis of Grit, Cooperation, Academic helplessness and Satisfaction with Life by Adolescents. *J. Emot. Behav. Disord.* **2021**, *37*, 61–79. [CrossRef]
44. Yoo, K. Structural Relationship Analysis between Positive and Negative Parenting Attitudes, Grit, and Academic Helplessness Felt by First Graders of Middle School Students. *J. Korea Contents Assoc.* **2021**, *21*, 140–154.
45. Buffart, L.M.; Ros, W.J.G.; Chinapaw, M.J.M.; Brug, J.; Knol, D.L.; Korstjens, I.; May, A.M. Mediators of physical exercise for improvement in cancer survivors' quality of life. *Psychooncology* **2014**, *23*, 330–338. [CrossRef] [PubMed]
46. Martinek, T.J.; Hellison, D.R. Fostering resiliency in underserved youth through physical activity. *Quest* **1997**, *49*, 34–49. [CrossRef]
47. Brown, H.E.; Pearson, N.; Braithwaite, R.E.; Brown, W.J.; Biddle, S.J. Physical activity interventions and depression in children and adolescents. *Sports Med.* **2013**, *43*, 195–206. [CrossRef] [PubMed]
48. Hrafnkelsdottir, S.M.; Brychta, R.J.; Rognvaldsdottir, V.; Gestsdottir, S.; Chen, K.Y.; Johannsson, E.; Arngrimsson, S.A. Less screen time and more frequent vigorous physical activity is associated with lower risk of reporting negative mental health symptoms among Icelandic adolescents. *PLoS ONE* **2018**, *13*, e0196286. [CrossRef]
49. McMahon, E.M.; Corcoran, P.; O'Regan, G.; Keeley, H.; Cannon, M.; Carli, V.; Wasserman, D. Physical activity in European adolescents and associations with anxiety, depression and well-being. *Eur. Child Adolesc. Psychiatry* **2017**, *26*, 111–122. [CrossRef]
50. Seligman, M.E. *Helplessness. On depression, Development and Death*; Freeman: San Francisco, CA, USA, 1975.
51. Kim, K.; Kim, J.H.; Won, H.T. *Korean Manual of Symptom Checklist-90-Revision (SCL90-R), The Brief Symptom Inventory (BSI)*; Chung Ang Aptitude Publishing: Seoul, Republic of Korea, 1989.
52. Derogatis, L.R. Symptoms checklist-90. Administration, scoring, and procedures manual for the revised version. *Baltim. Psychom. Res.* **1977**, *19*, 1–15.
53. National Health Insurance Service. *Inquiry of Health Examinations*; National Health Insurance Service: Seoul, Republic of Korea, 2009.
54. Kim, B.S. Korean Version of International Physical Activity Questionnaire (IPAQ). *Korean J. Fam. Med.* **2006**, *27*, 348–357.
55. Hong, S.Y.; Yang, Y.J.; Park, H.K.; Kim, B.S. Validation of Korean Youth Physical Activity Questionnaire (KYPAQ). *Korean J. Phys. Edu.* **2006**, *45*, 161–173.
56. Diener, E.D.; Emmons, R.A.; Larsen, R.J.; Griffin, S. The satisfaction with life scale. *J. Pers. Assess.* **1985**, *49*, 71–75. [CrossRef]
57. Anderson, J.C.; Gerbing, D.W. Structural equation modeling in practice: A review and recommended two-step approach. *Psychol. Bull.* **1988**, *103*, 411. [CrossRef]
58. Fornell, C.; Larcker, D.F. Evaluating structural equation models with unobservable variables and measurement error. *J. Mark. Res.* **1981**, *18*, 39–50. [CrossRef]
59. Abramson, L.Y.; Seligman, M.E.; Teasdale, J.D. Learned helplessness in humans: Critique and reformulation. *J. Abnorm. Psychol.* **1978**, *87*, 49–74. [CrossRef] [PubMed]
60. Schroder, K.E.; Ollis, C.L. The coping competence questionnaire: A measure of resilience to helplessness and depression. *Motiv. Emot.* **2013**, *37*, 286–302. [CrossRef]
61. Paykel, E.S. Basic concepts of depression. *Dialogues Clin. Neurosci.* **2008**, *10*, 279–289. [CrossRef] [PubMed]
62. Schloss, P.J. Classroom-based intervention for students exhibiting depressive reactions. *Behav. Disord.* **1983**, *8*, 231–236. [CrossRef]
63. Wainscott, M.C. The relationship of depression in middle school adolescents and their school extracurricular activities: A perspective for family therapy. Ph.D. Thesis, Texas Woman's University, Denton, TX, USA, 2005.
64. Kremer, P.; Elshaug, C.; Leslie, E.; Toumbourou, J.W.; Patton, G.C.; Williams, J. Physical activity, leisure-time screen use and depression among children and young adolescents. *J. Sci. Med. Sport* **2014**, *17*, 183–187. [CrossRef]
65. Oberste, M.; Medele, M.; Javelle, F.; Lioba Wunram, H.; Walter, D.; Bloch, W.; Zimmer, P. Physical activity for the treatment of adolescent depression: A systematic review and meta-analysis. *Front. Physiol.* **2020**, *11*, 185. [CrossRef]
66. Bélair, M.A.; Kohen, D.E.; Kingsbury, M.; Colman, I. Relationship between leisure time physical activity, sedentary behaviour and symptoms of depression and anxiety: Evidence from a population-based sample of Canadian adolescents. *BMJ Open* **2018**, *8*, e021119. [CrossRef]
67. Zullig, K.J.; White, R.J. Physical activity, life satisfaction, and self-rated health of middle school students. *Appl. Res. Qual. Life* **2011**, *6*, 277–289. [CrossRef]
68. Park, S. Associations of physical activity with sleep satisfaction, perceived stress, and problematic Internet use in Korean adolescents. *BMC Public Health* **2014**, *14*, 1–6. [CrossRef]
69. Løvoll, H.S.; Bentzen, M.; Säfvenbom, R. Development of positive emotions in physical education: Person-centred approach for understanding motivational stability and change. *Scand. J. Educ. Res.* **2020**, *64*, 999–1014. [CrossRef]
70. Fredrickson, B.L.; Branigan, C. Positive emotions broaden the scope of attention and thought-action repertoires. *Cogn. Emot.* **2005**, *19*, 313–332. [CrossRef]
71. Fredrickson, B.L.; Cohn, M.A.; Coffey, K.A.; Pek, J.; Finkel, S.M. Open hearts build lives: Positive emotions, induced through loving-kindness meditation, build consequential personal resources. *J. Personal. Soc. Psychol.* **2008**, *95*, 1045–1062. [CrossRef]
72. Neissaar, I.; Raudsepp, L. Changes in physical activity, self-efficacy and depressive symptoms in adolescent girls. *Pediatr. Exerc. Sci.* **2011**, *23*, 331–343. [CrossRef]

73. Filippello, P.; Buzzai, C.; Costa, S.; Orecchio, S.; Sorrenti, L. Teaching style and academic achievement: The mediating role of learned helplessness and mastery orientation. *Psychol. Sch.* **2020**, *57*, 5–16. [CrossRef]
74. Greenwood, B.N.; Fleshner, M. Exercise, learned helplessness, and the stress-resistant brain. *Neuromolecular Med.* **2008**, *10*, 81–98. [CrossRef]
75. Trout, J.; Graber, K.C. Perceptions of overweight students concerning their experiences in physical education. *J. Teach. Phys. Educ.* **2009**, *28*, 272–292. [CrossRef]

healthcare MDPI

Article

The Association between Physical Activity, Self-Compassion, and Mental Well-Being after COVID-19: In the Exercise and Self-Esteem Model Revised with Self-Compassion (EXSEM-SC) Perspective

Ming-Yu Claudia Wong [1,*], Hong-Wang Fung [2] and Guangzhe Frank Yuan [3,4]

1 Department of Health and Physical Education, The Education University of Hong Kong, Hong Kong, China
2 Department of Social Work, Hong Kong Baptist University, Hong Kong, China
3 South Carolina Smart State Center for Healthcare Quality, Arnold School of Public Health, University of South Carolina, Columbia, SC 29208, USA
4 Department of Health Promotion, Education, and Behavior, Arnold School of Public Health, University of South Carolina, Columbia, SC 29208, USA
* Correspondence: cmywong@eduhk.hk

Abstract: During the great life-altering challenges brought by Coronavirus 2019, school closures and lack of access to exercise and social interactions may have increased students' negative emotions. The current research acts as a follow-up study to the development of the EXSEM-SC, using the Repeated Measures Panel Analysis Framework (RMPAF) to examine the stability of the model in revealing the relationship between physical activity, self-compassion, and mental well-being among Hong Kong adolescents. It is also aimed at examining the changes in physical activity, self-compassion, and mental well-being among Hong Kong adolescents between, before, and after the peak of COVID-19 using the EXSEM-SC Model. The RMPAF has involved 572 (60% Female, *Mage* = 13.63, SD =1.31) Hong Kong secondary school students. Furthermore, using the abductive qualitative approach, a total of 25 (*Mage* = 14.84, *SD* = 1.40) students were involved in the in-depth interviews to further investigate the relationships within the EXSEM-SC. The quantitative results showed that the relationship between physical activity and self-compassion could be demonstrated by the EXSEM-SC, with a satisfactory goodness-of-fit index in the SEMs, as well as satisfying model construct consistency. Moreover, it showed no significant differences in the level of physical activity, self-compassion, and mental well-being during and after the peak of COVID-19. The qualitative results demonstrated two new categories within the EXSEM-SC variables, which are personality traits and injuries experiences. With the stability of the EXSEM-SC model among adolescents, it is expected that the physical activity intervention, which is based on the EXSEM-SC model, could also aim at easing Hong Kong adolescent's mental health issues. In addition, in terms of generating a long-term impact among students, the physical activity and self-compassionate intervention should be promoted among schools. However, the quantitative properties of the two new categories in the qualitative outcomes should be involved in future investigation.

Keywords: self-compassion; physical activity; mental well-being; adolescents

Citation: Wong, M.-Y.C.; Fung, H.-W.; Yuan, G.F. The Association between Physical Activity, Self-Compassion, and Mental Well-Being after COVID-19: In the Exercise and Self-Esteem Model Revised with Self-Compassion (EXSEM-SC) Perspective. *Healthcare* **2023**, *11*, 233. https://doi.org/10.3390/healthcare11020233

Academic Editor: Roberta Frontini

Received: 9 November 2022
Revised: 20 December 2022
Accepted: 29 December 2022
Published: 12 January 2023

1. Introduction

With its ongoing outbreak, the Coronavirus disease 2019 pandemic has not only caused a higher risk of death from the viral infection, but also led to great life-altering challenges. As the outbreak continues, youth's psychological problems may increase during the COVID-19 pandemic [1]. Youth are likely to be experiencing worry, anxiety, and fear [2]. School closures, lack of access to exercise and social interactions, boredom, or family poverty may increase students' negative emotions because they have less social support, which is essential for good mental health and well-being [3]. A cross-sectional study was conducted to assess a two-time point comparison between the months preceding the COVID-19 outbreak and two months after the social distancing and online schooling measures were implemented [4]. It indicated that adolescents showed a significant increase in depressive symptoms, anxiety, and poor parent-child relationship after the COVID-19 measures, while the COVID-19-related worries led to a significant decrease in life satisfaction as well [4]. Given that independence from parents and peer interaction are considered as the most important factors towards adolescents' development [5], school closures and the lack of peer support and interactions are likely to be the pertinent sources of stressors among adolescents, which affect their self-concept shaping and the estimation of self-worth [6], thus leading to high risk of vulnerability. Furthermore, adolescents have often been labelled as emotional and sensitive that their self-regulatory system is considered not yet mature until early adulthood [7]; therefore, fostering self-compassion among adolescents is considered a protective factor against adolescents' negative mental impact during COVID-19.

1.1. *Self-Compassion in COVID-19*

Self-compassion has been shown to improve adolescents' sense of well-being and mental health through providing oneself with self-kindness and reducing negative self-esteem [8,9]. Self-compassion is also seen as a coping mechanism in transforming negative feelings into neutral emotions, and towards a more productive emotion for oneself. It was discovered that a high level of self-compassion was associated with more emotion-focused coping mechanisms utilization, such as a positive reinterpretation and accepting their shortcomings [10]. Hence, self-compassion can act as a protective role in positive interventions to enhance the coping strategies of adolescents in regards to reacting to adversity during COVID-19 [11]. COVID-19-related research studies indicated that people who resulted in low levels of self-compassion tended to show anxiety and depression [12], and people with high levels of self-compassion tended to show better life satisfaction, despite self-quarantine [13]. Furthermore, a Hong Kong research study found that self-compassion is critical in influencing a person's adjustment to unprecedented problems [14], with self-compassion demonstrating a strong moderating influence between threats and perceived benefits of the pandemic (i.e., more time for rest and relaxation, learning new skills or knowledge), whereas persons with a higher degree of self-compassion exhibited a less positive relationship with the pandemic.

1.2. *Physical Activity and COVID-19*

During COVID-19, studies revealed the negative effects of social distancing measures, quarantining measures, and the lack of social support on adolescents' mental health. Several studies found a connection between social distancing measures, depression, and anxiety [15]. Furthermore, research has shown that reduced physical activity and social activities as a result of COVID-19 have led to higher scores of anxiety and depressive symptoms as well [16]. A study found that social restrictions had led to a drop in teenagers' physical activity participation, prolonged sedentary behavior, owing to online schooling and screen time, and irregular sleep patterns, creating long-term psychological health risks among adolescents during COVID-19 [17]. Among the Asian population studies, they revealed similar results on the reduced physical activity and increased sedentary behaviour among Chinese youths during COVID-19 [18]. As such, they revealed the importance of physical activity and a healthy lifestyle in mental health during COVID-19 [19].

1.3. *The Relationship between Physical Activity and Self-Compassion*

Given that the essential function of self-compassion in enhancing mental well-being has been validated, and programs such as the American College of Sports Medicine's Exercise is Medicine® represent the greatest way of preventing mental health problems [20], the impacts of regular physical activity on lowering mental health risk and boosting positive well-being cannot be refuted [21–24] conducted a comprehensive review and meta-analysis of the link between self-compassion and physical activity, and they found substantial relationships between self-compassion, physical activity, and physical activity intention. Moreover, Wong [24] have developed the model, named the Exercise Self-Esteem Model Revised with Self-Compassion (EXSEM-SC [24]), which significantly indicated the significant conceptualization among physical activity and self-compassion, with the involvement of exercise self-efficacy and body compassion. The EXSEM-SC Model has kept the variables of exercise self-efficacy, while replacing physical competence and acceptance with body compassion. It was anticipated that body compassion would be a more distinctive method to demonstrate the level of self-compassion of the physical self [25]. The significant result of the EXSEM-SC model demonstrates the possible influences of physical activity participation on adolescents' level of self-compassion. The EXSEM-SC version was changed based on Sonstroem and Morgan Exercise and Self-Esteem Model (EXSEM)developed in 1989, which at the start indicated the impact of bodily activity or exercise participation on character self-concept [26]. Despite the lack of evidence demonstrating the umbrella construct of self-compassion above self-esteem, Neff's argument on the mental hazards induced by self-esteem (i.e., self-enhancement bias, narcissism, and social comparison) and Deci and Ryan's conjecturing self-compassion as a type of "True self-esteem" [10,27–29] encourage the examination of self. As a result, the construction and adaptation of the EXSEM-SC model in showing the association between physical exercise and self-compassion in the current study is regarded robust and illustrative.

1.4. Research Gap and Purpose

Participating in self-based physical exercise is seen as autonomously accomplished under the notion of self, which could greatly lower emotional vulnerability during COVID-19. However, it is worth mentioning that only a few studies with mixed results compared the results of two-time points to investigate the impact of the COVID-19 pandemic on mental health and self-compassion in adolescents (during the peak of COVID-19 versus post-COVID-19 social distancing measures). Only two studies identified a significant negative correlation between COVID-19-related concerns, such as spending less time with friends and schooling, and negative mental well-being, such as loneliness, depression, and anxiety, among these few repeated measures or longitudinal studies [30,31]. The remaining studies, the majority of which looked at the Chinese population, found no significant differences in mental health status, such as depression, anxiety, stress, or suicidal thoughts, between the two time points [32–34].

Given that the COVID-19 pandemic has affected both adolescents' physical activity and psychological status, while documenting the importance of self-compassion in coping with adversity during COVID-19, the current research is aimed to examine the changes in physical activity, self-compassion, and mental well-being among Hong Kong adolescents between the peak of COVID-19 and after a certain release of the social distancing measures, using the Exercise Self-Esteem Model Revised with Self-Compassion (EXSEM-SC [24]). In addition to reviewing the impact of COVID-19, this research is also seen as a follow-up study of the development of EXSEM-SC, which is to investigate the stability and reliability of the model in demonstrating the relationship between physical activity, self-compassion, and mental well-being among Hong Kong adolescents. Furthermore, as a follow-up study of the EXSEM-SC, this study has conducted a qualitative interview to exploratively analyse the EXSEM-SC, as to explore the underlying interaction between physical activity and self-compassion. The qualitative study has abductively explored the EXSEM construct with self-compassion, which enabled the deductive analysis of the EXSEM-SC model, as well as the inductive analysis of the possible newly derived variables underneath the relationship between physical activity and self-compassion.

Based on the purpose of the study, the hypotheses of the study are,

Hypothesis 1. *There are significant mean differences between Time 1 and Time 2 (during COVID) in terms of the level of physical activity and self-compassion.*

Hypothesis 2. *A good-fit model is found for the EXSEM-SC when using a Repeated Measures Panel Analysis Framework.*

Hypothesis 3. *The interview outcomes are found to deductively support the EXSEM-SC and inductively derive additional variables for future modification.*

2. Methods

2.1. Participants and Procedures

Around 1000 students were recruited through convenience sampling in response to the sample size rule of thumb of structural equation modelling in the previous study [24]. Three government subsidized schools from the New Territories (n = 579), one school from Kowloon (n = 231), and one school from Hong Kong Island (n = 285) were recruited, as described in the earlier study by Wong et al. (2021). Notably, regardless of their degree of physical activity, all eligible secondary school students were able to participate in the current study. Students with any type of disability (including motor, visual, and hearing impairments, as well as intellectual and social difficulties) or who had been diagnosed with a mental or cognitive disorder were excluded from the study. The survey [24] was first conducted during the third wave of COVID-19 in Hong Kong (mid-to-late October 2020). In order to perform the repeated measure panel analysis, the students were invited to participate in the research survey after a 4 to 5 month interval for the retest, in which half-day face-to-face schooling started to resume. However, among the 1097 students involved in the previous model testing [24], only 589 students participated in the re-test survey. Among the 589 students, 20–30 participants were invited to participate in the in-depth interview as well. The students invited to be in the interview were required to be (1) Secondary school students, regardless of their physical activity participation level, and (2) students who were able to communicate fluently in either English or Chinese. Exclusion criteria were as follows: (1) Students with any kind of disability (i.e., motor impairment, visual or hearing impairment, intellectual or social disability) or diagnosed with any mental or cognitive illness, and (2) students who had undergone surgery that prevented them from participating in physical activity. In addition to this, students with past or current mental health issues, such as anxiety, stressfulness, or non-diagnosed depression, needed to seek school teachers' and parents' approval and had to be accompanied in order to participate in the interviews, or else they were excluded from the study.

2.2. Transparency and Openness

The University Research Ethics Committee granted ethical permission prior to the start of the study. After permission was granted, all data were collected at the schools. Before taking the questionnaire, all participants were required to sign a permission form stating that they understood the study's confidentiality agreement and that they were free to quit at any moment. Prior to data collection, all parents' informed consents were obtained through schools. We report how we determined our sample size, all data exclusions (if any), all manipulations, and all measures in the study, and we follow JARS [35]. All data, analysis code, and research materials are available upon request.

3. Measures

3.1. Self-Compassion

To determine the level of self-compassion, the Chinese version of the Self-compassion Scale [10,36] was used. The self-compassion measure is a 26 item, 5-point Likert scale derived from the 6 self-compassion components: self-kindness, common humanity, mindfulness, self-judgment, isolation, and over-identification (1 = nearly never, 5 = almost always). The test-retest reliability of the Chinese version of the self-compassion questionnaire was 0.89, with a Cronbach's alpha of over 0.80 among Chinese students [36,37].

3.2. *Body Compassion*

The Chinese-translated body compassion scale, which is able to enlighten both physical perception and self-compassion, was adopted to measure the level of body compassion. The body compassion scale is a 23-item scale with 3 subscales: defusion, common humanity, and acceptance. The items were rated on a 5-point scale (1 = almost never, 5 = almost always [10,38]. The Chinese-translated body compassion scale [24] showed satisfactory internal consistency and test-retest reliability, as well as adequate goodness-of-fit results, with X^2 (465.64)/227 = 2.05, $p < 0.001$, CFI = 0.916, TLI = 0.906, SRMR = 0.071, RMSEA = 0.069 (90% CI = 0.06 to 0.078).

3.3. *Exercise Self-Efficacy*

The Exercise Self-efficacy Scale [39–41] was used to assess how assured (or confident) individuals were in their ability to maintain a regular exercise regimen under a variety of settings. The Chinese version is based on Bandura's 17-item, 7-point Likert-type scale [42]. Cronbach's alpha score for the Chinese version of the scale was 0.944, indicating satisfactory reliability [36].

3.4. *Physical Activity Subjective Measure*

To acquire self-reported physical activity levels, the Chinese version of the Physical Activity Questionnaire for Adolescents (PAQ-A) was used. The questionnaire has nine questions on a 5-point Likert scale, 8 of which were utilized to calculate physical activity levels. The Chinese version of PAQ-A has a satisfactory Cronbach's alpha, ranging from 0.82 to 0.85, and a test-retest reliability of 0.81. It also had a moderate correlation value with the accelerometer-based physical activity objective measure [43].

3.5. *Mental Well-Being*

To assess people's overall mental health, the Chinese version of the Warwick-Edinburgh Mental Well-being Scale Short Form [44] was used. The WEMWBS is a 7-item scale with a 5-point Likert scale for the short version. Despite the fact that it is a short-form scale, the psychological components, such as affective-emotional, cognitive-evaluative, and psychological function, can be demonstrated and studied in a simple manner [45]. With a Cronbach's alpha of 0.93, an excellent test-retest reliability of 0.84 [44], and good convergent validity (CFI 0.986 and TLI = 0.979), the Chinese version demonstrated satisfactory internal reliability [46].

3.6. *Interview Setting*

The in-depth interviews each lasted for 30–45 min and were conducted via video conferencing (i.e., via Zoom) due to restrictions imposed by the COVID-19 pandemic. To ensure the theoretical sensitivity and trustworthiness of the qualitative research, a triangulation strategy was adopted, with each section of the interview involving more than one interviewer to provide multiple perspectives and follow-up questions. The interviewers (the authors) have no personal relationship with the interviewees, who work outside secondary schools. Yet, the author has been working closely with secondary schools and is familiar with the physical education system in Hong Kong, hence, shows a certain extent of understanding towards the interviewees' responses and the reality that students are facing.

The interview guide was formulated according to the hypothesized framework of the Exercise and Self-Esteem Model revised with self-compassion. The interview guide involved questions designed to explore the relationship between physical activity and self-compassion from a first-person perspective, through participants' daily experiences, exercise habits, and their feelings towards physical activities in light of the variables of the Exercise and Self-Esteem Model. This enabled the researchers to investigate how the participants indicated and described the components, as well as revealing the associations between physical activity and self-compassion, and to identify possible variables that were not included in the hypothesized model.

Moreover, the interview guide contained professional contributions to ensure accuracy and representativeness in illustrating the characteristics of self-compassion for the prospective relationship between physical activity and self-compassion (i.e., content validity). Hence, an expert in self-related concepts was invited to comment on the draft of the interview guide, until consensus was reached between the expert and the author regarding any discrepancies. Furthermore, five secondary school students were invited to participate in a pilot interview to evaluate the choice of words and the clarity of the questions.

4. Methodology and Data Analysis

4.1. Repeated Measure Panel Analysis Framework in Structural Equation Modeling

Through Rstudio [47], the models were constructed and tested in a Structural Equation Modelling Approach, with the full-information maximum likelihood estimator (FIML). The consistency and stability of the variables of the EXSEM-SC model was tested using the Repeated Measure Panel Analysis Framework. The EXSEM model revised with self-compassion is considered as a newly exploring model that variables relationship's stability is an essential concern. Hence, all the components within the proposed EXSEM structure, including self-compassion, were involved in the repeated measures, in which it is able to analyse whether the model structure is consistent over time and during the COVID-19 pandemic. Subsequently, the consistency of the model was tested based on the repeated measures panel analysis framework. The panel analysis framework allows an examination of both cross-sectional and 2-time point relations simultaneously. In the panel analysis framework, bivariate correlations among all variables were generated, and the first wave of the path analysis model had shown the path coefficients, either direct or indirect effects, between the model components. The second wave of the path analysis model had related to the relationships among the model components across the 2-time point in order to demonstrate the changes in the variables over time. These were identified by analysing the change of the path coefficients, the variation percentage (R^2) across a 2-time point, as well as the stability coefficients, for all the components within the panel model. It is acknowledgeable that with fewer variations and a high stability coefficient (0.70 or above), we can consider the structural model as consistent [48].

Various additional goodness-of-fit indicators were involved [49] and, with the following level of index, assumed to be a good fit: the minimum fit function (X^2), having chi-square to the degree of freedom ratio value range 2–5 as an acceptable fit [50]; Comparative Fit Index (CFI; [51]) and Tucker–Lewis index (TLI) rated as 0.90 or above [50]; Standardized Root Mean Square Residual (SRMR) value of 0.08 or below [51]; Root Mean Square Error of Approximation (RMSEA) value as between 0.05–0.08, with a 90% confidence interval [52].

4.2. Qualitative Procedures, Methodology and Analysis

The abductive grounded theory approach of Peirce [53] was utilized as a methodology to explore and investigate the hypothesized EXSEM revised with self-compassion model in order to conceptualize the theoretical construct systematically. The main purpose of abductive reasoning is to uncover the logic by having new ideas come into existence [53]. Tavory and Timmermans [54] summarized that using abductive analysis for generating theory should involve the capture of the narrative view of the targets and unfurl meaning making through interpreting their thoughts and experiences. This is a way leading to the process of theory construction; furthermore, it is an open and continuous process without a standardized meaning of interpretation. Nevertheless, during the abduction, the researcher should first recognize new ideas or breakdown anomaly to create a hypothetical inference, which can provide a meaningful explanation for the latent relations of the selected phenomenon. This is because abduction reasoning is proposed to observe the unknown cause and effect of familiar structures or phenomena [54]. Furthermore, Perice (1931–1958) conceptualized the reason for the abduction process being both logical and a flash of insight [53]. In order to be abductive, the research process should be as follows: First, with recognized phenomenon focus derived from literature reviews, the researcher should imply an established interpretive theory into the data collection process. While during the data synthesis and analysis, the interpretation of the aimed phenomenon should take the established interpretive theory into consideration. This process involves the unpacking and reforming of the dominating theory. Finally, it would then articulate a new interpretative theory from a new angle and a new connection that explains the targeted phenomenon. Abduction helps formulate groundwork interpretation with a theoretical contribution and would extend the bearing of the empirical findings and fill in the limitations of the examined theory. As a result, the abductive grounded theory approach was applied to deductively investigate the EXSEM-SC model and inductively confirm the model, as well as enumerate new variables for possible model modification.

The audio recordings of the interviews were transcribed verbatim, then translated from Chinese to English. The translated transcripts were screened by a second person to eliminate the translation variations, and the verbatim transcripts were returned to participants to verify the accuracy of the interview content, thus enhancing the credibility of the qualitative research. Nvivo 12 (QSR, [55]) was used to manage the empirical data through memo writing, coding, and categorizing until the data saturation was achieved. Conformability of the research was achieved by involving a second coder (that is, someone other than the author) in the coding and synthesis process, and collaboration occurred when the interpretation of data varied. The thematic synthesis approach was used in combination with grounded theory. In applying thematic synthesis, open codes were labelled with "descriptive" themes and then further "analytical" themes for the empirical data generated [56]. In addition, memos were written throughout the synthesis and analytic process to identify, develop, and keep track of theoretical ideas [57]. Furthermore, according to Haig [57], data collection and data analysis are to be done interactively in order to refine and enrich the empirical data subsequently [58,59]. Hence, data analysis has been engaged during the process of data gathering, for further data collection then ensuing data analysis continuously. Moreover, to consolidate and standardize the reporting of our qualitative research, the consolidated criteria for reporting qualitative research (COREQ checklist for interviews) was followed [60].

5. Results

Among the 1097 students, only 589 students participated in the re-test survey due to the change of school teaching schedule. While 11 cases with more than 20% missing data were deleted, 6 univariate and multivariate outlier cases were identified and deleted. The remaining missing data were replaced with the mean values of the items. The variables in the data set were normally distributed, with no items greater than 3.3 or less than −3.3. Finally, a total of 572 cases were included in the panel analysis, of which 59.5% and 40% were girls and boys, respectively, and the mean age was 13.63 (SD = 1.31). Additionally, the in-depth interviews were conducted with 25 (15 male, 10 female) secondary school students from both junior forms (n = 11) and senior forms (n = 14), with a mean age of 14.84 (SD = 1.40) years. Demographic information of the participants is indicated in Table 1.

5.1. Repeated Measure Panel Analysis Framework

The purpose of building the panel analysis framework is to show the stability and reliability of the Exercise and Self-esteem Model Revised with Self-Compassion and Mental Well-being among the adolescent population. On top of the first (Time 1) path analysis done on EXSEM-SC and EXSEM-SC with mental well-being, participants were involved in a re-test survey (Time 2) four to five months after the first data collection, thus enabling the development of the repeated measure panel analysis framework. Responding to hypothesis 1, Table 2 showed no significant differences in the level of physical activity, self-compassion, and mental well-being between, during and after COVID-19, while only the level of exercise self-efficacy and body compassion showed significant differences among the secondary school students. Table 3 showed the correlation matrix of all the model variables, including both Time 1 and Time 2 variables data. Variables showed a significant correlation with each other at the same time point. Each variable also showed a significant correlation with their respective repeated measure outcome.

Table 1. Demographic Information of the in-depth interview.

Participant's Code ID	Age	Gender	Form of Physical Activity	Type of Physical Activity
CKS1	14	Male	School-based	Table Tennis
CKS2	14	Male	Leisure-based	Swimming
CSK3	13	Male	Leisure-based	Swimming
CSK4	13	Male	Leisure-based & School-based	Running & Basketball
CSK5	12	Male	School-based	Basketball
CSK6	14	Male	School-based	Taekwondo
WGF1	16	Female	Leisure-based	Volleyball
WGF2	16	Male	Leisure-based	Basketball, Football & Running
WGF3	16	Male	Leisure-based	Running & Cycling
WGF4	16	Female	Leisure-based & School-based	Yoga & Volleyball
WGF5	16	Male	Leisure-based & School-based	Softball & Gym
WGF6	14	Male	School-based	Football
WGF7	14	Female	Leisure-based	Cycling
WGF8	14	Female	Leisure-based & School-based	Table Tennis & Volleyball
WGF9	14	Female	School-based	Table Tennis & Volleyball
WGF10	14	Female	Leisure-based& School-based	Table Tennis & Volleyball
LDF1	15	Female	Leisure-based	Basketball & Running
LDF2	15	Female	Leisure-based	Basketball & Cycling
LDF3	15	Female	Leisure-based	Basketball
LDF4	15	Male	School-based	Taekwondo
LDF5	15	Male	School-based	Fencing
LDF6	15	Male	Leisure-based	Fencing
LDF7	18	Female	Professional Athletes	Swimming
SJ1	18	Male	Professional Athletes	Swimming
SJ2	15	Male	Professional Athletes	Swimming

When comprising and comparing the Time 1 and Time 2 model, the panel analysis framework showed a good fit model in both the EXSEM model revised with self-compassion (X^2 (60)/16 = 53.75, CFI = 0.957, TLI = 0.957, SRMR = 0.043, and RMSEA = 0.072 (90% CI = 0.053–0.092), as well as the EXSEM model revised with self-compassion and mental well-being (X^2 (90.84)/26 = 3.49, CFI = 0.956, TLI = 0.94, SRMR = 0.049, and RMSEA = 0.068 (90% CI = 0.053–0.083). Furthermore, the consistency of the path coefficient and the R-square were looked into as well. Referring to Figures 1 and 2, all paths were significant with consistent path coefficients, with all changes within 0.1. Additionally, the R-square changes were within 0.03, which a low R-square change with variation of less than 30% indicated the structural model as consistent [48]. The research outcomes supported hypothesis 2, that the EXSEM-SC model was consistent over time, as well as during COVID-19, when the mental status of participants tended to fluctuate, which also supported the generalizability of the model within different social circumstances.

Table 2. Paired T-test.

		Mean Differences	Std. Deviation	t	df	Sig.
Pair 1	PA & R_PA	−0.02	0.92	−0.67	568	0.50
Pair 2	ESE & R_ESE	−0.3	2.57	−3.14	568	0.002
Pair 3	SC & R_SC	0.0	0.70	1.63	568	0.10
Pair 4	BC & R_BC	−0.10	0.69	−3.33	568	0.001
Pair 5	WB & R_WB	0.036	1.06	0.80	568	0.42

Note: PA = Time 1 physical activity; R_PA: Time 2 physical activity; ESE = Time 1 exercise self-efficacy; R_ESE = Time 2 exercise self-efficacy; SC = Time 1 self-compassion; R_SC = Time 2 self-compassion; BC = Time 1 body compassion; R_BC = Time 2 body compassion; WB = Time 1 mental well-being; R_WB = Time 2 mental well-being.

Table 3. Correlation Matrix Among All Variables Between Test and Re-Test.

	PA	R_PA	ESE	R_ESE	SC	R_SC	BC	R_BC	WB	Mean (*SD*)
PA	-									2.20 (0.78)
R_PA	0.30 **	-								2.18 (0.76)
ESE	0.57 **	0.15 **	-							4.62 (2.15)
R_ESE	0.17 **	0.54 **	0.24 **	-						4.96 (2.00)
SC	0.10 *	0.04	0.24 **	0.11 **	-					3.10 (0.50)
R_SC	0.06	0.25 **	0.11 *	0.38 **	0.14 **	-				3.05 (0.57)
BC	0.08 *	0.02	0.24 **	0.10 *	0.618 **	0.113 **	-			3.01 (0.47)
R_BC	0.01	0.15 **	0.004	0.20 **	0.08	0.57 **	0.09 *	-		3.11 (0.55)
WB	0.21 **	0.13**	0.23 **	0.15 **	0.51 **	0.15 **	0.48 **	0.09 *	-	3.30 (0.85)
R_WB	0.04	0.31 **	0.04	0.39 **	0.11 *	0.49 **	0.07	0.48 **	0.19 **	3.26 (0.82)

Note: * $p < 0.05$, ** $p < 0.01$. PA = Time 1 physical activity; R_PA: Time 2 physical activity; ESE = Time 1 exercise self-efficacy; R_ESE = Time 2 exercise self-efficacy; SC = Time 1 self-compassion; R_SC = Time 2 self-compassion; BC = Time 1 body compassion; R_BC = Time 2 body compassion; WB = Time 1 mental well-being; R_WB = Time 2 mental well-being.

5.2. Qualitative Interview Outcomes

The 25 participants participated in different kinds of exercise and were at different levels of participation, and some of the participants participated in more than one kind of exercise. Participants' level of participation was divided into three categories: Leisure-based physical activity, in which physical activity is engaged in for leisure purposes; school-based PA, in which participants had joined the school team and had participated in inter-school competitions; and professional athletes who trained with the Hong Kong team. Participants reported different psychological states and influences during participation in PA. They revealed positive psychological states and benefits during and after participating in PA. In general, participants stated that participation in PA relaxed them, increased their perseverance, and matured them in overcoming difficulties. Unlike such generalities, the Exercise and Self-Esteem model revised with self-compassion revealed particular categories.

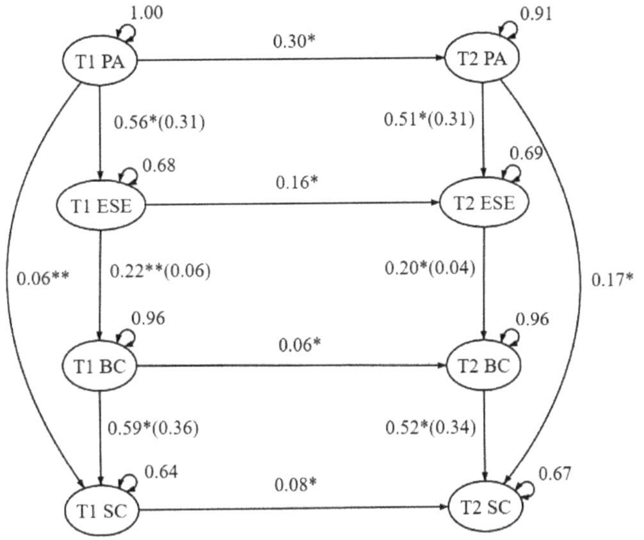

Figure 1. Exercise and Self-Esteem Model Revised with Self-Compassion—Panel Analysis Framework. Note. Standardized coefficients, total variance explained on the outcome (R^2) and errors are presented. R^2 is presented in brackets, in the form of $\beta(R^2)$. * $p < 0.05$, ** $p < 0.01$. T1 PA = Time 1 physical activity; T2 PA = Time 2 physical activity; T1 ESE = Time 1 exercise self-efficacy; T2 ESE = Time 2 exercise self-efficacy; T1 BC = Time 1 body compassion; T2 BC = Time 2 body compassion; T1 SC = Time 1 self-compassion; T2 SC = Time 2 self-compassion.

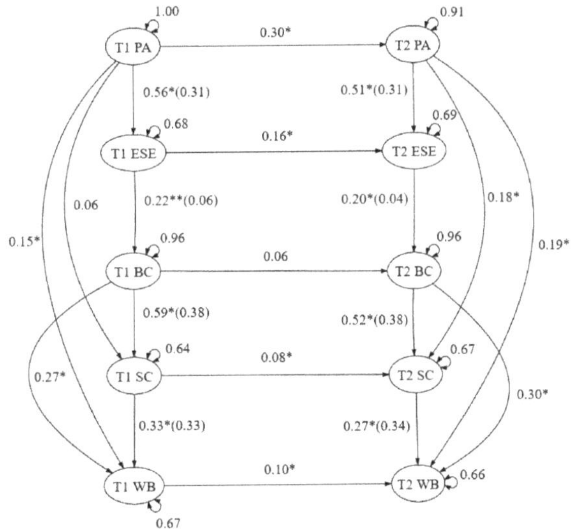

Figure 2. Exercise and Self-esteem Model Revised With Self-Compassion Including Mental Well-being—Panel Analysis Framework. Note. Standardized coefficients, total variance explained on the outcome (R^2) and errors are presented. R^2 is presented in brackets, in the form of $\beta(R^2)$. * $p < 0.05$, ** $p < 0.01$. T1 PA = Time 1 physical activity; T2 PA = Time 2 physical activity; T1 ESE = Time 1 exercise self-efficacy; T2 ESE = Time 2 exercise self-efficacy; T1 BC = Time 1 body compassion; T2 BC = Time 2 body compassion; T1 SC = Time 1 self-compassion; T2 SC = Time 2 self-compassion; T1 WB = Time 1 mental well-being; T2 WB = Time 2 mental well-being.

6. Exercise Self-Efficacy

Exercise self-efficacy refers to the degree to which one can successfully perform, adopt, and maintain an exercise behaviour. Several participants provided relevant statements regarding exercise self-efficacy. Most of the leisure-based PA and school-based PA participants showed positive exercise self-efficacy after experiencing a breakthrough in their exercises (Figure 3).

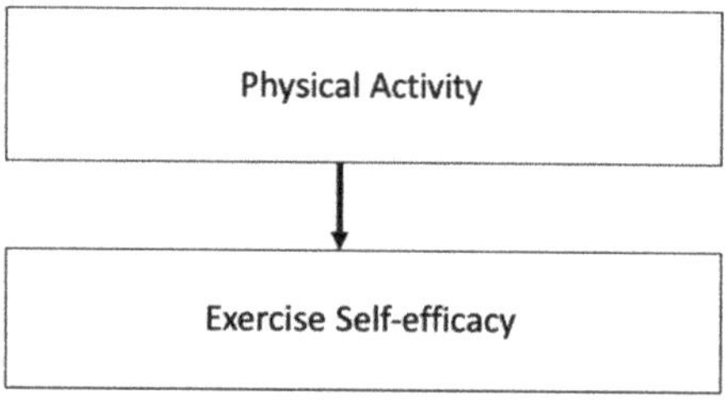

Figure 3. Relationship between Physical Activity and Exercise Self-Efficacy. Note. The figure demonstrate the path from physical activity to exercise self-efficacy, which in line with the original EXSEM.

A school-based PA participant (*CSK1*) stated, "After I have learned a new difficult table tennis technique, I feel accomplished, and have more self-confidence".

A leisure-time PA participant (*CSK4*) similarly stated, "After I have engaged in regular physical activity, I feel stronger and very happy just like someone who has overcome something difficult".

In addition, participants showed that the self-efficacy and self-confidence gained through participating in physical activity did not only apply to exercise performance or exercise behaviour maintenance, but also other experiences in their daily lives.

However, negative exercise self-efficacy was shown in the interview outcomes as well.

A professional athlete (*SJ1*) stated, "I tend to give up my main event if I fail to perform my personal best in the competition because I will never feel confident in performing it well again in the next competition".

Negative exercise self-efficacy was not restricted to the high-level competition of professional athletes. A school-based PA participant (*WKF4*) also stated that she would think of herself as a mess if she was not in good condition during exercising. Exercise self-efficacy was seen as a more shaped concept among secondary school students; hence, both young and older adolescents (junior form and senior form students) were able to describe and reveal their thoughts towards exercise self-efficacy, as well as not showing any substantial differences in the effect of physical activity on exercise self-efficacy.

7. Self-Compassion—Mindfulness vs. Over-Identified

Under the concept of self-compassion, mindfulness refers to focusing on the present moment and being aware of one's deficiencies in a neutral emotional state. Participants showed better self-awareness regarding their own difficulties through the calmness and the sense of focus brought on by doing physical activity and the gaining of positive experiences after having engaged in physical activity.

A leisure-based PA participant (*LDF1*) reflected, "Doing exercise helps me focus more on myself, as well as be more attentive when doing other work, so I think that exercise makes me more contemplative". Therefore, engaging in physical activity led to tranquil contemplation and having a calm mind, which helped participants to be more focused on themselves, as well as more self-aware in their daily issues. Moreover, participants with demonstrably positive exercise self-efficacy, regardless of the level of PA participation, showed the ability to be aware of their deficiencies in a neutral, reflectively way. Hence, they were regarded as being mindful of their daily issues under the concept of self-compassion. However, two of the professional athletes tended to show over-identification towards their deficiencies of performing poorly in their professional sports, which led to negative self-reflection and self-judgment.

Other than the differences shown among different levels of PA participation, junior form students showed a difference in the use of words, compared to that of senior form students when illustrating the effect of physical activity on being mindful. Junior form students tended to describe their mindful situation as, "I'm not thinking of anything". or "My brain was plain when I'm doing exercise", while senior form students tended to use the word "focus", "being more aware of", "to reflect". This indicated that senior form students were more aware than junior form students. However, it is worth noting that, the junior form students were able to be more aware or describe more in details about their inner status after the interviewer provided these keywords in the conversation.

8. Self-Compassion—Self-Kindness vs. Self-Judgment

Self-kindness means that individuals treat themselves with love and kindness, as opposed to self-judgment, which causes individuals to impose cruel judgment on themselves when facing their own deficiencies.

The current study found that people tended to undergo a process of self-reflection before they engaged in any acts of self-kindness or self-judgment. It was found that, after the mindful process during and after physical activity, participants tended to reflect on their failures, negativities, and deficiencies.

Some of the leisure-based PA (*WGF6, CSK2*) and school-based PA participants (*CSK6, LDF4*) stated that they looked at recordings of their workout or competition to figure out and reflect on where to improve.

After the self-reflection process, participants who were shown to be more positive and optimistic tended to engage in self-kindness. This involved, firstly, performing self-love by treating themselves, such as allowing time for video gaming, reading books, or listening to music, while some participants also mentioned that doing PA was in itself a kind of self-love act. Secondly, it involved showing self-acceptance towards their deficiencies. For instance, a leisure-based PA participant said, "After the process of being aware of what's wrong with me as well as the process of self-reflection, I tend to accept the current situation, and treat this case as an experience, and find further ways of improvement" (*WGF1*). Thirdly, upon self-acceptance, participants tended to shift the failure as a kind of motivation for improvement, stating, for example, "I tend to be motivated to deal with my other issues after doing exercises" (*WGF1*) and "I will apply this motivated attitude gained from doing exercise to overcome other daily difficulties, telling myself I could pass this difficulty just as I passed the hardship in training" (*LDF4*). Finally, participants with self-kindness would engage in positive self-talk stating, for example, "Everything has a second chance, I can do it over and over again until I do it well" (*WGF6*). As illustrated by the above statements, participants who showed themselves kindness tended not to impose cruel judgments or to self-criticism, but were positive instead. It is also worth noting that participants who showed self-kindness had a positive attitude towards themselves, stating, for example, "As we do our best, that's enough" (*CSK3*), and "I think the word criticize is too negative for me, therefore, I won't" (*CSK6*).

However, participants who were perfectionistic and demanding tended to show self-judgment towards their deficiencies before finding ways to improve or to tackle the issue. Participants showed disappointment in themselves by stating, for example, "I would keep looping my negativities, and I don't know why I still can't get out of this despite keeping on trying to improve and correct it" (*SJ1*), and "I would wonder whether I'm not working hard enough" (*CSK1*). Moreover, participants who engaged in self-criticism after the awareness process and after reflecting on their deficiencies displayed a cyclical loop of their negativities and liked sinking into a metaphorical hole that was full of their own failures, in which they thought they could not improve. Yet, the level of self-judgement was determined by the importance and the influencing effect of the failure.

A school-based PA participant (*CSK4*) reflected, "I will keep blaming myself and will force myself to do better and get back into good condition".

A professional athlete (*SJ1*) said, "I have to keep my mind on my training performance, and I will keep focusing on my deficiencies until I find ways to solve them or figure out what's wrong to me".

Despite being self-critical, the study showed that participants would go through a transition process between self-criticism and the release of criticism, which entailed engaging in common humanity, thus achieving a positive psychological state.

9. Self-Compassion—Common Humanity and Isolation

In the context of self-compassion, common humanity refers to the individual's ability to not take their life difficulties and failures too personally, but be able to relate to others who are in a similar situation. Most of the participants, both junior and senior form students, showed common humanity when suffering from failings, and they were willing to share their failing with their peers, parents, and teachers when necessary. A few participants noted that as most of their peers might have experienced a similar situation, talking with peers made them feel that their sadness was being shared (*CSK4, CSK1, LDF5, LDF6*). Other participants stated that communicating with teachers or parents could further assist positive self-awareness regarding their deficiencies, thus releasing stress and breaking their attachment to negative emotions (*LDF6, LDF7, WGF3, WGF8, SJ2*). However, a minority of participants chose to isolate themselves from their failures, especially after engaging in self-criticism.

A professional athlete (*SJ1*) stated, "I will tend to escape from that particular event at which I failed to perform at my personal best and try not to compete in that event anymore".

A participant who engaged in both leisure-based and school-based PA (*WGF4*) also mentioned that she might choose not to face that particular issue until she could find a proper solution.

10. The Relationship between Physical Activity and Self-Compassion

Figure 4 shows the conceptual framework of the relationship between physical activity and self-compassion. Firstly, the study outcomes have successfully indicated that physical activity can affect participants' exercise self-efficacy and lead to self-compassion through engaging in PA, as well as the efficacy gained through PA. In addition, the study has also shown that physical activity can lead directly to individual self-compassion, specifically the consistency of the calmness and sense of focus while doing physical activity.

The Processing of Self-Compassion Components

Although mindfulness, self-kindness, self-judgment, common humanity, and self-isolation are components of self-compassion, the outcomes of the interviews showed that the components also formed a series of processing stages, mediated by self-reflection.

A leisure-based PA participant (*LDF1*) stated, "When doing exercise on my own, like playing basketball or going for a run, that's a time for me to contemplate, it is a process for me to quietly reflect myself. (How about after reflecting?) I then acknowledge that there may be an issue and try to improve it, or think how to do it better next time".

It can thus be seen that individuals achieved mindfulness through the process of contemplation during PA and gained self-awareness of their deficiencies. Then, they would reflect and show themselves self-kindness by accepting the deficiency and courageously finding ways to improve, including approaching peers or coaches for their opinions.

Several participants who engaged in acts of self-judgment also went through the self-compassion processing stages; additionally, they displayed a release of pressure and stress, which can be regarded as resulting in better mental well-being. A leisure-based PA participant who fenced (*LDF6*) reflected as follows:

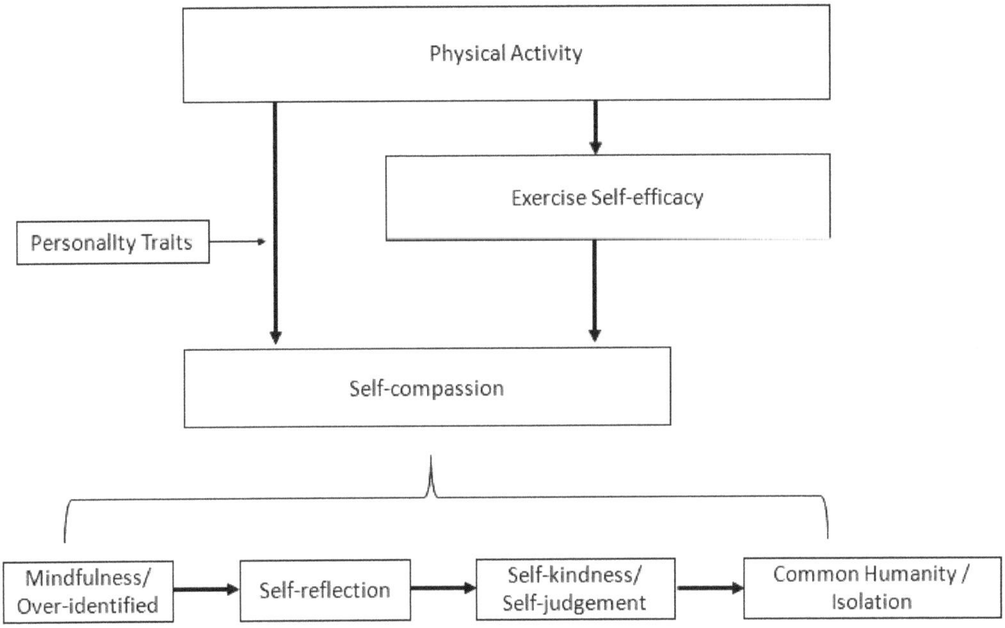

Figure 4. The Relationship between Physical Activity and Self-Compassion. Note. This figure indicated the path from physical activity to self-compassion through exercise self-efficacy. On the other hand, it also indicates the possible mediating effect of personality on physical activity and self-compassion. Additionally, the four sub-categories under self-compassion were shown and demonstrated their processing stage from mindfulness towards common humanity.

I become more persistent or could be called obsessed with my stuff after I have fenced. Fencing is an activity which requires different kinds of postures and these postures must be accurate; therefore, after I have fenced, I tend to be obsessed with those postures that I have done badly and may feel desperate when I keep thinking about why I can't I do the postures right. (Which means you will also become more persistent while doing other things and will also be obsessed when you do other things wrong?) Yes. (So, how would you overcome this obsession?) I will find my peers or even my coach to talk about it, then I will feel released that, oh, actually everyone will do it wrongly at the beginning, then I will stop being obsessed.

A school-based PA participant (*WGF5*) also stated:

I will blame or judge myself after a poor performance in a competition, maybe I will be sad or down for a couple of days after the competition, after that, I will try find my peers to talk about it to see how I can improve in the next competition. I think you definitely would blame yourself when you face difficulties, however, you also need to try finding ways to make a change, but not keep blaming yourself. I think it's just a process.

The study's outcomes indicated that after the process of acknowledging one's negativities or the particular issue, as well as reflecting on them, individuals who impose self-judgment regarding their failings would blame or criticize themselves for a shorter period of time. The period is not that long for most of the participants. Then, they would engage with common humanity in order to release their negative feelings. However, there was a minority among the participants who self-isolated instead. Additionally, the participants indicated that the experiences and feelings gained from doing PA had changed their way of thinking and attitude towards their daily life issues by osmosis. Despite professional athletes having to pay more attention to their sports performance, participants stated that they held similar attitudes when facing other daily issues, especially when facing academic-related issues. There were, thus no perceivable differences between leisure-based PA participants, school-based PA participants, and professional athletes. Furthermore, when discussing topics related to self-kindness and self-judgment, interviewees were asked whether they were used to thinking positively or negatively about daily issues. Responses showed that participants who typically thought positively and who were optimistic tended to show self-kindness and common humanity, while participants who typically thought negatively and were always being distracted by negative emotions showed self-judgment and isolation, as well as being less mindful. Therefore, personality traits can be regarded as moderating between PA and self-compassion.

11. Body Compassion

Body compassion combines the multidimensional concept of body image with self-compassion and indicates an individuals' level of compassion and acceptance towards their body in terms of appearance, competence, and health.

The interviews outcomes in this study showed participants changed their body perception after indicating their exercise self-efficacy. Participants who showed changes in exercise self-efficacy after physical injuries tended to show changes in body compassion. A school-based PA participant (*LDF5*) stated:

I had suffered from a muscle sprain about one year ago and stopped training for around half a year. I feel like I need to work extra hard to recover and build up the strength of that particular part of the muscle in order to get back to good physical condition for training. Therefore, I keep actively finding ways to solve this problem like consulting the physiotherapist.

Another school-based PA participant (*WGF5*) said,

I had suffered some small injuries before, not that serious, and I don't think it had affected my efficacy in doing exercise or recovering. Therefore, I just try to take some rest and won't consider much about it, everyone will get injuries when doing exercises.

A leisure-based PA participant (*WGF3*) stated,

I will keep being active despite having some slight injuries in order to improve my body, as I know what kind of exercise I need to do to tackle that injury. For example, I get injured in my back, you know that's already happened then you may choose some gym exercise that could train and strengthen the back muscles.

A professional athlete participant (SJ2) expressed the following:

There's a time I competed in a race with my hand injury, I keep mentally telling myself to just go through it even though it is painful. Surprisingly, I even got satisfying results in that race. Therefore, I think it just about your mentality sometimes, but not exactly the physical injuries that affect you.

According to the statements above, individuals with positive self-efficacy, in spite of injuries, showed positive body compassion by accepting their injuries and acknowledging that injuries resulting from physical activity are common, and by actively finding ways to strengthen the injured body part, or even to break through the mental blocks due to the injuries and regain their reduced exercise efficacy.

However, there were senior form participants who showed negative exercise self-efficacy, as well as negative body compassion, especially defusion. Two professional athletes (*SJ1*, *LDF7*) stated that they had thought of giving up an event or even their sport after a serious injury, while a school-based PA participant (*WGF9*) stated, "Without playing volleyball for more than half a year, my physical fitness and ball sense reduced, and I felt mentally so tired that I thought of just letting it go, just giving up".

These individuals showed that they tended to want to escape from the fact that they were suffering from an injury, instead of accepting the injury and finding positive ways to treat the injury. Compared to junior form participants who got injured due to physical activity, they showed more kindness and acceptability towards their injuries. They accepted the fact that they were injured, yet they also believed that they would be able to recover and reengage in physical activity in a short period of time.

A few participants, regardless of age, who did not suffer from injuries due to physical activities gave positive comments relating to body compassion and further demonstrated positive effects towards exercise self-efficacy (Figure 5). For example, a participant who engaged in both leisure-based and school-based PA (*WGF4*) stated, "Doing exercise, both cycling and volleyball, makes my muscles stronger and the shape of my leg muscles more appealing as well. But, as a girl, I don't think it bothers me, in the opposite, I tend to like this appearance and would like to keep it by keeping on doing exercise". Another school-based PA participant (*WGF5*) expressed the following:

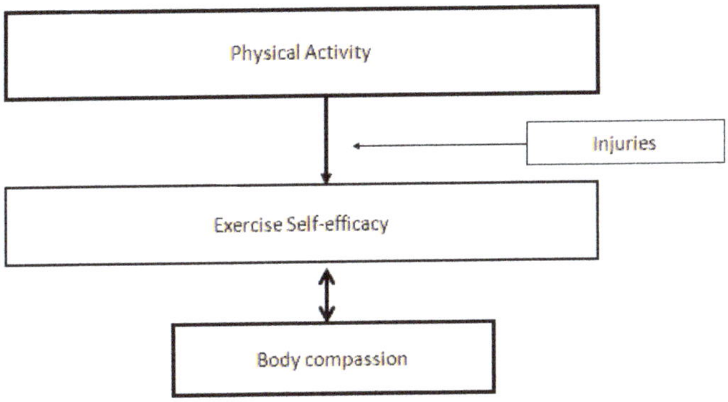

Figure 5. The Relationship between Exercise Self-efficacy and Body Compassion. Note. This figure indicated the path from physical activity to body compassion, which it is in lined with the EXSEM, with the replacement of body compassion. However, injuries is indicated as a possible mediator between physical activity and exercise self-efficacy, in order to reach body compassion. Besides, the relationship between exercise self-efficacy and body compassion could be indicated as inter-related.

Since I started to exercise from a young age, I felt that my physical fitness or cardiorespiratory function was better than others, because I have been doing sports for a long period of time. Hence, I felt more confident about my physical body, my exercise skills sometimes, which could help me perform better in a competition. So, I think doing exercises is valuable to my physical body.

However, the rest of the participants (*LDF1, LDF4, LDF6, WGF1, WGF2, WGF4*), who did not suffer from any physical injuries, only provided general comments regarding changes in their body, such as being physically stronger and having a better physical appearance, like being slimmer and looking healthier, while showing a neutral perception towards body compassion. These participants expressed that they felt no special thoughts about the value of their physical body and were less likely to relate their physical body with their inner emotions or thoughts.

12. Discussion

The study results indicated that the relationship between physical activity and self-compassion could be demonstrated by the EXSEM-SC, with a satisfactory goodness-of-fit index in the SEMs, as well as satisfying model construct consistency. Moreover, the study results showed no significant differences in the level of physical activity, self-compassion, and mental well-being during and after the peak of COVID-19, which, on the one hand, shows the insignificant impact of COVID-19 on physical activity and psychological status among Hong Kong adolescents, and, on the other hand, documented the stability and reliability of the EXSEM-SC and EXSEM-SC with mental well-being model among the Hong Kong adolescents population. The qualitative interview allows the hypothesized model to be linked with the ordinary experiences of the participants, which showed an interactive relationship between the data and the hypothesized EXSEM revised with self-compassion model that has combined with the existing EXSEM model [61,62]. The results demonstrated that the relationship between physical activity and self-compassion was mediated by exercise self-efficacy, which is expected based on the Exercise and Self-Esteem Model revised with self-compassion. Moreover, a new category, personality traits, was determined inductively from the outcomes and seen as a potential moderator in the direct association between physical activity and self-compassion. Self-compassion and the processing stages of self-compassion were shown to achieve further mental well-being as well. Since the body compassion category showed no interrelation between physical activity and self-compassion, a separate conceptual pathway was built between physical activity and body compassion through exercise self-efficacy. Additionally, a new category, injuries, was inductively determined from the outcomes and seen as a potential moderator between physical activity and exercise self-efficacy, which then influenced body compassion. Figure 6 shows the conceptual framework of the Exercise and Self-Esteem Model revised with self-compassion based on the abductive qualitative approach.

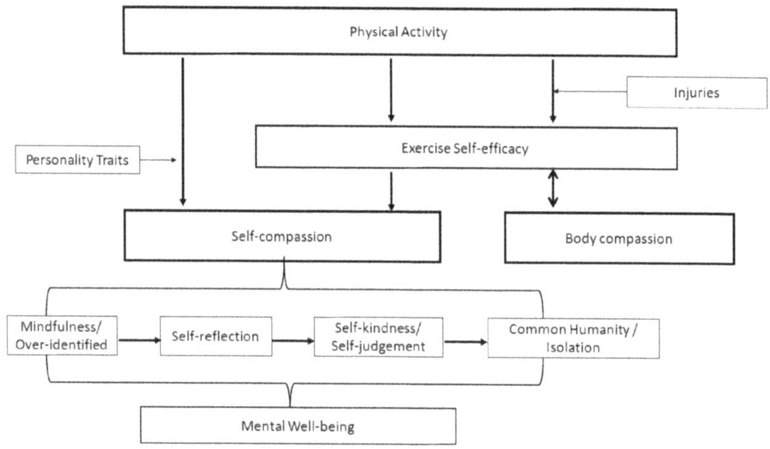

Figure 6. Exercise and Self-Esteem Model revised with self-compassion: An Abductive Qualitative Approach. Note. This figure demonstrates the final model of the interview outcomes. Self-compassion and body compassion have shown as two separate paths, without any inter-relationships. While, the figure also indicates the effect of physical activity and self-compassion in achieving mental well-being.

12.1. The Impact of COVID-19

Surprisingly, the current research showed no significant differences in adolescents' PA levels during and after the peak of COVID-19. In light of the fact that most of the research studies report significant declines in physical activity levels and healthy lifestyle behaviors [17], it was anticipated that external factors would play a role in helping Hong Kong adolescents maintain their PA levels. Research demonstrated that parents' education and parental support on the importance of maintaining healthy living during public health challenges were positively correlated with adolescents' PA level and maintained a sufficient PA level during COVID-19 [63]. In addition, environmental and psychosocial factors are considered to be critical in supporting adolescents' intrinsic motivation to engage in physical activity and their self-determination to pursue positive well-being [64]; therefore, based on the self-determination theory, adolescents should have been able to engage in physical activity autonomously under the support of schools and parents despite social distancing measures [65]. Based on empirical research, adolescents are likely to have scheduled their daily schedule, which includes engaging in various hobbies and physical activities, is well-organized, and reflects their adaptive coping abilities, contributing to subjective well-being [66]. Hence, it supports that people with a high level of social cognition, including self-efficacy and self-regulation, showed a higher level of PA during the COVID-19 pandemic as well.

As a result of these empirical findings, it can also be explained that Hong Kong adolescents' exercise confidence has increased as foreseeable obstacles to exercise engagement or other exercise barriers have been reduced as a result of COVID-19, and they are able and feel more confident to engage in physical activity with more time and capacity. Moreover, adolescents at the transformation stage of maturation and risk of identity crisis [67] are expected to have heightened attention towards health literacy and body image, thus resulting in engaging in preventive behaviour, such as physical activity, as well as demonstrating a higher level of exercise self-efficacy and body compassion. During COVID-19, despite there being research that indicated negative body image in women due to struggling with regular eating habits [68], another study indicated that students showed a decrease in unhealthy food intake and irregular eating habits [69]. In this way, Hong Kong adolescents are more likely to show kindness and compassion to their bodies and to realize that others may also be experiencing similar struggles during the lockdown or social isolation measures associated with COVID-19.

Apart from the unchanged PA level, Hong Kong adolescents' self-compassion was less likely to be affected by the COVID-19 pandemic. As mentioned in the literature review, self-compassion could act as a protective role and a positive coping strategy during COVID-19, resulting in better life satisfaction [13]. Moreover, empirical research studies demonstrated that adolescents with a higher level of self-compassion showed a direct association with psychological well-being [70], in which one would engage in reducing stress and fears brought by COVID-19 and show gratitude towards their concurrent life status [70]. However, there was limited research stating the impact of COVID-19 on self-compassion, except those of intervention studies. Self-compassion was less likely to be affected by COVID-19 because it is conceptualized as a psychological trait. It has always been found that self-compassion acts as an emotional protective factor for mental health problems, such as depression and anxiety, and that self-compassion measures are consistent across populations across time [71]. Therefore, self-compassion was conceptualized as a trait model similar to that of personality traits [72], which were commonly examined together in interpersonal and intrapersonal problems [71,73–75]. However, self-compassion is a modifiable trait [76]; it can only be cultivated or improved through intervention or practice, but is less likely to be affected by COVID-19 significantly.

12.2. The Newly Derived Variables from the Qualitative Interview

12.2.1. Personality Traits Moderating Physical Activity and Self-Compassion

The research outcomes showed that individuals with a more positive and optimistic mindset tended to demonstrate positive self-compassion; vice versa, individuals who were perfectionists and who tended to be obsessed with their failings demonstrated negative self-compassion. Hence, it could be interpreted that individual differences involving personality traits would affect the relationship between physical activity and self-compassion. The literature contains limited research regarding physical activity and self-compassion, never mind involving personality traits. Yet there was sufficient research stating the effect of personality on self-compassion. Research has shown that perfectionism reduced levels of self-compassion and, thus, increased the risk of depression [77], and this moderating relationship was shown to be more significant among adolescents [78]. People with personality disorders, including narcissistic and borderline personality disorder, showed a negative association with self-compassion and a positive association with self-criticism. Based on the Big Five personality traits, self-compassion was once regarded as being similar to neuroticism, hence neuroticism was tested and demonstrated a significant correlation with negative self-compassion [79]. Furthermore, other personality traits, including extraversion, agreeableness, conscientiousness, and openness, as well as their latent factors, demonstrated a significant positive correlation with positive self-compassion [79,80]. According to the above literature, personality traits can be regarded as a factor influencing individuals' levels of self-compassion. Despite physical activity having been shown to be a self-care method to improve self-compassion, the degree of improvement may be influenced by one's personality. Therefore, other than including personality traits as a testing component in the model, the potential effect of personality traits should be considered as an influencing factor or a covariance in future physical activity intervention research in order to identify the potential differences among personality traits regarding the effect of physical activity on self-compassion.

12.2.2. The Stages of Processing within Self-Compassion through Self-Reflection

The process cycle of the self-compassion facets has been discussed by Neff [27], showing that individuals with self-compassion could first mindfully acknowledge and become aware of their own sufferings, then alleviate them with kindness, while gentle comfort and soothing helps individual to accept their failings by relating themselves to others and the outside world. However, in Neff's [27] article, she only briefly mentioned the process of self-reflection together with self-kindness and self-judgement, but did not consider self-reflection as a separate stage within self-compassion. Moreover, a study of Chinese adults indicated that self-kindness and mindfulness could moderate the relationship between self-criticism and depression [81]. The current study, however, indicates that self-reflection is a perceivable stage within the three facets of self-compassion, in particular between mindfulness/over-identified and self-kindness/self-judgment. Participants demonstrated that they would process self-reflection first, regardless of whether it was gentle or cruel, about their failings and deficiencies, then they expressed their way of perceiving the deficiencies, as well as the reflections. Research has shown that individuals with increased mindfulness were associated with better self-awareness and self-reflection, thus leading to an increase of self-compassion [82]. This is because being mindful helps individuals to discover their boundaries easily and equips them with better self-knowledge, thus leading to better performance in self-acceptance and showing gentleness towards oneself [62,83]. Additionally, self-reflection was also regarded as a tool to emphasize oneself, where individuals who have performed self-reflection demonstrated positive emotions and enhanced the positive soothing effect, thus representing the achievement of self-kindness [84].

12.2.3. The Association between Body Compassion, Self-Compassion, and Psychological Status among Hong Kong Secondary School Students

Based on the significant association between body compassion and self-compassion reported in previous studies [24], it was expected that Hong Kong secondary school students would express a perceivable relationship between body compassion and self-compassion. Although a few participants mentioned this aspect, they showed a common feature in which was they all treated physical injuries and the effect on their physical activity engagement as the most important issue is their life, which showed a recognizable relationship within their conversation. Research studies have also supported that people with physical injuries would be paying more attention towards their body image and self due to bodily changes, and resulted in either positive or negative self-concept and body image [85]. Furthermore, a recent study indicated that illness and injuries had been shown to influence and cause variation in the relationship between body and physical activity. In particular, people who engaged in regular physical activities would tend to recall criticism or to reflect on their bodily change, as well as would intend to manage injury setbacks in sports [86]. Therefore, it supported the role of injuries in affecting the relationship between physical activity and body compassion.

Moreover, despite Hong Kong secondary school students being less likely to relate their physical body with their inner self, they experienced a release of distress and pressure after having engaged in physical activity, as well as having gone through the process of self-compassion. A systematic review and meta-analysis [87] revealed that physical activity intention and physical activity engagement were positively correlated with self-compassion. Furthermore, research studies that targeted Chinese college students indicated that individuals with a high level of self-compassion were negatively correlated with anxiety and depression and positively correlated with subjective well-being [88–90]. As already mentioned, Hong Kong adolescents displayed the processing cycle of achieving self-compassion, in which individuals with self-judgement would show common humanity for seeking references from the outside world. It is worth noting that one research study has reported that common humanity was shown as the moderator in the relationship between self-criticism and depression [81], which further supports the processing cycle of self-compassion revealed by the current study and, at the same time, further extending the Exercise and Self-Esteem Model revised with self-compassion by indicating the association with mental well-being.

12.3. Limitations

Regardless of the quantitative results showing consistent results over time, the qualitative interview revealed that most participants had a neutral attitude toward body compassion, acknowledging that physical activity engagement would contribute to improved exercise self-efficacy and body image, but are less likely to care about their body image or its effects on mental health. Although sex has been shown to play a significant role in body-related issues, including body satisfaction, female participants in this study showed no differences compared with male participants. As a result, this qualitative study could barely determine the relationship between body compassion and self-compassion. In fact, within the scarce literature regarding Chinese adolescence body image, research studies have demonstrated that self-compassion played a predictive effect on body dissatisfaction, which helped reduce body dissatisfaction and negative mental well-being [91]. Moreover, one study showed that individuals with a high level of self-compassion showed no association between body shame and depression [92]. According to the research outcomes, the majority of the participants tended to be optimistic and with positive self-compassion, which might explain the unexpected relationship between body compassion and self-compassion; yet, further investigation is needed.

12.4. Strengths and Applications

This current research indicated that Hong Kong adolescents' physical activity, self-compassion, and mental well-being were stable during the COVID-19 pandemic. Moreover, despite such tremendous daily life routine changes, the EXSEM-SC and EXSEM-SC with mental well-being model were still able to show notable statistical stability. This reveals the reliability of the models as well as the solidity of the relationship between physical activity and self-compassion. Therefore, owing to the significant mental health problems and high suicidal rate among Hong Kong adolescents regardless of the COVID-19 pandemic, it is expected that the physical activity intervention, which is based on the EXSEM-SC model, could also aim at easing Hong Kong adolescent's mental health issues. In addition, according to the Organisation for Economic Co-operation and Development (OECD), promoting well-being is being one of the key competencies of the global educational trend, while Hong Kong secondary education has also stated that mental well-being is being one of the components in the healthy lifestyle curriculum; therefore, in terms of generating a long-term impact, the physical activity and self-compassionate intervention should be promoted among schools through advocating as extra-curriculum and further being involved in regular physical education lessons. Furthermore, the stand-alone physical activity intervention program could also involve self-compassion psycho-educational components to further enhance its effect on improving self-compassion and mental well-being, then to disseminate through developing a manual for enhancing the health education materials in the future. Last, but not least, with the stability of the EXSEM-SC model among adolescents, the model can be applied to other populations, including older adults, young children, and athletes. Hence, it could be further explored and investigated the association between physical activity and self-compassion among other populations with mental health issues.

13. Conclusions

Using the Exercise and Self-Esteem Model revised with self-compassion, the current study has revealed the relationship between physical activity and self-compassion among Hong Kong secondary school students, as well as the steps toward mental wellbeing. Exercise and Self-Esteem Model is a well-known and well-established model, along with the self-concept model, that illustrates how exercise is linked to self-esteem. Self-compassion may be in line with the self-concept model, according to this study. In this research, physical activity is shown to contribute to self-compassion, both directly and indirectly, thus encouraging the use of physical activity as a tool toward self-compassion.

Author Contributions: Conceptualization, methodology, software, validation, formal analysis, data curation, writing—original draft preparation, M.-Y.C.W.; writing—review and editing, H.-W.F. and G.F.Y. All authors have read and agreed to the published version of the manuscript.

Funding: This research received no external funding.

Institutional Review Board Statement: The ethics application for this research has been approved by the Hong Kong Baptist University Research Ethics Committee (Ethics Code: REC/STUDENT/19-20/0560, date of approval: 31 March 2021).

Informed Consent Statement: Informed consent was obtained from all subjects involved in the study.

Data Availability Statement: Data will be available upon reasonable request.

Conflicts of Interest: The authors declare no conflict of interest.

References

1. Rajkumar, R.P. COVID-19 and mental health: A review of the existing literature. *Asian J. Psychiatry* **2020**, *52*, 102066. [CrossRef]
2. Mental Health and Psychological Resilience during the COVID-19 Pandemic. Available online: https://www.who.int/europe/news/item/27-03-2020-mental-health-and-psychological-resilience-during-the-covid-19-pandemic (accessed on 9 September 2022).
3. Children's Reactions to Lockdown: Need of Nurturing Resilience in Children Exposed to COVID-19 Pandemic: A Review. Available online: https://www.academia.edu/43555475/Childrens_Reactions_to_Lockdown_Need_of_Nurturing_Resilience_in_Children_Exposed_to_COVID_19_Pandemic_A_Review (accessed on 9 September 2022).
4. Magson, N.R.; Freeman, J.Y.A.; Rapee, R.M.; Richardson, C.E.; Oar, E.L.; Fardouly, J. Risk and protective factors for prospective changes in adolescent mental health during the COVID-19 pandemic. *J. Youth Adolesc.* **2021**, *50*, 44–57. [CrossRef]
5. Meuwese, R.; Cillessen, A.H.; Güroğlu, B. Friends in high places: A dyadic perspective on peer status as predictor of friendship quality and the mediating role of empathy and prosocial behavior. *Soc. Dev.* **2017**, *26*, 503–519. [CrossRef]
6. Competence, Autonomy, and Relatedness: A motivational Analysis of Self-System Processes. Available online: https://drjameswellborn.com/wp-content/uploads/2017/10/Connel-and-Wellborn-Chapter.pdf (accessed on 11 September 2022).
7. Somerville, L.H. The teenage brain: Sensitivity to social evaluation. *Curr. Dir. Psychol. Sci. J. Am. Psychol. Soc.* **2013**, *22*, 121–127. [CrossRef]
8. Bluth, K.; Roberson, P.N.; Gaylord, S.A.; Faurot, K.R.; Grewen, K.M.; Arzon, S.; Girdler, S.S. Does self-compassion protect adolescents from stress? *J. Child Fam. Stud.* **2016**, *25*, 1098–1109. [CrossRef]
9. Marshall, S.L.; Parker, P.D.; Ciarrochi, J.; Sahdra, B.; Jackson, C.J.; Heaven, P.C. Reprint of "Self-compassion protects against the negative effects of low self-esteem: A longitudinal study in a large adolescent sample". *Personal. Individ. Differ.* **2015**, *81*, 201–206. [CrossRef]
10. Neff, K.D. The development and validation of a scale to measure self-compassion. *Self Identity* **2003**, *2*, 223–250. [CrossRef]
11. Hussong, A.M.; Midgette, A.J.; Thomas, T.E.; Coffman, J.L.; Cho, S. Coping and mental health in early adolescence during COVID-19. *Res. Child Adolesc. Psychopathol.* **2021**, *49*, 1113–1123. [CrossRef] [PubMed]
12. Gutiérrez-Hernández, M.E.; Fanjul, L.F.; Díaz-Megolla, A.; Reyes-Hurtado, P.; Herrera-Rodríguez, J.F.; Enjuto-Castellanos, M.D.P.; Peñate, W. COVID-19 lockdown and mental health in a sample population in Spain: The role of self-compassion. *Int. J. Environ. Res. Public Health* **2021**, *18*, 2103. [CrossRef] [PubMed]
13. Li, W.; Zhang, Y.; Wang, J.; Ozaki, A.; Wang, Q.; Chen, Y.; Jiang, Q. Association of home quarantine and mental health among teenagers in Wuhan, China, during the COVID-19 pandemic. *JAMA Pediatr.* **2021**, *175*, 313–316. [CrossRef]
14. Lau, B.H.P.; Chan, C.L.W.; Ng, S.M. Self-compassion buffers the adverse mental health impacts of COVID-19-related threats: Results from a cross-sectional survey at the first peak of Hong Kong's outbreak. *Front. Psychiatry* **2020**, *11*, 1203. [CrossRef]
15. Duan, L.; Shao, X.; Wang, Y.; Huang, Y.; Miao, J.; Yang, X.; Zhu, G. An investigation of mental health status of children and adolescents in china during the outbreak of COVID-19. *J. Affect. Disord.* **2020**, *275*, 112–118. [CrossRef]

16. Fong, B.Y.F.; Wong, M.C.S.; Law, V.T.S.; Lo, M.F.; Ng, T.K.C.; Yee, H.H.L.; Leung, T.C.H.; Ho, P.W.T. Relationships between physical and social behavioural changes and the mental status of homebound residents in Hong Kong during the COVID-19 pandemic. *Int. J. Environ. Res. Public Health* **2020**, *17*, 6653. [CrossRef] [PubMed]
17. Bates, L.C.; Zieff, G.; Stanford, K.; Moore, J.B.; Kerr, Z.Y.; Hanson, E.D.; Barone Gibbs, B.; Kline, C.E.; Stoner, L. COVID-19 impact on behaviors across the 24-h day in children and adolescents: Physical activity, sedentary behavior, and sleep. *Children* **2020**, *7*, 138. [CrossRef]
18. Ng, K.; Cooper, J.; McHale, F.; Clifford, J.; Woods, C. Barriers and facilitators to changes in adolescent physical activity during COVID-19. *BMJ Open Sport Exerc. Med.* **2020**, *6*, e000919. [CrossRef] [PubMed]
19. Chi, X.; Liang, K.; Chen, S.T.; Huang, Q.; Huang, L.; Yu, Q.; Jiao, C.; Guo, T.; Stubbs, B.; Houssain, M.M.; et al. Mental health problems among Chinese adolescents during the COVID-19: The importance of nutrition and physical activity. *Int. J. Clin. Health Psychol.* **2021**, *21*. [CrossRef] [PubMed]
20. Thompson, W.R.; Hutber, A.; Stoutenberg, M. Response to the Letter to the Editor. *ACSM's Health Fit. J.* **2018**, *22*, 44. [CrossRef]
21. Jewett, R.; Sabiston, C.M.; Brunet, J.; O'Loughlin, E.K.; Scarapicchia, T.; O'Loughlin, J. School sport participation during adolescence and mental health in early adulthood. *J. Adolesc. Health* **2014**, *55*, 640–644. [CrossRef] [PubMed]
22. Rice, S.M.; Parker, A.G.; Rosenbaum, S.; Bailey, A.; Mawren, D.; Purcell, R. Sport-Related Concussion and Mental Health Outcomes in Elite Athletes: A Systematic Review. *Sport. Med.* **2018**, *48*, 447–465. [CrossRef]
23. Vella, S.A.; Gardner, L.A.; Swann, C.; Allen, M.S. Response: Sports participation and interventions to reduce risk of mental health problems during childhood: A response to Crowell (2018). *Child Adolesc. Ment. Health* **2019**, *24*, 152–153. [CrossRef]
24. Wong, M.-Y.C.; Chung, P.-K.; Leung, K.-M. Examining the exercise and self-esteem model revised with self-compassion among Hong Kong secondary school students using structural equation modeling. *Int. J. Environ. Res. Public Health* **2021**, *18*, 3661. [CrossRef] [PubMed]
25. Altman, J.K.; Zimmaro, L.A.; Woodruff-Borden, J. Targeting body compassion in the treatment of body dissatisfaction: A case study. *Clinical Case Studies* **2017**, *16*, 431–445. [CrossRef]
26. Sonstroem, R.J.; Morgan, W.P. Exercise and self-esteem: Rationale and model. *Med. Sci. Sport. Exerc.* **1989**, *21*, 329–337. [CrossRef]
27. Neff, K. Self-compassion: An alternative conceptualization of a healthy attitude toward oneself. *Self Identity* **2003**, *2*, 85–101. [CrossRef]
28. Neff, K.D.; Pisitsungkagarn, K.; Hsieh, Y.P. Self-compassion and self-construal in the United States, Thailand, and Taiwan. *J. Cross-Cult. Psychol.* **2008**, *39*, 267–285. [CrossRef]
29. Neff, K.D.; Rude, S.S.; Kirkpatrick, K.L. An examination of self-compassion in relation to positive psychological functioning and personality traits. *J. Res. Personal.* **2007**, *41*, 908–916. [CrossRef]
30. Chen, F.; Zheng, D.; Liu, J.; Gong, Y.; Guan, Z.; Lou, D. Depression and anxiety among adolescents during COVID-19: A cross-sectional study. *Brain Behav. Immun.* **2020**, *88*, 36–38. [CrossRef]
31. Ellis, W.E.; Zarbatany, L. Understanding processes of peer clique influence in late childhood and early adolescence. *Child Dev. Perspect.* **2017**, *11*, 227–232. [CrossRef]
32. Hawke, L.D.; Barbic, S.P.; Voineskos, A.; Szatmari, P.; Cleverley, K.; Hayes, E.; Relihan, J.; Daley, M.; Courtney, D.; Cheung, A. Impacts of COVID-19 on Youth Mental Health, Substance Use, and Well-being: A Rapid Survey of Clinical and Community Samples: Répercussions de la COVID-19 sur la santé mentale, l'utilisation de substances et le bien-être des adolescents: Un sondage rapide d'échantillons cliniques et communautaires. *Can. J. Psychiatry* **2020**, *65*, 701–709. [CrossRef] [PubMed]
33. Wang, C.; Pan, R.; Wan, X.; Tan, Y.; Xu, L.; Ho, C.S.; Ho, R.C. Immediate psychological responses and associated factors during the initial stage of the 2019 coronavirus disease (COVID-19) epidemic among the general population in China. *Int. J. Environ. Res. Public Health* **2020**, *17*, 1729. [CrossRef]
34. Zhu, S.; Zhuang, Y.; Ip, P. Impacts on children and adolescents' lifestyle, social support and their association with negative impacts of the COVID-19 pandemic. *Int. J. Environ. Res. Public Health* **2021**, *18*, 4780. [CrossRef] [PubMed]
35. Kazak, A.E. Journal article reporting standards. *Am. Psychol.* **2018**, *73*, 1–2. [CrossRef] [PubMed]
36. Tsai, C.L. Research on the Correlation between Exercise Self-efficacy, Exercise Participation and Emotional Intelligence of Elementary School Teachers. Master's Thesis, National Yunlin University of Science and Technology, Yunlin, Taiwan, 2008.
37. Lai, C.; Su, L. Mindfulness, Self-healing and psychological adaptation-th e mediating effects of self-compassion and self-disparagement. *Chin. J. O F Guid. Couns.* **2015**, *42*, 93–124.
38. Altman, J.K.; Linfield, K.; Salmon, P.G.; Beacham, A.O. The body compassion scale: Development and initial validation. *J. Health Psychol.* **2020**, *25*, 439–449. [CrossRef] [PubMed]
39. Bandura, A. Self-efficacy: Toward a unifying theory of behavioral change. *Psychol. Rev.* **1977**, *84*, 191–215. [CrossRef]
40. Guide for Constructing Self-Efficacy Scales. Available online: https://www.crcaih.org/assets/Resources/sample-scales.pdf (accessed on 9 September 2022).
41. Neupert, S.D.; Lachman, M.E.; Whitbourne, S.B. Exercise self-efficacy and control beliefs: Effects on exercise behavior after an exercise intervention for older adults. *J. Aging Phys. Act.* **2009**, *17*, 1–16. [CrossRef]
42. Likert-Type Scale Response Anchors. Available online: http://media.clemson.edu/cbshs/prtm/research/resources-for-research-page-2/Vagias-Likert-Type-Scale-Response-Anchors.pdf (accessed on 12 September 2022).
43. Li, X.; Kearney, P.M.; Keane, E.; Harrington, J.M.; Fitzgerald, A.P. Levels and sociodemographic correlates of accelerometer-based physical activity in Irish children: A cross-sectional study. *J. Epidemiol. Community Health* **2017**, *71*, 521–527. [CrossRef]

44. Translation and Validation of the Chinese Version of the Short Warwick-Edinburgh Mental Well-Being Scale for Patients with Mental Illness in Hong Kong. Available online: https://search.informit.org/doi/pdf/10.3316/informit.231617649345291?download=true (accessed on 10 September 2022).
45. Tennant, A.; Conaghan, P.G. The Rasch measurement model in rheumatology: What is it and why use it? When should it be applied, and what should one look for in a Rasch paper? *Arthritis Care Res.* **2007**, *57*, 1358–1362. [CrossRef]
46. Fung, S. Psychometric evaluation of the Warwick-Edinburgh Mental Well-being Scale (WEMWBS) with Chinese university students. *Health Qual. Life Outcomes* **2019**, *17*, 46–49. [CrossRef]
47. RStudio: Integrated Development for R. Available online: http://www.rstudio.com (accessed on 10 September 2022).
48. Lewis-Beck, M.; Bryman, A.E.; Liao, T.F. *The Sage Encyclopedia of Social Science Research Methods*; Sage: Marina View Asia Square Tower, Singapore, 2003; pp. 50–92.
49. Yusoff, A.S.M.; Peng, F.S.; Abd Razak, F.Z.; Mustafa, W.A. Discriminant validity assessment of religious teacher acceptance: The use of HTMT criterion. *J. Phys. Conf. Ser.* **2020**, *1529*, 042045. [CrossRef]
50. Fidell, S.; Tabachnick, B.; Mestre, V.; Fidell, L. Aircraft noise-induced awakenings are more reasonably predicted from relative than from absolute sound exposure levels. *J. Acoust. Soc. Am.* **2013**, *134*, 3645–3653. [CrossRef] [PubMed]
51. Hu, L.t.; Bentler, P.M. Cutoff criteria for fit indexes in covariance structure analysis: Conventional criteria versus new alternatives. *Struct. Equ. Model. A Multidiscip. J.* **1999**, *6*, 1–55. [CrossRef]
52. Jaccard, J.; Wan, C.K. *LISREL Approaches to Interaction Effects in Multiple Regression*; Sage: Marina View Asia Square Tower, Singapore, 1996; pp. 20–62.
53. Peirce, J.W. The northward motion of India since the Late Cretaceous. *Geophys. J. Int.* **1978**, *52*, 277–311. [CrossRef]
54. Tavory, I.; Timmermans, S. *Abductive Analysis: Theorizing Qualitative Research*; University of Chicago Press: Chicago, IL, USA, 2014.
55. Dhakal, K. NVivo. *J. Med. Libr. Assoc.* **2022**, *110*, 270–272. [CrossRef] [PubMed]
56. Barnett-Page, E.; Thomas, J. Methods for the synthesis of qualitative research: A critical review. *BMC Med. Res. Methodol.* **2009**, *9*, 59. [CrossRef]
57. Haig, B.D. Abductive research methods. *Int. Encycl. Educ. Third Ed.* **2010**, 77–82. [CrossRef]
58. Glaser, B.G.; Strauss, A. *The Discovery of Grounded Theory: Strategies for Qualitative Research*; Aldine Publishing Company: Chicago, IL, USA, 1967.
59. Strauss, A.; Corbin, J. *Basics of Qualitative Research Techniques*; Sage Publications: Thousand Oaks, CA, USA, 1998.
60. Tong, A.; Sainsbury, P.; Craig, J. Consolidated criteria for reporting qualitative research (COREQ): A 32-item checklist for interviews and focus groups. *Int. J. Qual. Health Care* **2007**, *19*, 349–357. [CrossRef]
61. Shank, T.M.; Lutz, R.A.; Vrijenhoek, R.C. Molecular systematics of shrimp (Decapoda: Bresiliidae) from deep-sea hydrothermal vents, I: Enigmatic "small orange" shrimp from the Mid-Atlantic Ridge are juvenile Rimicaris exoculata. *Mol. Mar. Biol. Biotechnol.* **1998**, *7*, 88–96.
62. Van Maanen, L.; Van Rijn, H. Accounting for subliminal priming in ACT-R. In Proceedings of the 8th International Conference on Cognitive Modeling, Ann Arbor, MI, USA, 27–29 July 2007; pp. 1–6.
63. Gilic, B.; Ostojic, L.; Corluka, M.; Volaric, T.; Sekulic, D. Contextualizing Parental/Familial influence on physical activity in adolescents before and during COVID-19 pandemic: A prospective analysis. *Children* **2020**, *7*, 125. [CrossRef]
64. Gu, X.; Solmon, M.A.; Zhang, T. Using expectancy-value model to examine students' physical activity engagement and cardiovascular fitness in physical education. *Int. J. Sport Psychol.* **2012**, *43*, 385–402. [CrossRef]
65. Developing a Motivationally-Supportive Environment to Promote Children' Physical Activity and Health in Youth Sports during the COVID-19 Pandemic. Available online: http://www.sports-media.org/index.php/abstracts/item/57-developing-a-motivationally-supportive-environment-to-promote-children-physical-activity-and-health-in-youth-sports-during-the-covid-19-pandemic (accessed on 10 September 2022).
66. Pigaiani, Y.; Zoccante, L.; Zocca, A.; Arzenton, A.; Menegolli, M.; Fadel, S.; Ruggeri, M.; Colizzi, M. Adolescent lifestyle behaviors, coping strategies and subjective wellbeing during the COVID-19 pandemic: An online student survey. *Healthcare* **2020**, *8*, 472. [CrossRef]
67. Identity Youth and Crisis. Available online: https://books.google.co.jp/books/about/Identity_Youth_and_Crisis.html?id=v3XWH2PDLewC&redir_esc=y (accessed on 10 September 2022).
68. Robertson, M.; Duffy, F.; Newman, E.; Bravo, C.P.; Ates, H.H.; Sharpe, H. Exploring changes in body image, eating and exercise during the COVID-19 lockdown: A UK survey. *Appetite* **2021**, *159*, 105062. [CrossRef]
69. Baceviciene, M.; Jankauskiene, R. Changes in sociocultural attitudes towards appearance, body image, eating attitudes and behaviours, physical activity, and quality of life in students before and during COVID-19 lockdown. *Appetite* **2021**, *166*. [CrossRef]
70. Nguyen, T.M.; Le, G.N.H. The influence of COVID-19 stress on psychological well-being among Vietnamese adults: The role of self-compassion and gratitude. *Traumatology* **2021**, *27*, 86. [CrossRef]
71. Raes, F. The effect of self-compassion on the development of depression symptoms in a non-clinical sample. *Mindfulness* **2011**, *2*, 33–36. [CrossRef]
72. Zuroff, D.C.; Clegg, K.-A.; Levine, S.L.; Hermanto, N.; Armstrong III, B.F.; Haward, B.; Thode, S. Beyond trait models of self-criticism and self-compassion: Variability over domains and the search for signatures. *Personal. Individ. Differ.* **2021**, *170*, 110429. [CrossRef]

73. Arslan, C. Interpersonal Problem Solving, Self-Compassion and Personality Traits in University Students. *Educ. Res. Rev.* **2016**, *11*, 474–481. [CrossRef]
74. Saricaoglu, H.; Arslan, C. An Investigation into Psychological Well-Being Levels of Higher Education Students with Respect to Personality Traits and Self-Compassion. *Educ. Sci. Theory Pract.* **2013**, *13*, 2097–2104. [CrossRef]
75. Tuncay, O.; Arslan, C. Adaptation of the rumination about an interpersonal offense scale into Turkish. *J. Cogn.-Behav. Psychother. Res.* **2017**, *6*, 101. [CrossRef]
76. Neff, K.D.; Germer, C.K. A pilot study and randomized controlled trial of the mindful self-compassion program. *J. Clin. Psychol.* **2013**, *69*, 28–44. [CrossRef]
77. Mehr, K.E.; Adams, A.C. Self-compassion as a mediator of maladaptive perfectionism and depressive symptoms in college students. *J. Coll. Stud. Psychother.* **2016**, *30*, 132–145. [CrossRef]
78. Ferrari, M.; Yap, K.; Scott, N.; Einstein, D.A.; Ciarrochi, J. Self-compassion moderates the perfectionism and depression link in both adolescence and adulthood. *PLoS ONE* **2018**, *13*, e0192022. [CrossRef]
79. Pfattheicher, S.; Geiger, M.; Hartung, J.; Weiss, S.; Schindler, S. Old wine in new bottles? The case of self–compassion and neuroticism. *Eur. J. Personal.* **2017**, *31*, 160–169. [CrossRef]
80. Di Fabio, A.; Saklofske, D.H. The relationship of compassion and self-compassion with personality and emotional intelligence. *Personal. Individ. Differ.* **2021**, *169*, 110109. [CrossRef]
81. Wong, C.C.Y.; Mak, W.W.S. Differentiating the role of three self-compassion components in buffering cognitive-personality vulnerability to depression among Chinese in Hong Kong. *J. Couns. Psychol.* **2013**, *60*, 162–169. [CrossRef]
82. Van Wietmarschen, H.; Tjaden, B.; van Vliet, M.; Battjes-Fries, M.; Jong, M. Effects of mindfulness training on perceived stress, self-compassion, and self-reflection of primary care physicians: A mixed-methods study. *BJGP Open* **2018**, *2*, bjgpopen18X101621. [CrossRef]
83. Viskovich, S.; de George-Walker, L. An investigation of self-care related constructs in undergraduate psychology students: Self-compassion, mindfulness, self-awareness, and integrated self-knowledge. *Int. J. Educ. Res.* **2019**, *95*, 109–117. [CrossRef]
84. Muris, P.; Petrocchi, N. Protection or vulnerability? A meta-analysis of the relations between the positive and negative components of self-compassion and psychopathology. *Clin. Psychol. Psychother.* **2017**, *24*, 373–383. [CrossRef]
85. Bailey, K.A.; Gammage, K.L.; van Ingen, C.; Ditor, D.S. "It's all about acceptance": A qualitative study exploring a model of positive body image for people with spinal cord injury. *Body Image* **2015**, *15*, 24–34. [CrossRef]
86. Beadle, E.S. Body Shame, Body Compassion and Physical Activity. Ph.D. Thesis, University of Hertfordshire, Hertfordshire, UK, 2020. [CrossRef]
87. Wong, M.Y.C.; Chung, P.K.; Leung, K.M. The relationship between physical activity and self-compassion: A systematic review and meta-analysis. *Mindfulness* **2020**, *12*, 547–563. [CrossRef]
88. Chu, R. The Relations of Self-Compassion, Implicit Theories of Intelligence, and Mental Health Outcomes among Chinese Adolescents. Master's Thesis, San Francisco State University, San Francisco, CA, USA, May 2016.
89. Ge, J.; Wu, J.; Li, K.; Zheng, Y. Self-compassion and subjective well-being mediate the impact of mindfulness on balanced time perspective in Chinese college students. *Front. Psychol.* **2019**, *10*, 367. [CrossRef]
90. Luo, Y.; Meng, R.; Li, J.; Liu, B.; Cao, X.; Ge, W. Self-compassion may reduce anxiety and depression in nursing students: A pathway through perceived stress. *Public Health* **2019**, *174*, 1–10. [CrossRef]
91. Chen, K.-M. Subjective poverty, deprivation, and the subjective well-being of children and young people: A multilevel growth curve analysis in Taiwan. *Child. Youth Serv. Rev.* **2020**, *114*, 105045. [CrossRef]
92. Sick, K.; Pila, E.; Nesbitt, A.; Sabiston, C.M. Does self-compassion buffer the detrimental effect of body shame on depressive symptoms? *Body Image* **2020**, *34*, 175–183. [CrossRef]

healthcare

MDPI

Article

Factors Associated with Mental Health among Malaysian University Music Students: Roles of Fear of COVID-19, Nomophobia, Loneliness, Sleep Quality, and Socioeconomic Status

Chunmei Zhuang [1] and Hashem Salarzadeh Jenatabadi [2,*]

1 Faculty of Creative Arts, University of Malaya (UM), Kuala Lumpur 50603, Malaysia
2 Department of Science and Technology Studies, Faculty of Science, Universiti Malaya, Kuala Lumpur 50603, Malaysia
* Correspondence: jenatabadi@um.edu.my

Abstract: Previous mental health studies have shown higher levels of anxiety, stress, and depression symptoms among university music students. In general, some similar findings have been observed for Malaysian music university students. In diagnosing the complications of mental health, there is consensus that it is essential to develop and evaluate a model oriented toward mental health illness prevention and treatment. To date, a suitable pattern for estimating mental health in terms of anxiety, stress, and depression among music university students is lacking. To fill this gap, we collected the necessary data from 691 music and 871 general students who were students for one year. The introduced pattern includes socioeconomic status, fear of COVID-19, nomophobia, sleep quality, loneliness, and mental health. Our data analysis proved that the levels of anxiety, depression, and stress of music students were lower than those of general students. Unlike some previous studies, in this study, the fear of COVID-19 and nomophobia didn't have the most significant impact on mental health. The most significant impacts were related to sleep quality and loneliness. These findings have the potential to inform health promotion and services in the music education system.

Keywords: music students' mental health; moderation analysis; quality of life; sleep quality; depression

Citation: Zhuang, C.; Jenatabadi, H.S. Factors Associated with Mental Health among Malaysian University Music Students: Roles of Fear of COVID-19, Nomophobia, Loneliness, Sleep Quality, and Socioeconomic Status. *Healthcare* **2023**, *11*, 18. https://doi.org/10.3390/healthcare11010018

Academic Editor: John H. Foster

Received: 30 September 2022
Revised: 13 November 2022
Accepted: 18 December 2022
Published: 21 December 2022

1. Introduction

There is strong evidence that university students in a variety of fields of study are vulnerable to mental illness [1,2]. College students experience a higher incidence of physical and psychological sickness than the general population, according to a study by Henning and Krägeloh [3]. Moreover, it has been discovered that university students suffer one or two mental diseases, such as anxiety and depression [4]. According to a different study by Suarez, Cardozo [5], anxiety symptoms are reported by 44.9% of medical students and 6.8% of the general population, while depression symptoms are recorded by 33.9% and 2.6% of people. Existing research suggests that music students have higher rates of stress, anxiety, and depression than their non-musical counterparts. Spahn, Strukely [6] compared four groups: 266 medical students and 247 music students, as well as 71 psychology and 71 athletics majors. The authors found that music students face higher levels of anxiety and depression compared to the other students. Araújo, Wasley [7] compared the health-promoting behaviors and general health of music (n = 208) and general (n = 65) students in the United Kingdom and found that the former group had lower levels of self-regulation and self-efficacy.

According to the findings of the studies cited above, even before the widespread spread of the COVID-19 virus, there have been growing worries in recent years regarding the mental health of college students. Students in higher education institutions are more likely to suffer from mental health issues as a direct result of the stressors and constraints brought on by the pandemic. This may have a detrimental effect on their academic performance, social relationships, and future opportunities in the professional and personal spheres. After a year and a half of the pandemic, this suffering among university students might be significant [8].

Previous research has taken a fragmented approach to investigating the elements that affect mental health. These studies have focused on certain aspects of mental health, such as social media [9], physical activities [10], technostress [11], nomophobia and sleep quality [12], anxiety and sleep quality during the pandemic [13,14], and socioeconomic background [15]. This study, on the other hand, takes a more holistic approach by taking into account a number of different aspects that are still significant, such as fear of COVID-19, nomophobia, loneliness, sleep quality, and socioeconomic status. The majority of the earlier studies that looked at these important components were carried out in a variety of research settings, with a general range of student populations and a narrow focus on particular aspects of the situation. As a result, the current study added to the body of literature by investigating the factors using a framework. Additionally, we took mental health into account as a latent variable, which is a combination of stress, anxiety, and depression. The study also takes place in a previously unstudied Malaysian musical and general educational context. Additionally, this investigation used Bayesian Structural Equation Modelling. It is employed to model the causal link between variables and identify the model's most significant influencing factors. The results of such a comprehensive approach will make it easier to create the most effective strategies for addressing many stakeholders, including educators, higher education institutions, and the government, in order to further promote mental health. With consideration of the above objectives, the present study aims to answer the following questions:

What is the status of anxiety, depression, and stress among Malaysian music university students and general students?

What are the rules of fear of COVID-19, nomophobia, sleep quality, loneliness, and SES in estimating mental health among Malaysian music and general university students?

2. Literature Review and Theoretical Framework

Fear has been the most prevalent psychological reaction in the populace throughout the current COVID-19 outbreak [16]. People are concerned about their health, so this response or reaction is crucial [17]. It is the most frequent physiological and mental response to significant societal or social problems, such pandemics or emerge, which results in psychologically uncomfortable behaviours [18]. It is also linked to high levels of anxiety, which can cause irrational thought. Such circumstances can lead to mental health problems in the general public and in universities during a pandemic scenario. Consequently, concern over COVID-19 may be a sign of mental health (including anxiety, stress, and depression). Additionally, it was discovered that nomophobia, or the fear of not being able to access and enjoy information through mobile phones, is one of the modern world's diseases that is already evident in young people [19].

Nomophobia, which is the fear of not having a phone or phone contact, was previously recognised as a modern disorder [20]. It is a problem that Yildirim and Correia [19] characterised as having three dimensions: (i) anxiety over losing contact with others, (ii) inability to get information through phones, and (iii) lack of convenience of smartphone applications. The dependence on cell phones has significantly expanded during the COVID-19 epidemic [21] as they are a crucial communication tool and offer additional advantages such as access to online courses, playing video games, listening to music, etc. If people are unable to use their smartphones, all of these activities could make people feel much more anxious [22]. According to a previous study by Tams and Legoux [23], nomophobia will cause stress if withdrawal control from the phone is poor or event uncertainty is high. In addition, Farooqui and Pore [24] have demonstrated that people are more likely to suffer fear, panic, depression, and anxiety when they are unable to access their smartphone. Additionally, empirical research conducted by Samaha and Hawi [25] provided support for the concept by demonstrating that people who suffer from nomophobia experience tension whenever their smartphones are not within reach. Given that the fear of COVID-19 and nomophobia have comparable symptoms, the effect that fear of COVID-19 has on mental health may be made worse by nomophobia. Those students who spent a significant amount of their time engaging in compulsive internet use, gaming addiction, and excessive use of social media reported high levels of despair, loneliness, poor sleep quality, and anxiety [26].

One of the world's most widespread adult difficulties is loneliness. Those who suffer from it have a "persistent and unfavourable psychological condition characterised by a sense of emotional isolation, a sense of being alone, and a sense of estrangement from others" [27]. The negative emotion known as loneliness results from a mismatch between the number of friends one has and the number of friends one would want to have [28]. Fan, Chen [29] presented that feelings of isolation, estrangement, and dissatisfaction in interpersonal connections characterise loneliness. These negative emotions have been linked to an increase in mortality and other health hazards [30]. Loneliness, for instance, is associated with clinical disorders such as stroke and cardiovascular sickness and is a predictor of psychological symptoms like despair, stress, and worry [31].

A good night's sleep is one of the most important factors in determining how effectively one can carry out the activities of daily living and how well one can function mentally [32]. During the epidemic, students had to make adjustments to their lifestyles and confront several problems, including adjusting to a modified teaching-learning structure, dealing with the loss of social connectedness, and more. This could have a detrimental impact on the quality of sleep that they get [33], and it could also lead to elevated levels of depression, anxiety, and stress [34]. Because good quality sleep is necessary for effective neurocognitive and psychomotor functioning as well as for optimal physical and mental health, poor sleep quality may lead to difficulties with attention and poor academic performance [35]. There is a correlation between poor sleep quality and a number of parameters, including psychological factors, physical activity, lifestyle factors, and chronic disorders [36].

3. Materials and Methods

3.1. Search Method

The online database from the Web of Science was used to search the literature on the mental health of music university students for works published between 2000 and 2022. Both "mental health" and "music students" were used as key phrases. A built model using the Bayesian SEM method was presented. The primary terms we searched from the start were "music students", "depression", "anxiety", "stress" and "structural equation modelling". We were aiming for "Fear of COVID-19" with "nomophobia" in the second phase. We combined "student mental health" with "loneliness", "socioeconomic" and "sleep quality" for the third phase.

3.2. Study Design

A quantitative cross-sectional methodology was used for this investigation. From January 2022 through July 2022, the survey was fielded. The Malaysian government issued a nationwide movement control order that effectively ended on-campus, face-to-face instruction at all levels of education from kindergarten through university. Most Malaysian college students had already taken three online courses, either in real-time or asynchronously.

3.3. Sampling

In this article, we used a cross-sectional analysis in which the required sample size is relevant to data collection at one point in time. According to Hair et al. [37], the sample size needed in the research should be related to the number of latent variables of the study which include the number of indicators inside the latent variables as described below:

- A minimum of 100 respondents with five or fewer latent variables, each of which must have three indications, are required.
- A minimum of 150 respondents with seven or fewer latent variables, each of which must have three indications, are required.
- 300 respondents are required, with certain latent variables having no more than three indications and no more than seven latent variables.
- 500 respondents are needed, and there are more than seven latent variables, some of which have fewer than three indications.

Our research framework includes six latent variables, and the educational level is categorized into two groups. Therefore, we expected to have at least 100 respondents for every group (music and general students). In total, we needed 200 respondents.

There was a concerted effort made to ensure sample consistency throughout this investigation. Ethical approval from the University of Malaya Research Ethics Committee (UMREC) was obtained prior to beginning data collection (UM.TNC2/UMREC 1582). Informed consent was obtained from all respondents after an explanation of the study's goals was provided. Respondents were emailed a Google form survey with several pre-set questions. Some of them were given out by their university course instructor. A total of 1562 responses were received from the survey. All protocols and laws were strictly adhered to while conducting the research.

3.4. Instrument

Questionnaires were distributed among the participants to achieve the research goals. The information on the participants was organized into a few categories based on the variables which include personal SES, Fear of COVID-19, nomophobia, loneliness, sleep quality and mental health. To describe the SES variable, we used three indicators: age group, working experience, and income per month. The age group of the participants is classified into five criteria, which are 'less than 21 years old', 'between 21 to 25 years old', 'between 26 to 30', 'between 31 to 35 years' and 'more than 35 years old' which coded to 1, 2, 3, 4 and 5, respectively. Respondents are asked about their duration of working experience where the responses are coded as 1 for 'no job experienced', 2 for 'between 1 to 3 years', 3 for 'between 4 to 6 years', 4 for 'between 7 to 10 years' and 5 for 'more than 10 years'. The responses to income per month are coded as 1, 2, 3, 4 and 5 for 'less than RM 1000', 'RM 1000 to RM 2000', 'RM 2000 to RM 3000', 'RM 3000 to RM 4000 and 'over RM 4000', respectively [RM: Ringgit Malaysia]. Subjects' mental health was evaluated using the DASS-21 [38], which has been found to be reliable and valid. There are 21 items in total; 7 each for stress, anxiety, and depression. A total DASS-21 score can be anywhere from 0 to 63, with a subscale score ranging from 0 to 21 and an item score ranging from zero (did not apply to me at all) to three (applied to me very much). Respondents' sleep quality was evaluated using the Pittsburgh Sleep Quality Index (PSQI) [32], a self-administered questionnaire that evaluates sleep quality over the preceding month. There are 19 parts which are arranged into seven components: subjective sleep quality, sleep latency, sleep duration, sleep efficiency, sleep disturbance, use of sleep medication, and daytime dysfunction. Loneliness was measured using a modified version of the Likert scale of Russell, Peplau [39], which has four points, ranging from 'never' to 'always'. Nomophobia was evaluated using an adapted version of the 7-point Likert scale that was developed by Yildirim and Correia [19]. The scale ranges from 1 (Definitely do not agree) to 7 (Definitely agree).

3.5. Statistical Method

From a mathematical and statistical modelling point of view, regression (bivariate or multivariate) [40,41] and ANOVA [42,43] are the most familiar techniques used for analyzing the associations between various factors and mental health among music university students. Structural Equation Modelling (SEM) has garnered a lot of attention in the last few decades thanks to studies that show its potential in the field of mental health [44]. This method makes it possible to estimate psychological well-being as a result of causal relationships (simple or complex) between observable and non-observable (latent) factors. Previous research has introduced several estimators for use in SEM analysis. Maximum likelihood (ML) is the estimator of choice for studies involving SEM analysis [45]. However, model misspecification is a common problem that undermines ML applications. Examples of overly restrictive models include those that require no residual correlations and exact zero cross-loadings [46]. It has been shown by Kolenikov [47] and Asparouhov and Muthén [48] that the ML estimator has a large parameter bias in factor correlations and factor loadings. Researchers have begun using alternative estimators in modelling to get around the shortcomings of ML in SEM analysis brought on by factors such as small sample sizes and the normal distribution of independent variables. Very few researchers have proposed replacing the ML estimator with a Bayesian one in SEM analysis [49], but this may be the key to getting around ML's limitations.

We used the SEM technique in this research because it has helped researchers to understand the concept of latent variables and the interactions within the model. SEM has the following features which are an advantage when applying this technique for mental health modeling.

- The ability to use latent variables, a feature of SEM that is unique in that they cannot be observed directly and are not used by other analysis techniques [50].
- The capacity to calculate and analyse the direct and indirect links between the research study's variables [51].
- The capacity to demonstrate relationships between dependent variables suggests the estimation of multiple exogenous and endogenous variables simultaneously [52].

3.6. Research Framework

The framework of the study is presented in Figure 1. The research framework of this study is being created by the combination of the theoretical framework with the addition of some new ideas. Independent and dependent variables in this research relate to each other by using the mediator to gain the output. The research framework includes six latent variables. Socio Economic Status (SES) is presented as an independent variable and mental health as a dependent variable. Our framework contains four mediators which are fear of COVID-19, nomophobia, loneliness and sleep quality. This research is delivered through a cross-sectional study design.

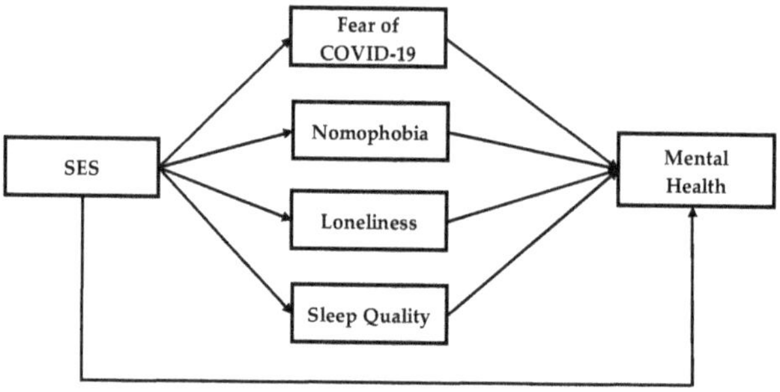

Figure 1. Research framework.

4. Results

4.1. Descriptive Statistics

At 15 universities in Malaysia, an online poll was conducted. Table 1 provides descriptive statistics for mental health status as well as the number of questionnaires that were completed at each educational level. We measured the severity of stress, anxiety, and depressive symptoms among Malaysian music and general university students using descriptive statistics.

Table 1. Descriptive statistics of mental health.

Criteria		Stress		Anxiety		Depression	
Music students (number Percentage) Total = 691							
4.21–5.00	Very High	109	15.8%	106	15.3%	120	17.4%
3.41–4.20	High	164	23.7%	128	18.5%	136	19.7%
2.61–3.40	Medium	166	24.0%	176	25.5%	165	23.9%
1.81–2.60	Low	165	23.9%	201	29.1%	187	27.1%
1.00–1.80	Very Low	87	12.6%	80	11.6%	83	12.0%
General students (number Percentage) Total = 221							
4.21–5.00	Very High	161	18.5%	169	19.4%	184	21.1%
3.41–4.20	High	271	31.1%	196	22.5%	284	32.6%
2.61–3.40	Medium	283	32.5%	284	32.6%	251	28.8%
1.81–2.60	Low	113	13.0%	186	21.3%	61	7.0%
1.00–1.80	Very Low	43	4.9%	37	4.2%	91	10.5%

4.2. SEM Analysis

4.2.1. Validity and Reliability

According to Fornell and Larcker [53], to test the validity and reliability of a survey, some conditions for SEM analysis need to fit. To examine the validity, every latent variable in the research should be equal to or higher than 0.7 for the Cronbach's alpha value. From Table 2, the Cronbach's alpha value for every latent variable is aligned with the condition that reinforces the validity of this research.

Table 2. Cronbach's alpha output.

Research Variables	Music Students	General Students
SES	0.77	0.77
Fear COVID-19	0.73	0.71
Nomophobia	0.79	0.74
Loneliness	0.81	0.80
Sleep Quality	0.76	0.75
Mental Health	0.78	0.71

Next, to test the reliability of this research, every latent variable indicator should have a factor loading value higher than 0.7.

Hence, after the elimination of indicators from research data, claiming the reliability of the research must comply with another condition i.e., all latent variables should have an equal or higher than 0.5 value of the average variance extracted (AVE). Table 3 shows the AVE output for this research, which indicates that the AVE of every latent variable was higher than 0.5. As the features of reliability are fulfilled, this research is confirmed.

Table 3. AVE output.

Research Variables	Music Students	General Students
SES	0.55	0.63
Fear COVID-19	0.58	0.65
Nomophobia	0.59	0.52
Loneliness	0.61	0.58
Sleep Quality	0.64	0.65
Mental Health	0.62	0.66

4.2.2. Model Fitting

The output of SEM model fitting is tabulated in Table 4. The range in the model fitting analysis that is endorsed should be above 0.9 to determine the suitability of the research model. The comparative fit index (CFI), normed fit index (NFI), relative fit index (RFI), incremental fit index (IFI), goodness of fit index (GFI), and Tucker Lewis index (TLI) value of the chosen BMI group levels were within acceptable ranges. Therefore, the model fitting of three groups of data is accepted.

Table 4. Model fitting analysis.

	Music Students	General Students
CFI	0.913	0.921
NFI	0.909	0.937
RFI	0.945	0.944
GFI	0.911	0.912
IFI	0.977	0.904
TLI	0.932	0.909

4.2.3. Structural Model

In the SEM analysis, we used the structural model to recognize the substantial connection between research variables that are linked to the considered conceptual model. Figures 2 and 3 show the output of the structural model for the music and general students. Based on Figures 2 and 3, the impact of each latent variable on mental health are significant for music and the general students' model.

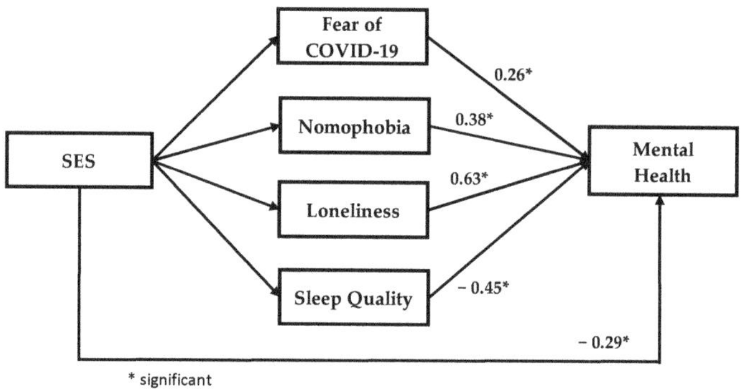

Figure 2. Output of mental health model (music students).

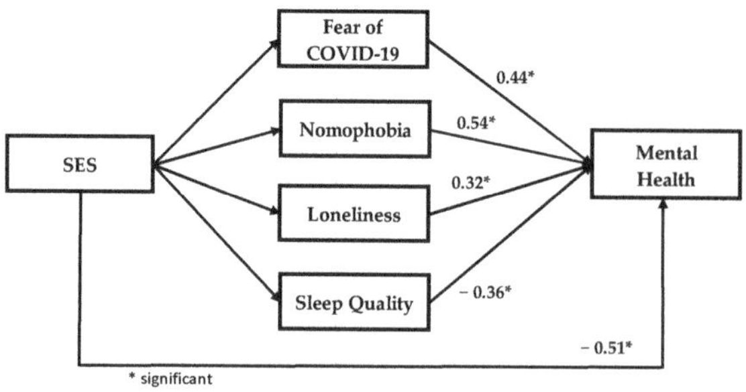

Figure 3. Output of mental health model (general students).

5. Discussion

During the course of their education, students go through a substantial transition unlike any other, from high school to university or college [54]. This transition marks the beginning of a significant period of psychological and social development, which can have a variety of effects on students' lives, including their health [55]. However, in the past two years, COVID-19 has caused massive disruptions throughout the world. The majority of university learning and evaluation processes have shifted from face-to-face courses to distance and/or online learning, which has made it more difficult for students to access learning and adjust to the new techniques. Second, students are separated from the general public. During a pandemic, they must remain at home, even if they are unable to see their families for many months. Thirdly, the students had financial difficulties. Due to the lockdown, many undergraduate and graduate students who previously worked to earn extra money are now unable to do so. All of these concerns may have contributed to an increase in stress, affecting anxiety and depression. Young university students may experience symptoms of depression as a result of the stress caused by these long-lasting, major changes, or they may first experience a condition of worry that could later progress to mental health issues.

The purpose of this study was to investigate the factors that influence the mental health (anxiety, depression, and stress) of music and general college students, specifically focusing on fear of COVID-19, nomophobia, sleep quality, loneliness, and socio-economic connections.

The findings indicated that of the variables shown to have a significant causal association with students' mental health, among music students, sleep quality status had the most direct negative relationship, with greater sleep quality scores being related with lower mental health (DASS scores). Silva et al.'s discovery of an independent link between mental health and sleep quality status among medical [56] and arts [57] students is supported by these findings. Poor sleep quality is associated with increased tension, irritability, anger, depression, anxiety, and confusion, according to a study conducted on university students during COVID-19 post epidemic era by Tang, Chen [58]. Therefore, university students with sleep quality issues still face multiple severe sources of stress, increasing their risk for developing or worsening existing mental health issues.

In our research, there is a strong positive correlation between loneliness and mental health. The outcomes concurred with earlier research showing that loneliness had strong significant relationships with mental health [59], including depression [60] and anxiety [61]. These results provide credence to Kim and Cho [62] that people with insecure attachments struggle to fully control their emotions and may experience feelings of loneliness because they lack healthy attachments. This result highlights the need to concentrate on various approaches to minimize social isolation and raise knowledge of the advantages of social relationships. In the specific situation of COVID-19, some of the possibilities could include making regulations on community interactions more flexible if the health prevention changes can be implemented, or promoting the creation of "safe social bubbles" in which a group of individuals with more controlled external interactions can gather with a limited number of people as long as everybody respects the health-preventive recommendations [63]. These options have the potential to reduce the risk of the spread of COVID-19 [63].

According to the results of our research, 78.4 percent of music students suffer from some degree of nomophobia. There were 16.3% of people with mild phobia, 53.12% with moderate, and 8.98% with severe phobia. These levels are lower than those found in previous investigations among teachers [51] and high school students [64]. Furthermore, the current study found that the third most important factor that significantly impacted mental health was nomophobia. Several studies demonstrate that nomophobia has a substantial impact on the mental health of university students. Farchakh, Hallit [28] demonstrated a substantial association between nomophobia and anxiety, depression, stress, and impulsivity. Moreover, Tung, Gan [65] revealed that students with severe nomophobia had greater anxiety and distress levels. A possible explanation is that a person with high levels may utilize a smartphone to research coping strategies for dealing with COVID-19. For example, if a student has greater levels of nomophobia in the context of COVID-19, as suggested by fear of COVID-19, the student may be driven to keep, protect, and construct a variety of resources in order to survive and sustain well-being. On the other side, stress and anxiety enhance the likelihood of phone addiction. Before COVID-19, a prior study by ÖZDEMİR, ÇAKIR [66] reported students with higher Internet addiction scores were more worried than those with lower scores. Those who reported high levels of gaming addiction, compulsive internet use, and social media use also reported significant levels of depression, avoidance, poor sleep quality, loneliness, and depression-related anxiety [26].

SES is the fourth important characteristic that has a detrimental effect on the mental health of music students. Lower socioeconomic status was related to greater DASS scores. This conclusion is consistent with the findings of Fernandes, Biswas [26], who found an independent association between mental health and socioeconomic status among Medical Sciences students. However, according to their research, SES has the most detrimental effect on mental health. However, according to our research, socioeconomic status has the fourth greatest impact on the mental health of musicians. A lower socioeconomic position is associated with a greater burden in a variety of aspects of day-to-day life as well as an increased exposure to stressful life situations. Therefore, unpleasant life events and other stressors are obviously related to socioeconomic position, and it is clear that lower parental education and lower family income were associated with higher stress levels regardless of whether or not the individuals in question were university students.

Fear of COVID-19 is the subject of numerous studies about the mental health of university students. COVID-19 had the least significant impact on mental health status among the five predictors examined in this study. In this study, fear of COVID-19, among music students, had a lesser effect on mental health than four other predictor variables: SES, sleep quality, loneliness, and nomophobia. However, this does not imply reduced worry of COVID-19. Young university students' fear of COVID-19 may have been strongly influenced by the quick spread of the disease, the enormous number of individuals affected, the rising number of fatalities, mistrust of the health care system, ignorance, and disinformation. This fear has been identified as a factor that affects depression, and the effects of this fear on depression may be exacerbated by the presence of anxiety. The majority of students live away from their families, are unable to return, and/or reside in poor conditions where it is difficult to remain healthy and make ends meet, causing them to experience more fear when they perceive they are in a more precarious and dangerous situation.

6. Conclusions

According to the findings of this study, music students' perceptions of uncertainty and risk might serve as a fertile breeding ground for stress, anxiety, and depression, resulting in a mental health concern. Recognizing the complexity of the interactions between these elements and developing mental health symptoms, we must rapidly develop intervention programs in universities to assist these music and general students in better coping with this type of situation. We found that the levels of anxiety, depression, and stress of music students are lower than those of general students. This study developed a framework for music students' mental health, which improved based on previous studies related to SES, fear of COVID-19, loneliness, nomophobia, and sleep quality. The most significant impacts among music students belonged to loneliness and sleep quality. However, among general students, the most significant impacts belong to nomophobia and SES. Nevertheless, a few limitations to this research have occurred as follows:

- Some studies involved "family chronic illness" and "mental wellbeing history" for analyzing anxiety, depression, and stress among university students [67,68]. However, we didn't consider it in this research, but we think that this is one of the indicators that affects the mental health of the respondents.

- The study's validity may be jeopardized because the data was self-reported. Because this method has been widely used in previous studies, we are confident that the data obtained are of high quality, and our data collectors stressed the confidentiality of all answers.
- Nomophobia may cause someone who is afraid of COVID-19 to use a smartphone to look for online help regarding their mental health. This should be researched further.
- We used nomophobia in our research model. "Technostress" is a well-known indicator that has been used in previous studies related to university students' academic performance [11], sleep quality [69], anxiety and depression [70]. It could be significant to use it for estimating university students' mental health.
- It would be prudent to repeat the study during later phases of the pandemic and under normal conditions, as our study may have been a snapshot geared toward coping with COVID-19 in Malaysia's last phases.
- This article describes a new study that used Bayesian SEM to examine the mental health of music university students at various educational levels. In the SEM technique, the significance of the variables is very important in measuring the strength of the relationship between variables. This would be a beneficial addition to future research to expand knowledge of mental health among music university students, which is becoming a serious issue that needs to be addressed.

Author Contributions: Conceived of and designed the study: H.S.J. and C.Z. Performed the study: H.S.J. and C.Z. Analyzed and interpreted the data: H.S.J. Wrote the manuscript text: H.S.J. and C.Z. All authors have read and agreed to the published version of the manuscript.

Funding: There is no funding for this research.

Institutional Review Board Statement: The study was conducted according to the guidelines of the Declaration of Helsinki and approved by University of Malaya Research Ethics Committee.

Informed Consent Statement: Informed consent was obtained from all subjects involved in the study (study code, UM.TNC2/UMREC 1582; date of approval, 22 October 2021).

Data Availability Statement: The datasets generated and analysed during the current study are available from the corresponding author.

Acknowledgments: We are thankful to all students who participated in this study.

Conflicts of Interest: The authors declare that they have no conflict of interest.

References

1. Ibrahim, N.; Amit, N.; Shahar, S.; Wee, L.-H.; Ismail, R.; Khairuddin, R.; Siau, C.S.; Safien, A.M. Do depression literacy, mental illness beliefs and stigma influence mental health help-seeking attitude? A cross-sectional study of secondary school and university students from B40 households in Malaysia. *BMC Public Health* **2019**, *19*, 544. [CrossRef]
2. Epstein, I.; Khanlou, N.; Balaquiao, L.; Chang, K.-Y. University students' mental health and illness experiences in health and allied health programs: A scoping review. *Int. J. Ment. Health Addict.* **2019**, *17*, 743–764. [CrossRef]
3. Henning, M.A.; Krägeloh, C.U.; Hawken, S.J.; Zhao, Y.; Doherty, I. The quality of life of medical students studying in New Zealand: A comparison with nonmedical students and a general population reference group. *Teach. Learn. Med.* **2012**, *24*, 334–340. [CrossRef] [PubMed]
4. Ramón-Arbués, E.; Gea-Caballero, V.; Granada-López, J.M.; Juárez-Vela, R.; Pellicer-García, B.; Antón-Solanas, I. The prevalence of depression, anxiety and stress and their associated factors in college students. *Int. J. Environ. Res. Public Health* **2020**, *17*, 7001. [CrossRef] [PubMed]
5. Suarez, D.E.; Cardozo, A.C.; Ellmer, D.; Trujillo, E.M. Short report: Cross sectional comparison of anxiety and depression symptoms in medical students and the general population in Colombia. *Psychol. Health Med.* **2021**, *26*, 375–380. [CrossRef]
6. Spahn, C.; Strukely, S.; Lehmann, A. Health conditions, attitudes toward study, and attitudes toward health at the beginning of university study: Music students in comparison with other student populations. *Med. Probl. Perform. Artist.* **2004**, *19*, 26–33. [CrossRef]
7. Araújo, L.S.; Wasley, D.; Perkins, R.; Atkins, L.; Redding, E.; Ginsborg, J.; Williamon, A. Fit to perform: An investigation of higher education music students' perceptions, attitudes, and behaviors toward health. *Front. Psychol.* **2017**, *8*, 1558. [CrossRef]
8. Dosil-Santamaria, M.; Ozamiz-Etxebarria, N.; Idoiaga Mondragon, N.; Reyes-Sosa, H.; Santabárbara, J. Emotional state of Mexican university students in the COVID-19 pandemic. *Int. J. Environ. Res. Public Health* **2022**, *19*, 2155. [CrossRef]

9. Mishna, F.; Regehr, C.; Lacombe-Duncan, A.; Daciuk, J.; Fearing, G.; Van Wert, M. Social media, cyber-aggression and student mental health on a university campus. *J. Ment. Health* **2018**, *27*, 222–229. [CrossRef]
10. Wilson, O.W.; Holland, K.E.; Elliott, L.D.; Duffey, M.; Bopp, M. The impact of the COVID-19 pandemic on US college students' physical activity and mental health. *J. Phys. Act. Health Aff.* **2021**, *18*, 272–278. [CrossRef]
11. Essel, H.B.; Vlachopoulos, D.; Tachie-Menson, A.; Johnson, E.E.; Ebeheakey, A.K. Technology-induced stress, sociodemographic factors, and association with academic achievement and productivity in Ghanaian higher education during the COVID-19 pandemic. *Information* **2021**, *12*, 497. [CrossRef]
12. Essel, H.B.; Vlachopoulos, D.; Tachie-Menson, A.; Nunoo, F.K.N.; Johnson, E.E. Nomophobia among Preservice Teachers: A descriptive correlational study at Ghanaian Colleges of Education. *Educ. Inf. Technol.* **2022**, *27*, 9541–9561. [CrossRef]
13. Xiang, M.-Q.; Tan, X.-M.; Sun, J.; Yang, H.-Y.; Zhao, X.-P.; Liu, L.; Hou, X.-H.; Hu, M. Relationship of physical activity with anxiety and depression symptoms in Chinese college students during the COVID-19 outbreak. *Front. Psychol.* **2020**, *11*, 582436. [CrossRef]
14. Alshammari, T.K.; Alkhodair, A.M.; Alhebshi, H.A.; Rogowska, A.M.; Albaker, A.B.; Al-Damri, N.T.; Bin Dayel, A.F.; Alonazi, A.S.; Alrasheed, N.M.; Alshammari, M.A. Examining Anxiety, Sleep Quality, and Physical Activity as Predictors of Depression among University Students from Saudi Arabia during the Second Wave of the COVID-19 Pandemic. *Int. J. Environ. Res. Public Health* **2022**, *19*, 6262. [CrossRef]
15. Nivyimana, W.; Mbasani, R.; Yollande, D.S.; Daan, Z.; Bayumvire, C.; Wang, M. Association between demographic, academic, and behavioral characteristics with physical activity levels among international students in China during COVID-19 pandemic. *Saudi J. Health Sci.* **2022**, *11*, 97.
16. Wang, C.; Pan, R.; Wan, X.; Tan, Y.; Xu, L.; Ho, C.S.; Ho, R.C. Immediate psychological responses and associated factors during the initial stage of the 2019 coronavirus disease (COVID-19) epidemic among the general population in China. *Int. J. Environ. Res. Public Health* **2020**, *17*, 1729. [CrossRef]
17. Lin, C.-Y. Social reaction toward the 2019 novel coronavirus (COVID-19). *Soc. Health Behav.* **2020**, *3*, 1. [CrossRef]
18. Ahorsu, D.K.; Lin, C.-Y.; Imani, V.; Saffari, M.; Griffiths, M.D.; Pakpour, A.H. The fear of COVID-19 scale: Development and initial validation. *Int. J. Ment. Health Addict.* **2020**, *20*, 1537–1545. [CrossRef]
19. Yildirim, C.; Correia, A.-P. Exploring the dimensions of nomophobia: Development and validation of a self-reported questionnaire. *Comput. Hum. Behav.* **2015**, *49*, 130–137. [CrossRef]
20. King, A.L.S.; Valenca, A.-M.; Silva, A.-C.O.; Baczynski, T.; Carvalho, M.R.; Nardi, A.E. Nomophobia: Dependency on virtual environments or social phobia? *Comput. Hum. Behav.* **2013**, *29*, 140–144. [CrossRef]
21. Beaunoyer, E.; Dupéré, S.; Guitton, M.J. COVID-19 and digital inequalities: Reciprocal impacts and mitigation strategies. *Comput. Hum. Behav.* **2020**, *111*, 106424. [CrossRef] [PubMed]
22. Contractor, A.A.; Frankfurt, S.B.; Weiss, N.H.; Elhai, J.D. Latent-level relations between DSM-5 PTSD symptom clusters and problematic smartphone use. *Comput. Hum. Behav.* **2017**, *72*, 170–177. [CrossRef] [PubMed]
23. Tams, S.; Legoux, R.; Léger, P.-M. Smartphone withdrawal creates stress: A moderated mediation model of nomophobia, social threat, and phone withdrawal context. *Comput. Hum. Behav.* **2018**, *81*, 1–9. [CrossRef]
24. Farooqui, I.A.; Pore, P.; Gothankar, J. Nomophobia: An emerging issue in medical institutions? *J. Ment. Health* **2018**, *27*, 438–441. [CrossRef] [PubMed]
25. Samaha, M.; Hawi, N.S. Relationships among smartphone addiction, stress, academic performance, and satisfaction with life. *Comput. Hum. Behav.* **2016**, *57*, 321–325. [CrossRef]
26. Fernandes, B.; Biswas, U.N.; Mansukhani, R.T.; Casarín, A.V.; Essau, C.A. The impact of COVID-19 lockdown on internet use and escapism in adolescents. *Rev. De Psicol. Clín. Con Niños Y Adolesc.* **2020**, *7*, 59–65. [CrossRef]
27. Cao, Q.; An, J.; Yang, Y.; Peng, P.; Xu, S.; Xu, X.; Xiang, H. Correlation among psychological resilience, loneliness, and internet addiction among left-behind children in China: A cross-sectional study. *Curr. Psychol.* **2020**, *41*, 4566–4573. [CrossRef]
28. Farchakh, Y.; Hallit, R.; Akel, M.; Chalhoub, C.; Hachem, M.; Hallit, S.; Obeid, S. Nomophobia in Lebanon: Scale validation and association with psychological aspects. *PLoS ONE* **2021**, *16*, e0249890. [CrossRef]
29. Fan, Z.; Chen, M.; Lin, Y. Self-Control and Problematic Internet Use in College Students: The Chain Mediating Effect of Rejection Sensitivity and Loneliness. *Psychol. Res. Behav. Manag.* **2022**, *15*, 459. [CrossRef]
30. Eslinger, P.J.; Anders, S.; Ballarini, T.; Boutros, S.; Krach, S.; Mayer, A.V.; Moll, J.; Newton, T.L.; Schroeter, M.L.; de Oliveira-Souza, R. The neuroscience of social feelings: Mechanisms of adaptive social functioning. *Neurosci. Biobehav. Rev.* **2021**, *128*, 592–620. [CrossRef]
31. Yanguas, J.; Pinazo-Henandis, S.; Tarazona-Santabalbina, F.J. The complexity of loneliness. *Acta Bio Med. Atenei Parm.* **2018**, *89*, 302.
32. Buysse, D.J.; Reynolds, C.F., III; Monk, T.H.; Berman, S.R.; Kupfer, D.J. The Pittsburgh Sleep Quality Index: A new instrument for psychiatric practice and research. *Psychiatry Res.* **1989**, *28*, 193–213. [CrossRef]
33. Altena, E.; Baglioni, C.; Espie, C.A.; Ellis, J.; Gavriloff, D.; Holzinger, B.; Schlarb, A.; Frase, L.; Jernelöv, S.; Riemann, D. Dealing with sleep problems during home confinement due to the COVID-19 outbreak: Practical recommendations from a task force of the European CBT-I Academy. *J. Sleep Res.* **2020**, *29*, e13052. [CrossRef]
34. Cao, W.; Fang, Z.; Hou, G.; Han, M.; Xu, X.; Dong, J.; Zheng, J. The psychological impact of the COVID-19 epidemic on college students in China. *Psychiatry Res.* **2020**, *287*, 112934. [CrossRef]

35. Giri, P.A.; Baviskar, M.P.; Phalke, D.B. Study of sleep habits and sleep problems among medical students of Pravara Institute of Medical Sciences Loni, Western Maharashtra, India. *Ann. Med. Health Sci. Res.* **2013**, *3*, 51–54. [CrossRef]
36. Lemma, S.; Gelaye, B.; Berhane, Y.; Worku, A.; Williams, M.A. Sleep quality and its psychological correlates among university students in Ethiopia: A cross-sectional study. *BMC Psychiatry* **2012**, *12*, 237. [CrossRef]
37. Hair, J.; Black, W.; Babin, B.; Anderson, R. *Multivariate Data Analysis: Pearson New International Edition*; Pearson/Prentice Hall: Upper Saddle River, NJ, USA, 2014.
38. Lovibond, P.F.; Lovibond, S.H. The structure of negative emotional states: Comparison of the Depression Anxiety Stress Scales (DASS) with the Beck Depression and Anxiety Inventories. *Behav. Res. Ther.* **1995**, *33*, 335–343. [CrossRef]
39. Russell, D.; Peplau, L.A.; Cutrona, C.E. The revised UCLA Loneliness Scale: Concurrent and discriminant validity evidence. *J. Personal. Soc. Psychol.* **1980**, *39*, 472. [CrossRef]
40. Akdemir, M.; Sönmez, Y.; Köse, F.; Şenol, Y.Y.; Gürpınar, E.; Aktekin, M.R. Psychological Changes of Music and Fine Arts Students in the Education Process: A Comparative Longitudinal Study. *Med. Probl. Perform. Artist.* **2022**, *37*, 165–175. [CrossRef]
41. Botha, M.; Panebianco, C.; Masenge, A. The Relationship between Perfectionism, Cognitive Rumination, Mindfulness and Mental Health in Music Students at a South African University. *Muziki* **2022**, *19*, 1–18. [CrossRef]
42. Rosset, M.; Baumann, E.; Altenmüller, E. A Longitudinal Study of Physical and Mental Health and Health-Related Attitudes Among Music Students: Potentials and Challenges for University Health Promotion Programs. *Front. Psychol.* **2022**, *13*, 885739. [CrossRef] [PubMed]
43. Gilbert, D. A Comparison of Self-Reported Anxiety and Depression Among Undergraduate Music Majors and Nonmusic Majors. *J. Music Teach. Educ.* **2021**, *30*, 69–83. [CrossRef]
44. Sun, J. Exploring the Impact of Music Education on the Psychological and Academic Outcomes of Students: Mediating Role of Self-Efficacy and Self-Esteem. *Front. Psychol.* **2022**, *128*, 841204. [CrossRef] [PubMed]
45. Jenatabadi, H.S.; Moghavvemi, S.; Mohamed, C.W.J.B.W.; Babashamsi, P.; Arashi, M. Testing students'e-learning via Facebook through Bayesian structural equation modeling. *PLoS ONE* **2017**, *12*, e0182311.
46. Cole, D.A.; Ciesla, J.A.; Steiger, J.H. The insidious effects of failing to include design-driven correlated residuals in latent-variable covariance structure analysis. *Psychol. Methods* **2007**, *12*, 381. [CrossRef]
47. Kolenikov, S. Biases of parameter estimates in misspecified structural equation models. *Sociol. Methodol.* **2011**, *41*, 119–157. [CrossRef]
48. Asparouhov, T.; Muthén, B. Exploratory structural equation modeling. *Struct. Equ. Model. Multidiscip. J.* **2009**, *16*, 397–438. [CrossRef]
49. Radzi, W.M.; Jasimah, C.W.; Salarzadeh Jenatabadi, H.; Alanzi, A.R.; Mokhtar, M.I.; Mamat, M.Z.; Abdullah, N.A. Analysis of Obesity among Malaysian University Students: A Combination Study with the Application of Bayesian Structural Equation Modelling and Pearson Correlation. *Int. J. Environ. Res. Public Health* **2019**, *16*, 492. [CrossRef]
50. Bollen, K.A. Latent variables in psychology and the social sciences. *Annu. Rev. Psychol* **2002**, *53*, 605–634. [CrossRef]
51. Kukreti, S.; Ahorsu, D.K.; Strong, C.; Chen, I.-H.; Lin, C.-Y.; Ko, N.-Y.; Griffiths, M.D.; Chen, Y.-P.; Kuo, Y.-J.; Pakpour, A.H. Post-Traumatic Stress Disorder in Chinese Teachers during COVID-19 Pandemic: Roles of Fear of COVID-19, Nomophobia, and Psychological Distress. *Healthcare* **2021**, *9*, 1288. [CrossRef]
52. Jeon, J. The Strengths and Limitations of the Statistical Modeling of Complex Social Phenomenon: Focusing on SEM, Path Analysis, or Multiple Regression Models. *Int. J. Soc. Behav. Educ. Econ. Bus. Ind. Eng.* **2015**, *9*, 1559–1567.
53. Fornell, C.; Larcker, D.F. Evaluating structural equation models with unobservable variables and measurement error. *J. Mark. Res.* **1981**, *18*, 39–50. [CrossRef]
54. Rababah, J.A.; Al-Hammouri, M.M.; Drew, B.L.; Aldalaykeh, M. Health literacy: Exploring disparities among college students. *BMC Public Health* **2019**, *19*, 14011. [CrossRef]
55. Rivas, R.; Shahbazi, M.; Garett, R.; Hristidis, V.; Young, S. Mental Health–Related Behaviors and Discussions Among Young Adults: Analysis and Classification. *J. Med. Internet Res.* **2020**, *22*, e17224. [CrossRef]
56. Maharjan, N.; Karki, P.K.; Adhikari, B.; Bhaila, A.; Shrestha, H. Association between sleep duration, sleep quality and body mass index in medical students. *J. Chitwan Med. Coll.* **2020**, *10*, 34–38. [CrossRef]
57. Zaidi, S.F.H.; Hanif, S.N.H.; Yusuf, S.; Abdul Mubin, N.N. Gender differences and prevalence of sleeping disorder among arts students in higher learning institutions. *Asian J. Prof. Bus. Stud.* **2021**, *2*, 1–9.
58. Tang, S.; Chen, H.; Wang, L.; Lu, T.; Yan, J. The Relationship between Physical Exercise and Negative Emotions in College Students in the Post-Epidemic Era: The Mediating Role of Emotion Regulation Self-Efficacy. *Int. J. Environ. Res. Public Health* **2022**, *19*, 12166. [CrossRef]
59. Nottage, M.K.; Oei, N.Y.; Wolters, N.; Klein, A.; Van der Heijde, C.M.; Vonk, P.; Wiers, R.W.; Koelen, J. Loneliness mediates the association between insecure attachment and mental health among university students. *Personal. Individ. Differ.* **2022**, *185*, 111233. [CrossRef]
60. Zhao, B.; Kong, F.; Nam, E.W. Assessing Knowledge, Preventive Practices, and Depression among Chinese University Students in Korea and China during the COVID-19 Pandemic: An Online Cross-Sectional Study. *Healthcare* **2022**, *9*, 433. [CrossRef]
61. Nurluöz, Ö. A Research on the Levels of Social Anxiety, Self-Esteem and Loneliness Among University Students: An Application at Northern Cyprus. *Anthropol.* **2016**, *23*, 79–84. [CrossRef]

62. Kim, E.; Cho, I.; Kim, E.J. Structural equation model of smartphone addiction based on adult attachment theory: Mediating effects of loneliness and depression. *Asian Nurs. Res.* **2017**, *11*, 92–97. [CrossRef] [PubMed]
63. Leng, T.; White, C.; Hilton, J.; Kucharski, A.; Pellis, L.; Stage, H.; Davies, N.G.; Keeling, M.J.; Flasche, S. The effectiveness of social bubbles as part of a Covid-19 lockdown exit strategy, a modelling study. *Wellcome Open Res.* **2020**, *5*, 213. [CrossRef]
64. Nguyen, B.T.N.; Nguyen, T.T.; Le, U.T.T. Nomophobia and stress among Vietnamese high school students in Covid-19 pandemic: A mediation model of loneliness. *J. Biochem. Technol.* **2022**, *13*, 34–40. [CrossRef]
65. Tung, S.E.H.; Gan, W.Y.; Chen, J.-S.; Kamolthip, R.; Pramukti, I.; Nadhiroh, S.R.; Chang, Y.-L.; Lin, C.-C.; Pakpour, A.H.; Lin, C.-Y. Internet-Related Instruments (Bergen Social Media Addiction Scale, Smartphone Application-Based Addiction Scale, Internet Gaming Disorder Scale-Short Form, and Nomophobia Questionnaire) and Their Associations with Distress among Malaysian University Students. *Healthcare* **2022**, *10*, 1448.
66. Özdemir, B.; Çakir, Ö.; Hussain, I. Prevalence of Nomophobia among university students: A comparative study of Pakistani and Turkish undergraduate students. *Eurasia J. Math. Sci. Technol. Educ.* **2018**, *14*, 1519–1532. [CrossRef]
67. Hamaideh, S.H.; Al-Modallal, H.; Tanash, M.A.; Hamdan-Mansour, A. Depression, anxiety and stress among undergraduate students during COVID-19 outbreak and "home-quarantine". *Nurs. Open* **2022**, *9*, 1423–1431. [CrossRef]
68. Chen, T.; Lucock, M. The mental health of university students during the COVID-19 pandemic: An online survey in the UK. *PLoS ONE* **2022**, *17*, e0262562. [CrossRef]
69. Yao, N.; Wang, Q. Technostress from Smartphone Use and Its Impact on University Students' Sleep Quality and Academic Performance. *Asia-Pac. Educ. Res.* **2022**, 1–10. [CrossRef]
70. Torales, J.; Torres-Romero, A.D.; Di Giuseppe, M.F.; Rolón-Méndez, E.R.; Martínez-López, P.L.; Heinichen-Mansfeld, K.V.; Barrios, I.; O'Higgins, M.; Almirón-Santacruz, J.; Melgarejo, O. Technostress, anxiety, and depression among university students: A report from Paraguay. *Int. J. Soc. Psychiatry* **2022**, *68*. [CrossRef]

healthcare

MDPI

Article

The Effect of Learning Burnout on Sleep Quality in Primary School Students: The Mediating Role of Mental Health

Lulu Qin [1], Si Chen [1], Bangan Luo [2,*] and Yiwei Chen [3,*]

[1] Department of Social Medicine and Health Management, School of Medicine, Hunan Normal University, Changsha 410013, China
[2] Department of Mental Health, Brain Hospital of Hunan Province (The Second People's Hospital of Hunan Province), Changsha 410007, China
[3] Department of Neurology, Xiangya Third Hospital, Central South University, Changsha 410017, China
* Correspondence: luo276@126.com (B.L.); cyw9778@163.com (Y.C.)

Abstract: Due to the growth of research on sleep, mental health, and learning burnout on healthy growth and its related public health significance of adolescents, this study aimed to provide a deeper understanding of the effect of mental health and learning burnout on sleep among primary school students. The sleep quality (subjective sleep quality, sleep time, sleep latency, sleep duration, sleep efficiency, sleep disturbance, and daytime dysfunction), mental health, and learning burnout (exhaustion, learning cynicism, and reduced efficacy) of 900 students of grades 3–6 in primary schools were assessed in 2020. The PSQI scores of participants were 4.19 ± 2.545, of which a number of 322 (39.03%) students had sleep disturbance (PSQI scores ≧ 5). Binary logistic regression analysis showed that screen time (*OR* = 1.518, 95% *CI*: 1.164–1.980), ranking status (*OR* = 0.659, 95% *CI*: 0.480–0.907), learning burnout (*OR* = 1.088, 95% *CI*: 1.067–1.108), and mental health (*OR* = 4.672, 95% *CI*: 1.954–11.173) were the influencing factors for sleep quality of grade 3–6 students. According to the mediation effect analyses, mental health played a mediating effect (58.73% of the total effect) on the relationship between learning burnout and sleep quality. In conclusion, primary school students in Hunan of China have prominent sleep problems, and the daytime dysfunction caused by sleep problems is the most serious. Learning burnout positively predicted poorer sleep quality, and mental health played a mediating effect on the relationship between learning burnout and sleep quality.

Keywords: primary students; sleep quality; learning burnout; mental health

check for updates

Citation: Qin, L.; Chen, S.; Luo, B.; Chen, Y. The Effect of Learning Burnout on Sleep Quality in Primary School Students: The Mediating Role of Mental Health. *Healthcare* **2022**, *10*, 2076. https://doi.org/10.3390/healthcare10102076

Academic Editor: Daniele Giansanti

Received: 26 September 2022
Accepted: 13 October 2022
Published: 19 October 2022

1. Introduction

Sleep is closely related to the healthy growth of adolescents and has extensive public health significance. The American Academy of Sleep Medicine proposes that school-age children need to ensure 9–12 h of sleep to maintain their physical and mental health [1] Good sleep quality is conducive to the healthy growth, study, and life of adolescents. However, many studies have reported that children have many sleep-related problems. Hawkins et al. reported that sleep deprivation occurred as early as age 6, and that sleep deprivation became more common with increased age and showed a social pattern [2]. Research by Norell-Clarke et al. found that fewer children and adolescents in Sweden got enough sleep over time, which may have an impact on their mental health and cognitive abilities [3].

Mental health is a state of well-being, in which every individual who realizes his or her own potential can cope with the normal stresses of life, can work productively and fruitfully, and is able to make a contribution to her or his community [4]. In the theory of psychological development, psychologist, Erickson, proposed that childhood (6–11 years old) is the basic stage of individual physical and mental health development and the key to ensuring adult mental health [5]. However, studies at home and abroad have shown that the incidence of children's mental health problems has become increasingly serious [6]. Compared with a decade ago, British teenagers had higher rates of depression and self-harm; parents reported higher levels of emotional difficulties, conduct problems, hyperactivity and peer problems, and less sleep [7].

Burnout is defined as a syndrome composed of three factors: Depersonalization, emotional exhaustion and reduced personal achievement [8]. With the gradual deepening of the research on burnout, learning burnout is summarized as a negative emotion caused by the long-term learning pressure and workload of students, leading to their loss of interest in learning activities [9]. Current studies show that learning burnout is common among college students, which can bring negative psychological and behavioral consequences, including anxiety, depression, and so on [10]. According to a study in Nanjing of China, the rate of learning burnout among college students reached a staggering 90.3% [11]. Primary school is the initial stage of learning, and a good learning attitude is conducive to improving the efficiency and quality of learning. However, current research on learning burnout mainly focuses on college students and professional learners, while the research on learning burnout of primary school students is lack obviously.

Many previous studies have shown that learning burnout is associated with sleep quality [7,11,12]. Meanwhile, it is known that learning burnout leads to many mental health problems, such as anxiety and depression [13]. In addition, mental health was related to one's sleep quality, for example, according to a Canadian study, sleep quality was correlated with screening measures for post-traumatic stress disorder (PTSD), depression, anxiety, social anxiety disorder, panic disorder, and alcohol-use disorder for all Public Safety Personnel categories [14]. A prospective study has shown that burnout can have an impact on mental health, with adverse symptoms such as insomnia, depressive symptoms, use of psychotropic and antidepressant medications, hospitalization for mental disorders, and poor mental health [15]. In China, previous studies have shown that the learning burnout of primary school students was at a medium level [16,17], and even some studies have reported high levels in China's primary students [18], which should be concerning as a serious problem. Primary school is only the initial stage of learning life; students will face heavier learning tasks and greater pressure as they grow up. However, in past studies, researchers used learning burnout, mental health, and sleep quality as outcome variables to explore their relationships with other factors. However, no study focuses on the direct connection between them and discusses the effect paths between them, such as mediating effects. Thus, early prevention of learning burnout in primary school students should be paid attention to, and good sleep quality and mental health may be conducive to reducing learning burnout and improving learning efficiency.

Due to the deficiency and importance of the study on the effect paths among the three variables (learning burnout, mental health, and sleep quality) among primary students, it is necessary to point out how the above factors affect each other. As far as we know, this is the first study to explore the effect on primary school students' sleep quality from the perspective of mental health and learning burnout. In this study, we took sleep quality as the dependent variable and planned to explore the sleep quality of primary school students from the perspective of mental health and learning burnout, as well as the mechanism and way that mental health and learning burnout affect sleep quality. Research hypothesis: H1: Learning burnout can positively predict the poor sleep quality of primary school students; H2: Mental health plays a mediating role in the relationship between sleep quality and learning burnout.

2. Methods

2.1. Participants and Procedures

This study was a cross-sectional survey conducted in the Hunan province of China. In consideration of reading and writing skills, primary students of grades 3–6 were selected as the survey objects by using the cluster sampling method. Data were collected through self-filling questionnaires, which were distributed and collected by researchers in the class in 7 primary schools. A number of 900 questionnaires were sent out in this survey, and a total of 825 valid questionnaires were collected with an efficiency rate of 91.67% (825/900).

2.2. Measuring Instruments

2.2.1. Socio-Demographic Information

Gender (boy or girl), age, grade, height (cm), weight (cm), learning performance (highly ranked: students' performance measured by teacher ranked in the top one-third of their class, middle-ranked: students' performance measured by teacher ranked in the middle one-third of their class, lower ranked: students' performance measured by teacher ranked in the bottom one-third of their class), screen time in a day (hours), myopia (yes or no), having brothers and sisters (yes or no), primary caregiver (parents or others), having the habit of an afternoon nap in the past month (yes or no). BMI was computed with the following formula: BMI = kg/m^2. Participants were defined as being lean, normal, overweight, or obese according to the Chinese standards of children [19]. Screen time was defined as time spent on screen devices, including time spent watching TV, using computers, using mobile phones, and using video games and e-readers [20].

2.2.2. Sleep Quality

The Chinese version of the Pittsburgh Sleep Quality Index (PSQI) was used to measure the sleep quality of primary students [21], which was used to evaluate the sleep quality of individuals in the past 30 days. PSQI is composed of seven factors: subjective sleep quality, sleep time, sleep latency, sleep duration, sleep efficiency, sleep disturbance, and daytime dysfunction. Each factor was scored by a four-level scale of 0–3, with a total score range of 0–21. PSQI $\geq$ 5 indicates significant sleep disturbance, and the higher the score, the worse the sleep quality. The PSQI was verified by Buysse et al. and showed good reliability; Cronbach's α was 0.83. The Chinese version of PSQI has been tested and proved to be an effective clinical tool with good reliability, and has proved to be suitable for investigation among children [22].

2.2.3. Mental Health

The Kessler Psychological Distress Scale (K6) [23] was used to measure the mental health of primary school students. This scale contains 6 items, and participants are required to self-evaluate according to the frequency of distress symptoms in the recent month. A five-level score of 0–4 is adopted, with a total score $\leq$12 indicating a low risk of psychological disorders and $\geq$13 indicating a high risk of psychological disorders. In recent years, K6 has been proven to be a good response to adolescent mental health in many studies, and its simplicity and strong predictive ability for mental illness have confirmed its usefulness in clinical and community settings [24]. In addition, Cronbach's α coefficient of the K6 was 0.89.

2.2.4. Learning Burnout

Adolescent Student Burnout Inventory (ASBI) [25] was used to evaluate the learning burnout of primary school students. The scale is a self-rating scale with three dimensions: exhaustion, learning cynicism, and reduced efficacy. There are a total of 16 items on the scale, and a five-point scoring method is adopted: "very consistent"—5 points, "somewhat consistent"—4 points, "not quite consistent"—3 points, "not quite consistent"—2 points, and "Very inconsistent"—1 point and some items in the scale need reverse scoring. ASBI has good reliability, validity, and internal consistency in primary school students [26]. Additionally, Cronbach's α coefficient of ASBI was 0.91.

2.3. Statistical Analysis

Epidata 3.1 software was used for data entry, SPSS 23.0 was used for data statistical analysis. Pearson correlation analysis was used to explore the relationship between learning burnout, sleep quality, and mental health. Binary logistic regression analysis with sleep quality as an independent variable was performed to explore the influencing factors of sleep quality of grades 3–6 primary students. Drawing using Amos 21.0 software [27].

The common method deviation test was performed using Harman single-factor test, the exploratory factor analysis was conducted on all items of primary school students learning burnout, mental health, and sleep quality. Meanwhile, model 4 in the SPSS process compiled by Hayes (2012) [28] (model 4 is a simple mediation model) was used to test the mediation effect of mental health in the relationship between learning burnout and sleep quality under the control of age, grade, ranking status, screen time, and whether they had the habit of napping in the past month (the level $\alpha = 0.05$).

3. Results

3.1. Socio-Demographic Information of Participants

Among the 825 primary students, 400 (48.5%) were boys and 425 (51.5%) were girls. A total of 558 (67.6%) students reported less than one hour of screen time per day, 216 (26.2%) students reported 1–2 h of screen time per day, and 51 (6.2%) students reported more than 2 h of screen time per day. More information about the participants is shown in Table 1.

Table 1. Socio-demographic information of participants ($n = 825$).

Variables		Number	Percentage (%)
Gender	Boy	400	48.5
	Girl	425	51.5
Age (years)	≤9	219	26.5
	10	237	28.7
	11	164	19.9
	≥12	205	24.8
Grade	The 3 grade	225	27.3
	The 4 grade	213	25.8
	The 5 grade	156	18.9
	The 6 grade	231	28.0
BMI (kg/m^2)	Lean	118	14.3
	Normal	573	69.5
	Overweight	134	16.2
Myopia	Yes	463	56.1
	No	362	43.9
Ranking status in class	The first one-third ranking	266	32.2
	The middle	518	62.8
	The last one-third rankings	41	5.0
Screen time	<1 h	558	67.6
	1–2 h	216	26.2
	>2 h	51	6.2
Only child in the family	Yes	327	39.6
	No	498	60.4
Main caregiver	Parents	762	92.4
	Others	63	7.6
The habit of napping in the past month	Yes	347	42.1
	No	478	57.9

3.2. Sleep Quality of the Primary Students in Grades 3–6 and Its Influencing Factors

The PSQI scores of 825 students of grades 3–6 were (4.19 ± 2.545), of which a number of 322 (39.03%) students were with sleep disturbance (PSQI scores ≥ 5). Among the seven dimensions of the PSQI, the highest score was daytime dysfunction and the lowest was hypnotic medication use (Table 2 and Tables S1–S3).

Table 2. PSQI total score and score details of each factor.

PSQI Scores	Minimum	Maximum	$\bar{x} \pm s$	Rank
Subjective sleep quality	0	3	0.88 ± 0.733	4
Sleep duration	0	3	0.96 ± 0.925	2
Sleep latency	0	3	0.15 ± 0.449	5
Sleep efficiency	0	3	0.10 ± 0.348	6
Sleep Disturbances	0	3	0.95 ± 0.541	3
Hypnotic medication use	0	3	0.02 ± 0.202	7
Daytime dysfunction	0	3	1.13 ± 0.898	1
Total scores	0	16	4.19 ± 2.545	

3.3. *Exploring the Influencing Factors of Sleep Quality of Grades 3–6 Students*

Binary logistic regression analysis showed that screen time (*OR* = 1.518, 95%*CI*: 1.164–1.980), ranking status (*OR* = 0.659, 95%*CI*: 0.480–0.907), learning burnout (*OR* = 1.088, 95%*CI*: 1.067–1.108), and mental health (*OR* = 4.672, 95%*CI*: 1.954–11.173) were the influencing factors for sleep quality of grade 3–6 students. The specific results are shown in Table 3 below.

Table 3. Binary Logistic regression analysis of sleep quality of the primary students in grades 3–6.

	β	*SE*	Wald	*p*	*OR*	95% *CI*
Screen time	0.417	0.136	9.474	0.002	1.518	(1.164, 1.980)
Ranking status	−0.416	0.162	6.576	0.010	0.659	(0.480, 0.907)
Learning burnout	0.084	0.010	77.025	0.000	1.088	(1.067, 1.108)
Mental Health	1.542	0.445	12.012	0.001	4.672	(1.954, 11.173)
Constant	−5.026	0.570	77.836	0.000	0.007	

3.4. *Mental Health and Learning Burnout and Its Correlations with Sleep Quality of Grades 3–6 Students*

The average score of mental health of primary school students in grades 3–6 was 4.46 ± 4.404, and 45 students (5.5%) scored 13 or above, indicating that the participants had a high risk of psychological disorders. (Supplementary Table S4).

The average score of learning burnout of the grades 3–6 students was 36.23 ± 10.383. Among the three dimensions of learning burnout, the reduced efficacy dimension scored the highest (17.33 ± 4.726), and the learning cynicism scored the lowest (8.71 ± 4.213) (Supplementary Table S5).

Correlation analysis showed that sleep quality significant positive correlated with mental health (r = 0.551, $p < 0.05$) and learning burnout (r = 0.505, $p < 0.05$). There was a significant positive correlation between mental health and learning burnout (r = 0.542, $p < 0.05$) (Supplementary Table S6).

3.5. *Mediating Effect of Mental Health on the Relationship between Learning Burnout and Sleep Quality*

Results from the mediating effect analysis showed that learning burnout had a significant predictive effect on sleep quality ($\beta = 0.126$, $t = 15.621$, $p < 0.001$), and the direct predictive effect of learning burnout on sleep quality was still significant ($\beta = 0.074$, $t = 8.415$, $p < 0.001$). Learning burnout has a significant positive predictive effect on mental health ($\beta = 0.241$, $t = 17.587$, $p < 0.001$); the positive predictive effect of mental health on sleep quality was also significant ($\beta = 0.215$, $t = 11.203$, $p < 0.001$). In addition, learning burnout can not only directly predict sleep quality, but also predict sleep quality through the intermediary effect of mental health. Mental health played a mediating effect (58.73% of the total effect) on the relationship between learning burnout and sleep quality (Tables 4 and S6 and Figure 1).

Table 4. Intermediary model test of mental health (n = 825).

Regression Equation (n = 825)		Fitting Index			Coefficient Significance	
Result Variable	**Predictive Variable**	**R**	**R^2**	**F(df)**	**β**	**t**
Sleep quality		0.54	0.29	55.10		
	Age				0.328	1.724
	Grade				−0.164	−0.888
	Ranking status				−0.512	−3.443
	Screen time				0.318	2.411
	Whether they had the habit of napping in the past month				−0.477	−3.080
	Learning burnout				0.126	15.621
Mental health				61.64		
	Age				0.284	0.875
	Grade				−0.073	−0.232
	Ranking status				−0.728	−2.878
	Screen time				−0.035	−0.155
	Whether they had the habit of napping in the past month				−0.651	−2.472
	Learning burnout				0.241	17.587
Sleep quality				72.34		
	Age				0.268	1.507
	Grade				−0.148	−0.862
	Ranking status				−0.356	−2.556
	Screen time				0.326	2.649
	Whether they had the habit of napping in the past month				−0.337	−2.329
	Mental health				0.215	11.203
	Learning burnout				0.074	8.415

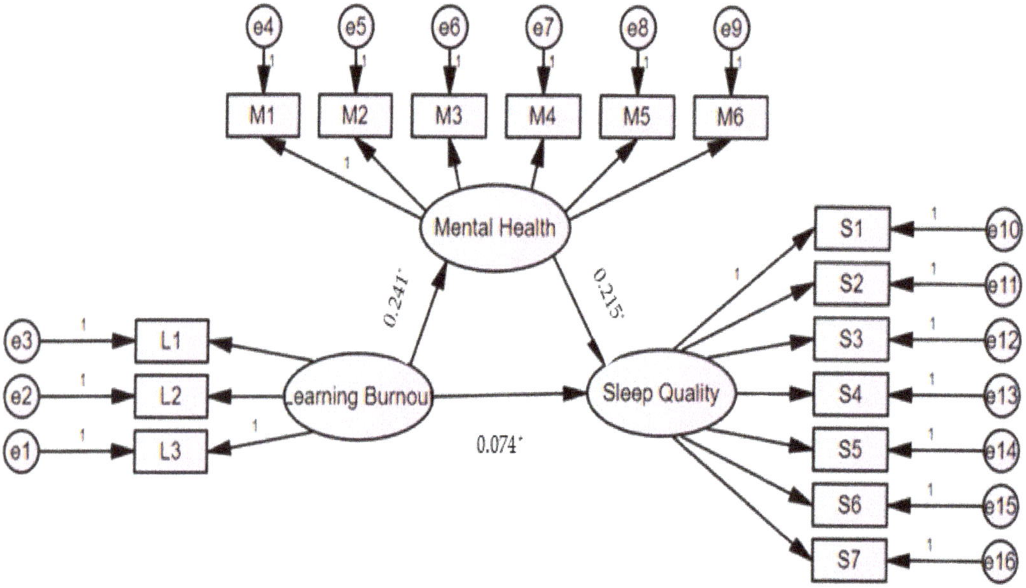

Figure 1. Mediating role of mental health. Note: L1, L2, and L3 are the three dimensions of learning burnout, respectively; M1–M6 are the 6 questions of K6, respectively; S1–S7 are seven dimensions of sleep quality, respectively; e1–e16 are the residual error to each variable; The number 1 means that the path coefficient (i.e., the influence coefficient) has a fixed value of 1; The asterisk (*) means that the path coefficient is statistically significant.

4. Discussion

4.1. Sleep Quality of the Primary Students in Grades 3–6

This study showed that the PSQI score of pupils in grades 3–6 of China was 4.19 ± 2.545, which was significantly lower than the critical value of 5 ($t = -9.136$, $p = 0.000$) and the global average score of PSQI ($t = -4.961$, $p = 0.000$). Compared with previous studies of Chongqing City of China in 2011 (PSQI score: 5.51 ± 2.57), Hunan primary school students have better sleep quality than them [29]. In 2021, a Portuguese study showed that the PSQI reported by children aged 6–10 was 4.05 ± 2.803, slightly lower than the score of this study [30].

The prevalence of sleep disorders in primary school students of grades 3–6 in Hunan Province was 39%, which was similar to developing countries. The prevalence of sleep disorders in children is estimated to be 20–50% and varies in different areas of the world, such as nearly 40% in Japan in 2013 [31] and 43.1% in Spain in 2016 [32]. According to the regulations of the Ministry of Education in China, the sleep time of primary school students should be more than 10 h [33]. Unfortunately, only 166 (20.12%) primary school students in this survey slept for 10 h and above, suggesting that the sleep problems of primary school students in Hunan were serious.

Among the seven dimensions of PSQI, the score of the daytime dysfunction dimension was the highest, suggesting that daytime dysfunction caused by sleep problems was more serious than others among the participants. The score of the hypnotic medication-use dimension was the lowest, which may be related to the careful thinking of parents. Parents always prefer to be very cautious when using drugs for children. According to the score of the sleep efficiency dimension, it was shown that the sleep efficiency of primary school students is relatively good in this study.

Logistic results showed that the sleep quality of primary school students was influenced by their ranking status, screen time, mental health, and learning burnout. Results showed that children's sleep quality was significantly correlated with their ranking status in the class. The lower the performance ranking, the worse the sleep quality. Firstly, poor sleep quality is closely related to the adverse effects on the cognitive process of the prefrontal cortex, which may have a negative impact on working memory and executive function [34]. Secondly, poor sleep quality will reduce daytime alertness, which, in turn, may decrease the attention effect and lead to impaired academic performance [35]. In addition, students at the last ranking will encounter greater learning pressure, which may affect the quality of sleep [1–4]. Screen time was positively correlated with the sleep quality score of primary school students, this may be due to the screen light stimulating the brain and inhibiting melatonin production, resulting in an increase in sleep latency [36].

4.2. The Mediating Role of Mental Health on the Influence of Learning Burnout on Sleep Quality of Primary School Students

Our study showed that learning burnout had a significant impact on sleep among primary school students. There are two main pathways to this effect: (1) one is that learning burnout directly affects sleep quality; (2) the other is the effect of learning burnout on sleep quality through the mediating effect of mental health, which was the first time that it was demonstrated that mental health played a mediating effect on the relationship between learning burnout and sleep quality.

As for the first hypothesis of this study: learning burnout can positively predict the poor sleep quality of primary school students, our results show that this hypothesis is valid. There was a moderately positive correlation between learning burnout and sleep quality score ($r = 0.505$, $p < 0.05$), that is, the higher the learning burnout degree, the worse the sleep quality. This is consistent with previous studies. A Finnish study on middle school students showed that burnout was related to sleep disorders and poor sleep quality [37]. Wolf and Rosenstock reported that pathological sleepiness was significantly associated with a higher incidence of burnout. Sleep deprivation is associated with significantly reduced occupational efficacy and higher fatigue scores [38]. Scholars in the United States found that learning burnout was related to the global Pittsburgh sleep quality total score and its seven subscales [39]. Thus, students with a low level of learning burnout have a strong sense of autonomy and competence. When encountering difficulties, they will actively try more solutions to improve learning efficiency and reduce the pressure brought by learning, which is conducive to developing good sleep.

In our second hypothesis, mental health plays a mediating role in the relationship between learning burnout and sleep quality. The results of the study show that this hypothesis is tenable. Mental health has a mediating effect between learning burnout and sleep quality, and mental health plays a "bridge" role, that is, learning burnout not only directly affects sleep quality, but also indirectly affects sleep quality through mental health. These findings are consistent with other studies [40]. On one hand, learning burnout will have an impact on mental health, and a high degree of burnout will bring many negative effects on mental health. Some Finnish scholars found that burnout is related to dropping out of school, dysfunction caused by mental health problems, and at least one mental illness at present [41]. The effect of learning burnout on mental health can be explained by the JDR model (Job Demands–Resources model) [42]. The JDR model proposed that the matching degree of adolescents' needs and resources in the school environment affects their school-related burnout. When school resources cannot meet their needs, adolescents may feel high academic pressure. Persistent high academic pressure can lead to physical and mental exhaustion, a lack of personal achievement in learning, and a sense of alienation in their relationship with teachers [40]. In addition, under high study pressure, teenagers tend to produce a series of emotion-related reactions, such as depression. All this evidence suggests that learning burnout can have a negative impact on mental health. On the other hand, the effect of mental health on sleep has been demonstrated in many studies, and a review by Lam [43] literature points to a significant and possible causal relationship between early childhood sleep disorders and the development of mental health problems such as anxiety, depression, and ADHD (Attention Deficit Hyperactivity Disorder) in adolescence. A study of sleep among primary school students in Iran also showed a significant correlation between sleep habits and mental health [44]. Therefore, it can be inferred that learning burnout can affect the mental health of primary school students through learning pressure factors, and the mental health of primary school students will further affect their sleep quality, so the mediating effect of mental health between the two is established.

In view of the results of our study, we intend to put forward some suggestions for education researchers and parents. Firstly, we need to pay enough attention to children's learning burnout, mental health, and sleep quality to help children grow up healthily. Secondly, teachers and parents should look at the role of study pressure dialectically; moderate study pressure may promote learning, but excessive study pressure may bring many negative effects [45,46]. It is necessary to think about how to maintain moderate study pressure to promote students' learning. In addition, considering the effective ways of learning burnout, mental health, and sleep quality of this study, some intervention strategies should be working together to provide a better scientific basis for the healthy growth of children and adolescents.

However, there are some limitations to this study and our results should be interpreted with caution. Firstly, we only measure subjective sleep quality. The assessment of objective sleep quality was not conducted in this study. In future studies, the objective sleep quality of children reported could be considered. In addition, due to the cross-sectional design, so the causation cannot be inferred, and future researchers can further verify the relationship using longitudinal methods and/or randomized control designs.

5. Conclusions

Primary school students in grades 3–6 have more prominent sleep problems, and the daytime dysfunction caused by sleep problems is the most serious in Hunan of China.

Learning burnout positively predicted poorer sleep quality and mental health played a mediating effect on the relationship between learning burnout and sleep quality.

Supplementary Materials: The following supporting information can be downloaded at: https://www.mdpi.com/article/10.3390/healthcare10102076/s1, Table S1: PSQI scores 1; Table S2: PSQI scores 2; Table S3: PSQI scores 3; Table S4: ASBI total score and score details of each factor. Table S5: Describe statistics and correlation analysis results; Table S6: Breakdown of total effect, direct effect and intermediary effect.

Author Contributions: Conceptualization, L.Q., B.L., Y.C. and S.C.; Data Curation, L.Q. and B.L.; Methodology, L.Q., B.L., Y.C. and S.C.; Funding Acquisition, L.Q. and S.C.; Resources, B.L. and Y.C.; Writing, L.Q., B.L., Y.C. and S.C.; Revising, L.Q., B.L., Y.C. and S.C. All authors have read and agreed to the published version of the manuscript.

Funding: This work was founded by Hunan Normal University School of Medicine Open Fund project (2020, 2022).

Institutional Review Board Statement: The study was conducted in accordance with the Declaration of Helsinki. Ethical approval was obtained from the institutional ethics committee of the Hunan Normal University (NO. 2021399).

Informed Consent Statement: All respondents were patients and signed an informed consent form.

Data Availability Statement: Data cannot be shared publicly because of potentially identifying and sensitive participants information. Data are available from the Hunan Normal University of China (contact via powerestlulu@hunnu.edu.cn) for researchers who meet the criteria for access to confidential data.

Conflicts of Interest: The authors declare no conflict of interest.

References

1. Sundell, A.L.; Angelhoff, C. Sleep and Its Relation to Health-Related Quality of Life in 3–10-Year-Old Children. *BMC Public Health* **2021**, *21*, 1043. [CrossRef] [PubMed]
2. Hawkins, S.S.; Takeuchi, D.T. Social Determinants of Inadequate Sleep in Us Children and Adolescents. *Public Health* **2016**, *138*, 119–126. [CrossRef] [PubMed]
3. Norell-Clarke, A.; Hagquist, C. Changes in Sleep Habits between 1985 and 2013 among Children and Adolescents in Sweden. *Scand. J. Public Health* **2017**, *45*, 869–877. [CrossRef] [PubMed]
4. World Health Organization. *Mental Health: A State of Well-Being*; WHO: Geneva, Switzerland, 2011. Available online: http://tinyurl.com/kmc523c (accessed on 17 May 2016).
5. Knight, Z.G. A Proposed Model of Psychodynamic Psychotherapy Linked to Erik Erikson's Eight Stages of Psychosocial Development. *Clin. Psychol. Psychother.* **2017**, *24*, 1047–1058. [CrossRef]
6. Troy, D.; Anderson, J.; Jessiman, P.E.; Albers, P.N.; Williams, J.G.; Sheard, S.; Geijer-Simpson, E.; Spencer, L.; Kaner, E.; Limmer, M.; et al. What Is the Impact of Structural and Cultural Factors and Interventions within Educational Settings on Promoting Positive Mental Health and Preventing Poor Mental Health: A Systematic Review. *BMC Public Health* **2022**, *22*, 524. [CrossRef]
7. Patalay, P.; Gage, S.H. Changes in Millennial Adolescent Mental Health and Health-Related Behaviours over 10 Years: A Population Cohort Comparison Study. *Int. J. Epidemiol.* **2019**, *48*, 1650–1664. [CrossRef]
8. Rehman, A.U.; Bhuttah, T.M.; You, X. Linking Burnout to Psychological Well-Being: The Mediating Role of Social Support and Learning Motivation. *Psychol. Res. Behav. Manag.* **2020**, *13*, 545–554. [CrossRef]
9. Xu, R.; Wang, Q.; Chin, N.S.; Teo, E.W. Analysis of Learning Motivation and Burnout of Malaysian and Chinese College Students Majoring in Sports in an Educational Psychology Perspective. *Front. Psychol.* **2021**, *12*, 691324. [CrossRef]
10. Mufarrih, S.H.; Naseer, A.; Qureshi, N.Q.; Anwar, Z.; Zahid, N.; Lakdawala, R.H.; Noordin, S. Burnout, Job Dissatisfaction, and Mental Health Outcomes among Medical Students and Health Care Professionals at a Tertiary Care Hospital in Pakistan: Protocol for a Multi-Center Cross-Sectional Study. *Front. Psychol.* **2019**, *10*, 2552. [CrossRef]
11. Douris, P.C.; Hall, C.A.; Jung, M.K. The Relationship between Academic Success and Sleep, Stress and Quality of Life During the First Year of Physical Therapy School. *J. Am. Coll. Health* **2021**, *9*, 1–10. [CrossRef]
12. Arbabisarjou, A.; Hashemi, S.M.; Sharif, M.R.; Haji Alizadeh, K.; Yarmohammadzadeh, P.; Feyzollahi, Z. The Relationship between Sleep Quality and Social Intimacy, and Academic Burn-out in Students of Medical Sciences. *Glob. J. Health Sci.* **2015**, *8*, 231–238. [CrossRef]
13. Koutsimani, P.; Montgomery, A.; Georganta, K. The Relationship between Burnout, Depression, and Anxiety: A Systematic Review and Meta-Analysis. *Front. Psychol.* **2019**, *10*, 284. [CrossRef]

14. Angehrn, A.; Sapach, M.J.N.T.; Ricciardelli, R.; MacPhee, R.S.; Anderson, G.S.; Carleton, R.N. Sleep Quality and Mental Disorder Symptoms among Canadian Public Safety Personnel. *Int. J. Environ. Res. Public Health* **2020**, *17*, 2708. [CrossRef]
15. Salvagioni, D.A.J.; Melanda, F.N.; Mesas, A.E.; González, A.D.; Gabani, F.L.; De Andrade, S.M. Physical, Psychological and Occupational Consequences of Job Burnout: A Systematic Review of Prospective Studies. *PLoS ONE* **2017**, *12*, e0185781. [CrossRef]
16. Gan, C. *Investigation on the Current Situation of Learning Burnout of the Rural Primary School Student*; Qufu Normal University: Qufu, China, 2021.
17. Wang, A.Y. *Study on Current Situation and Influencing Factors of Learning Burnout in Primary School Students*; Shanghai Normal University: Shanghai, China, 2019.
18. Liu, S. Investigation on learning burnout of primary school students in urban and rural junction department. *Ment. Health Educ. Prim. Second. Sch.* **2020**, *19*, 19–21.
19. Group of China Obesity Task Force. Body mass index reference norm for screening overweight and obesity in Chinese children and adolescent. *Chin. J. Epidemiol.* **2004**, *25*, 97–102.
20. Sun, F.F. *The Relationship between Screen Time, Physical Activity and Sleep Quality in Junior Middle School Students*; Nanjing Normal University: Nanjing, China, 2021.
21. Dietch, J.R.; Taylor, D.J.; Sethi, K.; Kelly, K.; Bramoweth, A.D.; Roane, B.M. Psychometric Evaluation of the Psqi in U.S. College Students. *J. Clin. Sleep Med.* **2016**, *12*, 1121–1129. [CrossRef]
22. Wang, B.R. *Study on the Relationship between Child Behavior Problems of Children Aged 6–11 Years and Coping Style Sleep Quality and Mental Health of Family Members in Shandong Province*; Jining Medical University: Jining, China, 2021.
23. Kessler, R.C.; Andrews, G.; Colpe, L.J.; Hiripi, E.; Mroczek, D.K.; Normand, S.-L.; Walters, E.E.; Zaslavsky, A.M. Short Screening Scales to Monitor Population Prevalences and Trends in Non-Specific Psychological Distress. *Psychol. Med.* **2002**, *32*, 959–976. [CrossRef]
24. Ferro, M.A. The Psychometric Properties of the Kessler Psychological Distress Scale (K6) in an Epidemiological Sample of Canadian Youth. *Can. J. Psychiatry Rev. Can. Psychiatr.* **2019**, *64*, 647–657. [CrossRef]
25. Wu, Y.; Dai, X.Y. The Development of Adolescent Student Burnout Inventory. *Chin. J. Clin. Psychol.* **2010**, *18*, 152–154.
26. Xie, X.D.; Yu, C.P.; Li, D.D. Future Orientation and Learning Burnout among Adolescents in the Pearl River Delta: The Mediating Role of Coping Style. *China J. Health Psychol.* **2016**, *24*, 1468–1472.
27. Wu, M.L. *Structural Equation Modeling—Operation and Application of AMOS*; Chongqing University Press: Chongqing, China, 2009.
28. Hayes, A.F.; Scharkow, M. The Relative Trustworthiness of Inferential Tests of the Indirect Effect in Statistical Mediation Analysis: Does Method Really Matter? *Psychol. Sci.* **2013**, *24*, 1918–1927. [CrossRef]
29. Yong, N.; Wang, H.; Hu, H.; Meng, Q.H.; Chen, P.H.; Du, L.; Qu, Y.; Zou, Z.L.; Wang, T.; Zhao, W.J.; et al. Relationship among Child-Abuse, Depressive Symptoms and Sleep Quality in Grade 4–6 Primary Students. *Chin. Ment. Health J.* **2011**, *25*, 616–621.
30. Gomes, A.M.; Martins, M.C. Child Perception and Parent's Perception About Child Sleep Quality. *Sleep Sci.* **2021**, *14*, 342–347. [CrossRef]
31. Iwadare, Y.; Kamei, Y.; Oiji, A. Study of the Sleep Patterns, Sleep Habits, and Sleep Problems in Japanese Elementary School Children Using the Cshq-J. *Kitasato Med. J.* **2013**, *43*, 595–604.
32. Lucas-de la Cruz, L.; Martinez-Vizcaino, V.; Alvarez-Bueno, C.; Arias-Palenica, N.; Sanchez-Lopez, M.; Notario-Pacheco, B. Reliability and validity of the Spanish version of the Children's Sleep Habits Questionnaire (CSHQ-SP) in school-age children. *Child Care Health Dev.* **2016**, *42*, 675–682. [CrossRef]
33. Circular of the General Office of the Ministry of Education on Further Strengthening the Physical Health Management of Primary and Secondary School Students. Bulletin of Ministry of Education of the People's Republic of China. 2021. Available online: http://www.moe.gov.cn/srcsite/A17/moe_943/moe_947/202104/t20210425_528082.html (accessed on 23 October 2021).
34. Takeuchi, H.; Taki, Y.; Nouchi, R.; Yokoyama, R.; Kotozaki, Y.; Nakagawa, S.; Sekiguchi, A.; Iizuka, K.; Yamamoto, Y.; Hanawa, S.; et al. Shorter Sleep Duration and Better Sleep Quality Are Associated with Greater Tissue Density in the Brain. *Sci. Rep.* **2018**, *8*, 5833. [CrossRef]
35. Arnsten, A.F.T.; Shanafelt, T. Physician Distress and Burnout: The Neurobiological Perspective. *Mayo Clin. Proc.* **2021**, *96*, 763–769. [CrossRef]
36. Kohyama, J. Factors Affecting the Quality of Sleep in Children. *Children* **2021**, *8*, 499. [CrossRef]
37. Lehto, J.E.; Kortesoja, L.; Partonen, T. School Burnout and Sleep in Finnish Secondary School Students. *Sleep Sci.* **2019**, *12*, 10–14. [CrossRef]
38. Wolf, M.R.; Rosenstock, J.B. Inadequate Sleep and Exercise Associated with Burnout and Depression among Medical Students. *Acad. Psychiatry J. Am. Assoc. Dir. Psychiatr. Resid. Train. Assoc. Acad. Psychiatry* **2017**, *41*, 174–179. [CrossRef] [PubMed]
39. May, R.M.; Bauer, K.N.; Seibert, G.S.; Jaurequi, M.E.; Fincham, F.D. School Burnout Is Related to Sleep Quality and Perserverative Cognition Regulation at Bedtime in Young Adults—Sciencedirect. *Learn. Individ. Differ.* **2020**, *78*, 101821. [CrossRef]
40. Yan, Y.W.; Lin, R.M.; Su, Y.K.; Liu, M.Y. The Relationship between Adolescent Academic Stress and Sleep Quality: A Multiple Mediation Model. *Soc. Behav. Personal. Int. J.* **2018**, *46*, 63–78. [CrossRef]
41. Nagy, G.A.; Fang, C.M.; Hish, A.J.; Kelly, L.; Nicchitta, C.V.; Dzirasa, K.; Rosenthal, M.Z. Burnout and Mental Health Problems in Biomedical Doctoral Students. *CBE Life Sci. Educ.* **2019**, *18*, 27. [CrossRef]
42. Katariina, S.A.; Katja, U. Developmental Trajectories of School Burnout: Evidence from Two Longitudinal Studies. *Learn. Individ. Differ.* **2014**, *36*, 60–68.

43. Lam, L.T.; Lam, M.K. Sleep Disorders in Early Childhood and the Development of Mental Health Problems in Adolescents: A Systematic Review of Longitudinal and Prospective Studies. *Int. J. Environ. Res. Public Health* **2021**, *18*, 11782. [CrossRef]
44. Shamsaei, F.; Daraei, M.M.; Aahmadinia, H.; Khalili, A.; Seif, M. The Relationship between Sleep Habits and Mental Health in Iranian Elementary School Children. *Sleep Sci.* **2019**, *12*, 94–99. [CrossRef]
45. Almojali, A.I.; Almalki, S.A.; Alothman, A.S.; Masuadi, E.M.; Alaqeel, M.K. The Prevalence and Association of Stress with Sleep Quality among Medical Students. *J. Epidemiol. Glob. Health* **2017**, *7*, 169–174. [CrossRef]
46. Jayanthi, P.; Thirunavukarasu, M.; Rajkumar, R. Academic Stress and Depression among Adolescents: A Cross-Sectional Study. *Indian Pediatr.* **2015**, *52*, 217–219. [CrossRef]

MDPI
St. Alban-Anlage 66
4052 Basel
Switzerland
www.mdpi.com

Healthcare Editorial Office
E-mail: healthcare@mdpi.com
www.mdpi.com/journal/healthcare

www.ingramcontent.com/pod-product-compliance
Lightning Source LLC
Chambersburg PA
CBHW061505210926
51850CB00008B/1824
9783725809929